Lecture Notes of the Institute for Computer Sciences, Social Informatics and Telecommunications Engineering 195

More information about this series at http://www.springer.com/series/8197

Ombretta Gaggi · Pietro Manzoni
Claudio Palazzi · Armir Bujari
Johann M. Marquez-Barja (Eds.)

Smart Objects and Technologies for Social Good

Second International Conference, GOODTECHS 2016
Venice, Italy, November 30 – December 1, 2016
Proceedings

 Springer

Editors
Ombretta Gaggi
Università degli Studi di Padova
Padua
Italy

Armir Bujari
Università degli Studi di Padova
Padua
Italy

Pietro Manzoni
Universitat Politècnica de València
Valencia
Spain

Johann M. Marquez-Barja
Trinity College Dublin
Dublin
Ireland

Claudio Palazzi
Dipartimento di Matematica
Università degli Studi di Padova
Padua
Italy

ISSN 1867-8211   ISSN 1867-822X   (electronic)
Lecture Notes of the Institute for Computer Sciences, Social Informatics
and Telecommunications Engineering
ISBN 978-3-319-61948-4   ISBN 978-3-319-61949-1   (eBook)
DOI 10.1007/978-3-319-61949-1

Library of Congress Control Number: 2017946065

Printed on acid-free paper

This Springer imprint is published by Springer Nature
The registered company is Springer International Publishing AG
The registered company address is: Gewerbestrasse 11, 6330 Cham, Switzerland

Preface

The GOODTECHS 2016 Conference was the second edition of a conference that wants to become a point of attraction for researchers in the area and it was held in the beautiful city of Venice, a worldwide renowned historical, academic, and cultural center. In GOODTECHS we were interested in experiences with the design, implementation, deployment, operation, and evaluation of smart objects and technologies for social good. Clearly, we were not considering only the so-called first world as the scenario for this evolution; we also referred to those areas where ICT is currently less widespread, hoping that it may represent a societal development opportunity rather than a source for further divide.

It was our honor to have prominent international scholars as speakers. The conference program embodied technical papers selected through peer reviews by the Technical Program Committee members and keynote speakers that provided even more insight into this area. We would like to thank the EAI for the support and all the members of the conference committees and the reviewers for their dedicated and passionate work. None of this would happened without the support and curiosity of the authors that have sent their papers to this event. Finally, we would like to encourage current and future authors to continue working in this direction and to participate in forums like this conference in order to exchange knowledge and experiences and to make ICT actually helpful to society.

October 2016

Ombretta Gaggi
Pietro Manzoni
Claudio Palazzi

Organization

GOODTECHS 2016 was organized by the Università degli Studi di Padova, Italy, and the Universitat Politècnica de València, Spain, in cooperation with EAI (European Alliance for Innovation).

Executive Committee

Steering Committee Chair

Imrich Chlamtac — Create-Net Trento, Italy

General Co-chairs

Ombretta Gaggi — Università degli Studi di Padova, Italy
Pietro Manzoni — Universitat Politècnica de València, Spain
Claudio Palazzi — Università degli Studi di Padova, Italy

Technical Program Committee Chair

Armir Bujari — Università degli Studi di Padova, Italy

Special Session on: Persuasive Systems Design for Promoting Health and Well-being Co-chairs

Silvia Gabrielli — CREATE-NET, Italy
Ahmed Salih Fadhil — FBK, Italy
Dario Betti — CR-GPI, Italy

Open Challenges in Online Social Networks Co-chairs

Laura Ricci — University of Pisa, Italy
Barbara Guidi — CNR, Italy

ICT4D: Information and Communication Technologies for Persons with Disabilities Co-chairs

Fulvio Babich — University of Trieste, Italy
Eric Medvet — University of Trieste, Italy
Gianni Ramponi — University of Trieste, Italy

Smart Things for Active and Assisted Living (ST4AAL) Co-chairs

Susanna Spinsante — Università Politecnica delle Marche, Italy
Lorena Rossi — INRCA, Italy
Chris Nugent — University of Ulster, UK

Interdisciplinary Topics Co-chair

Pamela Kato   Coventry University, UK

Networking in Challenging Scenarios Co-chairs

Aloizio P. Silva   Federal University of Minas Gerais, Brazil
Vinicius F.S. Mota   Federal University of Minas Gerais, Brazil

Serious Games Co-chair

Elif Sürer   Middle East Technical University, Turkey

**Smart, Internet-Connected Objects and Applications in Dynamically Evolving
Cities and Communities Co-chairs**

Vivian Kiousi   INTRASOFT International S.A., Greece
George Dimitrakopoulos   Harokopio University of Athens, Greece

Semantic Technology Co-chair

Valentina Presutti   CNR, Italy

Publications Chair

Johann M. Marquez-Barja   CONNECT Research Centre, Trinity College Dublin,
                           Ireland

Web Chair

Carlos Calafate   Universitat Politècnica de València, Spain

Publicity and Social Media Co-chairs

Carlos Calafate   Universitat Politècnica de València, Spain
Matteo Ciman   University of Geneva, Switzerland
Daniele Ronzani   Università degli Studi di Padova, Italy

Local Co-chairs

Sabina Rossi   Università Ca Foscari Venezia, Italy
Andrea Marin   Università Ca Foscari Venezia, Italy

Conference Manager

Lenka Laukova   European Alliance for Innovation

Program Committee

Antonella Molinari   Università Mediterranea di Reggio Calabria, Italy
Danda Rawat   Georgia Southern University, USA

Antonio Jara	HES-SO University of Applied Sciences Western Switzerland
Dario Maggiorini	Università degli Studi di Milano, Italy
Enrique Hernández-Orallo	Universitat Politècnica de València, Spain
Francisco J. Martinez	University of Zaragoza, Spain
Giancarlo Fortino	University of Calabria, Italy
Guglielmo De Angelis	ISTI-CNR, Italy
Gianluca Rizzo	HES SO Valais, Switzerland
Joel Rodrigues	University of Beira Interior, Portugal
Juan Carlos Cano	Universitat Politecnica Valencia, Spain
Katarzyna Wac	University of Copenhagen, Denmark
Laura Anna Ripamonti	Università degli Studi di Milano, Italy
Ling-Jih Chen	Academia Sinica, Taiwan
Lito Kriara	Disney Research Zürich, Switzerland
Luigi Atzori	University of Cagliari, Italy
Marco Picone	University of Parma, Italy
Marco Roccetti	Università degli Studi di Bologna, Italy
Daniele Ronzani	Università degli Studi di Padova, Italy
Armir Bujari	Università degli Studi di Padova, Italy
Maria Luisa Sapino	University of Turin, Italy
Matteo Ciman	University of Geneva, Switzerland
Nadjib Achir	University of Paris XIII, France
Mohammad Pourhomayoun	University of California at Los Angeles, USA
Monica Aguilar	Universitat Politècnica de Catalunya, Spain
Piedad Garrido	University of Zaragoza, Spain
Schahram Dustdar	Vienna University of Technology, Austria
Silvia Mirri	University of Bologna, Italy
Marco Furini	Università degli Studi di Modena e Reggio Emilia
Siraj Shaikh	Coventry University, UK
Uichin Lee	Korea Advanced Institute of Science and Technology, KAIST, Republic of Korea
Matteo Dell'Amico	Sophia-Antipolis, France
Pedro Garcia Lopez	Rovira i Virgili University, Spain
Barbara Guidi	University of Pisa, Italy
Kalman Graffi	University of Düsseldorf, Germany
Andrea Marino	University of Pisa, Italy
Anna Monreale	University of Pisa, Italy
Paolo Mori	CNR, Italy
Amir H. Payberah	Swedish Institute of Computer Science, Sweden
Laura Ricci	University of Pisa, Italy
Giulio Rossetti	CNR, Italy
Fulvio Babich	University of Trieste, Italy
Silvio Bonfiglio	BARCO Company, Italy
Zeljka Car	University of Zagreb, Croatia
Barbara Carminati	University of Insubria, Italy

Thiago Henrique Silva	Universidade Tecnológica Federal do Parana, Brazil
Yacine Ghamri-Doudane	Université de La Rochelle, France
José Marcos Silva Nogueira	Universidade Federal de Minas Gerais, Brazil
Waldir Moreira	Lusofona University, Portugal
Scott Burleigh	JPL-NASA/Caltech, USA
William D. Ivancic	NASA Glenn Research Center, USA
Elif Sürer	Middle East Technical University, Turkey
Pamela Kato	Coventry University, UK
Vivian Kiousi	INTRASOFT International S.A., Greece
George Dimitrakopoulos	Harokopio University of Athens, Greece
Valentina Presutti	CNR, Italy

Sponsoring Institutions

Università degli Studi di Padova, Italy
Universitat Politècnica de València, Spain
EAI (European Alliance for Innovation)

Contents

Indoor Activity Monitoring for Mutual Reassurance

Fabio Veronese, Simone Mangano, Sara Comai, Matteo Matteucci, and Fabio Salice$^{(\boxtimes)}$

Politecnico di Milano, Polo Territoriale di Como, Via Anzani, 42, 22100 Como, Italy
{fabio.veronese,simone.mangano,sara.comai,matteo.matteucci,
fabio.salice}@polimi.it
http://atg.deib.polimi.it

Abstract. Population ageing is rising issues concerning the sustainability of older seniors assistance. A possible solution can be avoiding early retirement in nurse houses by providing the family and the senior(s) with an unobtrusive monitoring system, mainly based on motion sensors, capable of extending their independent living. The presented system processes the collected data to infer when the person exits and enters, his/her position inside the house, and the occupancy of the house areas. Such information is made available to the family through a set of purposefully designed graphical interfaces and prompt notifications. Preliminary results are satisfying, showing it is possible to restore *Mutual Reassurance*.

Keywords: Ageing · Smart home · Activity monitoring

1 Introduction

In recent years population studies are evidencing a growth of the elderly population. Based on a report of the United Nations [1] the number of the seniors aged over 60 is expected to be 2 billions by 2050, three times their number in 2000. Since the process of population ageing is expected to be *unprecedent, pervasive*, and *enduring*, one of the main concerns regards the rapid rise of elderly care costs. Health-care facilities and seniors hospitalization have a significant impact on the life of the older person, while they can be also not affordable for the family. Active and Assisted Living (AAL) has been proposed as a paradigm to overcome such problems, suggesting active and independent ageing in place [2].

To prevent the hospitalization process, it is necessary to preserve the conditions (in terms of needs) of both the seniors and their relatives, according to Maslow's hierarchy [3]. In particular, restoring the awareness of the senior's status and activity can reassure the elderly person as well as the family, providing what we defined in previous works *Mutual Reassurance* [4]. This proficient awareness can be achieved thanks to an unobtrusive monitoring system, delivering the information necessary and notifying undesired happenings.

© ICST Institute for Computer Sciences, Social Informatics and Telecommunications Engineering 2017
O. Gaggi et al. (Eds.): GOODTECHS 2016, LNICST 195, pp. 1–10, 2017.
DOI: 10.1007/978-3-319-61949-1_1

The challenges related to the aforementioned issues are addressed by the Assistive Technology Group (ATG) of Politecnico di Milano, working in close collaboration with a social counterpart: CRAIS[1] (*Resource Center for Autonomy and Social Inclusion*). Within this project CRAIS contributed with its professionals in the identification of the needs and the expected activities to be performed by a person: the set of conditions agreed between the senior and his/her family represents a *life agreement* and may concern eating activities, expected daily and nightly movements, indoor presence or absence, etc. In order to provide notifications to the family as soon as undesired happenings are recognized (e.g., unexpected nightly activity, or medicines take time, etc.) we propose a system based on a wireless sensor network monitoring the senior and visualization tools showing information about the inhabitant activities with the possibility to review his/her history. The proposed methodology for live monitoring is based mainly on Home Automation (HA) sensors detecting human activity in areas of interest inside the house. The overall system architecture refers to the project BRIDGe: *Behavior dRift compensation for autonomous and InDependent livinG* is a project on which ATG has been working in recent years [4]. The project aims at creating strong connections between a person living independently at home and his/her social environment by implementing monitoring, and focused interventions according to the user's need.

The rest of this publication is structured as follows: next section reports and analyses previous works based on similar sensors. Section 3 refers to the architecture of the monitoring system, detailing the exploited sensors, the data collection and the processing platform; moreover, Sect. 4 concerns the methodology applied for the activity monitoring and the proposed family perspectives. Finally, Sect. 5 reports the preliminary evaluation outcome obtained with the application of the presented methodology to synthetic data, and Sect. 6 contains the conclusions and the future perspectives.

2   State of the Art

Concerning the development of unobtrusive systems for the enhancement of elderly everyday life, several research projects are devoted to the identification of the action performed by the inhabitant, often referred to as ADL (i.e. Activity of Daily Living). In the proposed settings though the aim is to infer the activity of the person in its broadest sense, presenting the information in an aggregate manner to a remote user.

In such perspective, several projects rely on movement and domotic sensors to collect information in the home environment. As presented in the review by Peetoom et al. [5], the results in terms of identified activities, and precision vary among systems, as well as the acceptance and the stress level reported by inhabitants and caregivers.

Developing probably one of the first projects in this field, Yamaguchi et al. [6] use simple devices (PIR and door sensors) to monitor the human behavior in

---

[1] http://crais.eu.

indoor environments. The aim was to unobtrusively monitor a person along nine months, proving it is possible to observe the daily cycle of a person's life without him or her being aware of it.

In Dalal et al. [7] a system for elderly people living alone is presented, its aim is to provide warnings in case of emergency conditions and to recognize health issues through the identification of anomalies in IADLs (Instrumental Activities of Daily Living) patterns. PIR sensors and an instrumented bed are used to collect data, on which a rule-based approach is applied to associate sensors groups with specific actions.

In Zhang et al. [8] the same sensor technology is used to build a dense network at floor level to track heat sources as they move around in the house. The aim is to track the persons position and motion direction in house rooms.

Other research projects have a different approach, involving more elaborate systems and pervasive instrumentation. Damarla et al. [9] propose a complex system where different sensors (e.g., chemical, electrostatic, PIR, cameras, etc.) collect information joined to monitor the inhabitant's life. Even if the aim is the same of the previous systems, cameras and extended sensorization have a negative impact on system acceptance.

Kaye et al. [10] propose a system for indoor monitoring with simple and unobtrusive home devices. The main source of information is the extended network of PIR sensors, for fine person localization, enriched with the details obtained by door sensors. The data in this work are also transferred to a remote SQL database, approaching to the architecture of cloud services.

Higher level analyses are performed by Yang and Hsu [11], who propose a set of *activity features* measuring the intensity, the frequency, the regularity, and the anomalies of the activity patterns. The results show how it is possible to estimate the daily activities rhythms and to detect unusual behavior in unexpected situations.

3   System Architecture

The core of the BRIDGe project is a wireless sensor-actuator network that enables home automation as well as user activity monitoring through a rich and flexible communication system toward the relatives and the carers. The basic infrastructure is composed of two subsystems, one residing inside the dwelling and one standing in the cloud.

3.1   Domotic Sensors

Active and Assisted Living (AAL) and Home Automation (HA) technologies are attracting much attention and their growth and diffusion bring the comfort pervasive home control. Nonetheless such expansion also provides a wide choice of market devices to be exploited to monitor and assist fragile people at home.

Focusing on the type of sensors, the choice of unobtrusive devices has fundamental importance. Cameras and microphones are known to be not well accepted by people, especially in their dwelling: to respect privacy and to limit the perceived invasiveness of the system, we choose HA devices that are not even acquiring personal information. Thus the hereby presented system relies only on HA devices sensing and acting on the home environment and not the inhabitant. The only exception is represented by motion sensors, being well tolerated.

Smart Homes devices market is highly competitive and many different solutions in terms of technologies, standards and companies are available nowadays. The choice of the technology to employ is crucial, since it brings a wide set of opportunities but also inevitable restrictions [12]. The BRIDGe system technological choice is Z-Wave [4], drawn considering many factors as suggested in the analysis by Saidinejad et al. [13]. Above all, thanks to the wireless communication, the battery power supply, the small dimensions design, and the modularity Z-Wave devices can be easily integrated in the existing electric plant of a house.

3.2   Data Collection and Processing

In order to provide the high level information about activity monitoring, a device inside the dwelling is needed to collect and the process the data. To approach such issue we exploited a Raspberry Pi 2[2], equipped with a Z-Wave daughter board and the Z-wave.ME[3] software stack. Such solution has several advantages: the hardware is low cost, easily purchasable and installable. This home server is capable of interacting with the HA sensors network, retrieving, processing and buffering the data, before forwarding them to the remote subsystem.

There are two possible moments to process the data: right after they are collected by the home server, or remotely and asynchronously when received by the remote server. This implies that depending on its aim it may be advisable to perform the computation on the most suited subsystem. More explicitly, the processing requiring low delay (ideally real time), the operations triggering immediate responses on the actuators, the extraction of information requiring prompt notification, etc. need to be performed on the home server.

Considering the scope of this work, the computation is performed on the home server. The data collected live from the Z-Wave HA network are fed continuously to a stream processing engine. The chosen software for this task is Esper[4], an event series analysis and event correlation engine. It is programmable to perform queries and processing over dynamic sets of real-time changing data, exploiting the Event Processing Language (EPL). Its peculiarity is the possibility to express pattern semantics and complex temporal consequentiality. Moreover, EPL capabilities can be extended thanks to the integration of extra custom components written in Java. About the remote subsystem, it is important to stress that it provides the web applications to visualize and store efficiently the history of all the data, both collected and obtained by processing.

---

[2] www.raspberrypi.org.

[3] http://z-wave.me.

[4] www.espertech.com.

3.3   Data Visualization

The data collected (both directly from the HA network and after the processing), have to be provided in a proper form to the family or the relatives of the inhabitant. At this aim the remote server provides a specific web application for the visualization of the data. In particular, two main channels are available to transfer the information between the remote and the home servers. The first channel is used by the house server to periodically (once per minute) upload messages to the remote server, this channel is mono-directional and is implemented using a REST (REpresentational State Transfer) API on the remote server. The second channel is a bidirectional one based on the publish and subscribe paradigm implemented through an open source library called crossbar.io, this second mechanism enables real time communication also in the opposite direction (from the remote server to the house server) in order to offer remote access to house services from outside, using the remote server as gateway. Indeed it is worthy to mention that all the information from the remote server is accessible only after authentication of the user.

4   Indoor Activity Monitoring

The core of the proposed work is the possibility to provide aggregate and immediate information to the family, through visualizations or prompt notifications.

Probably one of the simplest way of providing coarse information regarding the indoor activity of a home sensorized with HA devices, is being aware of where the person is inside the house, in terms of *area*. When using the concept of *area* we refer to (an entire or to) a specific portion of a room: the presence of the person in such space implies a high probability he/she is performing an interesting task, induced by the objects/furniture. The areas distribution has to be defined depending on the specific needs of the person and his/her family, with the assistance of social professionals [12]. Similarly, also the definition of the requirements for the visualization and notification of information should be carried out by the family and the seniors with the aid and assistance of professionals, in order to find the most fitting solution.

4.1   Localization and Presence

The target of the implemented HA data processing is to define the person position inside the house. Using a set of PIR motion sensors, their activations follow the position of the person along the dwelling. However these sensors remain in *active* status for a certain lapse of time, resulting also in several active sensors at the same time. It is necessary to associate each sensor with its field of view, and with its house area, in order to infer where the person is when triggering a specific sensor. Moreover, sensors become inactive if the person stops (e.g., sits at a table, on the sofa, lays on the bed); intuitively, the person position is related the activation of motion sensors, giving more importance to the most recent information and recalling the last valid position when sensors turn off.

Given a set of areas $\mathcal{A}$, the focus is to infer which $A_i \in \mathcal{A}$ contains the person position $\mathbf{x}_p$. HA sensors response can be exploited to infer the person's position depending on the interaction with them.

In detail, associating to each sensor s_i its *space* σ_i, i.e. the fraction of the house in which the person can activate its response, we can estimate the instantaneous position of the person starting from the active areas. To take into account the sensors activation persistence, we introduced an exponential weighting of the activations:

$$w_i(t) = \exp\left(\frac{t_{last} - t_{a,i}}{\tau}\right);$$
(1)

where the further the sensors activation $(t_{a,i})$ is, with respect to the last activation – taking into account all the sensors – (t_{last}) the lower its space contributes to the final position estimation, depending on a decay parameter τ. The reference of the decay is t_{last} rather than the current time instant because the person is more likely to be in the last visited space. Otherwise, if the person moves to another space σ_i, it is expected to trigger the sensor s_i accordingly, updating t_{last}.

The person coordinates $\mathbf{x}_p$ are estimated based on the set of weighted sensors spaces, by applying the barycenter function $B(\cdot)$:

$$\hat{\mathbf{x}}_p = B\left(\bigcup_i \{w_i\sigma_i : s_i \text{ is active}\}\right)$$
(2)

To simplify the computation and reduce the processing load, the barycenter function is reduced to a discrete form. In particular a grid $\mathcal{G}$ of evenly spaced points $\mathbf{x}_g \in \mathcal{G}$ is distributed across the home. Let's also introduce the activation function f as:

$$f(s_i, t) = \begin{cases} 1 & s_i \text{ is active} \\ 0 & \text{otherwise} \end{cases}.$$
(3)

Each space σ_i is then considered: based on the activation function and the temporal weighting, the barycenter is obtained as a weighted summation. Formally:

$$\hat{\mathbf{x}}_p(t) = \frac{\sum_i \left[f(s_i, t)w_i(t) \cdot \sum_{\mathbf{x}_g \in \sigma_i} \mathbf{x}_g\right]}{\sum_j \left[f(s_j, t)w_j(t)\#(x_g \in \sigma_j)\right]};$$
(4)

where $\#(x_g \in \sigma_j)$ is the number of grid points included in the space σ_j.

Furthermore the obtained position $\hat{\mathbf{x}}_p$ is compared to the areas in $\mathcal{A}$ to obtain their expected occupation given the estimated person position.

Even if very important, the information concerning the presence in home might not be sufficient to the awareness required by the family. A needed enhancement concerns the identification of the absence of the person, or more precisely, the detection of the moments when the person enters and exits the house. To such aim, we can identify two models representing entrance and exit. Let us formalize them in the following simplified statements:

Exit. The sensors activations detected before the main door opening and closure are all followed by the corresponding deactivations, within a time lapse compatible with their normal functioning in absence of the inhabitant; Person status changes from present to absent;

Entrance. The inhabitant was absent, while now any of the sensor detects activity; Person status changes from absent to present.

It is clear how for both these statements the temporal sequence is relevant. Indeed the hereby presented model neglects burglar intrusion and other happenings, considering them out of the scope of this work.

Both the position and the occupation data are stored first on the home server and then on the remote subsystem, where the family and the relatives can access them.

4.2   On-Demand Information Delivery

Indeed one of the fundamental phases of the mutual reassurance is the information delivery to the family. The simplest way of providing such information is a set of multimodal visualization tools integrated in a web application. In particular we propose three data representations, characterized by different elements and capabilities strongly complementary.

The first data representation is a *live perspective* of the house (Fig. 1): it shows the instantaneous status of all the sensors and HA devices deployed, as well as the person's position and the areas occupation. Such view is designed to provide a prompt and clear perception of the instantaneous house status and to have an idea of the ongoing activity.

The second visualization, called *time machine* (Fig. 2) allows the exploration of the historic data. The appearance is very similar to the live perspective, but the data displayed are extracted from the database: the user can set a specific date and time, play the activations at custom time scale, seek along the day for a specific condition, etc. This tools enables to manually verify the inhabitant behavior in an asynchronous way.

Third, we propose a *bubbles diagram* (Fig. 3), for the aggregated and synthetic visualization of the house areas occupation along time. This enables to visualize the time spent in each house area: the wider the circle hovering the corresponding area, the longer the overall time spent there. Indeed, variations of the inhabitant behavior that imply changes in the daily routine, modify the distribution of the presence in the house. These are better to be investigated: a sick person would spend much more time in the bedroom, or would not exit from the house, or even spend an anomalous lapse of time at the toilet, etc. In all these situations the family may require to be aware of such happenings and changes.

4.3   Notifications

When monitoring the activity of an elderly person whose independence is threatened by the possibility of domestic accidents, it is important not only to recognize and detect them, but also to get notified right after they have taken place.

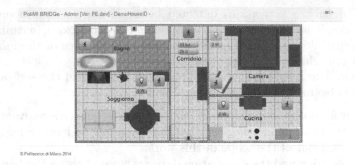

Fig. 1. Live perspective of the house status. In this visualization the person is localized in the corridor (cyan ring), and the corresponding movement sensor (in red) is triggered. (Color figure online)

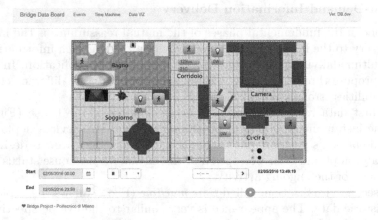

Fig. 2. Time machine visualization: the inhabitant is shown in the kitchen (cyan ring) right after lunch. The horizontal bar enables to browse the visualized instant in time.

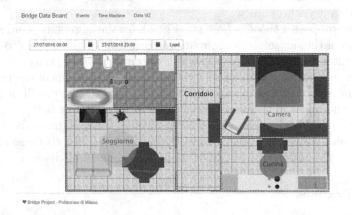

Fig. 3. Bubbles diagram visualization: the rooms occupancy is displayed, the wider the circle the longer the time.

Depending on the content of *life agreement*, the system should provide some pieces of information as soon as possible through notifications. Two simple examples can be: a prompt notification to the family when the person enters or exits the house, or a daily notification about the time spent in the bedroom.

We propose as notification tools two widespread general purpose communication media: e-mail and Twitter[5]. Since these modern communication technologies provide lightweight free client applications for smartphones, where to receive instantaneous notifications, it is convenient to leverage them. Concerning the reliability of such communication channels, it would be indeed worthy to analyze their Quality of Service; however we believe that this analysis stands out of this work's scope. In details the home server generates a notification, through e-mail and/or Twitter, whenever an interesting happening takes place.

5   Experimental Results

Even if testing the system with real-world data would have been interesting, it was impossible to retrieve a dataset with specific situations, as advisable for this work scope. Given these conditions, we exploited synthetic simulated data of a smart home. The simulator we used, called SHARON [14], enables the configuration of the person's behavior in terms of basic needs (e.g. eat, sleep, etc.), of place and time routines of the performed activities, but also the design of the all virtual environment (e.g. map of the place, areas, appliances, sensors, etc.). The results proved the validity of the approach on simulated data.

However, the evaluation of the system on real world data is surely more interesting. To such aim the project is currently in recording data on two pilot installations and trying to recruit more testers. The preliminary results of this testing phase are encouraging.

6   Conclusions

In the hereby presented work we propose an integrated system for the monitoring of indoor activity of independent elderly people, which is intended to be a tool to restore the mutual reassurance between the family and the seniors living alone.

The system comprises the collection, transmission, storage and analysis of HA data, to provide aggregate synthetic information: the coarse scale person localization, the house rooms occupancy, the presence at home and other customizable complex events. The set of visualizations and the notification mechanism enables the family to have an insight of the inhabitant activity.

Preliminary results on synthetic data and real world installation are encouraging: further tests will be carried out. To such extent it would be interesting to evaluate also the visualization system on an audience of testers.

---

[5] http://twitter.com.

References

1. United Nations: World population ageing: 1950–2050. UN (2002)
2. AAL Programme: Strategy 2014–2020 for the active and assisted living programme (2014)
3. Maslow, A.H., Frager, R., Fadiman, J., McReynolds, C., Cox, R.: Motivation and Personality, vol. 2. Harper & Row, New York (1970)
4. Mangano, S., Saidinejad, H., Veronese, F., Comai, S., Matteucci, M., Salice, F.: Bridge: mutual reassurance for autonomous and independent living. IEEE Intell. Syst. **30**(4), 31–38 (2015)
5. Peetoom, K.K., Lexis, M.A., Joore, M., Dirksen, C.D., De Witte, L.P.: Literature review on monitoring technologies and their outcomes in independently living elderly people. Disabil. Rehabil.: Assist. Technol. **10**(4), 271–294 (2015)
6. Yamaguchi, A., Ogawa, M., Tamura, T., Togawa, T.: Monitoring behavior in the home using positioning sensors. In: Proceedings of the 20th Annual International Conference of the IEEE Engineering in Medicine and Biology Society, vol. 4, pp. 1977–1979. IEEE (1998)
7. Dalal, S., Alwan, M., Seifrafi, R., Kell, S., Brown, D.: A rule-based approach to the analysis of elders activity data: detection of health and possible emergency conditions. In: AAAI Fall 2005 Symposium, pp. 2545–2552 (2005)
8. Zhang, Z., Gao, X., Biswas, J., Wu, J.K.: Moving targets detection and localization in passive infrared sensor networks. In: 2007 10th International Conference on Information Fusion, pp. 1–6. IEEE (2007)
9. Damarla, T., Kaplan, L., Chan, A.: Human infrastructure & human activity detection. In: 2007 10th International Conference on Information Fusion, pp. 1–8. IEEE (2007)
10. Kaye, J., Maxwell, S.A., Mattek, N., Hayes, T.L., Dodge, H., Pavel, M., Jimison, H.B., Wild, K., Boise, L., Zitzelberger, T.A.: Intelligent systems for assessing aging changes. J. Gerontol. Ser. B Psychol. Sci. Soc. Sci. **66**, i180–i190 (2011)
11. Yang, C.-C., Hsu, Y.-L.: Remote monitoring and assessment of daily activities in the home environment. J. Clin. Gerontol. Geriatr. **3**(3), 97–104 (2012)
12. Veronese, F., Comai, S., Saidinejad, H., Salice, F.: Elderly monitoring and AAL for independent living at home: human needs, technological issues, and dependability. In: Optimizing Assistive Technologies for Aging Populations, pp. 154–181 (2015)
13. Saidinejad, H., Radaelli, J., Veronese, F., Salice, F.: Mixed technical and market evaluation of home automation networks for AAL solutions. Assist. Technol.: Res. Pract. Assist. Technol. Res. Ser. **33**, 865–870 (2013)
14. Veronese, F., Proserpio, D., Comai, S., Matteucci, M., Salice, F.: Sharon: a simulator of human activities, routines and needs. Stud. Health Technol. Inform. **217**, 560–566 (2014)

IoT-Based Health Monitoring System for Active and Assisted Living

Ahmed Abdelgawad[1], Kumar Yelamarthi[1(✉)], and Ahmed Khattab[2]

[1] School of Engineering and Technology, Central Michigan University,
Mt. Pleasant, MI 48859, USA
{abdella,yelamlk}@cmich.edu
[2] Electronics and Electrical Communications Department, Cairo University,
Giza 12613, Egypt
akhattab@ieee.org

Abstract. The Internet of Things (IoT) has been widely used to interconnect the available medical resources and offer smart, reliable, and effective healthcare service to the elderly people. Health monitoring for active and assisted living is one of the paradigms that can use the IoT advantages to improve the elderly lifestyle. In this paper, we present an IoT architecture customized for healthcare applications. The proposed architecture collects the data and relays it to the cloud where it is processed and analyzed. Feedback actions based on the analyzed data can be sent back to the user. A prototype of the proposed architecture has been built to demonstrate its performance advantages.

Keywords: Health monitoring · Internet of Things (IoT) · Medical devices · Sensors · Platform implementation · Cloud computing

1 Introduction

Remote healthcare has become a vital service with the growing rate of senior citizens. Health monitoring, rehabilitation, and assisted living for the elderly and medically challenged humans is an emerging challenge because they require seamless networking between people, medical instruments, and medical and social service providers. This motivates the need for affordable, low-power, reliable, and wearable devices that will improve the quality of life for many elderlies and physically challenged people.

The Internet of Things (IoT) platform offers a promising technology to achieve the aforementioned healthcare services, and can further improve the medical service systems [1]. IoT wearable platforms can be used to collect the needed information of the user and its ambient environment and communicate such information wirelessly, where it is processed or stored for tracking the history of the user [2]. Such a connectivity with external devices and services will allow for taking preventive measure (e.g., upon foreseeing an upcoming heart stroke) or providing immediate care (e.g., when a user falls down and needs help).

Recently, several IoT systems have been developed for IoT healthcare and assisted living applications. A multiple communication standard compatible IoT system for medical devices was designed by Wang et al. in [3]. Xu et al. proposed a resource-based

O. Gaggi et al. (Eds.): GOODTECHS 2016, LNICST 195, pp. 11–20, 2017.
DOI: 10.1007/978-3-319-61949-1_2

data accessing method (UDA-IoT) that is suitable for healthcare information-intensive applications [4]. Kolici et al. proposed and implemented a medical support system considering Peer-to-Peer (P2P) and IoT technologies. They used a smart box to control the situation of patients. Moreover, they performed several experiments to evaluate the implemented system for few different scenarios [5]. Sandholm et al. proposed an on-demand Web Real-Time Communication (WebRTC) and IoT device tunneling service for hospitals. The proposed system relies on intercepting key parts of the WebRTC Javascript Session Establishment Protocol (JSEP) and using local network gateways that can multiplex traffic from multiple concurrent streams efficiently without leaking any WebRTC traffic across the firewall except through a trusted port [6]. An acquisition and management of biomedical data using IoT has been proposed by Antonovici et al. They developed an Android application that aims to record the data measured (SBP-Systolic Blood Pressure, DBP - Diastolic Blood Pressure and Heart Rate) by the electronic sphygmomanometer that communicates via Bluetooth. The proposed system offers the possibility of transmitting medical data using any mobile device. Data will be compared with the normal values and when an abnormality is observed, the patient is notified. In the worst case, the emergency service and doctors will be notified as well. The patient with vision impairment who are suffering from diabetes, hypertension or obesity is also supported by adapting a "Text To Speech" engine that allows data to be transmitted as type string to the device [7]. Krishnan et al. presented a real-time Internet application with distributed flow environment for medical IoT. If the patient is out of range for the Wi-Fi, or the server is unavailable, the patent's data will be stored locally and sent to the server when the patient arrives back in range of connectivity [8]. Azariadi et al. proposed an algorithm for electrocardiogram (ECG) signal analysis and arrhythmia detection on IoT-based embedded wearable medical platform, as suitable for 24-h continuous monitoring. A Galileo board is used to implement the design [9].

Mohan presented a cyber security framework for IoT Personal Medical Devices (PMDs) that enable enhanced mobility for the patient. In the meantime, it is facilitating better monitoring of the patient's condition while moving. He presents the security threats and limitations of PMD IoT that makes addressing these threats challenging. He also presents some initial solution approaches in order to address these security threats [10]. Yeh et al. presented a cloud-based fine-grained health information access control framework for lightweight IoT devices with dynamic auditing and attribute revocation. They handled the potential security challenges and the cloud reciprocity issues. The results show that the proposed scheme is promising for cloud-based Personal Health Information (PHI) platform [11]. Porambage et al. proposed a secure lightweight authentication and key establishment protocol for end-to-end communication for constrained devices in IoT-enabled ambient assisted living systems. They used proxy-based approach to assign the heavily computational operations to more powerful devices in the neighborhood of the used medical sensors. The results are promising for the real world applications [12].

Yelamarthi and Laubhan [13] have designed and implemented a portable electronic travel aid for the blind. Utilizing ultrasonic range finders mounted on the belt, the assistive device was able find obstacles in front of the user, and provide respective navigation directions through a Bluetooth headphone. However, this device is limited in the distance and localization of obstacles with high accuracy. Yelamarthi et al. [14, 15] have presented a depth sensor based navigation system to detect obstacles in front of the user with high accuracy, and inform user of the same through vibro tactile feedback in the hand gloves. However, a limitation in majority of the work presented is lack of connectivity to the cloud to continually monitor the user data, and storage for health analysis when necessary.

Addressing this limitation, in this paper, we present a cloud-based IoT system that is applicable in different healthcare and active/assisted living applications. The proposed system is composed of 6 modules: the physical sensors that collects the user's information and provides the needed feedback, a sensor interfacing circuit, an indoor positioning module that helps locating the user, a low-power microcontroller that manages the data collection and forwarding process, a wireless transceiver that connects the system to the Internet, and a cloud server in which the data storage and processing take place. A prototype of the proposed system is built and tested to illustrate its different performance aspects.

The remainder of the paper is organized as follows. In Sect. 2, we present the proposed IoT health monitoring architecture. A preliminary set of result of a prototype of this architecture is presented in Sect. 3. The paper is concluded in Sect. 4.

2 Wearable Active and Assisted Living System

In this section, we propose a portable and customizable IoT system that can be used to collect the data needed to facilitate the independent living of senior and challenged citizens to improve their quality of life. The proposed system design philosophy targets having a low-power system that can be worn during the day and be turbo charged as necessary. The system is designed to be light and comfortable to wear. Furthermore, the system is implemented using low-cost components, which makes it an affordable system. An overview of the proposed wearable IoT system is shown in Fig. 1. The system is composed of six main components that are described as follows.

2.1 Physical Sensors

In order to collect the user information that reflect its activity and medical signs, multiple sensors are needed. These sensors are lightweight in order to be wearable. A pulse oximeter sensor is used to measure the amount of oxygen dissolved in the user's blood, based on the detection of Hemoglobin and Deoxyhemoglobin. Such a sensor is useful in the situation in which the user's oxygenation is unstable, and in need for supplemental oxygen or even intensive care. An electrocardiogram (ECG) sensor is used to obtain a side set of cardiac information such as the rate and rhythm of the heart, the patterns of abnormal electric activity that may predispose the user to abnormal cardiac rhythm disturbances, and how the heart is placed inside the chest cavity. Furthermore, the ECG sensor provides evidences of damages that occur to different parts of the heart muscle, any acutely impaired blood flow to the heart muscle, and increased thickness of the heart muscle. A nasal/oral airflow sensor is used to measure

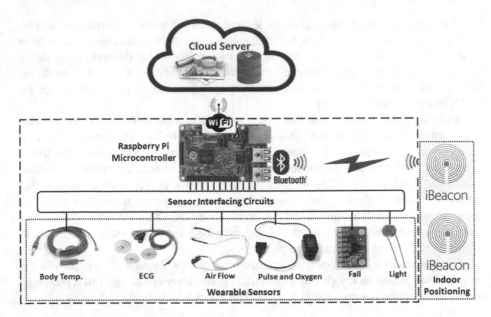

Fig. 1. Proposed IoT wearable system for active and assisted living

the breathing rate of the user to determine whether or not he or she is in need of respiratory help. A temperature sensor is used to measure the temperature of any part of the body, and can be moved easily in order to be placed over the body part where temperature measurement is needed.

In addition to the above medical sensor that capture the user's health signs, light and fall detection sensors are also used. The light sensor provides the information that can help the user adjust his/her ambience light, so as to help him/her navigate around with ease. For example, when the ambience light decreases, readings from this sensor can be used to turn on extra lights. The fall detection sensor is an accelerometer that is used to determine whether the user has fallen abruptly, such that warnings signals can be generated to provide the needed care.

2.2   Indoor Positioning Module

The second module of the proposed system is a Bluetooth Low-Energy (BLE) iBeacon which is widely used for indoor positioning [16]. Instead of using latitude and longitude information to determine the user's location, iBeacon transmits a Bluetooth low energy signal to infer the existence within its vicinity. Several iBeacon devices are installed in the environment in which the user is located. When the user moves to the proximity of an iBeacon, its ID is read by the microcontroller wirelessly using BLE. The iBeacon ID is sent to the cloud server to obtain the user's location. The BLE technology allows the iBeacon to be powered by a single coin cell battery for extended time intervals.

2.3   Sensor Interface Circuits

The signals representing the different sensed phenomena (e.g., blood oxygen level, body temperature, etc.) are then conditioned to be ready for input to the microcontroller. This is achieved through the use of sensor interfacing circuitry that converts any analog signals coming from the sensors into the corresponding digital format and performs any further signal conditioning functionality to ensure compatibility with the used microcontroller.

2.4   Microcontroller

The microcontroller is the core of the system. It is responsible for collecting the data of the different sensors interfaced to it, and communicating such a data to the cloud server for further processing, or for retrieving the iBeacon location information. We use the single-board Raspberry Pi 2 single-board microcontroller that is powered through a 3.7 V Li-Ion battery in our front-end nodes [17]. The Raspberry Pi is equipped with an on-board communication module that controls the data flow between the different sensors and the microcontroller using the I^2C protocol.

2.5   Wireless Transceivers

The proposed system has BLE and IEEE 802.11 WiFi wireless transceivers interfaced to the Raspberry Pi 2 microcontroller. The BLE transceiver is responsible for locating the system using the deployed iBeacons. It can be also used to provide feedback to the user through Bluetooth headsets for example. The WiFi transceiver is used to connect the proposed system to the Internet, and hence, the cloud server. The collected sensor data and the iBeacon location information transferred over the WiFi wireless interface.

2.6   Cloud Server

The collected user's data is communicated to a cloud server which is responsible for facilitating the accessibility of such a data anywhere through the Internet. The cloud server implements a wideset of data management services including data storage, data analytics, and data visualization in addition to providing an appropriate application program interface (API) and software tools through which the data can be accessed and manipulated. Our implementation of the cloud server is shown in Fig. 2.

The cloud server core is a large database that has enough space to accommodate the huge amounts of data for the different sensors for long times to track the history of the system user. The database is interfaced to a wide set of data analysis algorithms and APIs such as Google Sheets for data visualization. Data can be accessed through the Internet using dynamic webpages as shown in Fig. 2.

In our implementation of the cloud server, both Apache and MySQL run on the same virtual machine (VM) running Ubuntu 14.04. This VM is just one of the many VMs that constitute a larger VSphere implementation. The VSphere control panel is

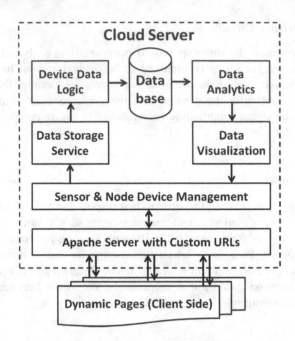

Fig. 2. Cloud server architecture.

used to increase the resource allocation of the VM (such as memory and disk space) with a minimal downtime and without data corruption. It is worth noting that if the health monitoring system requirement exceeds the available hardware resources, the implemented VM can be easily moved to a dedicated cloud hosting platform such as an EC2 instance on Amazon Web Services (AWS).

3 Experimental Evaluation

As a proof of concept, a prototype system has been implemented to evaluate the proposed IoT active and assisted living healthcare system. The system has been configured to collect data from all the listed sensors. However, in what follows, we only present the data of the indoor positioning, the fall detection, and the light sensor. The readings of the other wearable sensors have been validated in the lab as well.

Figure 3 shows the results of the fall detector sensor. In this experiment, we have the user walking for a few seconds then abruptly fall on the ground, to mimic real-world scenario. As shown in Fig. 3(a) and (b) the x- and y-axis acceleration of the user changes while the user is walking, but not the acceleration on z-axis. When, the user falls down, there was a small change in acceleration in x- and y-axis, and a significant spike in the acceleration of z-axis demonstrating that the proposed system can detect sudden falls, as applicable in health care sector.

Figure 4 shows the indoor positing results using the iBeacon sensors. We deployed several iBeacon transmitters in the building where the experiment was conducted.

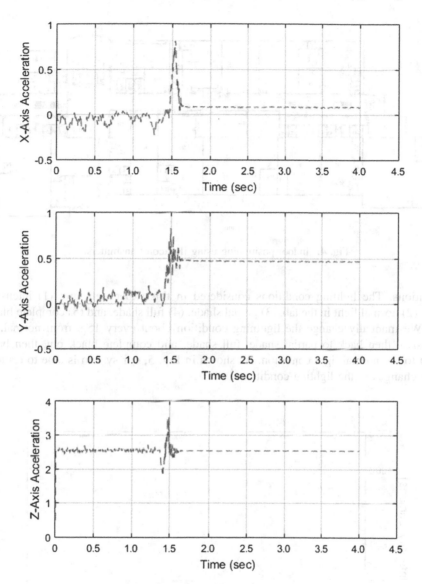

Fig. 3. The results of the fall detector.

When the IoT system worn by the user moves close to any iBeacon, the current location of the user is obtained from the cloud server. The user's current position, the red circle, is stored in the cloud and keep track the all the position history. Moreover, the user or any authorized person can check the user's location.

Light condition is critical for some elderly; some time we need to control the light according to the health condition of the user. The proposed system can monitor the light condition and control it accordingly. Figure 5 shows the light sensor data. The light sensor reports different voltage values in accordance with the different lighting

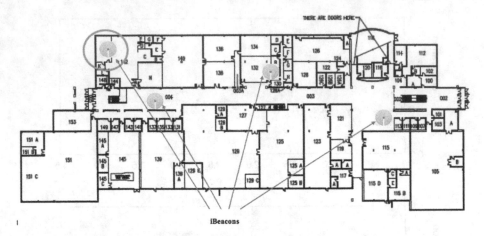

Fig. 4. Indoor positioning using iBeacon transmitters.

conditions. The lighting conditions considered in this experiment are: (1) intensive light, (2) normal light in the lab, (3) partial shade, (4) full shade, and (5) complete black out. We manually change the lightning condition about every 15 s from normal, to intensive, then back to partial shade, full shade, and complete black out, then back again to the normal light condition. As shown in Fig. 5, our system is able to capture these changes in the lighting conditions.

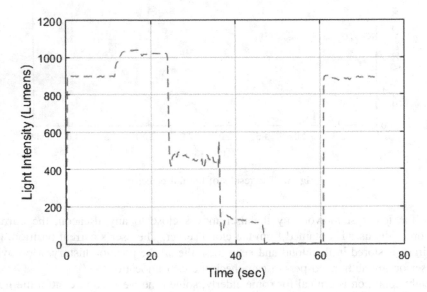

Fig. 5. Lighting condition results.

4 Conclusion

In this paper, we have presented a low-power wearable IoT system for active and assisted living healthcare applications. We have outlined the main components of the proposed system and explained their implementation details. We have built a prototype to illustrate the different performance aspects of the proposed system. The preliminary performance evaluation results have demonstrated the efficiency of the proposed system – despite being a low-cost one. This makes the proposed system a good candidate for implementing a wide set of wearable healthcare systems. Our future work will include how to secure the access of the data and will develop a mobile application that allows access of the data on handheld devices.

References

1. Yin, Y., Zeng, Y., Chen, X., Fan, Y.: The Internet of Things in healthcare: an overview. J. Ind. Inf. Integr. **1**, 3–13 (2016)
2. Sullivan, H.T., Sahasrabudhe, S.: Envisioning inclusive futures: technology-based assistive sensory and action substitution. Futur. J. **87**, 140–148 (2017)
3. Wang, X., Wang, J.T., Zhang, X., Song, J.: A multiple communication standards compatible IoT system for medical usage. In: IEEE Faible Tension Faible Consommation (FTFC), Paris, pp. 1–4 (2013)
4. Xu, B., Xu, L.D., Cai, H., Xie, C., Hu, J., Bu, F.: Ubiquitous data accessing method in IoT-based information system for emergency medical services. IEEE Trans. Ind. Inf. **10**(2), 1578–1586 (2014)
5. Kolici, V., Spaho, E., Matsuo, K., Caballe, S., Barolli, L., Xhafa, F.: Implementation of a medical support system considering P2P and IoT technologies. In: Eighth International Conference on Complex, Intelligent and Software Intensive Systems, Birmingham, pp. 101–106 (2014)
6. Sandholm, T., Magnusson, B., Johnsson, B.A.: An on-demand WebRTC and IoT device tunneling service for hospitals. In: International Conference on Future Internet of Things and Cloud, Barcelona, pp. 53–60 (2014)
7. Antonovici, D.A., Chiuchisan, I., Geman, O., Tomegea, A.: Acquisition and management of biomedical data using Internet of Things concepts. In: International Symposium on Fundamentals of Electrical Engineering, Bucharest, pp. 1–4 (2014)
8. Krishnan, B., Sai, S.S., Mohanthy, S.B.: Real time internet application with distributed flow environment for medical IoT. In: International Conference on Green Computing and Internet of Things, Noida, pp. 832–837 (2015)
9. Azariadi, D., Tsoutsouras, V., Xydis, S., Soudris, D.: ECG signal analysis and arrhythmia detection on IoT wearable medical devices. In: 5th International Conference on Modern Circuits and Systems Technologies, Thessaloniki, pp. 1–4 (2016)
10. Mohan, A.: Cyber security for personal medical devices Internet of Things. In: IEEE International Conference on Distributed Computing in Sensor Systems, Marina Del Rey, CA, pp. 372–374 (2014)
11. Yeh, L.Y., Chiang, P.Y., Tsai, Y.L., Huang, J.L.: Cloud-based fine-grained health information access control framework for lightweight IoT devices with dynamic auditing and attribute revocation. IEEE Trans. Cloud Comput. **PP**(99), 1–13 (2015)

12. Porambage, P., Braeken, A., Gurtov, A., Ylianttila, M., Spinsante, S.: Secure end-to-end communication for constrained devices in IoT-enabled ambient assisted living systems. In: IEEE 2nd World Forum on Internet of Things, Milan, pp. 711–714 (2015)
13. Yelamarthi, K., Laubhan, K.: Space perception and navigation assistance for the visually impaired using depth sensor and haptic feedback. Int. J. Eng. Res. Innov. 7(1), 56–62 (2015)
14. Laubhan, K., Trent, M., Root, B., Abdelgawad, A., Yelamarthi, K.: A wearable portable electronic travel aid for the blind. In: IEEE International Conference on Electrical, Electronics, and Optimization Techniques (2016)
15. Yelamarthi, K., DeJong, B.P., Laubhan, K.: A kinect-based vibrotactile feedback system to assist the visually impaired. In: IEEE Midwest Symposium on Circuits and Systems (2014)
16. What is iBeacon? (2016). https://support.apple.com/en-gb/HT202880
17. Raspberry Pi 2 Model B (2016). https://raspberrypi.org/products/raspberry-pi-2model-b/

DrivingStyles: Assessing the Correlation of Driving Behavior with Heart Rate Changes

Javier E. Meseguer$^{(\boxtimes)}$, Carlos T. Calafate, and Juan Carlos Cano

Department of Computer Engineering, Universitat Politècnica de València,
Camino de Vera S/N, 46022 Valencia, Spain
jmesegue@upvnet.upv.es, {calafate,jucano}@disca.upv.es

Abstract. Driving safety is of utmost importance in our society. The number of fatalities due to car accidents is still very high, and reducing this trend requires as much attention as possible. There are situations where the emotional conditions of drivers vary due to either reasons beyond their control, or because they decide to change their driving style. Hence, we consider that such frequent situations deserve more scrutiny. In this paper we designed an Android application able to monitor in real-time both physiological data from the driver and diagnostic data from the vehicle to study their correlation. More specifically, we study the connection between driving aggressiveness and heart rate. The vehicle diagnostic data is obtained using an OBD-II connector. Among the various non-invasive biomedical sensors available nowadays, in this work we focus on heart rate sensors, either packaged in belts or in smart watches.

Keywords: Driving styles · Android smartphone · OBD-II · Neural networks · Driving behavior · Heart rate · Heart rate belt · Eco-driving · Consumption · Road safety

1 Introduction

It is known that prolonged or repeated stress, such as long traffic jams or driving on severely congested roads, is related to increased aggressiveness. In fact, authors like Gibson and Wiesenthal [1], Cohen [2], and Gravina et al. [3,4] have identified a potentially dangerous aggressiveness level as a result of driver stress. Thus, any method or system that can help at lowering the levels of aggressiveness when driving is welcome.

Our proposal just needs basic devices, such as a mobile phone, and an On Board Diagnostics (OBD-II) device [5–7], available for less than 20 dollars, along with a heart rate band or a smart watch. Our novel DrivingStyles architecture adopts data mining techniques and neural networks to analyze and generate a classification of the driving styles based on an analysis of the characteristics of the driver along the route followed. It ensures that the driver can be constantly aware of its level of aggressiveness and driving stress, and how this affects to his heart rate. In a previous study [8], we developed a methodology to calculate, in

© ICST Institute for Computer Sciences, Social Informatics and Telecommunications Engineering 2017
O. Gaggi et al. (Eds.): GOODTECHS 2016, LNICST 195, pp. 21–30, 2017.
DOI: 10.1007/978-3-319-61949-1_3

real-time, the impact that the driving style will have on the consumption and environmental impact of spark ignition and diesel vehicles. We demonstrated that an aggressive driving style increases the fuel consumption, as well as the emission of greenhouse gases.

In this paper we go one step forward and demonstrate that a more aggressive driving behavior also leads to a heart rate increase of at least three beats per minute with respect to a quiet behavior. The analysis has been carried out with 460 min of driving, taking 27663 direct samples (obtained from the vehicle's ECU and the driver's heart rate band), which corresponds to 5532 time windows where the driver behavior and road types are analyzed. Our platform is able to assist drivers in correcting their bad driving habits, while offering helpful recommendations to improve fuel economy, and driving safety.

This paper is organized as follows: in the next section we present the DrivingStyles architecture. The method used for the analysis of the variables is presented in Sect. 3. We present experimental results in Sect. 4. Finally, in Sect. 5, we review the main conclusions and discuss future work.

2   General Overview of the DrivingStyles Architecture

Our proposed architecture applies data mining techniques to generate a classification of the driving styles of users based on the analysis of their mobility traces using neural networks. Such classification is generated taking into consideration the characteristics of each route, such as whether it is urban, suburban, or highway. To achieve the overall objective, the system is structured around the following two elements:

1. An application for Android-based smartphones which is responsible for collecting data from the car and the driver's heart rate band or smart watch, which also analyzes routes and driver behavior using neural networks.
2. A cloud-based data center to collect large data sets sent by different users concurrently. Subsequently, these data are analyzed using data mining and expert systems, in order to generate useful information.

2.1   Android Application

Using an OBD-II Bluetooth interface, the Android application (see Fig. 1b) collects information such as speed, acceleration, engine revolutions per minute, throttle position, and the vehicle's geographic position. It also obtains information from a wearable heart rate monitor, chest belts and smart watches. This information is analyzed on the device itself, performing the analysis of driver behavior and road type (using neural networks), instantaneous fuel consumption, greenhouse gas emissions, and heart rate measurement.

We then provide feedback from the device to the user in a way that, when the application detects high levels of aggressiveness, (above a certain threshold), the device generates an acoustic signal to alert the driver. Furthermore, if the

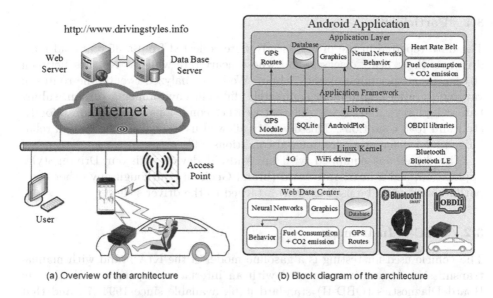

(a) Overview of the architecture   (b) Block diagram of the architecture

Fig. 1. System architecture of DrivingStyles: overview and block diagram architecture.

user has a wearable device, such as a smart watch, it is notified by a vibration event as well.

Eventually, the user uploads the route data to the remote data center for a more comprehensive analysis. The Android application is a key element of our system, proving connectivity to the vehicle and to the DrivingStyles web platform. The application, which is available as a free download in the DrivingStyle's website and from Google Play Store[1], has achieved nearly 6000 downloads from different countries in just one year. This indicates the great interest of this type of user-level applications. For more detailed information please refer to [8,9].

2.2   Data Center

Our data center[2] is able to collect large data sets sent by different users (see Fig. 1a). There are currently 485 registered users and 411 routes sent for study. The data center allows users and administrators to access data about routes and per-user statistics. In particular, users can access all the routes they have uploaded.

3   Research Strategy and Methodology

We now present the methodology we have followed in order to correlate driving aggressiveness and driver heart rate by using the data provided by our DrivingStyles architecture.

---

[1] https://play.google.com/store/apps/details?id=com.driving.styles.
[2] http://www.drivingstyles.info.

3.1 Participant

The data reported in the present study were collected from a 35 years old male driver, without heart diseases, and whose heart rate while at rest lies between 70 bpm (beats per minute) and 75 bpm. We have analyzed twenty-one routes of varying durations, and under completely different environments (urban, suburban or highway), and also at different weather conditions (rainy, sunny, cloudy, etc.) and road conditions. This diversity allowed us to analyze the system reliability under different environmental conditions [10].

The driver was equipped with an Android device with our DrivingStyles application, and a heart rate band (brand Geonaute, although any other compatible band could be used as well) attached to the driver's chest.

3.2 OBD-II Instrument

The vehicle used for testing is a gasoline model of the KIA brand with manual transmission. It was instrumented with an interface compatible with the On Board Diagnostics (OBD-II) standard [5,6], available since 1994 [7], and that has recently become an enabling technology for in-vehicle applications due to the appearance of Bluetooth OBD-II connectors [7,11]. These connectors enable a transparent connectivity between the mobile device and the vehicle's Electronic Control Unit (ECU).

3.3 Heart Rate Monitor (HRM)

Regarding heart rate monitor (HRM) devices, there are mainly two types on the market: the smart-watch (or other wrist band) and the chest strap. Smart-watch models tend to be less accurate than chest-strap HRMs. Tests were conducted with different models of both types. The first devices used were wrist devices, including the Motorola 360 smartwatch. In this model the back of the watch hosts the heart rate sensor. Despite using oximeter technology pulse measurement, in our tests, the sampling frequency of the smart watch was too low and, in combination with the high battery consumption when the heart rate measurement is activated, made us disregard this device from the beginning. So, we opted for the heart rate belt device instead.

Heart rate belt operation is simple, an electrical signal is transmitted through the heart muscle in order for it to contract. This electrical activity can be detected through the skin. The transmitter part of the heart rate monitor is placed on the skin around the area that the heart is beating, and picks up this signal. The transmitter then sends an electromagnetic signal containing heart rate data to the wrist receiver which displays the heart rate.

As we can see in Fig. 2, the Android app displays the heart rate in real-time, as well as a map representation of the heart rate compared with the average of the route undertaken so far, being red if it is higher than average, and green otherwise. It is mandatory that the mobile device used supports Bluetooth Low Energy (Bluetooth LE, BLE) to connect with the heart rate monitor.

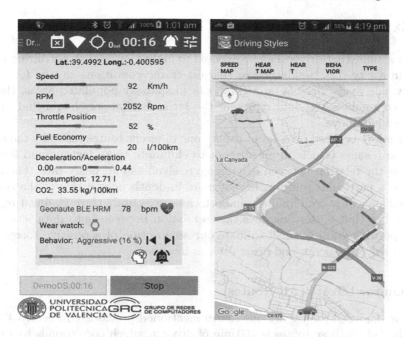

Fig. 2. Snapshots of the main screen and the heart rate module. (Color figure online)

Table 1. Mean, standard deviation, and range of route time, speed, and heart rate.

	Mean	SD	Range
Route time (*minutes*)	24.63	26.37	6.32–81.44
Speed (*km/h*)	67.44	41.30	0–135
Heart rate (*bpm*)	79.73	10.87	55–115

3.4   Measurement Result

The total time of the twenty-one routes considered for this study has been 7 h and 40 min (460 min). Regarding the heart rate, 27663 direct samples (one sample every second) have been obtained. Also 5520 driving behavior measures calculated by the neural network have been used in the test, reflecting the behavior of the driver at measurement time (behavior analysis is performed with data from 5 s before performing the calculation). See Table 1 for further information.

Before performing the statistical calculations, the samples were normalized between 0 and 1. The neural network developed returns a value between 0 and 100, as a result of analizing each type of behavior. These values must also be normalized before the statistical study.

In Sect. 4 we proceed to analyze the correlation between driving behavior and the driver's heart rate.

4   Experimental Results and Evaluation

We can assume that drivers can be exposed to higher levels of stress during rush-hours in a city [12]. Similarly, the sparsest traffic conditions can be found on country side roads, driving on highways or in sparsely populated areas. Hence, these two conditions should represent the far ends that we should find in the routes under analysis.

Our study is based on a set of twenty-one different routes made by the same driver on a same vehicle in an attempt to eliminate these factors, and focuses solely on the relation between driving aggressiveness and heart rate. Then, we focus on a particular route to have a more in-depth perspective of the results obtained and the overall findings. In both cases, we obtain through linear regression the line that better describes the correlation between both data sets. This way, a positive gradient shall validate our assumption of a positive correlation between driver behavior and heart rate, as intended.

4.1   On-road Tests (All Routes)

First, we analyzed the twenty-one routes mentioned previously in Sect. 3.4. The total time of all these routes is 460 min of driving, which corresponds to a total of 27663 direct samples and 5532 behavior samples calculated by the system. Notice that the developed neural network evaluated the three types of driver behavior at once, generating an output score for each that allows generating an output in the range from 0 to 1.

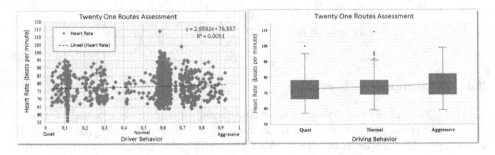

Fig. 3. Correlation between heart rate and driving behavior.

Fig. 4. Box and wisker plot of heart rate vs driving behavior.

Figures 3 and 4 show the correlation plots between heart rate and behavior of the 27663 samples obtained for the study. Table 2 shows the equation of the corresponding slope-intercept form, where the slope given by m, which equals to 2.959, and the y-intercept by b, which is equal to 76.557 (see Fig. 3). As it can be observed, the intended correlation between driving styles and heart rate R is 0.071. The correlation value obtained is not as significant when compared to result for a particular route, as shown in the following section.

Table 2. Slope-intercept form equation of single route and all routes.

	y	m	R^2	R
Behavior single route				
Quiet-normal	$8.692x + 72.72$	8.692	0.172	0.414
Normal-aggressive	$5.667x + 74.049$	5.667	0.041	0.203
Quiet-normal-aggressive	$6.937x + 73.362$	6.937	0.173	0.416
Behavior all routes				
Quiet-normal-aggressive	$2.959x + 76.557$	2.959	0.005	0.071

These results were mostly expected since the driver remains seated in all cases, and so the additional physical burden requiring a higher heart beat is not comparable to more demanding situations. It is noteworthy mentioning, though, that in this section we are studying routes of many types, some from urban scenarios and other from highway scenarios, being the behavior less aggressive for the latter. So, overall, we find that the difference between a quiet behavior and an aggressive behavior for a specific driver is a heart rate increase of 3.72%. Figure 4 shows the box and wisker plot of heart rate vs driving behavior. We find that the difference in heart rate between quiet and aggressive behavior is 3.25% (about three beats per minute).

4.2 On-road Tests (Single Route)

In this second part of the analysis, we study a specific route chosen from the set of twenty-one routes analyzed in this paper. The DrivingStyles platform, in addition to analyzing the behavior, is also able to compute the route type.

In particular, this route has a duration of 6 min and 33 s, circulating at an average speed of 24 km/h and a maximum speed of 57 km/h, covering a total of 2.17 km; this corresponds to 381 behavior type samples, also including data about the driver's heart rate that we use in the statistical analysis.

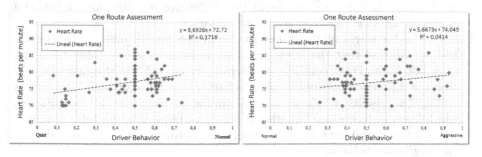

Fig. 5. Correlation between heart rate and driving behavior (quiet-normal).

Fig. 6. Correlation between heart rate and driving behavior (normal-aggressive).

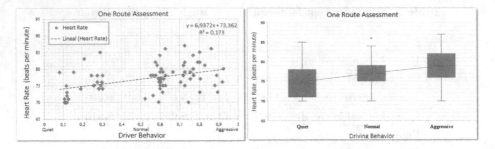

Fig. 7. Correlation between heart rate and driving behavior.

Fig. 8. Box and wisker plot of heart rate vs driving behavior.

After normalizing the data as explained in Sect. 3.4, we split our analysis into three parts: the difference in terms of heart rate between quiet and normal behavior (see Fig. 5), the same difference between normal and aggressive behavior (see Fig. 6), and a full comparison between quiet, normal, and aggressive driving (see Figs. 7 and 8):

1. Concerning the first case study i.e., when comparing the heart rate between a quiet behavior and normal behavior (see Fig. 5), we find that the linear trendline has a positive slope (8.69) and the *R-squared* value or coefficient of determination is 0.17 (how close the data are to the fitted regression line). As shown in this figure, there is a clear correlation between heart rate and driver behavior, being the heart rate when the system detects normal behavior about 10.67% higher compared to a quiet behavior.
2. In Fig. 6 we compare the normal driver behavior against an aggressive behavior for the same route. We find that the slope of the regression line is lower than for the plot previously discussed (quiet behavior vs normal behavior), having a value of 5.66, being the coefficient of determination significantly lower, with a value of 0.04. Observing both plots (see Figs. 5 and 6), we find that, regarding the outputs of the neural network implemented, the computation of the driver's behavior tends to provide as outcome that is either a quiet behavior or an aggressive behavior in most cases, being intermediate values more scarce. In this case, the heart rate difference is 7.20% higher between aggressive behavior and the normal behavior.
3. In the third scenario, all the system's outputs were jointly analyzed (see Figs. 7 and 8). We find that the linear trendline remains positive, being the slope value of 6.93, and the coefficient of determination is 0.17. In this last analyzed case the difference between a quiet behavior and an aggressive behavior is 8.61%. The results obtained are very similar to the first plot (see Fig. 5), which leads us to consider whether it would be interesting, in future studies, to train the neural network to have only two outputs instead: quiet behavior and aggressive behavior.

Finally, the box and whisker plot (see Fig. 8) displays the differences between quiet, normal, and aggressive driving behavior vs heart rate; for this test subject, an aggressive driving provoked an increased heart rate. If we look at the value of the median in the three types of behavior (quiet, normal and aggressive) we see that the difference in heart rate between a quiet and normal behavior is 2.78% (about two beats per minute); similarly, between a normal and an aggressive behavior, this difference is 2.41% (about two beats per minute as well). Summarizing, according to our findings, the driver's pulse increased by 5.18% (slightly more four beats per minute) when the driver switched to a more aggressive driving compared to a quite driving style.

5   Conclusions and Future Work

In this paper we studied the correlation of the driver heart rate with respect to his driver behavior. We based our study on the use of our novel DrivingStyles architecture, that combines new technologies such as smartphones and wearable body sensors with the modern software implementations of artificial neural networks.

The results of the present study indicated that aggressive driving causes an increase in the heart rate, being able to rise it by up to three beats per minute on average. Based on our experimental results, we have reached the conclusion that the difference in terms of heart rate between a quiet and aggressive behavior can become very noticeable. In statistical terms, we also found that, as the number of samples increases, the correlation between the driver behavior and heart rate becomes lower. This was expected since increasing the number of routes whose behavior is largely quiet, makes the percentage of values with an aggressive behavior to decreases, i.c., an urban route that causes stress and aggressiveness will get closer to our results that a long highway route where the stress is nonexistent or scarce. Since this study has been conducted taking a middle-aged male subject as reference, in future works we will expand the scope of our study to women, and also to drivers of different ages, which will help at covering a wider range of possible cases. This will allow us to study the differences between various age segments, as well as to differentiate driving aggressiveness and heart rate based on the driver's gender.

Acknowledgments. This work was partially supported by the Ministerio de Economa y Competitividad, Programa Estatal de Investigacin, Desarrollo e Innovacion Orientada a los Retos de la Sociedad, Proyectos I+D+I 2014, Spain, under Grant TEC2014-52690-R.

References

1. Gibson, P.M., Wiesenthal, D.L.: The driving vengeance questionnaire (DVQ): the development of a scale to measure deviant drivers. LaMarsh Research Programme Report Series, no. 54, June 1996
2. Cohen, S.: Aftereffects of stress on human performance and social behavior: a review of research and theory. Psychol. Bull. **88**, 82–108 (1980)

3. Gravina, R., Fortino, G.: Automatic methods for the detection of accelerative cardiac defense response. IEEE Trans. Affect. Comput. **7**(3), 286–298 (2016)
4. Andreoli, A., Gravina, R., Giannantonio, R., Pierleoni, P., Fortino, G.: SPINE-HRV: a BSN-based toolkit for heart rate variability analysis in the time-domain. In: Lay-Ekuakille, A., Mukhopadhyay, S.C. (eds.) Wearable and Autonomous Systems. LNEE, vol. 75, pp. 369–389. Springer, Heidelberg (2010). doi:10.1007/978-3-642-15687-8_19
5. Keyword Protocol 2000: International Organization for Standardization (1999)
6. ISO: ISO 9141-2:1994/Amd 1:1996,1196. Technical report, International Organization for Standardization (1996)
7. Niazi, M.A.K., Raza, A.: Development of an on-board diagnostic (OBD) kit for troubleshooting of compliant vehicles. In: 2013 IEEE 9th International Conference on Emerging Technologies (ICET) (2013)
8. Meseguer, J.E., Calafate, C.T., Cano, J.C., Manzoni, P.: Assessing the impact of driving behavior on instantaneous fuel consumption. In: 12th IEEE Consumer Communications and Networking Conference (CCNC 2015) (2015)
9. Meseguer, J.E., Calafate, C.T., Cano, J.C., Manzoni, P.: DrivingStyles: a smartphone application to assess driver behavior. In: 18th IEEE Symposium on Computers and Communications (ISCC 2013) (2013)
10. Riener, A.: Subliminal persuasion and its potential for driver behavior adaptation. IEEE Trans. Intell. Transp. **13**(1), 71–80 (2012)
11. Elm Electronics Circuits: ELM327DS. OBD to RS232 Interpreter. Hobbyist (2010)
12. Lajunen, T., Parker, D., Summala, H.: Does traffic congestion increase driver aggression? Transp. Res. Part F **2**, 225–236 (1999)

Understanding Needs, Identifying Opportunities: ICT in the View of Universal Design

Ilaria Garofolo$^{(\boxtimes)}$, Eric Medvet, Fulvio Babich, and Giovanni Ramponi

Department of Engineering and Architecture, University of Trieste, Trieste, Italy
garofolo@units.it

Abstract. This article provides food for thoughts elaborated by peer researchers who, basing on their studies and on current literature on relationships between Universal Design (UD) and Information and Communication Technologies (ICT), wish to share few key issues related to the challenges offered by the involvement of final users in designing product and services. Referring to approaches from different disciplines, key questions will be highlighted on which a debate could start, focused on the issue of promoting inclusion and how a close relationship among these different areas of knowledge can contribute to bridge the gap between the potential of new technologies and the real and diversified need by persons. Thus, actively contributing toward the empowerment of the community of belonging.

Keywords: Accessibility · Usability · Design for All · Inclusive and Universal Design · Internet of Things

1 ICT as a Driving Force for Inclusion and People Empowerment

In order to implement the UN Convention on the Rights of Persons with Disabilities (CRPD), the EU Commission launched the "European Disability Strategy 2010–2020: A Renewed Commitment to a Barrier-Free Europe", which aims to increase the participation of people with disabilities in society and economy, and enable them to fully exercise their rights.

Analysing the areas for joint action between the EU and Member States pointed out in the Strategy, it becomes clear that for most of these (and in particular for Accessibility, Participation, Equality, Employment, Education and training, Social protection, and Health) the role of support represented by ICT to overcome discrimination and to achieve the goal of a wider inclusion is crucial.

The UN CRPD [1] further states that "to ensure and promote the full realization of all human rights and fundamental freedoms for all persons with disabilities without discrimination of any kind on the basis of disability" States Parties shall "undertake or promote research and development of, and to promote the availability and use of new technologies, including information and communications technologies [...] suitable for persons with disabilities, giving priority to

© ICST Institute for Computer Sciences, Social Informatics and Telecommunications Engineering 2017
O. Gaggi et al. (Eds.): GOODTECHS 2016, LNICST 195, pp. 31–40, 2017.
DOI: 10.1007/978-3-319-61949-1_4

technologies at an affordable cost" (Art. 4); the Convention recognises therefore to persons with disabilities (PwD) the right to access, on an equal basis with others, "information and communications, including information and communications technologies and systems". It commits the States "to promote access for persons with disabilities to new information and communications technologies and systems, including the Internet" (Art. 9-g) and "to promote the design, development, production and distribution of accessible information and communications technologies and systems at an early stage" (Art. 9-h), to enable PwD to live independently and participate fully in all aspects of life, thus pursuing the goal of social inclusion.

Bearing in mind the ageing of the population in Europe, the envisaged actions in the strategic plan will specifically affect the quality of life of an important and increasing segment of population that includes, other than PwD, those who experiment disability in their lifetime due to aging or temporary reduced functionalities. ICT, with *assistive and enabling technologies* can be regarded as strategic drivers for the social evolution of a community: if truly usable and affordable, they are a fast, economic and reliable way to foster the inclusion of disadvantaged people and to tackle discrimination.

Nevertheless, to avoid the risk linked with the uncertain relationship between products and success/failure, innovative approaches to the design process should be based on a different values range, which considers what can effectively meet a user's need, perhaps latent at the moment, instead of what can be an exclusively technological achievement. This is a winning strategy in step with the idea that man should be placed again in the spotlight, with his/her needs, desires, tastes and disposition. And, above all, differences. Once again UN CRPD suggests the approach into achieving inclusive solutions, by means of Universal Design: that is "the design of products, environments, programs and services to be usable by all people, to the greatest extent possible, without the need for adaptation or specialized design. Universal Design shall not exclude assistive devices for particular groups of persons with disabilities where this is needed" (Art. 2).

The best option will certainly be to mainstream the UD approach and the related Design-for-All principles as much as possible in goods and services, making them economically viable and avoiding the necessity for consumers with special needs, like the elderly and persons with disability, to look for specific products or to depend on others for their daily activities.

In this context, accessibility can be seen as a *key enabling knowledge* that allows everybody to manage at their best their relationship with the surrounding environment (that is with living spaces, goods, services). According to the Classification of Functionality, Disability and Health (ICF) [2], to provide the environment with facilitating elements that enable the largest number of persons means to affect positively the "disability threshold", above which they can participate actively to life, according to their capabilities, with the largest autonomy and at the best possible conditions. Promoting accessibility in a proactive way, thus, (i) benefits society and the economy in general making life easier for everyone; (ii) supports an active and productive participation of older persons in their communities and labour market participation of PwD; and (iii) enables informal carers to reconcile work and care duties.

Researchers working in the field of UD are deeply (and often painfully) aware of the economic aspects of their studies. A recent EU study [3] demonstrates the socio-economic importance, and the related costs, of improving the accessibility to PwD of goods and services; among these services, ICT is a priority. Public financial support is managed differently in different countries, but in general countries with high investments and thus high accessibility standards in the built environment, transport, and ICT are those where the highest levels of employment of both older women and men are found; they are also those which perform best in terms of Healthy Life Years indicators [4].

The other way around, what can ICT do to increase the effectiveness of policies for the empowerment of PwD? One possible answer is to enable all stakeholders to make informed decisions. For this purpose, ICT is a fundamental source of data for the economic evaluation of the costs/benefits of a given policy. Understanding and exploiting the tools that contemporary studies in the economic assessment of health technologies employ is essential for people working in the UD field, to effectively interface with the agencies that define the spending policies of a country. One example of such tools is the Disability-Adjusted Life Year (DALY) indicator [5,6]. It is defined as the sum of two terms, evaluated in a selected test group: the reduction of the average duration of life due to the disability (Years of Life Lost, YLL), plus the quality loss in the life span (Years Lost due to Disability, YLD), which in turn is the product between the reduction of life quality and the average life duration with disability. The DALY can be determined using the data that are collected by ICT-based tools, and provides an a-posteriori estimate of the benefits of a given project.

2 Beyond Accessibility to Design ICT: Involving Users to Investigate Needs

UD, despite not being a new concept, is nowaday seen as innovative by an increasing number of stakeholders, including the final users who benefit from it and who, at the same time, are involved as *experts* into the participative process of conceiving the products. UD is based on the assumption that accessibility to spaces, objects and services is the key prerequisite to use them.

Before going any further, we need to set the meaning of some words we use hereinafter. In the field of computer science and ICT in particular, *accessibility* primarily refers to the distinguishing qualities that the design of devices and systems should have to allow their use by PwD. The World Wide Web Consortium (W3C) defines Web accessibility as an attribute through which "people with disabilities can perceive, understand, navigate, and interact with the Web, and they can contribute to the Web" [7]. Web accessibility includes all types of disabilities that impact access to the Web and thus includes visual, hearing, physical, and speech impediments, cognitive and neurological disabilities; elderly users benefit too from adherence to Web accessibility principles.

In a wider and cross-disciplinary view, accessibility is the basic requisite to use goods and navigate spaces, and it does not necessarily refer only to PwD; indeed, transposing the W3C definition we can assume that "accessibility is an attribute through which people can perceive, understand, navigate, and interact with the living environment, and they can contribute to the growth of the community".

The citizens' community lives and acts within an often unfriendly environment, which prevents persons to take an active role in daily life, and affects their independence and autonomy in respect of their capabilities and functionalities. Making the environment accessible, thus, means to integrate or to provide it with facilitating elements (for example using compensative solutions, eliminating barriers or resorting to Design for All resources) to raise its level of accessibility and allow its use by a wider range of persons. In the ICT field, while the focus of accessibility is disabilities, research and development in accessibility brings benefits to everyone, particularly users with situational limitations, including device limitations and environmental limitations [8].

The *usability* concept includes emotionally engaging a person by positively exciting him/her, thus fully meeting his/her expectations. The International Standards Organization's standard ISO 9241 defines usability as the "effectiveness, efficiency, and satisfaction with which specified users achieve specified goals in particular environments". A less formal interpretation defines usability as "an attribute of quality that refers to the promptness with which users learn to use something, the efficiency they attain while making use of it, how easy it is for them to remember how to use it, how error-prone it is, and the level of satisfaction that they attain from using it" [9].

In the ICT field, usability is slowly improving; however, the focus is still mainly on accessibility rather than on Design for All. While some ICT companies have developed accessibility devices to enable persons with disabilities to access their products, many people (among which especially the elderly) often feel excluded from a wide range of e-products and services which could otherwise be relevant to them. There is a genuine risk of departure of products from the real needs of users—that's typical in any field of innovation.

The slogan of the disability rights movement has long been "nothing about us without us". Far from being a mere challenging approach, asserting an attitude in claiming, it stresses the idea that PwD can contribute to the growth of a community moving from *passive recipients* to *co-producers* while involved in the process of visioning strategies, making policies, designing goods and services. It is truly PwD who understand best what PwD need: they just have a different opinion and different priorities than the current providers and decision makers. But as the movement progresses, and seeks the actions to realize its vision, difficult questions arise about exactly how self-determination can shape strategies and actions in the field of ICT. Key questions need to be asked, among which whether the modern disability movement is itself sufficiently inclusive of PwD and how to set requirements and pattern flows to ensure a proper and successful user participation in development and production processes. PwD are a heterogeneous group, and the specific issues which shape their life opportunities are just as diverse; moreover, the risk of "divergence of effect" [10] is rather high when design process based on the theoretical principles of UD are developed avoiding an effective users participation. In a sense, there is the need to create a standard for the participation of the user [11].

A proper engagement of persons could allow the *mutual* adaptation between the different users capabilities and the performances required by a very often complex outer environment and its "devices" (spaces, goods, services).

Engaging people in the development of a new product/service is the ultimate result of the evolvement from the "products designed for the user" approach to "the development of user inputs" and finally the active involvement of users by designers: a current practice, focused on identifying the most relevant requirements expressed by targeted user categories and on testing of released products/prototypes. Nevertheless, optimal solutions vary greatly depending on the specific users and contexts of use, and this is more evident when target groups are (or involve) PwD. Very often, considering their needs we face the risk that labelling these as "special" leads to think in terms of separate, special solutions, thus highlighting the inherent contradiction between diversity and "special" needs: everyone has unique needs and resources [12].

An Inclusive and Universal Design (I&UD) can offer different thought patterns if the starting point is to realize that one-size-fits-all solutions seldom meet every person's needs and that accessible features can benefit the majority of the population. Therefore, as argued by Page, a shift in design thinking is required to consider the "normality of doing things differently" [13].

Engagement of users introduces divergent thinking and implies that different users should first reciprocally accommodate their specific needs and expectations, which are very often deeply different if not conflicting. If it is true that seeing problems from diverse perspectives and looking for solutions in different ways can locate more potential innovations [12], the setting of user groups including diverse PwD implies raising their awareness on the real scale of differences, expectations, needs "by all". And makes them aware that aiming to a solution that benefits all implies a high level of adaptiveness "by all" to the best of possible solution.

3   A Case Study: IoT and Inclusive Design

The deployment of the ever-increasing number of systems that belong to the so-called Internet of Things (IoT) is a concrete example that we can consider as a case study. Indeed, the forthcoming evolution of 5G technology foresees a pervasive wireless scenario, in which a huge number of devices will concur to support IoT applications, including intelligent metering, infrastructure management, health support, home automation, public transportation, safety, and security. The number of devices that will be wirelessly connected in the IoT are estimated to be around 20 billion by the beginning of the next decade [14].

IoT is interesting because it is a still relatively small field experiencing a very fast growing rate, due to the combination of several favorable conditions. Some of these depend on its huge potential market (that in turn brings large available investments), others are more technical conditions related to the ICT world and concern this paper. For example:

- Electronics: IoT needs low-cost, high-volume, mature technologies on which research and development efforts have already been made by the electronic industry. The largest companies, indeed, have added to their traditional suite of products (such as sensors, analog and mixed signal components, microcontrollers, energy management devices) various dedicated development environments [15] that can be devoted to this purpose. In particular, IoT networks that are meant for the factory environment may be particularly suited to I&UD due to their attention to security and reliability [16].
- Telecommunications: the convergence towards an all IP solution for the telecom network, that started with 4G, and the seamless integration between the core telecom network and the local and the sensor networks, all based on international communication standards, allows now the development of a fully interacting system, connecting people and devices (things), leading towards the smart and fully connected society foreseen by 5G development, and avoiding the barriers deriving from the widespread utilization of "private standards" that have delayed and slowed down the full exploitation of the system capabilities [17].

A huge flow of information is expected to be available in IoT systems, not only that which is needed for the goals of the system, but also that coming as a byproduct of the system operation ("exhaust" data; e.g., in an inventory keeping system, the rate at which the quantities of the different goods change). A part of these data is used by the system itself (in home automation, to manage instantaneous power consumption by the different appliances), but in many cases an interaction with the user may be advisable. The user should be able to set the amount of data he/she is capable or willing to manage.

At the same time, since the flow of information is bi-directional, the IoT systems will also often collect data about the user (in a shop, the time spent in different sectors, the way goods are selected, etc.). It is widely acknowledged that this generates increasing privacy problems. If a person with disabilities is involved, the risk is even stronger; for example, the existence of the disability itself can be disclosed, which can be deeply undesirable for the user.

Under an economic viewpoint, the concept of exhaust data is in the focus of the attention of those who devise new business opportunities: data that have no value for the main purpose of the system could be extremely important for other potential users. For example, the long-term maintenance data of cars collected in a service station may become useful information for an insurance company. The presence of these data should be carefully considered also with respect to the potential benefits for a PwD. An open-minded design of an IoT system could provide these benefits at no or small cost for the owner. National and EU funding agencies should provide a financial support for the deployment of such systems, having verified the existence of such benefits.

A fundamental but still open issue is the one of standardization. To fully exploit the IoT capabilities and to avoid further digital divides, all the stakeholders should influence the standard development. Unfortunately, the main driving forces are the big companies and the standard bodies, while the SME and the consumer organizations are almost absent from the standardization process. One possible solution may be to invest some money to involve the user representatives in the standard activities [18].

However, given the high degree of flexibility of the standard under development, the robustness and the safety of which must be addressed by the standardization bodies and the big manufacturers, the user involvement may be addressed by I&UD which should work on the personalization and the interoperability of the communicating devices, to allow them to be really used by all [19].

4 Ongoing Research

We survey some recent works in which systems, tools, or methods related to the IoT have been proposed that were thought or adaptable for categories of weak users; we also consider studies which explicitly investigated about the relation between IoT and PwD. The aim is to understand if, to which degree, and in which form PwD have been involved in the design process.

The opportunities of the IoT for PwD depend on the involved technologies, which have to be related to different kinds of disability (e.g., hearing impaired, visually impaired). Some reference scenarios can be devised and discussed in detail from the technological point of view: for instance, the case in which a visually impaired person is assisted when autonomously shopping at a store. This approach is used in [20], and permits to outline some present research challenges: the paper acknowledges that the foremost consists in customizing and adapting the IoT for person with disabilities. However, the direct inclusions of those users in the design process is not explicitly mentioned. When the IoT belongs to a larger integrated IT environment (e.g., aimed at providing a so called Ambient Intelligence), a balance between Universal Design and adaptation is needed to cope with the design of tools or services for persons with disabilities; a fine-grained set of options should be considered for this purpose [21].

The inclusion of the final user in the design of IoT solution is instead the main focus of [22], where the EU project SOCIOTAL is presented. It lays down a "co-creation" approach in which the services arise from citizens for tackling their needs rather than being proposed by commercial service providers. From this point of view we are in line with the authors of the cited paper, who propose inclusion as a main requirement for designing effective IoT services; on the other hand, they do not mention disabled persons. A similar thesis is proposed also in [23], where the authors suggest that trust, user control, and transparency should be at the heart of IoT.

An interesting experimental study about the involvement of disabled or elder users in the design phase of an IoT-based tool is shown in [24]. The authors consider three relevant scenarios (smart homes, smart offices, and e-voting) and elaborate on the impact of users' inclusion in the design stage on users' trust in the resulting tool. In particular, they show the results of a study with 85 subjects (including visually impaired and persons affected by dyslexia) who were asked to evaluate an IoT system in its early stage: the subjects found the system itself useful, but suggested several improvements on the user interface; the system design was hence adjusted to meet the subjects' recommendations.

Visual impairment is a disability for which many IT based system have been proposed or designed in principle, ranging from shopping assistants [25,26], to tools for enabling social interactions [27,28], or for allowing interaction with visual-based online social networks [29]. The degree of inclusion of the specific category of disabled persons in the design of the system greatly varies and is not clearly related with the degree of development of the system itself. For instance, we observed cases with no mentions to inclusion [26,30], cases where normally sighted subjects wearing a blindfold were included in experimentation [25], and cases where actual visually impaired persons were included, either by collecting experimental data [31], or by participating in interviews aimed at guiding design choices [29], or by testing a system prototype [32].

5   Final Remarks

The good news in ICT, and specifically for the rapidly growing Internet of Things, is that a designer of a system can (and should) devote a large part of his/her attention to human aspects, since the basic technical tools suitable to build many types of network have already been made available. A 2015 McKinsey report provides impressive figures and facts about the impact of IoT [33]. However, among the different fields of application, from homes to factories to vehicles, the "human" field (especially related to health and social issues) is the one whose prediction has the largest uncertainty: it ranges from 170 to 1590 billion $ in 2025. We can easily deduce that much of this spread is related to the level of user's acceptance. Thus, this is a significant example of a field in which I&UD principles should be employed from the start. In fact, it has already been observed that "At a minimum, all parties involved in the development of IoT devices and applications should commit to upholding the principles of universal design" [34]. Engagement of final users is pivotal in shaping the Internet of the future, for the use of digital technologies to be successful to allow the Internet of Things to become the *Internet for People*.

References

1. Hendricks, A.: UN convention on the rights of persons with disabilities. Eur. J. Health L. **14**, 273 (2007). http://www.un.org/disabilities/convention/conventionfull.shtml
2. WHO: International Classification of Functioning, Disability and Health: ICF. Technical report, World Health Organization (2001). http://www.who.int/classifications/icf/en/
3. Deloitte: Study on the socio-economic impact of new measures to improve accessibility of goods and services for people with disabilities (2014). http://ec.europa.eu/social/BlobServlet?docId=14842

4. Eurostat: Healthy life years statistics. Technical report, Eurostat (2016). http://ec.europa.eu/eurostat/statistics-explained/index.php/Healthy_life_years_statistics

5. Drummond, M.F., Sculpher, M.J., Claxton, K., Stoddart, G.L., Torrance, G.W.: Methods for the Economic Evaluation of Health care Programmes. Oxford University Press, Oxford (2015)

6. Murray, C.J., Vos, T., Lozano, R., Naghavi, M., Flaxman, A.D., Michaud, C., Ezzati, M., Shibuya, K., Salomon, J.A., Abdalla, S., et al.: Disability-adjusted life years (DALYs) for 291 diseases and injuries in 21 regions, 1990–2010: a systematic analysis for the Global Burden of Disease Study 2010. Lancet **380**(9859), 2197–2223 (2013)

7. W3C-WAI: Introduction to Web Accessibility. Technical report, Web Accessibility Initiative (2005). https://www.w3.org/WAI/intro/accessibility.php

8. Henry, S.L., Abou-Zahra, S., Brewer, J.: The role of accessibility in a universal web. In: Proceedings of the 11th Web for all Conference, p. 17. ACM (2014)

9. Nielsen, J., Loranger, H.: Prioritizing Web Usability. Pearson Education, Upper Saddle River (2006)

10. Arenghi, A., Garofolo, I., Lauría, A.: On the relationship between "Universal" and "Particular" in architecture. In: Universal Design 2016: Learning from the Past, Designing for the Future, pp. 31–39. IOS Press (2016)

11. Brynn, R.: Universal design and standardisation-can user participation be standardized? In: Universal Design 2014: Three Days of Creativity and Diversity: Proceedings of the International Conference on Universal Design, UD 2014 Lund, Sweden, 16–18 June 2014, vol. 35, p. 307. IOS Press (2014)

12. Hedvall, P.O.: I have never been universal. In: Reklamebyrå, H.K. (ed.) Trends in Universal Design. Lund University Press, Lund (2013)

13. Page, S.E.: Making the difference: applying a logic of diversity. Acad. Manag. Perspect. **21**(4), 6–20 (2007)

14. Nathan, E.: Gartner: 21 Billion IoT Devices to Invade by 2020. Technical report (2015). http://www.informationweek.com/mobile/mobile-devices/gartner-21-billion-iot-devices-to-invade-by-2020/d/d-id/1323081

15. STM32 Open Development Environment (2015). http://www.st.com/STM32ODE

16. Weiss, J., Yu, R.: Wireless Sensor Networking for the Industrial Internet of Things. Technical report, Linear Technology white paper WP007f (2015). http://www.linear.com/docs/47097

17. ISO: International standards and "private standards". Technical report, ISO: International Organization for Standardization (2010). http://www.iso.org/iso/private_standards.pdf

18. Jakobs, K., Wagner, T., Reimers, K.: Standardising the internet of things: what the experts think. Int. J. IT Stan. Stand. Res. (IJITSR) **9**(1), 63–67 (2011)

19. McLoughlin, E.: Inclusive design: manufacturing, design, and retail expert views. Technical report (2016). http://www.pocklington-trust.org.uk/project/inclusive-design-manufacturing-design-retail-experts-views/

20. Domingo, M.C.: An overview of the internet of things for people with disabilities. J. Netw. Comput. Appl. **35**(2), 584–596 (2012)

21. Mikołajewska, E., Mikołajewski, D.: Integrated IT environment for people with disabilities: a new concept. Open Med. **9**(1), 177–182 (2014)

22. Kranenburg, R., Stembert, N., Moreno, M.V., Skarmeta, A.F., López, C., Elicegui, I., Sánchez, L.: Co-creation as the key to a public, thriving, inclusive and meaningful EU IoT. In: Hervás, R., Lee, S., Nugent, C., Bravo, J. (eds.) UCAmI 2014. LNCS, vol. 8867, pp. 396–403. Springer, Cham (2014). doi:10.1007/978-3-319-13102-3_65

23. Moreno, M.V., Hernández, J.L., Skarmeta, A.F., Nati, M., Palaghias, N., Gluhak, A., Van Kranenburg, R.: A framework for citizen participation in the internet of things. In: 2014 28th International Conference on Advanced Information Networking and Applications Workshops (WAINA), pp. 815–820. IEEE (2014)

24. Schulz, T.: Creating universal designed and trustworthy objects for the internet of things. In: Zaphiris, P., Ioannou, A. (eds.) LCT 2014. LNCS, vol. 8524, pp. 206–214. Springer, Cham (2014). doi:10.1007/978-3-319-07485-6_21

25. Tekin, E., Coughlan, J.M.: An algorithm enabling blind users to find and read barcodes. In: 2009 Workshop on Applications of Computer Vision (WACV), pp. 1–8. IEEE (2009)

26. Mathankumar, M., Sugandhi, N.: A low cost smart shopping facilitator for visually impaired. In: 2013 International Conference on Advances in Computing, Communications and Informatics (ICACCI), pp. 1088–1092. IEEE (2013)

27. Bonetto, M., Carrato, S., Fenu, G., Medvet, E., Mumolo, E., Pellegrino, F.A., Ramponi, G.: Image processing issues in a social assistive system for the blind. In: 9th International Symposium on Image and Signal Processing and Analysis (ISPA), pp. 216–221. IEEE (2015)

28. Carrato, S., Fenu, G., Medvet, E., Mumolo, E., Pellegrino, F.A., Ramponi, G.: Towards more natural social interactions of visually impaired persons. In: Battiato, S., Blanc-Talon, J., Gallo, G., Philips, W., Popescu, D., Scheunders, P. (eds.) ACIVS 2015. LNCS, vol. 9386, pp. 729–740. Springer, Cham (2015). doi:10.1007/978-3-319-25903-1_63

29. White, G.R., Fitzpatrick, G., McAllister, G.: Toward accessible 3D virtual environments for the blind and visually impaired. In: Proceedings of the 3rd International Conference on Digital Interactive Media in Entertainment and Arts, pp. 134–141. ACM (2008)

30. Bhargava, B., Angin, P., Duan, L.: A mobile-cloud pedestrian crossing guide for the blind. In: International Conference on Advances in Computing and Communication (2011)

31. Carrato, S., Marsi, S., Medvet, E., Pellegrino, F.A., Ramponi, G., Vittori, M.: Computer vision for the blind: a dataset for experiments on face detection and recognition. In: 2016 39th International Convention on Information and Communication Technology, Electronics and Microelectronics (MIPRO), pp. 1206–1211, May 2016

32. Stearns, L., Du, R., Oh, U., Wang, Y., Findlater, L., Chellappa, R., Froehlich, J.E.: The design and preliminary evaluation of a finger-mounted camera and feedback system to enable reading of printed text for the blind. In: Agapito, L., Bronstein, M.M., Rother, C. (eds.) ECCV 2014. LNCS, vol. 8927, pp. 615–631. Springer, Cham (2015). doi:10.1007/978-3-319-16199-0_43

33. Manyika, J., Chui, M., Bisson, P., Woetzel, J., Dobbs, R., Bughin, J., Aharon, D.: Unlocking the Potential of the Internet of Things. Technical report, McKinsey Global Institute (2015). http://www.mckinsey.com/business-functions/business-technology/our-insights/the-internet-of-things-the-value-of-digitizing-the-physical-world

34. G3ict: Internet of Things: New Promises for Persons with Disabilities. Technical report, Global Initiative for Inclusive Information and Communication Technologies (2015)

A Microservice Architecture Use Case for Persons with Disabilities

Andrea Melis[1]([✉]), Silvia Mirri[2], Catia Prandi[2], Marco Prandini[2],
Paola Salomoni[2], and Franco Callegati[1]

[1] Department of Electrical and Information Engineering,
Universitá di Bologna, Bologna, Italy
[2] Department of Computer Science and Engineering,
Universitá di Bologna, Bologna, Italy
{a.melis,silvia.mirri,catia.prandi2,marco.prandini,paola.salomoni,
franco.callegati}@unibo.it

Abstract. Applications supporting the independent living of people with disabilities are usually built in a monolithic fashion for a specific purpose. On the other hand, a crucial sector for the livability of urban spaces such as mobility is undergoing a deep transformation, heading towards flexible composition of standardized services. This paper shows how this approach allows to build better applications for people with specific needs, making them seamlessly integrated in the most modern approach to smart mobility.

Keywords: Mobility-as-a-Service · Microservices · Mobility aids for blind persons

1 Introduction

The advent of smart mobility has enabled the creation and development of applications for mobility support addressed to different categories of people, including those with disabilities [1–3]. Yet, the majority of these development paradigms provides vertical applications for accessible mobility, separated from the wealth of services available for average-capability travelers. For these applications, the integration of collected data, the possibility to share common sub-services, and the ability to interact with the same standards is rather difficult.

On the other hand, the rapidly growing diffusion of ICT solutions in every field of mobility is fostering the creation of novel approaches, such as the so-called *Mobility-as-a-Service* (MaaS) paradigm [4]. The enabling factor for these approaches to succeed is a strong drive towards standardization of data formats and access methods. According to the most modern model, every access to a piece of data, as well as every execution of a simple computation is offered as a service [5]. The collection of domain-specific services, completed by a set of commonly used infrastructural services, composes a service-oriented architecture, on which it is comparatively simple and fast to develop any application by orchestrating the needed services [6].

© ICST Institute for Computer Sciences, Social Informatics and Telecommunications Engineering 2017
O. Gaggi et al. (Eds.): GOODTECHS 2016, LNICST 195, pp. 41–50, 2017.
DOI: 10.1007/978-3-319-61949-1_5

The purpose of this paper is to present a specific use case that shows how it is possible to create a scalable and integrated mobility service for blind users, as a result of the coordination of reusable components on a microservice architecture. After discussing goals and purposes of the MaaS philosophy in Sect. 2, we introduce our microservice development approach in Sect. 3, focusing in particular on the advantages that this paradigm introduces on the basis of a real, currently developing infrastructure, which is called *Smart Mobility for All* (SMAll). Then, Sect. 4 details our use case developed in the urban region of the city of Bologna. Finally, Sect. 5 concludes the paper with some final remarks and directions for future work.

2   The MaaS Approach

Mobility as a Service [4] is an innovative approach that aims to break the barrier between public and private transport. It is made viable by the integration in a coordinated infrastructure of the technologies exposed by every single operator. Born in the city of Helsinki [4], this paradigm is starting to spread throughout Europe and beyond, aiming to establish standards for the interoperability between different (even in terms of country) operators, and to encourage the creation of alternative solutions to the standard "winner-take-all" paradigm. For our purpose, this approach can be seen from 2 different point of view, the business one and the technological one.

2.1   The Business Logic

Very briefly, the principle of MaaS is that as long as every detail of the demand and supply for transportation services is known in real-time, there is no need for passengers to commit on specific means. Instead, they will enjoy a broad spectrum of alternatives from which to choose, taking into account the needs of the moment. For example, one could specify a very strict set of constraints in terms of comfort and timing, likely to result in a choice of premium means, while another could simply express the need for reaching a destination at the best price, getting a virtual ticket, and receiving real-time instructions about which means to use to complete the trip. Many business models are possible [7].

In its simplest form, a MaaS operator could be a smart broker for planning and paying trips on existing networks. A more innovative approach would be that of selling mobility packages allowing travelers to use pre-configured amounts of travel on different means. From the transport operators viewpoint, a MaaS platform could be a great opportunity to leverage integration and to exploit unused capacity. For example, a taxi company exposing vehicle availability and position in real-time could offer lower prices during off-peak times, thus appearing as a good alternative to mass transit; data-mining could allow operators to foresee correlations between various conditions (events, weather, accidents) and transportation needs, to allocate materials in the best possible way [8].

Also the role of public administration can undergo a significant change. Some administrations could choose to play the role of a central MaaS operator, exerting a stronger control on the local mobility agenda. Others could leave the field to private companies, hoping to benefit from market-driven optimization of citizens' patterns of mobility. They could also accurately monitor citizens, using collected data to plan investments and direct incentives towards specific goals [9].

In this context, our use case became interesting. Typically, scenarios with few users involved, and that require specific technologies, as it happens in the case of people with disabilities, have always been profitable only through a heavy vertical investment [10] Thanks to the MaaS principle, where single services can be shared and public administrations can direct investments on the development of specific needs, even this kind of use case can be seen as an opportunity for MaaS operators.

2.2   The Technological Side

To effectively support the creation of MaaS providers, we envision the creation of an ecosystem of reusable components within a Service-Oriented Architecture, where standardized services efficiently and flexibly combine heterogeneous data sources, such as available transport options, real-time data regarding vehicles and infrastructures, pricing, etc., to provide customized travel planning, information and ticketing to final users, as well as monitoring and planning tools to policy-makers.

This infrastructure aims to create services to track timing, position, and availability of trains, buses, subways, shared bikes, shared cars, and to enable crowdsourcing of users' report, crowdsensing through devices [11,12], etc. in an overall effort of opening data and standardizing the interfaces to access them. Both operators and users can benefit from this plethora of mobility services.

A real example of this kind of infrastructure is the one that we are currently developing as a marketplace for mobility services, within the EIT Digital[1] called *Smart Mobility for All* (SMAll) [13]. In our vision, SMAll is the enabling technology to solve the challenges of the MaaS market, from developing user-contributed, crowdsourced applications, to launching a MaaS operator, to planning effective and sustainable transport policies for smart cities [14].

3   The Microservice Architecture Paradigm

The microservice architecture is a development style inspired by service-oriented computing that has recently started gaining popularity [15]. A microservice architecture can be defined as: "a distributed application where all its modules are microservices [16]."

The reasons why this architecture has been proposed is to try to overcome the limits of the so-called monolithic architecture [17]. In addition, we have to

---

[1] http://www.eitdigital.eu/.

consider the fact that this paradigm is a reasonable consequence of a world that is more and more oriented to the development on cloud, and therefore the need of connection and interoperability between the different platforms is increasing. Defined as [18] "a single-tiered software application in which the user interface and data access code are combined into a single program from a single platform", the main limits of the monolithic approach are:

- The maintain process.
- The dependency chain of libraries and modules explode.
- The deployment phase
- The scalability of the program.

It is clear that this kind of architecture is obsolete and it cannot be the right solution for today's service-oriented developments.

On the other side, the microservice architecture has been proposed with a diametrically opposite approach. Rather than having a single block composed of several force-dependent modules from each other, the microservice philosophy extracts each module making an independent and autonomous microservice following the statement "everything can be a microservice" [19].

This kind of distributed compositionality becomes his greatest strength. As described in [16], even the internal components of software are autonomous services, independent components conceptually deployed alone with dedicated technologies, both software and hardware. This means that this architectural style does not foster or forbid any particular programming, but it provides only a partition structure of the component the developer has to follow. Since all the components of a microservice architecture are microservices, its distinguishing behavior derives from the composition and coordination of its components via messages. Thus, the core of a microservice platform will be the orchestration phase, namely the composition of microservices, tools, and processes invoked, and the connection and automation of workflows that create the final service [20].

However, the microservice paradigm introduces also new challenges and enlarges known threats. The distributed programming nature is at the same time its main advantage (as shown earlier) and disadvantage. As described in [21], preventing programming errors in this context is harder, and the programmer has to face and work with different technologies that typically have different means of specifying contracts for the composition of services.

Other issues introduced by the microservice architecture are the ones related to the security aspects. These issues are certainly not new, as they apply to SOA and in general to distributed computing, but they become even more challenging in the context of microservices. Description of this kind of issues can be found in [22–24].

In Fig. 1 is represented a microservice platform, to enable the creation of mobility services. This architecture is inspired from our project SMAll [6].

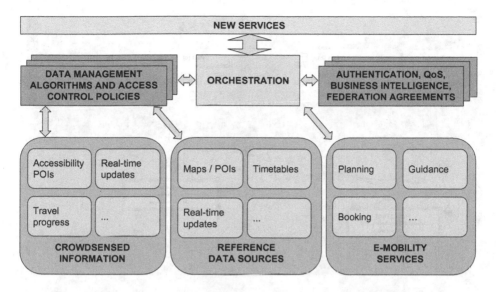

Fig. 1. A microservice platform to enable the creation of mobility services

4 A Use Case

In this section we describe a specific use case which has been developed by means of the SMAll platform. The goal of such a use case is to show how the microservice architecture can be exploited in the context of smart mobility, meeting different kinds of users' needs.

In particular, we present a scenario of a use case illustrating a blind user who requests a personalized path along the city of Bologna (Italy), by using his own smartphone. In particular, let us consider a male undergraduate student equipped with a white cane who uses to move across Bologna from home to reach the University campus and among offices and classrooms of the University, which are spread all over the city.

He has set up his profile with preferences related to the crossing facilities (he LIKEs zebra crossings, traffic lights, and audible traffic lights, since it is much easier for him crossing streets by exploiting such urban elements), surfaces (he LIKEs tactile pavings, which help him in walking on the street in an independent and safe way), bus and bus stops characteristics (he LIKEs tactile information and acoustic cues and announcements), and other urban elements (such as pathways, obstructions and so on). He LIKEs steps and stairs because they represent a landmark, helping him in orientating while he is wandering the city.

In this use case, our user asks for a specific path (including bus routes) starting from the School of Engineering and Architecture to reach the School of Art, Humanities and Cultural Heritage of the University of Bologna. The most commonly used geospatial mapping platforms (such as Google Maps) usually propose the path shown in Fig. 2.

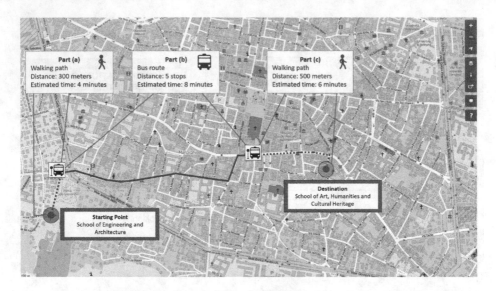

Fig. 2. The shortest path between the starting point and the destination

Such a path is the shortest one (it is expected to take 18 min) and it is structured in three parts, as follows:

1. a walking part to reach the bus stop; this part is supposed to take 4 min (for a 300 m distance);
2. a part of a bus route (between the bus stop icons); this part is supposed to take 8 min (with five in-between stops);
3. another walking part from the arrival bus stop to the final destination; this part is supposed to take 6 min (for a 500 m distance).

Taking into account the preferences shown in Listing 1 (in JSON format), the path depicted in Fig. 2 presents some issues our blind citizen has to face: (i) the absence of tactile pavings and of acoustic traffic lights; (ii) the absence of tactile information and of acoustic cues at the bus stops; (iii) the absence of acoustic announcements and of tactile information on the bus of that line; (iv) the information about bus arrival time is derived from a time table, instead of referring to the real bus position and availability.

When our user asks for a path from the starting point to the destination, then our system computes a personalized route taking into account the user?s profile (i.e. avoiding those barriers which affect him and including as much as possible the LIKEd facilities).

Our system computes a personalized path, by taking into account real data about bus availability and the user?s profile, in terms of barriers to avoid and LIKEd facilities to include as much as possible. In particular, our system matches the user's preferences with the information about the aPOIs (accessibility Points of Interest [2]) all over the city and real time open data about the public means of transport. A personalized path that meets these issues, computed by our system is shown in Fig. 3.

Such a personalized path is longer than the original one, and it is expected to take 24 min. According to a survey [25], citizens would face a longer path in urban environments if it meets their preferences. In particular, 88% of them were ready to face a path up to 30% longer to reach their destination if such a route was tailored to their preferences and needs, while 12% of the users would face a personalized path more than 30% longer.

Listing 1. User's profile fragment

```
{  "user_profile": {
        "crossing": {
            "zebra_crossings": {
                "-type": "facility",
                "-pref": "like"
            }, "traffic_lights": {
                "-type": "facility",
                "-pref": "like"
            }, "audible_traffic_lights": {
                "-type": "facility",
                "-pref": "like"
            }
        }, "surface": {
            ...
            "tactile_paving": {
                "-type": "facility",
                "-pref": "like"
            }
        }, ...
        "bus_stop": {
            ...
            "tactile_info": {
                "-type": "facility",
                "-pref": "like"
            },
            "acoustic_cues": {
                "-type": "facility",
                "-pref": "like"
            }
        }, "bus": {
            ...
            "acoustic_stop_announcements": {
                "-type": "facility",
                "-pref": "like"
            },
            "audible_output_devices": {
                "-type": "facility",
                "-pref": "like"
            }
        }
    }
}
```

The personalized path of our use case is structured in three parts, which involve a different bus line in its second part. In particular, such a path lets the user exploits urban facilities he declared as "LIKE" in his profile (e.g. zebra crossings, tactile pavings, acoustic traffic lights, bus stops equipped with tactile and acoustic cues), which improve his independence in moving across the city. During the third part of his personalized route, the user meets two stairs. Incidentally, his smartphone senses them, thanks to our system, making the user also a provider of sensed data related to urban barriers.

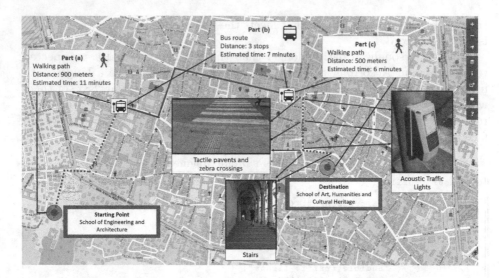

Fig. 3. The personalized path between the starting point and the destination

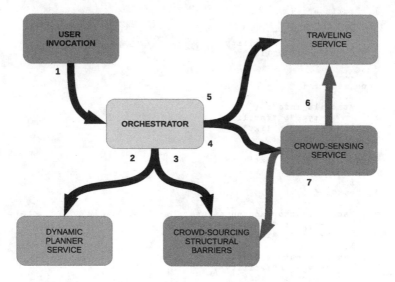

Fig. 4. The use case workflow represented as a microservice architecture in SMAll

A representation of the workflow of this use case in a microservice architecture is shown in Fig. 4. The user, in our case the blind user, invokes the routing service (1). The orchestrator intercept this call and he is the one in charge to create the correspondent workflow based on the invocation parameters. The invocation parameter are represented as the profile LIKES, and the orchestrator invoke the routing algorithms of the dynamic planner service (2) and the crowdsourcing service that map the structural barriers (3) based on the on this preferences. Once the trip has been proposed and choose the orchestrator call at the same time the traveling service (5) and the crowdsensing one (4). The traveling service manage the assistance phase, guiding the blind user and exposing the information with in an appropriate manner, e.g. voice synthesizer. The crowdsensing service otherwise as twofold goal. Based on the hardware device used he will collect (possibly) new information about the path in place at that time, e.g. such as the presence of stairs, obstacles or other temporary interruptions. This information will be used to immediately interact with the user notifying him warnings or advisories and at the same time this information will feed the crowdsourcing service enriching its database for future requests.

5 Conclusion

Smart mobility is a key element to support citizens in their daily activities and to offer them a livable smart city. Information about urban transportation (including taxis, bus, train, car-sharing, etc.), urban barriers and facilities, pedestrian and multimodal paths would be of great benefit in this context, as well as all the information about the whole experience of traveling and wandering the city, including travel planning and payments. In order to provide a platform to manage such services and features, we designed and prototyped an infrastructure as a marketplace for mobility services, called Smart Mobility for All (SMAll). A prototype of such infrastructure has been developed and its microservice architecture has been described in the paper. A use case involving a blind user moving across a urban environment is detailed in the paper and it shows the feasibility and the potentialities of our approach.

References

1. Cardonha, C., Gallo, D., Avegliano, P., Herrmann, R., Koch, F., Borger, S.: A crowdsourcing platform for the construction of accessibility maps. In: Proceedings of the 10th International Cross-Disciplinary Conference on Web Accessibility, p. 26. ACM (2013)
2. Mirri, S., Prandi, C., Salomoni, P.: A context-aware system for personalized and accessible pedestrian paths. In: 2014 International Conference on High Performance Computing and Simulation (HPCS), pp. 833–840. IEEE (2014)
3. Palazzi, C.E., Teodori, L., Roccetti, M.: Path 2.0: a participatory system for the generation of accessible routes. In: 2010 IEEE International Conference on Multimedia and Expo (ICME), pp. 1707–1711. IEEE (2010)
4. Pippuri, S., Hietanen, S., Pyyhti, K.: Maas finland. maas.fi/
5. Banerjee, P., Friedrich, R., Bash, C., Goldsack, P., Huberman, B., Manley, J., Patel, C., Ranganathan, P., Veitch, A.: Everything as a service: powering the new information economy. Computer **3**, 36–43 (2011)
6. Melis, A., Mirri, S., Prandi, C., Prandini, M., Salomoni, P., Callegati, F.: Crowdsensing for smart mobility through a service-oriented architecture. In: 2016 IEEE International Conference on Smart Cities Conference (ISC2). IEEE (2016)
7. Melis, A., Prandini, M., Sartori, L., Callegati, F.: Public transportation, IoT, trust and urban habits. In: Bagnoli, F., Satsiou, A., Stavrakakis, I., Nesi, P., Pacini, G., Welp, Y., Tiropanis, T., DiFranzo, D. (eds.) INSCI 2016. LNCS, vol. 9934, pp. 318–325. Springer, Cham (2016). doi:10.1007/978-3-319-45982-0_27

8. El Fassi, A., Awasthi, A., Viviani, M.: Evaluation of carsharing network's growth strategies through discrete event simulation. Expert Syst. Appl. **39**(8), 6692–6705 (2012)
9. Kupfer, D., Finger, M., Bert, N.: Mobility-as-a-Service: from the Helsinki experiment to a European model? Technical report, Observer European Transport Regulation (2015)
10. Sampo Hietanen, I.-F.: The new transport model? Technical report, MaaS Finland (2014)
11. Bujari, A., Licar, B., Palazzi, C.E.: Movement pattern recognition through smartphone's accelerometer. In: 2012 IEEE Consumer Communications and Networking Conference (CCNC), pp. 502–506. IEEE (2012)
12. Prandi, C., Ferretti, S., Mirri, S., Salomoni, P.: Trustworthiness in crowd-sensed and sourced georeferenced data. In: 2015 IEEE International Conference on Pervasive Computing and Communication Workshops (PerCom Workshops), pp. 402–407. IEEE (2015)
13. Callegati, F., Giallorenzo, S., Melis, A., Prandini, M.: Data security issues in maas-enabling platforms. In: International Forum on Research and Technologies for Society and Industry (2016)
14. Mirri, S., Prandi, C., Salomoni, P., Callegati, F., Campi, A.: On combining crowdsourcing, sensing and open data for an accessible smart city. In: 2014 Eighth International Conference on Next Generation Mobile Apps, Services and Technologies, pp. 294–299. IEEE (2014)
15. Fowler, M., Lewis, J.: Microservices. http://martinfowler.com/articles/microservices.html
16. Dragoni, N., Giallorenzo, S., Lluch-Lafuente, A., Mazzara, M., Montesi, F., Mustafin, R., Safina, L.: Microservices: yesterday, today, and tomorrow. CoRR, vol. abs/1606.04036 (2016)
17. Merkel, D.: Docker: lightweight linux containers for consistent development and deployment. Linux J. **2014**(239), 2 (2014)
18. Machado, R., El-Khoury, R.: Monolithic Architecture. Prestel Publishing, Munich (1995)
19. Newman, S.: Building Microservices. O'Reilly Media Inc., Sebastopol (2015)
20. Erl, T.: Service-Oriented Architecture: Concepts, Technology, and Design. Prentice Hall PTR, Upper Saddle River (2005)
21. Christensen, E., Curbera, F., Meredith, G., Weerawarana, S.: Web Services Description Language (WSDL) 1.1, Official Specification, W3C (2001). http://www.w3.org/TR/wsdl. Accessed 15 Mar 2001
22. Greene, W.: Providing secure data and policy exchange between domains in a multi-domain grid by use of a service ecosystem facilitating uses such as supply-chain integration with RIFD tagged items and barcodes. US Patent App. 11/069,479, 1 March 2005
23. Greene, W.: System and method for use of mobile policy agents and local services, within a geographically distributed service grid, to provide greater security via local intelligence and life-cycle management for RFLD tagged items. US Patent App. 10/913,887, 5 August 2004
24. Lea, G.: Microservices security: all the questions you should be asking (2015). http://www.grahamlea.com/2015/07/microservices-security-questions/
25. Mirri, S., Prandi, C., Salomoni, P.: Personalizing pedestrian accessible way-finding with mPASS. In: 2016 13th IEEE Annual Consumer Communications and Networking Conference (CCNC), pp. 1119–1124. IEEE (2016)

Performance Comparison of H.265/HEVC, H.264/AVC and VP9 Encoders in Video Dissemination over VANETs

Cristhian Iza Paredes[✉], Ahmad Mohamad Mezher,
and Mónica Aguilar Igartua

Universitat Politècnica de Catalunya (UPC), 08034 Barcelona, Spain
cristhian.iza@entel.upc.edu

Abstract. Video consumption over VANETs will increase significantly bandwidth and will occupy an important part of the overall data traffic. To decrease the load on the VANET infrastructure and reduce bandwidth taken by video, high efficiency video codecs have been developed. In this work, a benchmarking of H.265/HEVC, H.264/AVC and Google VP9 has been conducted by means of objective and subjective evaluations, assuming an urban VANET scenario. Considering a wide range of bit rates from very low to high, results show a clear advantage of HEVC with average bit rate savings of 27% when compared to VP9 and 49% when compared to AVC.

Keywords: HEVC · H.265 · H.264 · AVC · VP9 · VANETs · Video dissemination

1 Introduction

Supporting video dissemination over Vehicular Ad Hoc Networks (VANETs) is an attractive feature for many road safety applications. A key component to efficiently transport video with its stringent playout deadlines and bursty traffic characteristics, is using the most-efficient available encoding format. The current video codec standard H.264/AVC provides a better compression efficiency compared to other standards such as H.262/MPEG-2 or VP8. The goal behind the H.264 standard was to provide high quality video at lower bit rates. However, the emerging of a more efficient next generation video coding standard is a high demand at the moment. Two main contenders for the position of the next state of the art video standard are H.265/HEVC [1] and Google VP9 [2]. H.265/HEVC is the latest video coding standard, which achieves an increase of about 50% in coding efficiency compared to its predecessor H.264/AVC [3]. On the other hand, VP9 is an efficient open source video codec developed as part of the WebM Project by Google to get a royalty-free compression standard with efficiency superior to AVC [4].

In our previous work [5,6] H.265/HEVC appeared to provide the best compression efficiency compared to H.264/AVC. In this work we aim to evaluate

© ICST Institute for Computer Sciences, Social Informatics and Telecommunications Engineering 2017
O. Gaggi et al. (Eds.): GOODTECHS 2016, LNICST 195, pp. 51–60, 2017.
DOI: 10.1007/978-3-319-61949-1_6

the efficiency of the video compression standards H.265/HEVC and VP9. Our interest is centered on using a video dissemination mechanism in an urban scenario where vehicles' traffic is relatively dense and the communications are more exposed to interferences and radio obstacles.

The rest of the paper is organized as follows: Sect. 2 describes the features of selected encoders. Section 3 discusses the main approach aimed towards an effective solution for video dissemination over VANETs. The performance comparison of encoders and simulation results are discussed and presented in Sect. 4.3. Finally, conclusions and future work are drawn in Sect. 4.4.

2   Selected Encoder Implementations

In this section, a brief overview of the selected representative encoders is presented.

VP9 Encoder. Google started an Open Source project to develop royalty-free video codecs for the web entitled the WebM Project. The codec developed in the WebM project called is VP9 and is currently being served extensively by Google Chrome and YouTube. To evaluate VP9 compression efficiency, we use the open source libvpx encoder in its version 1.6.0 [2]. It has a two-pass run option which results in the improved rate distortion performance and which is also used in our work.

H.264/AVC Encoder. The latest version of JM reference software model (JM 19) was used for encoding video sequences with AVC [7]. The H.264/AVC standard has proven to be very fast, reliable, and efficient. Similarly as VP9, H.264/AVC has a two-step run option. At the first pass, a file with the detailed statistic data about every input frame is generated. At the second step, this information is used to improve the encoder rate-distortion performance.

H.265/HEVC Encoder. For evaluating H.265/HEVC-based encoding [1], we selected the latest reference model 16 (HM 16.9) in its simplified model to estimate the compression efficiency of the H.265/HEVC standard. To get constant QP (Quantization Parameter) on each frame we modified *Qpoffset* values of the GOP (Group of Pictures) structure in the configuration file.

The configuration parameters for HEVC, AVC and VP9 were set so that similarity was ensured between the three codecs to avoid any penalization. More details about the configurations can be found in Table 1.

2.1   Dataset

The comparison was carried out on the video sequences listed in Table 3. Four video sequences were downloaded from [8] and were used in the simulations, with different spatial, temporal characteristics and frame rates.

Table 1. Selected parameters and settings for the AVC, HEVC, and VP9 codecs.

Codec	Version	Parameters
HEVC	HM 16.9	**TAppEncoderStatic** -c encoder_lowdelay_P_main10.cfg (Default main low-delay profile with P frames) -c Traffic.cfg -b encoded sequence.bin -o decoded sequence.yuv -q <QP>
AVC	JM 19	**lencod** -f encoder.cfg -p FrameRate=<FR> -p QPISlice=<QP> -p QPPSlice=<QP> -p QPBSlice=<QP> -p Bitrate= -p SourceWidth=<W> -p SourceHeight=<H>
VP9	v1.6.0-326	**vpxenc** --codec=vp9 --profile=0 --fps=<FR> --static-thresh=0 --drop-frame=0 --good --auto-alt-ref=1 --kf-min-dist=8 --kf-max-dist=8 --cq-level=<QP> --max-intra-rate=8 --target-bitrate= --static-thresh=4 -w <W> -h <H> --limit=500 <inFile>.yuv -o <outFile>.webm

Each video file was encoded with all three evaluated codecs. Since fixed QP[1] configuration was used to control the quality of AVC, HEVC, and VP9 compressed bitstreams, the sequences were encoded at various QP values trying to cover the full quality scale for each content.

We aim to compare maximum video compression efficiency provided by the latest standards. Based on our previous work [6], we selected Low-Delay-P (LP) coding configuration to reflect the real-time application scenario for all encoders. In this mode the first frame is an intra-frame while the others are encoded as generalized P frames. This makes this mode more vulnerable to packet losses since it needs to wait to receive an entire GoP before decoding the video frames. To mitigate large dependencies between frames and trying to achieve a better packet loss resilience, the GOP size was set to 8 pictures and the Intra Period was set to 25 and 30 pictures for 25 and 30 fps contents, respectively. Table 2 reports the final sets of targeted (R1'–R4') and actual (R1–R4) bit rates, with corresponding QPs, for each codec.

3   Video Dissemination in VANET

The realization of a reliable transmission of video over VANETs is extremely challenging mainly due to the network's dynamic topology and stringent requirements of the video streaming service. The high velocity and limited communication range of the vehicles incur frequent link disconnection and even network partition. To evaluate the efficiency of the video compression standards over

---

[1] The Quantization Parameter (QP) regulates how much spatial detail is saved. When QP is very small, almost all that detail is retained. As QP is increased, some of that detail is aggregated so that the bit rate drops, but at the price of some increase in distortion and some loss of quality.

Table 2. Target R_i' and actual R_i bit rates (kbps) including the corresponding QP values for each codec.

Sequence	Codec	R1'	R1	QP	R2'	R2	QP	R3'	R3	QP	R4'	R4	QP
Highway	AVC	375	384	30	750	747	24	1500	1574	15	2500	2515	11
	HEVC	375	336	27	750	776	24	1500	1450	21	2500	2717	18
	VP9	375	390	28	750	749	25	1500	1486	22	2500	2833	19
Hall monitor	AVC	375	385	32	750	779	25	1500	1590	17	2500	2877	13
	HEVC	375	363	28	750	675	25	1500	1319	22	2500	2452	19
	VP9	375	416	30	750	787	26	1500	1640	22	2500	2370	20
City	AVC	256	242	58	512	520	33	1024	1010	23	2048	2087	12
	HEVC	256	235	35	512	508	29	1024	1392	24	2048	2041	19
	VP9	256	253	37	512	535	31	1024	1126	25	2048	2195	20
Bus	AVC	256	251	54	512	539	43	1024	1006	34	2048	2038	22
	HEVC	256	248	40	512	514	34	1024	997	29	2048	2089	23
	VP9	256	267	41	512	512	36	1024	1080	30	2048	2192	24

VANETs, we use a smart dissemination protocol known as RCP+ that we proposed in previous works [5,6]. The proposed mechanism is built on top of IEEE 1609.3 by adding a layer to select next forwarder vehicles based on the information of the environment and an estimation of the congestion of the communication channel. RCP+ ensures a large dissemination in the network to rebroadcast the video content.

3.1 Scenario Description

We focus the situation on the immediate consequences of a traffic accident. The crashed vehicle starts to generate and transmit a real-time SOS message to alert the vehicles in the network about the incident and to the appropriate emergency centers (e.g. 112 or 911). The emergency message includes a short video of a few seconds before the crash. We consider a real street environment imported from OpenStreetMap [9]. Under the street model, vehicles are generated and their moving patterns are controlled by SUMO [10]. Shadowing models are used to reproduce the attenuation of a radio signal induced by obstacles, such as

Table 3. Test video sequences have a resolution of 352×288 pixels

Sequence	Frame rate	Number of frames
Highway	25 fps	2000
Hall monitor	30 fps	300
City	30 fps	300
Bus	25 fps	150

Table 4. Simulation parameters.

	Parameter	Value
Physic and MAC Layers IEEE 802.11p	Channel; Bandwidth	178, 5.89 GHZ; 10 MHz
	Transmission range	230 m
	Transmission power	20 mW
	Obstacle model	Defined in [11,12]
	Beacon [CW_{min}, CW_{max}], AIFSN	[15,1023], 6
	Data [CW_{min}, CW_{max}], AIFSN	[7,15], 3
	Bit rate	6 Mbit/s
RCP+ [5,6]	RSS_{th}, RSS_{max}	−89 dBm, −20 dBm
	Time slot	13 μs
	Time window	10 s
	δ (Waiting Time)	[1, 11] μs
	Beacon frecuency, Beacon size	1 Hz, >=32 bytes
Scenarios	Number of runs per point	10
	Time to live (TTL)	90 s

buildings or other structures blocking the direct line of sight. A set of 4 RSUs (Road Side Units) have been strategically located at 20 m, 300 m, 600 m, and 1200 m from the accident scene. The distance between the RSUs and the road is 3 m. RSUs are traffic sinks used to measure the quality of the received video at different distances from the accident.

4   Performance Evaluation

This section provides simulation results on the coding performance of the three video coding standards under evaluation. We first present the simulation setup used, including models and scenarios. Then, we present the comparison of the compression efficiency between HEVC, VP9 and AVC by means of objective and subjective evaluations in the considered VANET video streaming scenario.

4.1   Simulation Setup

To carry out the performance comparison, each run uses a different random scenario that fulfills the requirements of the study. For each point in all figures we have calculated the average from 10 simulation runs. This let us obtain a standard error less than 5% in a 95% confidence interval. The packet error and Medium Access Control (MAC) layer models adopted are based on the IEEE 802.11p, using a data rate of 6 Mbit/s, a transmission power of 20 mW, and a receiver sensitivity of −89 dBm. In addition, all hello messages use the same Access Category (AC_BE), thus with the same values of Contention Window

(CW) and Arbitration Inter-Frame Spacing (AIFSN). Table 4 contains a summary of the simulation parameters common to all simulation scenarios.

We assume that each vehicle is equipped with a GPS device to obtain its geographical location in current time. A preloaded digital map provides information about roads. We assume that vehicles periodically exchange their own physical location, moving velocity and direction information enclosed in their periodic hello messages. They are sent at the frequency of 1 Hz. Finally, vehicles are assumed to be equipped with IEEE 802.11p wireless technology and computation capabilities.

4.2 Performance Measures

We use three performance metrics to evaluate the quality of video transmitted over VANETs:

Frame Delivery Ratio: It is defined as the ratio between the number of frames delivered and the total number of frames received during a time interval of T seconds.

PSNR(Peak Signal-to-Noise Ratio): It is an objective metric used to assess the application-level QoS of video transmissions. PSNR measures the error between the reconstructed image and the original one, frame by frame. We assume that in case an individual frame was lost, the decoder would display the last successfully received frame of the same type. So if a frame is dropped, we need to compare the source frame to the previous streamed frame.

MOS(Mean Opinion Score): It is a subjective metric used to provide a numerical indication of the perceived quality from the users's point of view of the received video. In a MOS assessment test, video sequences are presented in a predefined order to a group of subjects, who are asked to rate their visual quality on a rating scale. The MOS score is expressed in the range from 1 to 5, where 5 is the highest perceived quality and 1 is the lowest perceived quality.

4.3 Results and Discussion

In a first set of experiments, we used the Bjøntegaard model [13] to calculate the coding efficiency between different codecs. This metric allows us to compute the average gain in PSNR or the average per cent saving in bitrate between two rate-distortion curves. Also, we used another model based on subjective quality scores [14]. This model computes the average MOS difference and average bit rate difference between two sets of subjective results corresponding to two different codecs. This model reports the average bit rate difference, ΔR, for a similar perceived visual quality. Table 5 provides the results in terms of BD-Rate[2] and ΔR results. Results based on the Bjøntegaard model show that the average bit rate reduction of HEVC relative to AVC and VP9 is 49.73% and 27.12%,

---

[2] Bjøntegaard Delta-Rate (BD-Rate) is the average bit rate difference in percentage for the same PSNR.

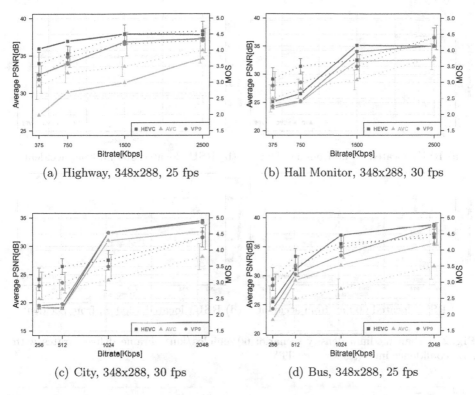

(a) Highway, 348x288, 25 fps   (b) Hall Monitor, 348x288, 30 fps

(c) City, 348x288, 30 fps   (d) Bus, 348x288, 25 fps

Fig. 1. PSNR (solid line) curves and subjective MOS (dashed line) values, for each bit rate and each video content. 95% confidence intervals are shown.

Table 5. Comparison of the three evaluated coding algorithms in terms of bit rate reduction for similar PSNR and MOS. Negative values indicate actual bit rate reduction.

Sequence	HEVC vs AVC		VP9 vs AVC		HEVC vs VP9	
	BD-Rate	ΔR	BD-Rate	ΔR	BD-Rate	ΔR
Highway	−47.41%	−40.11%	−32.48%	−36.58%	−41.19%	−42.79%
Hall monitor	−32.60%	−23.70%	−27.38%	−20.08%	−9.57%	−12.80%
City	−51.11%	−47.01%	−42.89%	−34.29%	−21.66%	−26.16%
Bus	−67.82%	−65.62%	−52.64%	−50.44%	−36.05%	−39.25%
Average	−49.73%	−44.11%	−38.85%	−35.35%	−27.12%	−30.25%

respectively. Also, the average bit rate reduction of VP9 relative to AVC is 38.85%. On the other hand, results based on the subjective ratings indicate an average bit rate saving of 44.11% and 30.35% for HEVC when compared to AVC and VP9, respectively. Furthermore, the bit rate reduction achieved by VP9 relative to AVC is 35.35%. As it can be seen, HEVC encoder provides better results than all the other codecs avaluated.

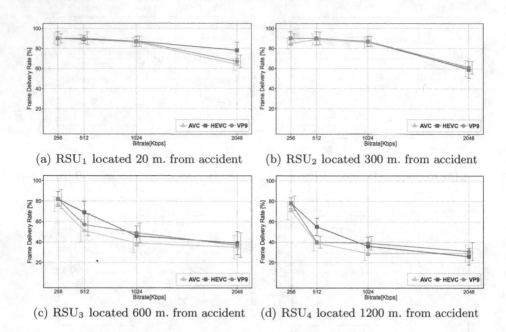

(a) RSU$_1$ located 20 m. from accident   (b) RSU$_2$ located 300 m. from accident

(c) RSU$_3$ located 600 m. from accident   (d) RSU$_4$ located 1200 m. from accident

Fig. 2. Urban medium density scenario: 60 vehicles/km^2. Frame delivery rates with 95% confidence intervals for the CITY.

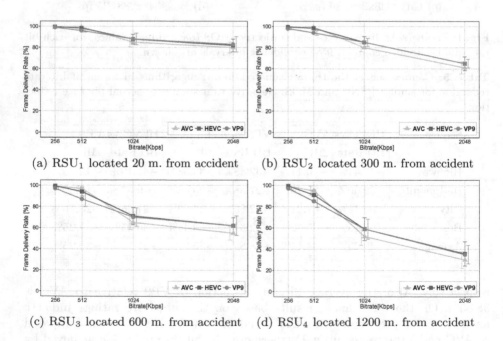

(a) RSU$_1$ located 20 m. from accident   (b) RSU$_2$ located 300 m. from accident

(c) RSU$_3$ located 600 m. from accident   (d) RSU$_4$ located 1200 m. from accident

Fig. 3. Urban high density scenario: 120 vehicles/km^2. Frame delivery rates with 95% confidence intervals for the CITY.

As a next step, we carry out a comparative assessment for the Low-Delay-P (LP) configuration of H.265/HEVC, VP9, and H.264/AVC encoders. Figure 1 shows the Rate-Distortion curves based on PSNR measurements and subjective ratings based on MOS measurements for all sequences. Based on PSNR measurements, HEVC outperforms VP9 by 0.5 to 3.5 dB, while VP9 provides a gain ranging from 0.5 to 8.45 dB when compared to AVC. For all video contents and bit rates, objective measurements show that HEVC outperforms both VP9 and AVC coding algorithms. The subjective results show similar trend to objective measurements: HEVC provides the best visual quality for a similar bit rate and outperforms AVC in most cases. Also, VP9 achieves better visual quality than AVC. However, in some cases (in particular, at high bit rates), HEVC and VP9 have similar ratings and there is no sufficient statistical evidence indicating differences in performance between these codecs at these bit rates.

Finally, we compare the effectiveness of the RCP+ scheme in terms of frame delivery rate for each codec. In the urban scenario, we define three densities: 30, 60 and 120 vehicles/km^2. These densities can be considered as Low, Medium, and High densities of vehicles. These network densities cover a range from low (normal or night time) to high vehicular traffic density (rush hour). A vehicle operating in a sparse traffic density is said to be in a totally disconnected neighborhood if it has no vehicle neighbor within its transmission range. In this case, simulation results (not shown here due to space limits) indicate that only the RSU_1 and RSU_2 located 20 and 300 m from the accident, received the complete trace. This makes it difficult to evaluate the codec in this scenario. On the other hand, the performance of our mechanism in Medium and High densities are presented in Figs. 2 and 3, respectively. As it is clearly seen, the HEVC encoder provides gains in terms of Frame Delivery Ratio compared to both VP9 and AVC encoders. Also, as the distance from the accident increases for the RSU, the delivery ratio decreases since probability of collisions or network failure increases. This result is expected, because the urban scenario shows more aggressiveness in the packet loss due to the existence of buildings. Besides, dynamic topology networks in VANET causes temporary disconnections, interrupting the video message dissemination and compromising the delivery of the video frames.

4.4 Conclusion

In this paper we have studied compression efficiency of the current video compression standard and candidates for the next generation video coding standard over VANETs in an urban traffic scenario. The high bandwidth required for video dissemination can be tackled through the use of recent encoders that allow doubling the efficiency coding, reducing almost half the bit rate for similar levels quality. The results have shown the superior compression efficiency of H.265/HEVC coding standard over H.264/AVC and VP9 encoders. The possible drawback of using H.265/HEVC is a higher computational complexity. As future work, we will seek an efficient forwarding mechanism to enhance video QoE (Quality of Experience) according with the VANET safety applications' requirements.

Acknowledgments. This work was partly supported by the Spanish Government through projects TEC2014-54435-C4-1-R (INcident monitoRing In Smart COmmunities. QoS and Privacy, INRISCO) and AGAUR Information Security Group (ISG) project - 2014 SGR 1504. Cristian Iza Paredes is recipient of a grant from Secretaria Nacional de Educación Superior, Ciencia y Tecnología SENESCYT. Ahmad Mohamad Mezher is a postdoctoral researcher with the Information Security Group in the Department of Network Engineering at the Universitat Politècnica de Catalunya (UPC). Additional funding supporting this work has been granted to UPC by the Spanish Ministry of Economy and Competitiveness (MINECO) through the "Anonymized Demographic Surveys (ADS)" project, ref. TIN2014-58259-JIN, under the funding program "Proyectos de I+D+i para Jóvenes Investigadores".

References

1. High efficiency video coding (HEVC). https://hevc.hhi.fraunhofer.de/. Accessed 17 May 2016
2. The webm project. http://www.webmproject.org/. Accessed 5 Sep 2016
3. Grois, D., Marpe, D., Mulayoff, A., Itzhaky, B., Hadar, O.: Performance comparison of h.265/MPEG-HEVC, vp. 9, and H.264/MPEG-AVC encoders. In: Proceedings of the Picture Coding Symposium (PCS), pp. 394–397, December 2013
4. Sharabayko, M.P., Markov, N.G.: Contemporary video compression standards: H.265/HEVC, vp9, vp10, daala. In: Proceedings of the International Siberian Conference Control and Communications (SIBCON), pp. 1–4, May 2016
5. Iza-Paredes, C., Mezher, A.M., Aguilar Igartua, M.: Evaluating video dissemination in realistic urban vehicular ad-hoc networks. In: The 19th ACM International Conference on Modeling, Analysis and Simulation of Wireless and Mobile Systems, MSWiM 2016, Malta. ACM (2016)
6. Iza-Paredes, C., Mezher, A.M., Aguilar Igartua, M.: Adaptive video-streaming dissemination in realistic highway vehicular ad-hoc networks. In: Performance Evaluation of Wireless Ad Hoc, Sensor, and Ubiquitous Networks, PE-WASUN 2016, Malta. ACM (2016)
7. H.264/avc software coordination (AVC). http://iphome.hhi.de/suehring/tml/. Accessed 17 May 2016
8. Derf's dataset. https://media.xiph.org/video/derf/. Accessed 22 Mar 2016
9. OpenStreetMap. http://www.openstreetmap.org. Accessed 22 Mar 2015
10. SUMO – Simulation of Urban MObility. http://goo.gl/uvvD4N. Accessed 22 Mar 2015
11. Boban, M., Vinhoza, T.T.V., Ferreira, M., Barros, J., Tonguz, O.K.: Impact of vehicles as obstacles in vehicular ad hoc networks. IEEE J. Sel. Areas Commun. **29**(1), 15–28 (2011)
12. Sommer, C., Joerer, S., Segata, M., Tonguz, O.K., Cigno, R.L., Dressler, F.: How shadowing hurts vehicular communications and how dynamic beaconing can help. IEEE Trans. Mob. Comput. **14**(7), 1411–1421 (2015)
13. Bjøntegaard, G.: Calculation of average PSNR differences between RD-curves. ITU-T SG16/Q6, Austin, Texas, USA (2001)
14. Hanhart, P., Ebrahimi, T.: Calculation of average coding efficiency based on subjective quality scores. J. Vis. Commun. Image Represent. **25**(3), 555–564 (2014). QoE in 2D/3D Video Systems

PIR Probability Model for a Cost/Reliability Tradeoff Unobtrusive Indoor Monitoring System

Fabio Veronese, Sara Comai, Simone Mangano, Matteo Matteucci, and Fabio Salice[✉]

Politecnico di Milano, Polo Territoriale di Como,
Via Anzani, 42, 22100 Como, Italy
{fabio.veronese, sara.comai, simone.mangano, matteo.matteucci, fabio.salice}@polimi.it

Abstract. PIR (Pyroelectric InfraRed) sensors can be used to detect the presence of humans without the need for them to wear any device. By construction, the fields of view of the sensors are not uniform both in terms of vision space and of sensitivity. The aim of this work is twofold: to provide a probabilistic model of the sensors' detection sensitivity with respect to the movement of the person and of his/her emission surface, and to identify the probability of detection within an area covered by multiple PIR sensors. This allows the computation of the coverage of the PIRs and their optimal arrangement that maximizes the probability of detection of the person.

Keywords: Pyroelectric infrared sensors · PIR sensor model · Presence detection

1 Introduction

The 2010 United Nations report of the department of economic and social affairs population division [1] states that ageing population is one of the most distinctive demographic events of the twentieth century. The slow, but steady, increase of the average population age has a deep, but unavoidable, impact on the social, economic and political conditions of all countries. In particular, the inter-generational social support systems will be unsustainable in the long-term.

One way to develop sustainable solutions in such a forthcoming scenario, consists in enforcing the autonomous and independent life of elderly through social support and the use of technologies, by monitoring the elderly at home and let the caregivers know in which condition the person is.

Methods proposed in the literature range from user location and biological monitoring using wearable devices to the gathering of data from environmental sensors. The cost of the system and the level of required cooperation from the person are key factors. Other not negligible aspects are system reliability and fault tolerance related to both devices and human. This paper provides a model for PIRs stochastic characterization (focusing on real industrial devices) and discusses the effect of their placement and interaction.

© ICST Institute for Computer Sciences, Social Informatics and Telecommunications Engineering 2017
O. Gaggi et al. (Eds.): GOODTECHS 2016, LNICST 195, pp. 61–69, 2017.
DOI: 10.1007/978-3-319-61949-1_7

The paper is organized as follows: next section reports previous works regarding PIR modelling. Then, we introduce our stochastic model for PIRs and show how PIR models are merged to characterize, from a probabilistic point of view, the sensitivity of interacting sensors. Finally, we validate our model by presenting experimental results of two industrial products and discuss its application in a real environment.

2   Previous Works

Most of literature on PIR devices describe them through very simple and deterministic models: the approaches in [2–4] adopt a 0/1 model, where the activation is "1" if a person crosses the sensible area of the sensor, otherwise it is "0". The authors in [5, 6] propose a "simplified imperfect binary sensing" model for a ceiling-mounted sensor, where the target is always detected within an inner disk of radius R_{in} and is detected with some nonzero probability in an annulus between this inner disk and the outer disk of radius R_{out}. This model improves the 0/1 model since it considers the distance from the sensitive element. However, it ignores factors like the speed of movement of the person, the size of his/her emitting surface, the period of insensitivity of the sensor. Indeed, in real physical devices, the activation value is a function of such factors: however, the parameters of the corresponding relationship can be only roughly estimated due to the uncertainty condition of the system: therefore, [7] propose an approach to represent, experimentally and using fuzzy sets, the detection distance as a function of the other parameters.

A stochastic model considering the Euclidean distance between the sensor and the object is proposed in [8], but it does not take into account the speed of the object and the inactivity time. The authors in [9] propose a motion-tracking pyroelectric detector: by using multiple sensor clusters in different orientation, they are able to track a human motion. Unfortunately, their approach requires a detailed sensor model for sensible elements and lenses, and is not general. However, they show that the detector sensitivity can be increased by using four sensors, one at each corner of the room; that the spatial sensitivity is not uniform at different distances and for different walking speed; and that there are dead points where the detection sensitivity is very low.

In this paper we propose a general stochastic model, experimentally calibrated for the detection of a moving person, which takes into account the speed, the direction of movement, and the distance from the sensing element. The model is used to evaluate the sensor position (location and orientation) in the different rooms of the house with the aim to identify a tradeoff between increasing the probability of detection and reducing the cost of the proposed solution.

3   Model and Characterization of a Single PIR

A Pyroelectric Infrared Sensor (PIR) is a passive device that measures the changes in the infrared (IR) radiation levels emitted by surrounding objects and returns "1" when it detects a variation within its viewing range. A PIR can detect any object emitting IR radiation, heat or changes in the background IR level, and is generally used for motion detection.

A PIR sensor is characterized by a, so called, *detection degradation*, which is a function of the direction (radial or tangential) and speed of the moving object, distance from the sensible element, the environment temperature, and the surface of the object. To detect people in their houses, our model becomes independent from the emitting surface (moving object are persons) as well as from the environment temperature (houses and apartments).

The proposed PIR model is obtained by combining a *geometric model* and a *motion model*.

The *geometric model* is characterized by the maximum detection angle (field of view), the discretization of the detection angle into sectors, and the detection depth with its discretization into traces. Figure 1 depicts an example of a PIR sensor (radial) model which takes into account the maximum angle of view (for ceiling-mounted sensors this is 360° and for wall-mounted sensors it is a parameter provided by the producer), the angle discretization (sectors) and the maximum detection distance from the sensing element discretized over the distance (traces).

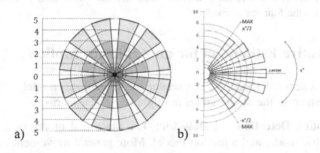

Fig. 1. The PIR radial geometric model - (a) the ceiling-mounted and (b) the wall mounted.

The *motion model* is characterized by the direction of the movement (radial or tangential) and the user speed. Each elementary geometric area, i.e., sector, is characterized by a probability to detect a movement with respect to the movement direction and speed. The proposed model considers 4 speed intervals (slow movement, slow step, normal step and quick step - see Table 1), and computes the activation probabilities by series of experiments.

Table 1. The four speeds models with their minimum, maximum and average speeds.

#	Name	Speed [m/s] min-avg-max
1	Slow Movement (SM)	0.2–0.3–0.4
2	Slow Step (SS)	0.4–0.6–0.8
3	Normal Step (NS)	0.8–1.2–1.6
4	Quick Step (QS)	1.6–2.0–2.4

By repeating the same compatible movement (speed in the interval and direction) several times, we can estimate activation probabilities for any cell in the planar geometric model, obtaining 8 probabilistic models, i.e., one for each speed for each movement direction. The combination of the geometric and motion models becomes the functional model of the sensors; an example of such model for a wall-mounted sensor is depicted in Fig. 2: slow motion is detected with lower probability.

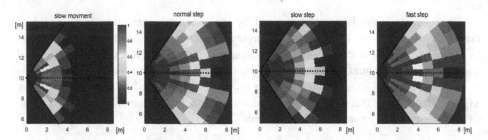

Fig. 2. Sensor functional model for a wall-mounted detector (horizontal direction) located at (0,10) obtained for the four speed models.

4   PIR Sensitive Estimation for an Arbitrary Motion

Based on the functional model of the sensor, a probabilistic model is extracted for arbitrary movement in the single and a multiple sensors scenario.

Arbitrary Motion Detection – 1 Detector: The functional model of a sensor combines a geometric model and a motion model. More general movement patterns could be modeled by considering that a generic movement direction can be always decomposed in two components: the radial and tangential directions:

$$P_{ics} = P_{\|ics}(1 - |\sin(\beta_c)|) + P_{\perp ics}|\sin(\beta_c)| \qquad (1)$$

where P_{ics} is the probability of activation in the c-th cell of the i-th sensor with a subject speed of s, $P_{\|cs}$ and $P_{\perp ics}$ are the radial and tangential probabilities at cell c, and β_c is the angle between the motion direction and crossed sector (see Fig. 3(a)).

Figure 3 depicts an example where the detection probabilities are shown for a quick step movement (b) along the central axis, and (c) at an angle of 45° with respect to the central sensor axis.

Arbitrary Motion Detection – k Detectors: in case of K interacting PIR sensors, the detection probability is obtained by combining the detection probabilities of all the sensors according to the following formula:

$$P_{cs} = 1 - \Pi_{j=1..k}(1 - P_{jcs}) \qquad (2)$$

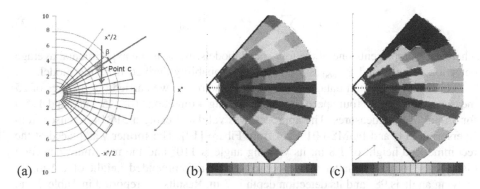

Fig. 3. (a) Angle with respect to the movement trajectory calculated at point c; (b) probability of detection along the central axis, and (c) at an angle of 45°.

where P_{cs} is the detection probability in the cell c with subject speed s, while P_{jcs} (j = 1..k) is the detection probability at the same speed in the same cell for sensor j.

The example in Fig. 4 depicts the detection probability for 3 sensors for the four motion models, at an angle of 45° with respect to the central sensor axis. The dotted lines represent the central axes of the PIRs. The dimension of the room is 8 × 6 m² - sensor sensitivity in the center axes is 8 m.

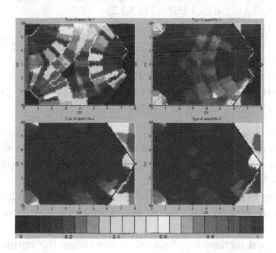

Fig. 4. Detection probability with 3 sensors at an angle of 45°, for each motion model.

5   Experimental Results

To evaluate the model we used the following figure of merit:

$$\varepsilon = \sum\nolimits_{i=1..4} \left(A_{iexp} - P_{imod} \right) \tag{3}$$

where each i represents one of the four speed models, $A_{i\,exp}$ is the experimental average detection activity, and $P_{i\,mod}$ is the detection probability derived from the model.

For the experimental data, given a point in the room, we carried out a series of 25 measurements for the four speed models and along 4 directions (0°, 45°, 90° and 135°) for a total of 400 measures. The approach was validated using a SP814-1 sensor from Everspring [11] and FGMS-001 V2.4 from Fibaro [12]. The former was placed at the recommended height of 1.8 m: its viewing angle is 110° and the maximum detection distance is 10 m. The latter was mounted at the recommended height of 2.4 m: its viewing angle is 98° and its detection depth is 7 m. Results are reported in Table 2 and Fig. 5, where $d_i = (x,y,\alpha)$ denotes the position of each PIR sensor d_i, where (x,y) are the coordinates with respect to the origin of the axis (0,0) and α is the angle between the middle ray of the detector and the horizontal axis. P(x,y) is the position of the measurement point. L and W represent the length and the width of the room, respectively. Notice that in case of large rooms the limited detection depth of the FIBARO sensor does not allow to detect P.

Table 2. Model validation with sensor type everspring – SP814-1 and FIBARO.

Experiment setting	Error everspring	Error FIBARO
L = 9 m–W = 6 m; d_1(0,3,0°), d_2(9,3,180°); P(4.5,1.2)	0.033	Not detected
L = 6 m–W = 5 m; d1(0,2.5,0°), d2(6,2.5,180°); P (3,0,1.3)	0.052	0.038
L = 7 m–W = 4 m; d1(0,1,0°), d2(0,3,180°); P(6,2)	2.540	1.590
L = 6 m–W = 2.5 m; d1(0,0.5,0°), d2(0,2, 0°); P(5,1.2)	0.709	0.280
L = 5 m–W = 5 m; d1(0,4,0°), d2(4,0,90°); P(4,4)	0.587	0.125
L = 8 m–W = 5 m; d1(0,3,0°), d2(6,0,90°); P(7,4)	0.218	Not detected

Figure 5 depicts the results of the model in a 9×6 m^2 room with a sensor placed at $d_1 = (0,3,0°)$, and a second one at $d_2 = (9,3,180°)$; the point is in position x = 4.5 m and y = 1.2 m (P(4.5, 1.2)).

It is worth noting that, as reported in the tables, the model always underestimates the real behavior of the system; thus, the proposed approach is suitable for a worst case analysis.

Finally, models and method can be used to determine the optimal positioning of PIRs. Figure 6 reports two different coverage scenarios using two PIRs: (a) is slightly better than (b) with respect to the entire room coverage.

Currently, the model is under test in a real situation where a person with a mild cognitive disability is experimenting his autonomy. The tradeoff between the cost (given by the number of PIRs used to detect the position) and the system's ability to detect the person's position was considered.

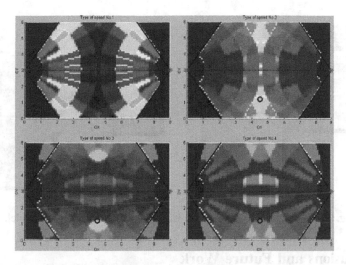

Fig. 5. Detection probability with 3 PIR sensors and 45° motion direction, for each speed model.

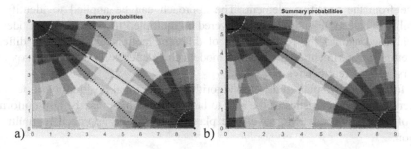

Fig. 6. Two scenarios with 2 PIR for covering a 6 × 9 m² room: (a) 97.03% coverage, 0.67 avg. probability detection, (b) 95.50% coverage, 0.64 avg. probability detection.

Figure 7 shows the final configuration: in the bed room (left-hand side room) two PIRs (PIR1 and PIR2) have been placed, even if PIR1 alone could cover the entire room; their combined effect increases the detection probability to detect the presence of the person near the door and in the center of the room. In the kitchen (in the upper/right part of the map) two different situations can be discriminated with the combination of PIR4 and PIR5: the user is in the kitchen but not at the table (only PIR4 is active) and the user is in the kitchen (both PIRs are active). It is worth noting that the duplication of PIRs allows also the identification of a PIR failure without losing the complete control of the "status" of the person.

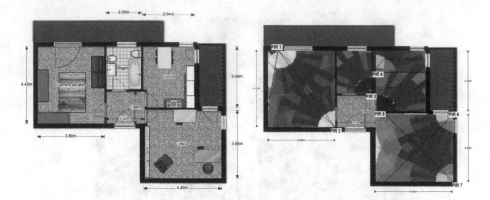

Fig. 7. An apartment instrumented with PIR using the proposed model.

6 Conclusions and Future Work

In this paper we have described a probabilistic model of the sensors' detection sensitivity that considers factors such as the speed of movement of the person and the distance from the sensitive element. The approach can be applied to identify the probability of detection within an area covered by multiple PIR sensors. The model has been validated against the real behavior of different motion detectors with different room settings: experiments show that our model can be effectively used to approximate the worst case of real behaviors.

As future work we plan to develop algorithms for optimal positioning of detectors considering the characteristics of the area to be covered, which may be non-uniform in terms of detection needs. Moreover, we plan to extend the approach to multi-user detection.

Acknowledgments. We wish to thank Victoria Grulenko and Ekaterina Ivanova for their precious contribution to this work.

References

1. United Nations report on world population ageing 1950–2050 (2002). http://www.un.org/esa/population/publications/worldageing19502050/
2. Feng, G., Liu, M., Guo, X., Zhang, J., Wang, G.: Genetic algorithm based optimal placement of PIR sensor arrays for human localization. In: International Conference on Mechatronics and Automation (ICMA), pp. 1080–1084 (2011)
3. Gopinathan, U., Brady, D.J., Pitsianis, N.P.: Coded apertures for efficient pyroelectric motion tracking. Opt. Express **11**(18), 2142–2152 (2003)
4. Shrivastava, N., Mudumbai, R., Madhow, U., Suri, S.: Target tracking with binary proimity sensors. ACM, Trans. Sens. Netw. **5**(4), 1–33 (2009)

5. Wang, Z., Bulut, E., Szymanski, B.K.: Distributed target tracking with imperfect binary sensor networks. In: Proceedings of the GLOBECOM 2008, Ad Hoc, Sensor and Mesh Networking Symposium, pp. 1–5, November 2008
6. Hsiao, R.-S., Lin, D.-B., Lin, H.-P., Cheng, S.-C., Chung, C.-H.: Indoor target detection and localization in pyroelectric infrared sensor networks. In: Proceedings of the 8th APWCS 2011, Singapore, August 2011
7. Cornel, B.: Localization system using video and PIR information fusion. In: 2nd International Workshop on Soft Computing Applications, SOFA 2007, pp. 21–23 (2007). doi:10.1109/SOFA.2007.4318299
8. Ammari, H.M.: Challenges and Opportunities of Connected k-Covered Wireless Sensor Networks: From Sensor Deployment to Data Gathering. Studies in Computational Intelligence. Springer, Heidelberg (2009). ISBN 978-3642018763
9. Shankar, M., Burchett, J.B., et al.: Human-tracking systems using pyroelectric infrared detectors. Opt. Eng. **45**(10), 106401-1–106401-10 (2006)
10. Z_Wave motion detector manual. http://www.vesternet.com/downloads/dl/file/id/47/z_wave_everspring_sp814_motion_detector_manual.pdf
11. Fibaro motion sensor manual. http://www.fibaro.com/manuals/en/Motion-Sensor/Motion-Sensor_EN_5.3.14.pdf

Cultural Heritage and Disability: Can ICT Be the 'Missing Piece' to Face Cultural Heritage Accessibility Problems?

Alberto Arenghi[1(✉)] and Maria Agostiano[2]

[1] DICATAM, Università di Brescia, Via Branze 43, 25123 Brescia, Italy
alberto.arenghi@unibs.it
[2] Ministero dei Beni e delle Attività Culturali e del Turismo,
Via di San Michele 22, 00153 Rome, Italy
maria.agostiano@beniculturali.it

Abstract. Improving the usability conditions for all is one of the basic concepts underlying the enhancement of cultural heritage. Usability must be declined both in terms of physical accessibility and sensory-perceptive of the places of cultural interest, both as accessibility of contents of which they are witnesses.

In this field, ICT technology can become very useful especially in terms of communication and thus effective before and during the visiting of a site.

ICT technology is analyzed, also by examples, by identifying the limits, mainly due to the fact that in most cases the means are preferred rather than the goal, and the potential that is very promising if the same are designed to support undifferentiated users with the aim of transmitting cultural and not spectacular messages.

Keywords: Cultural heritage · Accessibility · Disability · ICT · Universal Design

1 Introduction. Accessibility to Cultural Heritage: A Multifaceted Question

> *"...Vengo anch'io? No, tu no*
> *Ma perché? Perché no..."*[1]
> [Enzo Jannacci]

Article 2 of the *Faro Convention*, adopted by the Council of Europe in 2005, describes cultural heritage as «a group of resources inherited from the past which people identify, independently of ownership, as a reflection and expression of their constantly evolving values, beliefs, knowledge and traditions»[2]. In other words, cultural heritage includes all the tangible (movable and immovable) and intangible (language, customs, traditions, etc.) assets with which the identity of a nation is expressed.

---

[1] Translation by the authors: "Can I come too? No, not you/But why? Because you can't".
[2] The *Framework Convention on the Value of Cultural Heritage for Society* (informally known as *Faro Convention*) emphasises the contribution of cultural heritage to the construction of a democratic and peaceful society and to its sustainable development [1].

© ICST Institute for Computer Sciences, Social Informatics and Telecommunications Engineering 2017
O. Gaggi et al. (Eds.): GOODTECHS 2016, LNICST 195, pp. 70–77, 2017.
DOI: 10.1007/978-3-319-61949-1_8

In Italy this idea was explained for the first time in 1967 when the *Franceschini Commission* suggested the following definition of cultural heritage: «any material evidence of civilization (...) all types of property having reference to the history of civilization belong to the cultural heritage of the Nation»[3]. This description has expanded the concept of cultural assets from an idea of uniqueness and rarity based on a purely aesthetic and artistic judgment (the so-called *Fine Arts*) to a historical and ethno-anthropological evaluation by which an object has a cultural value not for what it intrinsically stands for, but for what it can represent (*witness*).

In this sense, the concept of cultural heritage is strictly connected with that of communication, as highlighted significantly in the ICOMOS *Ename Charter*: «every act of heritage conservation - within all the world's cultural traditions - is by its nature a communicative act»[4].

But, over time, means and content of communication have changed according to the times, living situations and technological developments. In the last years much attention is paid to the new digital technology that seems to have the potential for making significant improvement in many fields; such as, allowing persons with disabilities to enhance their social, cultural, political and economic integration as acknowledged by the UNESCO *New Delhi Declaration*[5].

ICT can play a key role in particular, with cultural heritage, in facilitating the enjoyment of a historical site by everyone, taking into account not only the various forms of disability, but also cultural diversity both in terms of different nationality and personal education. In this sense and according to the article 30 of the United Nations Convention on the Rights of Persons with Disabilities [5], ITC may approach accessibility interventions to the principles of Universal Design with a significant advantage not only for users, avoiding marginalizing situations, but also for the protection of cultural heritage itself by reducing the works to be carried out (less facilities and devices, limited impact and lower costs of implementation, management and maintenance).

Otherwise, as noticed by Baraldi: «It is not just a problem of the methodology of conservation, but rather the dynamic nature of the interconnection between culture and society, a cornerstone of the democratic development (...) If we assume that culture is the basis for the development of critical skills for democratic participation, conceptual accessibility becomes a form of social responsibility» [6]. Knowing the past is essential to understand the present times and to guarantee democratic development. For this

---

[3] The *Commission of Inquiry for the Protection and Enhancement of Historic, Artistic, Archaeological and Landscape Assets* (commonly called the *Franceschini Commission* after the minister Francesco Franceschini who presided over it) was established in 1964 with the aim to conduct a research on the state of cultural heritage in Italy. The Commission's work ended in 1967 and was summarized in 84 Declarations, the first of which contains the aforesaid notion of cultural heritage [2].

[4] The *Charter for the Interpretation and Presentation of Cultural Heritage Sites* (informally known as the *Ename Charter*) emphasizes the need for clear principles for interpretation and presentation of worldwide heritage sites as essential components of heritage conservation efforts and as a means of enhancing public appreciation and understanding of cultural heritage [3].

[5] The *New Delhi Declaration on Inclusive ICTs for People with Disabilities: Making Empowerment a Reality* (2014) aims to highlight the power of technological and scientific progress for inclusion and empowerment of persons with disabilities [4].

reason, it is necessary to pay specific attention to the social role of cultural heritage which motivates and requires the most extensive and effective understanding of the intrinsic value of cultural assets by the community itself. And for the same reason, access to culture is a right that must be guaranteed to everyone, regardless of ability or disability. So quoting Sørmoen: «Before starting the work with ramps, lighting, braille text etc. we need to have this basic understanding of the function of heritage (...). Physical access in itself does not mean a lot if one does not have access to the message, the values, or the meaning thereof» [7].

2 The Role of ICT in Communicating Cultural Heritage Accessibility

C'è il boom della comunicazione tutti a comunicare che stanno comunicando[6]
[Altan]

The visit to a place of cultural interest begins (or should begin) almost always by collecting documentation and instructions on the site and its contents regarding both the *level of accessibility* and access modalities. Nowadays the most common methods is the use of the *internet* where some information can often be found. But how true is the information? When was it last updated? Whom and with what preparation has accessibility been judged? What usually happens is that the information (exclusively referring to *physical* accessibility), is fairly generic and refer to a phone contact. Certainly the issues do not depend on the means with which they are provided[7]. However, in these cases the use of ICT could have a potential that no other means can provide for example through the development of an *app* that, by exploiting the GPS, guides the visitor along the accessible route using *Google Maps*.

Arriving on the site the necessary information concerns both the usability of the site, and the cultural content it offers. Regardless of the *material* and *immaterial* dimensions of communication, the first question to be faced is whether it is necessary to distinguish the ways and means according to the user and, therefore, whether it is necessary to have different systems. In general, according to the Universal Design approach, it is wrong to *atomise* the users and thus it is always preferable to have a single support that can be useful for as many users as possible.

On the other hand, especially in cultural sector, the content (information and communication) to be transmitted may not be the same for a child or for an expert in the field, just like the means of communication with the blind and deaf should be defferent. Universal Design must be declined by seeking maximum flexibility in order to adapt the solutions to the greatest number of possible needs such that they can be

---

[6] Translation by the authors: "There is the boom of the communication, everyone communicates that they are communicating".

[7] It should be underlined that «Communication, therefore, has a "material" dimension concerning the means to implement it, and an "immaterial" dimension, which includes the different uses of the words, of languages and images» [8].

customized for user profiles. In this perspective the use of ICT can become an extraordinary resource to specialize the information for user profile as long as the technology does not become the goal, but only a means to achieve the results of transmission and communication of knowledge [9].

A recent example of what has just been mentioned is the project *Le chiese di Milano...in tutti i sensi*[8] concerning the study, design and manufacture of plastic type panels made with the so-called *adduction technique* (Fig. 1).

Fig. 1. Basilica di San Marco, Milan. The tactile information panel with the QR Code and NFC to download the audio-video with the translation in LIS (Italian Sign Language).

On each panel there is a short text in Italian and English, with basic information on the building. The central part is occupied by the church plant, an essential tool to facilitate the orientation of everyone, with a numerical indication for each individual

---

[8] The project (*The churches of Milan ... in every sense*) has been developed mainly by Tactile Vision Onlus and Lettura Agevolata Onlus. It includes fifteen churches in Milan and it was completed in July 2016.

part, reported in the corresponding legend. Through *QR Code* and *NFC* (Near Field Communication) an audio-visual guide to help read each panel is also provided. This art-historical enrichment is supplied in various ways: audio for the blind and visually impaired people, videos for deaf people (with subtitles and translation of texts in LIS - Italian Sign Language). To access the contents of the guide a *smartphone* or *tablet* with internet connection and with QR Code software or equipped with NFC is needed[9].

In many sites there are the *classic* 3D video reconstructions, often downloaded from Internet or purchased on the site on DVD support, which go towards *story-telling*, hardly usable by people with visual disabilities, and that somehow overcome and/or support books. These products therefore are not necessarily related to an *in situ* use.

More recently, ICT technology has been developed, especially in archeology, so that it reconstructs the place in real life size, therefore giving the visitor an idea of how the site could have been presented in ancient times. These reconstructions are neither a means of overcoming physical barriers, depending on the nature of the specific place, nor the perceptual barriers (contrary are perceptual barriers especially for the blind and visually impaired). Beyond their quality and scientific level, this technology represents a tool for accessibility to content and, unlike the previous ones, must be used only *in situ*. Among them two examples can be mentioned: the *virtual journey* inside the *Domus Romane* in Palazzo Valentini (Rome) and the experience of reality increases in the Archaeological Park of Brescia with the use of *ARt-Glass*®. In the first case with a sophisticated system of video projections, of light and sound shows the visitor can see *reborn* walls, rooms, peristyles, kitchens, baths, decorations and furniture, taking a virtual trip into a great ancient Roman Domus. The visitor can therefore grasp dimensional and chromatic aspect of spaces as they could have been.

In the second case, thanks to the augmented reality that is superimposed on the real world, the visitor wearing the *ARt-Glass*® glasses can see the reconstruction of the buildings[10] which was made possible thanks to the data which emerged from the excavations, the studies and archaeological investigations: the *Capitolium* overlooking Piazza del Foro; the central cell with the statue of Jupiter; the long flights of stairs in white marble; the shadow of the columns on the porches; the Cidneo hill behind with another important temple that standing on it. It then moves to the Roman theater, capable of seating 20,000, the taverns, the *domus*, and, in the distance, the walls, with the city gate facing Verona (Fig. 2).

An experience that the visitor can live along the points of interest with 3D reconstructions and immersive virtual reality scenarios, allowing effectiveness to have a good rendering accompanied by a narrative sequence.

---

[9] When using technology that needs Internet it is essential to make sure there is signal coverage, fact not so obvious and common in indoor places, perhaps hypogeous, with very thick walls, or in isolated outdoor venues.

[10] The reconstruction of the ancient state with geo-referenced and settled buildings was carried out according to the findings of the excavations, the archaeological investigations and studies.

Fig. 2. Archeological Park, Brescia. The Capitolium as it is and the view wearing the *ARt-Glass®*.

3 The Role of ICT to 'Compensate' Cultural Heritage Inaccessibility

"Potevamo stupirvi con effetti speciali e colori ultravivaci,
ma noi siamo scienza, non fantascienza"[11]
[Italian Spot by Telefunken]

The impossibility of ensuring full physical or sensorial accessibility to a historical site must not automatically lead to declaring it *inaccessible*, precluding any possibility of enjoying it. If there can be actual barriers (inherent to the characteristics of the places or protection requirements), for physical and sensorial accessibility, there are no limits for the potential development of communicative measures even concerning people with specific disabilities.

The more inaccessible a cultural site is, the more communicative measures must be implemented, reaching the extreme case of buildings or works of art that have been lost or destroyed, for which only through communication can their testimonial value still be disclosed (*virtual accessibility*).

So in the case of inaccessible sites, the so-called *compensatory solutions*, which can - albeit indirectly - provide knowledge and enhancement at least of the most significant areas of the site (exhibition areas, museums, multimedia work stations, live CCTVs, publications, three-dimensional models, etc.), are fundamental to make up for the impossibility of direct access to specific areas if not the entire cultural complex. In these cases, lacking direct contact with the site (we are talking unavoidably of *off-site*

---

[11] Translation by the authors: "We were able to surprise you with special effects and ultra-vivid colors, but we are science, not science fiction".

solutions), it is necessary to include specific instruments allowing the perception of the site's real consistency: dimensions, planimetric and elevation profile, but also colors, characteristics of the materials, etc. Moreover, having to replace the emotional experience connected to a direct approach to a cultural asset, compensatory measures cannot be limited to a simple and cold list of data, images and events; they should recreate the lost experience as much as possible, stimulating sensory and emotional involvement.

The painted tombs of the necropolis of Monterozzi at Tarquinia (near Rome), a unique and exceptional testimony to the ancient Etruscan civilization, are an interesting example. The archaeological area as a whole is quite accessible, but there is great difficulty in reaching the various painted rooms. The tombs are, in fact, cut into the rock and they are all underground. The entrance is reached along a narrow corridor with steep steps (physical inaccessibility). Furthermore, to ensure their preservation, the burial chamber has been sealed with glass barriers placed at the entrance (inaccessibility for protection requirements). The glass barriers keep the microclimate conditions inside unchanged, avoiding the deterioration of paintings, and, at the same time, allow a good, but partially limited view, of the interior of the tomb. Unfortunately, it is not possible to appreciate the details of the wall paintings closely. As a compensatory measure, visitors can enjoy a virtual visit of the so-called *Tomba della Caccia e della Pesca*, thanks to a 3D digital model obtained by a laser scanning technique, coupled with high-resolution images of the painted walls. A screen has been installed near the entrance of the tomb. The Superintendence aims at creating the analogous virtual reconstruction of the whole archaeological area. A specific itinerary has been created instead for the *Tomba della Pulcella*, the only painted hypogeum of the necropolis with an almost flat corridor leading to the burial chamber. A multisensory workstation has been placed at the beginning of the path, with an information panel, aids in LIS (Italian Sign Language) for the hearing impaired and an audio support for the visually impaired.

4   Conclusions

> "...Capire tu non puoi
> tu chiamale se vuoi emozioni..."[12]
> [Lucio Battisti]

Today it is possible to see many sites that offer virtual visits to museums or cities of art or 3D reconstructions of complex and monuments with historical, artistic or archaeological interest. By contrast, in most cases, in such proliferation a parallel awareness of the value and potential of virtual products as communication tools is not accompanied. In other words, only the view of explored environments is offered to the user too frequently, without the virtual tour being guided and enhanced by the contents relating to what is presented in an eye-catching and great-looking graphic design.

---

[12] Translation by the authors: "...You can not understand/if you like you can call them emotions ...".

The problem lies in the fact that technology is not a means to an objective, but constant and adaptable to different purposes. The research on the enhancement and enjoyment of cultural heritage should be addressed so as to become *concept-driven*. Technology is only a means to reach a purpose. Besides it is necessary that the research is also *case-based*. It is an error to think that a given technology can work for every site, on the contrary it must always be designed and conducted as *site-specific* bearing in mind the users profile to which it is intended.

The contribution of ICT can provide useful support to improve the communicative dimension for the comprehension of sites that are usually difficult to understand. On the contrary, ICT cannot substitute physical accessibility in an exhaustive manner because the unique way to have real knowledge of cultural heritage comes from being there, walking through the architecture, having a direct experience.

The visit to a cultural site must always be designed so that it has first and foremost has a cultural value and becomes an experiential path that has a significant impact on our being citizens of the world through emotions and not ephemeral illusions.

References

1. COUNCIL OF EUROPE: Framework Convention on Value of Cultural Heritage for Society (Faro Convention), Council of Europe Treaty Series – No. 199 (2005). http://www.coe.int/t/dg4/cultureheritage/heritage/Identities/default_en.asp
2. Per la Salvezza dei Beni Culturali in Italia: Atti e Documenti della Commissione d'Indagine per la Tutela e la Valorizzazione del Patrimonio Storico, Archeologico, Artistico e del Paesaggio, vol. 3. Colombo, Rome (1967)
3. ICOMOS: Charter for the Interpretation and Presentation of Cultural Heritage Sites (2008). http://www.icomos.org/charters/interpretation_e.pdf
4. UNESCO: Outcome Document - The New Delhi Declaration on Inclusive ICTs for People with Disabilities: Making Empowerment a Reality (2014). http://unesdoc.unesco.org/images/0023/002320/232026e.pdf
5. UNITED NATIONS: Convention on the Rights of Persons with Disabilities (2006). http://www.un.org/disabilities/convention/conventionfull.shtml
6. Baraldi, L.: Sense beyond perception: conceptual accessibility and social inclusion. In: Arenghi, A., Garofolo, I., Sørmoen, O. (eds.) Accessibility as a Key Enabling Knowledge for Enhancement of Cultural Heritage, pp. 29–40. Franco Angeli, Milano (2016)
7. Sørmoen, O.: Access to life. An accessibility rethink. In: Arenghi, A., Garofolo, I., Sørmoen, O. (eds.) Accessibility as a Key Enabling Knowledge for Enhancement of Cultural Heritage, pp. 41–48. Franco Angeli, Milano (2016)
8. Garofolo, I., Paoletti, G.: How do places and messages communicate. In: Arenghi, A., Garofolo, I., Sørmoen, O. (eds.) Accessibility as a Key Enabling Knowledge for Enhancement of Cultural Heritage, pp. 148–163. Franco Angeli, Milano (2016)
9. Antinucci, F.: Musei virtuali. Come non fare innovazione tecnologica. Edizioni Laterza, Roma (2007)

Designing an Engaging and Informative Application About First Aid: Gamification and Humor as Design Elements in a Serious Game

Nicolai Foldager, Hans Hansen, Mikkel Skovsmose Tewes, and Thomas Bjørner$^{(\boxtimes)}$

Department of Architecture, Design and Media Technology, Aalborg University, A.C. Meyers Vænge 15, 2450 Copenhagen, SV, Denmark
tbj@create.aau.dk

Abstract. This study aimed at developing an engaging and informative application within first aid and CPR for people who are already certified in first aid. The paper outlines discussions within definitions of serious games, humor, gamification and engagement. Further we suggest specific elements for implementation and evaluation of humor and gamified elements. Two prototypes were developed: one with gamification elements and one without. A between-group design was used, in which two different groups tested one prototype each. Data were gathered through data logging, in-depth interviews (with use of a verbal numeric rating scale) and observations of participants' facial expression. The Facial Action Coding System (FACS) was used for analysis. The results showed very little difference between the gamified and non-gamified version. Important elements within gamification are focuses and thoughtfulness within the implementation of challenge, rewards, achievements, feedback and the overall visual theme.

Keywords: Serious game · Gamification · Enjoyment · Humor · Engagement · Qualitative · Observations

1 Introduction

Out-of-hospital cardiac arrest is a major health problem associated with poor outcomes [1, 2]. Every year, 3,500 people experience an out-of-hospital cardiac arrest in Denmark, and only 57.9% receive cardiopulmonary resuscitation (CPR) before an ambulance arrives. The number of CPR recipients has increased over the last 10 years [1], which could be due to a focus on supportive ubiquitous technology solutions, e.g., the large amount of applications as life-saving tools and use of GPS for exact location and nearby automated external defibrillator (AED) heart starters. Training courses with first aid (and CPR) are also mandatory in Danish state schools and are a condition for obtaining a driver license. The number of people receiving CPR can, however, still increase,

© ICST Institute for Computer Sciences, Social Informatics and Telecommunications Engineering 2017
O. Gaggi et al. (Eds.): GOODTECHS 2016, LNICST 195, pp. 78–87, 2017.
DOI: 10.1007/978-3-319-61949-1_9

considering that receiving CPR triples the survival rate [1, 2] and improves long-term outcomes [1, 2]. One important factor (and sometimes one that is overlooked) is to focus on keeping the already-trained layman up-to-date with CPR knowledge. This paper presents a study in which a mobile application is developed with a focus on different game design elements. The aim is to motivate people who have already been trained in CPR to refresh their first-aid knowledge using a serious game. The research question is as follows: how can game design elements be used to develop an engaging and informative application about first aid for people who are already trained? Previous research had similar approach [28, 29], however one element in this paper is also to evaluate gamification elements and humor to gain the objectives of an engaging and informative application.

There is no consensus on the definition of serious games, and they are used in divergent ways, focusing on various perspectives within purposes, players'/users' goals, and intended content [7, 23]. Some general requirements embedded in serious games are suggested as follows [23]. 1. The game play is intrinsically motivating. 2. There is immediate feedback in the game environment. 3. The content can have or has learning opportunities. One suggested definition of serious games that might also work as a starting point is "Any form of interactive computer-based game software for one or multiple players to be used on any platform and that has been developed with the intention to be more than entertainment" [23, p. 6]. However, within this definition, there still might be some unsolved categorical problems of what "a game" is and what "entertainment" actually means. The main problem is still that the various definitions of serious games are too generic, and we would rather use the term gamification. Though there are many different perspectives within gamification, there is, however, some agreement that gamification can be seen as the process of game-thinking and game mechanics to engage users to solve problems within a non-game context [3, 4]. The purpose of using gamification elements is improving the user experience, which includes engagement. Engagement is defined as "the desire to continue playing" [5] which can be seen as a prerequisite for the experience of other conceptualizations such as engrossment, flow, fun, enjoyment, immersion, involvement, and incorporation because a player first needs to desire continue playing before these other aspects of the player experience can be experienced [5]. There is significant hype around gamification, and even though there are some good examples, there are also great risks for failure. This can be due to poor design and a lack of knowledge about the target group. Careful thought is also necessary about both the advantages and disadvantages of the design methods.

2 The Design as Engaging and Informative

Scholars have come up with different definitions of engagement and suggestions for increasing players' engagement [5, 8–10]. There seems to be some agreement on the importance of motivation, challenge, and flow. O'Brien and Toms [9] suggest that engagement shares attributes such as intrinsic motivation with flow. Motivation is needed to interest users in the activity and is what makes a user enjoy an activity [13]. Challenge is an important attribute for engagement [9, 11] and is also described as flow [13, 14], in which the player's skills and challenge must be closely matched [14, 15].

Based on the theoretical framework, especially that of O'Brien and Toms [9] and Sweetser and Wyeth [11], the game design was developed with the following criteria:

1. Several scenarios. The application should consist of several different scenarios to maintain users' interest and motivation and to gain specific and different learning goals within CPR. As two-thirds of cardiac arrest cases occur at home, it was a prerequisite that a "home scenario" was implemented in different situations, e.g., in terms of different numbers of bystanders (0–3).
2. Implementation of humor. Because the target group for this application is young individuals (20–28 years of age) different elements involving humor were implemented. In the literature, it is described how humor attracts attention and can be used to make a dull subject more interesting [17–19] and even enhance learning [20]. Because first aid is a subject that can be quite tiresome to read about, we designed some of the answering options in the challenges to have humoristic formulations. This should help users obtain a certain amount of enjoyment, which is a part of the positive effect [9, 11]. All users are not motivated by the same things; some prefer hard fun, and others prefer easy fun [18]. It is therefore crucial to have in-depth qualitative user insight for implementing humor as intended.
3. Implementation of rewards in the application. Rewards can give the user clear visual feedback based on performance, which can motivate the user to try the scenarios more than once [9, 11, 12]. Furthermore, the users will be unable to continue to scenario 2 [see Fig. 1 for example] if they received less than two stars in the first scenario. Stars were chosen to indicate points because they are an already well-known reward symbol (as known from, e.g., Angry Birds).
4. Implementation of achievements. Achievements can be a motivational factor [9] because they provide clear feedback when showing users their progress. They also give users a reason to continue using the application (meaning they are engaged [5]), especially if they want to unlock as many scenarios as possible [see Fig. 1 for example]. The achievements will be shown as highlighted with a bright yellow color to give a clear indication of the user's accomplishments. The user will be shown a popup that enters the screen from the top to give them instant feedback as an important element in game flow [9, 11].
5. Implementation of challenge. It is important that the difficulty level of the content in the application is higher than the user's skill level [9]. The challenge will be implemented by different questions about CPR.
6. Implementation of feedback. A horizontal progress bar was implemented that fills up based on the user's progress (see Fig. 1), similar to how hit point bars and energy bars usually are displayed in games. Furthermore, the color of the progress bar was set to be red because it would match the rest of the theme in the application. The progress bar itself is not a motivational factor; however, as progress and clear visual feedback both are motivational factors [9, 11], it can be used to visualize progress for the users and thus motivate them to proceed through the entire application and all of the scenarios.
7. Visual theme resembles the topic. The visual theme of the application was determined to match the topic; therefore, red and white were used for most of the text and buttons in the game. These colors are generally associated with first aid (see

Fig. 1 as an example). The background color was decided to be a neutral blue color to avoid a conflict with the red buttons and make interactive objects more noticeable.

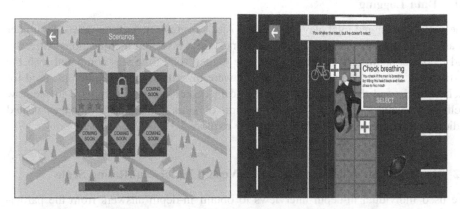

Fig. 1. Two screen shots from the game. Accomplishments and progress bar (*left*) and one of the scenarios with implemented questions and options (*right*). (Color figure online)

3 Methods

Unity3D was used to develop the application. Two different versions of the application were used for testing: one with gamified elements (gamification) and one without gamification elements. The gamified version was implemented with challenges, achievements, and rewards (as described in Sect. 2). A between-group test design was used in which each participant tried either of the two versions. The participants were not told to which group they belonged or what the test was evaluating. In total, there were 20 participants, with 10 in each group. There was an equal number of male and females in each group.

The application was installed on tablets. As we used camera observations of the participants' facial expressions (described in 3.3), the tablet was inclined by 25° to make more of their faces visible to the camera. It was placed approximately 140 cm in front of the participants and approximately 35 cm below the participant's eye level at an angle of 10°.

Quota sampling was used to recruit participants. The criteria for the target group were set to the following: 1. prior certified knowledge with first aid, 2. aged between 20 and 28, and 3. speaks and understands Danish. The age criterion was derived from the first aid certificate requirements for having a driver's license in Denmark, introduced in 2006. However, the first-aid certificate expires after two years.

All participants were informed about the procedure and the observations and signed an informed consent prior to the test. Participants were secured anonymity with an ID number, and their facial expressions not would be disclosed outside of the researchers in this study. Participants in the gamified version were labelled with a 'G' in front of the ID number and an 'NG' for the non-gamified group.

3.1 Data Logging

The prototype logged total play time, page visits, progression and stars earned, number of attempts for each scenario, how many times they answered the questions correctly, and incorrect answers for each attempt. The logged total time was compared with the participants' perceived time to detect if they were time distorted. The attempts used for each scenario and the number of correct and incorrect answers were used to see how well participants performed. The progression of stars and number of pages visited indicated how much of the application they explored.

3.2 In-Depth Interviews with Use of a Verbal Numerical Rating Scale

We used individual in-depth interviews to obtain in-depth answers from the participants. The main advantage of the interviews was the flexible design in having the participants verbally elaborate on their answers and that it was possible to ask follow-up questions. During the interview, we used a verbal numerical rating scale (VNRS), which is a projective technique used to have participants express their feelings or thoughts on a specific topic [26]. The VNRS ranged from 0–10; 0 was the lowest score, and 10 was the highest. The participants were asked to verbally rate seven elements from the application with regard to different attributes of engagement [9]: perceived time, aesthetics, feedback, challenge, enjoyment, interest, and goals. They were asked two different VNRS questions within each element. After the interview, participants were given a piece of paper with a scenario similar to those in the application. They were then asked four questions. These questions were asked to state whether they recalled what to do in terms of first aid and CPR.

3.3 Observations

The participants were video recorded while they used the application for detecting and analyzing their here-and-now facial expressions compared to their progression in the application. The purpose was to measure signs of concentration and happiness (and the function of the intended humoristic elements implemented). Happiness can be detected by lip-corner pulls, raising the cheeks, and narrowing the eyes by raising the cheeks [24, 25]. Concentration can be detected by narrowing of the eyes and lowering and bringing together the eyebrows [24, 25].

Krippendorff's Alpha (KALPHA)s for both the interviews and the observations (both with 3 coders) was calculated to check for intercoder reliability [27]. KALPHA for coding the interviews was 0.537 for participants for the gamified version and 0.546 for the non-gamified version. KALPHA for the observations was 0.320 for participants within the gamified version and 0.364 for the non-gamified version.

4 Humor in a Serious Game

Humor in serious games is highly complex, as it can have both different functions and specific experiences and outcomes in game play [20, 21]. However humor is associated with pleasure as an overall function [20] and might cause laughter and moments of shared fun. Besides pleasure, humor might also contain emotional responses, such as playfulness, surprise, or other responses associated with mirth [20]. In the implementation, we wanted to use humor for emotional and cognitive functions [20], both for maintaining engagement as well as attention and awareness. The name of some of the achievements was designed to be humorous. When users reached 50% progress, they were awarded an achievement stating "50% - Whoa, we're half way there," which is a reference to Bon Jovi's song "Livin' on a Prayer." Achievement 6 was unlocked when participants had opened all of the subpages on the "Learn CPR" page and stated "You should consider a job as a lifesaver!" Also, humor elements were implemented in the soundscape, e.g., there was the screeching of tires down the road with the arrival of an ambulance.

The participants that reported the highest amount of perceived time were G3 and NG3. They were also the participants with most positive evaluation in terms of the implemented humor. In the interviews, they stated that the application was "fun and serious but still game-like" (G3) and "had good basics and was more fun than traditional learning of CPR" (NG3). Other participants also mentioned that "it was done in a humorous way" (G2). However, some participants were confused by the humor and did not think the implemented humoristic elements were funny. Participant NG7 stated that she was "confused by the humor which suddenly occurred." This means that there might be a mismatch between the genre expectations and the actual content in the application, but to be humorous, the content must also be a surprise [20]. NG7 was also uncertain whether the purpose of the humoristic elements and scores were partly to compare them with friends (social function) or if the game was actually was an application for testing knowledge level (cognitive function).

Seven participants stated that it was a "fun experience" (G1, G3, G6, NG4, NG5, NG8, and NG10). Furthermore, only two participants did not smile through the usage of the application. However, the observed facial expressions related to participants' happiness did not reveal much difference between the gamified and non-gamified application (Table 1). Based on the observations, it can be questioned how enjoyable the application actually was. The findings of these observations is taken to a methodological level as being very difficult to actually observe and interpret participants' facial expressions. Table 1 shows the coders' ratings of the participants' enjoyment/happiness.

It is rather problematic using only self-reports (e.g., interviews and questionnaires) as the sole method for user feedback and evaluation. Users might have difficulties expressing their feelings and behaviors towards the application, and self-reports are often based on an evaluation after the event or "disturbing" the flow during usage. This is the reason why self-reports with advantages could be supplemented. However, observations and psychophysiological measurements (e.g., electroencephalography and skin conductance) can be very difficult to both set up and interpret in gaming. The idea is to come closer to what users do, feel, and think and guess what they have on their minds.

Table 1. Average number of signs of enjoyment/happiness (three coders), based on FACS codes [24, 25]

	Definition	Gamified	Non-gamified	Difference, N-G
1. Somewhat happy	Small lip-corner pull	2.36	2.17	0.21
2. Moderately happy	Medium lip-corner pull with mouth closed. Raising cheeks	2.2	2.2	0
3. Very happy	High lip-corner pull with mouth open. Narrowing the eyes by raising the cheeks	0.43	0.93	0.50

However, as many scholars have argued, information on causal relationships between discrete brain structures and their putative functions is still rather limited [6, 16].

5   Engaged or Not Engaged

In general, there was not much difference between the gamified and non-gamified group in terms of their VNRS ratings for six of the seven engagement elements (perceived time, aesthetics, feedback, enjoyment, interest, and goal). The only main difference was seen in "challenge," for which the participants were asked how challenging the application was. The question was rated on an average of 5.0 (0 lowest and 10 highest) for the gamified group and 2.9 for the non-gamified group. This could be interpreted as the gamified group feeling more challenged than the non-gamified group. Some participants in the gamified group stated that the achievements and points were a challenge for them to obtain, which might be the reason why they felt more challenged.

We assumed that the participants who used the gamified version would spend more time on the application compared to those who used the non-gamified version. However, the result was opposite. The group that used the gamified version had an average play time of 564 s (perceived time of 654 s) and the non-gamified had an average play time of 619.5 s (perceived time of 648 s). There is no significant difference between the difference in play time and perceived time between the two groups ($p < .2123$, Wilcoxon rank sum test). The minor difference in the two groups' perceived time and play time could be due to the participants not being in the flow [13, 14] or being engaged [9]. One reason could be the intrinsic motivation in the content of the application, but several participants also mentioned external factors, e.g., G7 stated several things that distracted from her experience (e.g., background noises and the artificial set up for the test).

The logged data revealed that the gamified group played scenario 1 more frequently (on average 0.4 more often) compared to the non-gamified group. This could be explained by a higher level of interest within the gamified version for scenario 1 and the fact that scenario 2 was seldom retried by either group. Scenario 2 had too high of a similarity with scenario 1 (not enough new content), which affected the interest. The average numbers of tries for scenario 2 was 0.7 for the gamified version and 0.8 for the non-gamified version.

The non-gamified group had an average of 78.9% progression, and the gamified group had an average of 77.4%. The gamified group's progression was lower than expected; however, all of the gamified group's participants had visited all of the pages in the application, but two participants of the non-gamified group missed a few. A general comment from the interview was that the questions/challenge were too easy. However, even though that we could not see much difference in the VNRS ratings (except the challenge questions), observations, or logged data, the comments from the interviews highlight major differences between the two groups, e.g., G2 stated, "The progression bar kept me going ...' G1 stated, "I liked and felt motivated by the achievements, and I wanted to unlock all of them ... I wanted to know how I could get all the achievements." However, in both groups, there were explicit statements mentioning that "it was a fun experience" (G1, G2, G3, NG4, NG8, and NG10).

After the interview, all participants were given a scenario on paper regarding a drowning accident to see if they recalled any of the information given in the application (cognitive learning perspective). Of 80 questions (four per participant), only 14 questions were answered incorrectly, and there was no difference between the two groups. The only difference was a total of one more correct answer for the non-gamified group for questions 1 and 4.

6 Conclusion

The topic of first aid had an impact in terms of participants' interest. Several participants stated that they knew it was an important topic but felt they did not need to know anything about it (again) because they believed they would never be in a situation where CPR was needed. This was mostly as expected. The idea behind this study was motivating people already trained in CPR to refresh their first-aid knowledge with the support of a serious game with gamified elements. With regard to this aim, the application was a success. An after-evaluation to test the knowledge gained revealed very few incorrect answers.

However, several topics can be further investigated within both the game design and the methods for evaluating engagement and gamified elements. The scenarios in this game should have been more challenging; nearly everyone who attempted the scenarios scored a high number of correct answers on their first attempt. The lack of challenge in the scenarios affected motivation, interest, and perceived time. If users do not feel challenged, there is less of a chance that they will be engaged in the game and may grow bored and lose interest in the application.

In general, there was not much difference between the gamified and non-gamified groups in terms of both the VNRS ratings from the interviews, time spent, and perceived time from the data logging. However, further research with more participants and better control set up is needed to determine the actual effects of gamified versus non-gamified elements.

Our conclusion reveals that it is rather difficult to both implement and measure humor in a serious game. The elements of humor were evaluated differently, both among the game developers and test subjects. In that sense, the conclusion is part of the already well-known trap for game developers. Game developers tend to make serious games fun using such heuristics as game interface, game mechanics, game story, and game play [22], but the implemented humor might not match either the overall purpose or the players' interest. However, the triangulated methods for measuring humor provided some insight. The FACS codes used to observe participants' facial expressions combined with the interviews could be one way of measuring humor, but this is rather time-consuming, and training is necessary both for detecting facial expressions and conducting the interviews. Intercoder reliability is an important tool for findings and reporting and in the design process. Besides an indication of reliability, it also gives the design developer a better common understanding of the application, as necessary discussions, definitions, and decisions can be made on the basis of better common understandings due to intercoder indications.

References

1. Wissenberg, M., et al.: Association of national initiatives to improve cardiac arrest management with rates of bystander intervention and patient survival after out-of-hospital cardiac arrest. JAMA **310**(13), 1377–1384 (2013)
2. Committee on the Treatment of Cardiac Arrest: Strategies to Improve Cardiac Arrest Survival: A Time to Act. National Academies Press, Washington, D.C. (2015). Current Status and Future Directions, Board on Health Sciences Policy; Institute of Medicine
3. Zichermann, S.C., Cunningham, C.: Gamification by Design. O'Reilly Media Inc., Sebastopol (2011)
4. Burke, B.: Gamify: How Gamification Motivates People to Do Extraordinary Things. Gartner Inc., Brookline (2014)
5. Schønau-Fog, H., Bjørner, T.: "Sure, I would like to continue": a method for mapping the experience of engagement in video games. Bull. Sci. Technol. Soc. **32**(5), 405–412 (2012)
6. LeDoux, J.E.: A neuroscientist's perspective on debates about nature and emotion. Emot. Rev. **4**(4), 375–379 (2012)
7. Lee, M.: Ticky ends: employing thinly-sliced narratives in serious games for mobile platforms. Int. J. Multimedia Ubiq. Eng. **9**(10), 349–362 (2014)
8. Yannakakis, G.N., Hallam, J.: Real-time game adaptation for optimizing player satisfaction. IEEE Trans. Comput. Intell. AI Games **1**(2), 121–133 (2009)
9. O'Brien, H.L., Toms, E.G.: The development and evaluation of a survey to measure user engagement. J. Am. Soc. Inf. Sci. Technol. **61**(1), 50–69 (2009)
10. Quesenbery, W.: The five dimensions of usability. In: Albers, M.J., Mazur, M.B. (eds.) Content and Complexity: Information Design in Technical Communication. Lawrence Erlbaum, New York (2003)
11. Sweetser, P., Wyeth, P.: Gameflow: a model for evaluating player enjoyment in games. Comput. Entertain. **3**(3), 1–24 (2005)
12. Marczewski, A.: Even Ninja Monkeys Like to Play: Gamification, Game Thinking and Motivational Design. Gamified, Addlestone (2015)
13. Csikszentmihalyi, M.: The Evolving Self A Psychology for the Third Millennium. Perennial, New York (1993)

14. Csikszentmihalyi, M.: Flow: The Psychology of Optimal Experience. Harper Perennial, New York (1990)
15. Keller, J., Bless, H.: Flow and regulatory compatibility: an experimental approach to the flow model of intrinsic motivation. Pers. Soc. Psychol. Bull. **34**(2), 196–209 (2008)
16. Gardhouse, K., Anderson, A.: Objectives and subjective measurement in affective science. In: Armony, J., Vuilleumier, P. (eds.) The Cambridge Handbook of Human Affective Neuroscience, pp. 57–81. Cambridge University Press, Cambridge (2013)
17. Weinberger, M.G., Gulas, C.S.: The impact of humor in advertising a review. J. Advert. **21**(4), 35–59 (1992)
18. Lazzaro, N.: Why we play games: four keys to more emotion without story. In: Game Developers Conference, 8 March (2004)
19. Dillon, R.: On the Way to Fun: An Emotion-based Approach to Successful Game Design. A. K. Peters, Natick (2010)
20. Dormann, C., Biddle, R.: A review of humor for computer games: play, laugh and more. Simul. Gaming **40**(6), 802–824 (2009)
21. Carr, D.: Contexts, gaming pleasures, and gendered preferences. Simul. Gaming **36**, 464–482 (2005)
22. Wang, H., Shen, C., Ritterfeld, U.: Enjoyment of digital games: what makes them "seriously" fun? In: Ritterfeld, U., Cody, M., Vorderer, P. (eds.) Serious Games: Mechanics and Effects. Routledge, New York and London (2009)
23. Ritterfeld, U., Cody, M., Vorderer, P.: Introduction. In: Ritterfeld, U., Cody, M., Vorderer, P. (eds.) Serious Games: Mechanics and Effects. Routledge, New York (2009)
24. Rozin, P., Cohen, A.B.: High frequency of facial expressions corresponding to confusion, concentration, and worry in an analysis of naturally occurring facial expressions of americans. Emotion **3**(1), 68–75 (2003)
25. Cohn, J.F., Ambadar, Z., Ekman, P.: Observer-based measurement of facial expression with the facial action coding system. In: Cohn, J.A., Allen, J.B. (eds.) The Handbook of Emotion Elicitation and Assessment. Oxford University Press Series in Affective Science, Oxford (2006)
26. Bjørner, T.: Data collection. In: Bjørner, T. (ed.) Qualitative Methods for Consumer Research. Hans Reitzels Forlag, Denmark (2015)
27. Hayes, A.F., Krippendorff, K.: Answering the call for a standard reliability measure for coding data. Commun. Methods Meas. **1**(1), 77–89 (2007)
28. Oak, J.W., Bae, J.H.: Development of smart multiplatform game app using UNITY3D engine for CPR education. IJMUE **9**(7), 263–268 (2014)
29. Kelle, S., Klemke, R., Specht, M.: Effects of game design patterns on basic life support training content. J. Educ. Technol. Soc. **16**(1), 275–285 (2013)

IOM–Internet of Mobility: A Wearable Device for Outdoor Data Collection

Francesco Frulio[1], Erfan Sheikhi[2], Lucia Rossazza[2],
Gabriele Perfetto[2], Andres Calvachi[1], Gianluca Picco[2],
and Sara Comai[1(✉)]

[1] Politecnico di Milano, Piazza L. Da Vinci 32, 20133 Milan, Italy
{francesco.frulio,andres.calvachi}@mail.polimi.it,
sara.comai@polimi.it
[2] Politecnico di Torino, Corso Duca degli Abruzzi, 24, 10129 Turin, Italy
{erfan.sheikhi,lucia.rossazza,gabriele.perfetto,
gianluca.picco}@studenti.polito.it

Abstract. Current technology allows the collection of data about cities by communities collaborating for the wellbeing of the city. The solution described in this paper is a wearable device ecosystem, called IOM (Internet of Mobility), consisting of a wearable device collecting environmental data through sensors to be visualized on a mobile or web platform. The paper focuses on the requirements analysis involving different types of target users and on the design of the wearable device.

Keywords: Wearable device · Smart city · Environmental data collection

1 Introduction

Emerging technologies, such as wireless sensor networks and internet-based mobile applications, have been reshaping our urban environments, making them smarter. According to the Digital Agenda for Europe smart cities are defined as places where the traditional networks and services are made more efficient with the use of digital and telecommunication technologies, for the benefits of its inhabitants and businesses. One of these enabling technological processes for smart cities is represented by the Wearable Technology, a rapidly evolving field expected to rocket dramatically in the next years. Although so far fitness and activity trackers have led the wearable device market, advances in material science, decreasing size and consumption of some sensors, collaborative platforms and social media, cloud computing, Internet of Thing (IoT) and Big Data science provide new potentialities and possibilities.

In this paper we present IOM, a wearable device prototype for gathering data about cities, processing and returning them to citizens in the form of customized maps and paths. The single user will acquire a deeper and wider knowledge about the city, feeling more comfortable to move in it and more embedded in the community, since his/her data will be used to build meaningful maps exploited by everyone. The core of this innovative service consists of raw, anonymous and open source data, accessible not

© ICST Institute for Computer Sciences, Social Informatics and Telecommunications Engineering 2017
O. Gaggi et al. (Eds.): GOODTECHS 2016, LNICST 195, pp. 88–95, 2017.
DOI: 10.1007/978-3-319-61949-1_10

only to the users but also to third parties. The latter would be able to carry out analysis on these data and probably bring to light valuable and hidden information exploitable to improve life conditions in the city as well as the city itself.

Thanks to the multidisciplinarity of the team, made of both engineers and designers with different expertise, both a functional prototype and a 3D printed prototype of the wearable device design have been produced. Furthermore, different issues, concerning user-centred design as well as hardware, software and business requirements, have been considered all along the process to propose a reasonable and practicable solution.

The paper is organized as follows: in Sect. 2 related work is reported; Sect. 3 reports requirements analysis. Section 4 describes the IOM solution, focusing on the wearable device prototype. Finally, Sect. 5 draws the conclusions.

2 Related Work

Wearable technology has emerged recently and several applications have been proposed. The fact that this technology can be worn and then taken everywhere, has favoured the emergence of a new phenomenon of participatory sensing or, as defined by Guo et al. [1], of Mobile Crowd Sensing (MCS), where everyday mobile devices form a network enabling people to gather, analyse and share local knowledge (Burke et al.) [2].

As pointed out by Delmastro et al. [9], "nowadays users not only represent the final utilizers of the technology, but they actively contribute to its evolution by assuming different roles: they act as humans, by sharing contents and experiences through social networks, and as virtual sensors, by moving freely in the environment with their sensing devices".

Of the same line is the work of Andrienko et al. [10]: they explain how the increasing market of wearable devices can provide new opportunities for applications that improve citizens quality of life, and show that the emerging phenomena of smart cities is giving rise to numerous challenges that can constitute a new interdisciplinary field of research.

aGrisu [3], Smart Citizen [4], and Netatmo [5] are examples of companies and projects producing wearable devices or services in part similar to our proposal, exploiting sensors to measure data about the environment. aGrisu [3] provides different products and apps including an environmental outdoor/indoor monitoring unit to collect data such as CO_2 level, VOC (Volatile Organic Compound), and Carbon Monoxide. Similar is the P-Sense wearable presented by Mendez et al. [6], for pollution monitoring and control of urban areas, allowing users and institutions to access such data for their benefit; however, they do not provide any real time interactive and customizable maps. Smart Citizen Kit [4] is an open-source environmental monitoring platform consisting of an arduino-compatible hardware, a data visualization web API, and a mobile app that has been used mostly for research purposes. It allows the visualization of measurements about CO, NO_2, light, humidity and temperature and sharing of data with other users of the community. Netatmo [5] offers a weather station. Although not in the field of wearable devices, it provides features and services close to IOM: a map with all the weather stations outdoor data is updated every few minutes, showing details about altitude, date and time of the last update/data measurement, temperature, humidity, pressure, and other useful data.

We considered also accessibility problems. Indeed, IOM exploits the algorithms of the MEP Project [7] to collect accessibility information in the city by exploiting mobile device sensors. Among the related projects, Wheelmap [8] is an online and worldwide map for finding and marking wheelchair accessible places: it enriches maps with information about accessibility, which is however collected manually, using a collaborative approach.

Table 1 summarizes the main characteristics (types of sensors, devices and platforms for data collection and visualization, etc.) of such proposals and compares them with our proposed system.

Table 1. Comparison of the characteristics of similar projects and products.

Product	MEP-WEAR	Netatmo	Smart Citizen	aGrisu API	Wheelmap
Hardware	Mobile/wear	Fixed	Fixed	Mobile/wear	N/A
Web platform	Yes	Yes	Yes	No	Yes
Mobile app	Yes	Yes	Yes	Yes	Yes
Environmental data	Yes	Yes	Yes	Yes	No
Indoor/outdoor	Both	Indoor	Indoor	Both	N/A
GPS	Yes	No	No	Unknown	N/A
Bluetooth	Yes	No	No	Unknown	N/A
Humidity and temp	Yes	Yes	Yes	Yes	N/A
UV	Yes	No	No	Yes	N/A
Ambient light	Yes	No	Yes	Yes	N/A
Pollution	No	Yes	Yes	Yes	N/A
Sound/noise	Yes	Yes	Yes	No	N/A
Motion detection	Yes	No	No	Yes	N/A
Accessibility map	Yes	No	No	No	Yes
Cost	$80–$100	$190	$155	N/A	Free

3   Requirements Analysis

To identify the needs of the target users and collect their requirements, we carried on a survey that has been spread over the Web among very different customers' classes in terms of geographical provenience, culture, and age. Beside collecting data about users' profiles, questions tried to better understand users' attitudes and interest about the wearable technology sector. The survey allowed us to identify important and remarkable trends in relation to age, gender and customs of the possible final users.

The survey has been filled by a sample of two hundred and twenty people, with an age ranging from fifteen to sixty years. Figure 1 shows the age distribution among males and females.

On the basis of the results of the survey and users analysis, we identified six main personas/target users: the Movement Impeded, the Runner, the Walker, the Biker, the

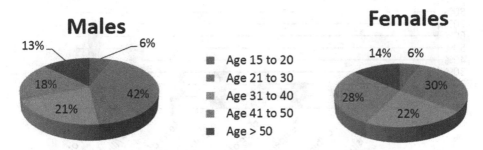

Fig. 1. Age distribution among males and females.

Exploiter (stakeholders interested to the collected data) and the External User (e.g., producers, advertisers, etc.). The performed analysis acquired a critical role directing the project activity, both at the level of hardware/software features specification and at the products' design.

As can be seen in Fig. 2, where one of the collected results is shown, the design of the device was another critical challenge considered in the survey since, as the set of sensors inside and the fact that has to be worn over the clothes, have influenced its final shape and material construction.

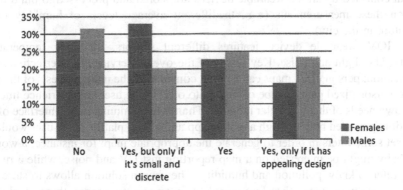

Fig. 2. Percentage of likeness of a possible wearable device.

Beside acquiring general information about the gender and the age of the sample, we tried to understand if users prefer to explore new areas or, on the contrary, they always choose the same paths. The former has come out to be the most chosen answer (60% against 40% for the latter) with no relevant difference with regard to the gender. With respect to the age it is noticeable that the only age band having a systematic preference towards the exploration of new areas is the highest one (older than fifty years).

Figure 3 shows the percentage of the preferred information that the users would like to know with the usage of the proposed system (multiple answers were allowed in this question), considering all the types of target users.

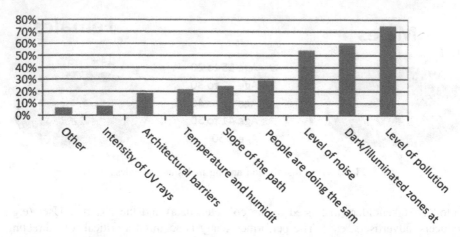

Fig. 3. Users' favorite information on personalized maps.

4 IOM Solution

The proposed solution is called IOM (Internet of Mobility), and consists of a wearable device that collects data in the city, and a mobile/Web platform for their visualization. The data collected by all the wearable devices are stored and processed to build maps based on these measurements (e.g., thedifferent average levels of humidity or of temperature in the city).

The IOM wearable device features different sensors, including temperature, humidity, UV, light and noise. Key points of the overall service are inter activity and customization: personalized maps can be built considering the main interests of the user and also personalized paths can be computed to offer to the user an experience fitted to his/her own needs of that particular moment. Thanks to an intuitive user interface of the application, provided both through a mobile app and a Web platform, the user would be able to set some filters in order to generate the appropriate map: for instance, a woman with a baby might be interested on a map reporting just UV and noise, while a runner would prefer to know pollution and humidity. The chosen solution allows to store and process anonymous data, therefore enabling everyone to access them, including external stakeholders which could use them to build new services. The IOM Mobile Application and the IOM Open Web Platform will work side by side with the wearable device designed in order to collect the data from the users that are moving around the city, allowing to have a better understanding of the condition of the city.

The hardware of the wearable device consists of different components including sensors, a subsystem for data handling and communication, and a power subsystem. Each sensor or module is connected to the main processor (an STM32F4xx microcontroller in our prototype) through different communication protocols such as UART, SPI, I2C, GPIO, etc. Figure 4 shows the overall schematic of the prototype. In the choice of which sensors to include we made a trade-off between the preferences expressed in the survey and the feasibility of the solution. Indeed, we excluded the level of pollution as directly measured data since to have a meaningful information

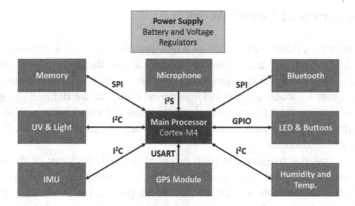

Fig. 4. Overall schematic of the prototype.

different sensors should be used and this would arise other issues on power consumption and size of the device.

Also the aesthetic of the wearable device was designed and built around the sensors board (Fig. 5). The device can be worn on clothes as a pin, in order to be always in contact with the environment, but can turn into a wristband if needed. We tried to satisfy the users' requirements emerged from the survey, i.e. a discrete and small device at the same time with an appealing design (Fig. 6).

Fig. 5. Different views of the IOM wearable device.

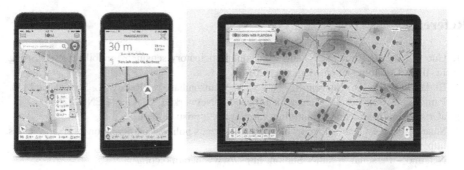

Fig. 6. Screenshot of the designed mobile application and web platform.

5   Conclusions and Future Work

IOM operates in the upcoming scenario of a new paradigm shift that the world is living in these days, in which IoT and connected devices are re-shaping our lives and cities, giving an idea of what the future might bring to us soon. We built and test a device prototype, in order to touch on real environmental data and we defined the electronic design of the miniaturized board taking into account the combination of the several requested functions, the power consumption constraints and the trade-off between hardware quality and costs.

We believe that our solution has high potential. Indeed, the heart of the concept is the open source cities data, and such valuable data could definitely give raise to strongly positive implications on the society development. In the future we may see prospects for the birth and improvement of products, services and business. For example, knowing which paths people are used to do, can be very interesting for planning the new shops, restaurant, public and private services; environmental data are instead exploitable by real estate companies, energy service provider or photovoltaic system provider. Moreover, since IOM is based on a dynamic and "living" network, where every citizen represents a moving measuring station, a scenario is forecast where it would be possible to have near real-time, continuous, widespread and detailed monitoring of our environment, not only cities but every place reachable by human beings.

A possible future service development can be related to a new IOM device that is equipped also with a heart rate sensor. Although we have already tested this kind of sensor on our prototype, we knowingly decided to not insert it in our solution; however, it could be very useful to identify correlations between heart monitoring and environmental parameters, especially for people with health problems.

Acknowledgements. This research has been funded by the Alta Scuola Politecnica (ASP) program which is an honor program restricted to 150 young and exceptionally talented students, selected solely on the basis of merit, among the applicants to the Master of Science in Engineering, Architecture, and Design at Politecnico di Milano and Politecnico di Torino. We are particularly thankful to Matteo Matteucci, Secil UgurYavuz, Raffaella Mangiarotti, and Daniele Caltabiano.

References

1. Guo, B., Yu, Z., Zhou, X., Zhang, D.: From participatory sensing to mobile crowd sensing. In: IEEE Communication Magazine (2014)
2. Burke, J., Estrin, D., Hansen, M., Parker, A., Ramanathan, N., Reddy, S., Srivastava, M.B.: Participatory sensing. In: Center for Embedded Networked Sensing (CENS) (2006)
3. aGrisù – Environmental Monitoring. http://www.a-grisu.com
4. Smart Citizen – Open source technology for citizens political participation in smarter cities. https://smartcitizen.me/
5. Netatmo – Personal Weather Station. https://www.netatmo.com/

6. Mendez, D., Perez, A.J., Labrador, M.A., Marron, J.J.: P-Sense: a participatory sensing system for air pollution monitoring and control. In: IEEE Communication Magazine (2011)
7. Bobrova, N., Comai, S.: MEP-wear – wearable devices for data logging about cities. https://www.politesi.polimi.it/handle/10589/119262
8. Wheelmap – Map of Wheelchair Accessible Places. http://wheelmap.org/en/
9. Delmastro, F., Arnaboldi, V., Conti, M.: People-centric Computing and Communications in Smart Cities. In: IEEE Communication Magazine (2016)
10. Andrienko, G., Gunopulos, D., Ioannidis, Y., Kalogeraki, V., Katakis, I., Morik, K., Verscheure, O.: Mining urban data. Inf. Sys. (2016)

IoT: Science Fiction or Real Revolution?

Marco Furini[1(✉)], Federica Mandreoli[2], Riccardo Martoglia[2],
and Manuela Montangero[2]

[1] Dipartimento di Comunicazione ed Economia,
Universta di Modena and Reggio Emilia, 42121 Reggio Emilia, Italy
marco.furini@unimore.it
[2] Dipartimento di Fisica, Informatica e Matematica,
Universta di Modena and Reggio Emilia, 42121 Modena, Italy
{federica.mandreoli,riccardo.martoglia,manuela.montangero}@unimore.it

Abstract. It's been many years since media began talking about the wonders of the IoT scenario, where a smart fridge checks the milk expiration date and automatically compiles the shopping list, but in the real life how many people have this smart fridge in the kitchen? Yet the interest around the IoT scenario is growing every day, so in this paper we try to figure out if IoT is science fiction or a real revolution. In particular, we describe in simple terms the IoT scenario, what can be done with current technologies, what are the main obstacles that limit the success and the wide use of IoT and we highlight directions that can make IoT a true reality.

Keywords: Internet of Things · Smart home · Smart city · Health-care · Retail industry · Smart factory

1 The IoT Scenario

In recent years, the term Internet of Things (IoT) is receiving considerable attention by governments, researchers, managers, media, etc. IoT refers to a scenario where people and physical objects (e.g., sensors, devices, etc.) are connected and able to communicate with each other with the result of transforming the physical world that surrounds us. Vehicles, home appliances, smartphones, home sensors, wearable sensors, environment devices are examples of objects that can be transformed into smart objects in order to be part of an IoT scenario. Indeed, by providing these objects with the ability to communicate, we allow them to capture and share data, we can control and analyze their actions to take decisions and to produce intelligent services able to transform our personal and professional life [1].

To clarify the idea, here is an example of how smart objects can change some everyday actions. In the morning, the alarm clock does not just wake us up, but it also turns on the coffee machine; the mattress turns on the room lights when we get up; the bathroom lights are switched on when we touch the door; television and lights are turned on when we go into the kitchen and the coffee machine begins pouring the coffee into the cup. Before going out, the umbrella handle lights if rain is expected and when we close the door all the house lights go off and the blinds are lowered. In the evening, when we get home, the heating is turned on by our smartphone that uses the GPS to check whether we are close to home or not; the house lights are turned on when we open the door. This is just an example of how our private life will change thanks to IoT technologies, but the scenario is definitely wider: a city may become smart by using sensors and devices to monitor and manage traffic, to improve the efficiency of waste management, to plan urban and transportation changes; health-care may become smart by using sensors and devices to improve emergency services, to provide elderly assistance and medical aids; industries may use IoT to improve security in automotive transportation, to make logistics more efficient, to improve industrial automation; energy providers may use IoT to intelligently mange energy distribution [2,3]. Needless to say, the IoT scenario is expected to transform every aspect of our life [3–7].

Millions of physical objects are being connected to the Internet [8] and several research reports agree that by 2020 the IoT scenario will include more than 20 billion of smart objects. These objects are enabled by several technological changes that caused, among others, a lowering of the production costs of sensors and devices, an increase of computational capacity and an ubiquitous networking coverage. In this scenario, objects are equipped with sensors and/or actuators and with suitable communication protocols that make them integral part of the Internet [4,9]. To clarify, the IoT can be thought of as the interconnection of objects with the Internet, as shown in Fig. 1. At objects level we have sensors that perform actions like "feel", "ear", "measure", "check" (i.e., sensors have different abilities like acoustic, liquid, temperature, pressure, force, etc.) and we have actuators that perform actions through electrical, hydraulic, pneumatic or mechanical movements. All these objects communicate with each other through sensor networks [8,10,11] that use data link protocols like NFC, RFID, LTE, Wi-Fi, Zigbee, etc., and communicate with the platform and with the application levels through Internet communication technologies.

Briefly speaking, the IoT architecture allows to extend today's Internet infrastructure with additional and innovative services. For this reason, different ICT consulting firms foresee an exponential growth of the IoT over the next few years. For instance, Gartner[1] forecasts that the IoT will generate revenue exceeding $300 billion in 2020, resulting in $1.9 trillion in global economic value-add through sales into diverse end markets; whereas [12] estimates that the whole annual economic impact caused by the IoT is in the range of $2.7 trillion to $6.2 trillion by 2025. The importance of this scenario is also highlighted by the amount of fundings that public governments are reserving to IoT research: the European Union is supporting different projects in the IoT area; the UK government, in March 2015, committed around €50 million to IoT research; Germany has earmarked up to €200 million to projects related to internet-based manufacturing;

---

[1] https://www.gartner.com/doc/2625419/forecast-internet-things-worldwide-.

France reserves €50 million to digital development projects related to embedded software and connected objects [13].

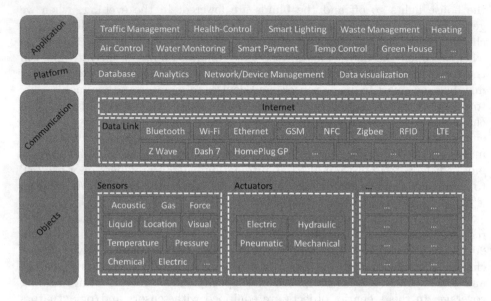

Fig. 1. The IoT archicture.

However, although many researches state that IoT technologies will affect several domains, there are some open issues like interoperability, security and privacy, that need to be addressed. In the following, after describing the most promising application domains for the IoT, we focus on these open issues and we provide some future directions that might help removing these burdens.

2   Fields of Applications

In recent years, academic and private researches proposed many different fields of applications for the IoT, from the well-know smart home to the less known smart agriculture. In all these fields of applications, the use of IoT aims to resolve in the rationalization of resources, and consequently monetary gain, while making the application field safer. Since it is useless to list all the IoT fields of application, in the following, we first describe two well-known IoT fields of applications and then we focus on three most promising ones.

Smart Home. Smart home is a firm and important field of application with a market expected to reach $121 billion by 2022 [14]. Comfort, security and energy efficiency are among the main benefits that a smart home can bring [15]. For instance, house owners might use their smartphone to control Wi-Fi enabled home electronics (e.g., appliances, heaters, hot water heaters, air conditioning, coffee machines, etc.) from anywhere, might increase home security (e.g., by using Wi-Fi connected cameras, sensors, and alarms) and might mange energy more efficiently (e.g., by using Wi-Fi outlets to turn off electronics when not in use). Gartner estimates that the number of devices and appliances currently connected in our houses is about 600 million[2] including lighting, security and access control, heating and air conditioning managing, entertainment systems and smart kitchen.

Smart City. Smart cities market is estimated to grow from $52 billion in 2015 to $147 billion by 2020 [16]. Smarter utilization and deployment of public resources (e.g., lights, roads, parkings), better efficiency of services (e.g., garbage collection, public transport), better quality life (e.g., pollution and traffic control) and, in general, a reduction of wastes and costs for the public administration are among the main benefits that a smart city can bring [4]. For instance, simple objects equipped with LoRaWAN and Sigfox communication technologies can transform the act of parking, allowing citizens to detect available parking spots in an easy way. This would not only save citizens time, but it would also help to reduce pollution, thus improving the lives of citizens. Another example of how IoT can improve the lives of citizens is transforming the waste collection into smart collection: smart trashcans[3] monitor their content by means of GPS traceable wireless fill-level sensors and, when they need to be emptied, they send a real-time alert to the municipal services through LoRa, Sigfox and cellular networks. All reports are accessible by a Web secure platform that suggests the best (also from an economical point of view) collection route. Thus, waste collection can be rationalized avoiding too empty bins and preventing overflows in others.

Health-Care. Medical and health-care are a very attractive application area for IoT [3] and the market is expected to create about $1.1–$2.5 trillion in value by 2025 [12]. Cost efficiency, reliability and safety are among the main benefits that smart health-care can bring: patients monitoring might be done in remote and in real-time through the use of smart objects and sensors, smart objects might be used to replace human regular checks of patients vital signs, home health might be improved by issuing alerts if some irregularity is detected. For example, smart prescription bottles[4] have sensors that register actions on bottles (as opening, or reducing their content) and are rechargeable using a standard micro-USB port. Bottles use the cellular technology to (world wide) communicate with the servers of the service provider that check on the patient activity in real time. If the patient does not stick to his/her medical prescription and forgets to take his/her medications or takes an overdose, the patient is immediately alerted with land-line or cell phone calls, text messages, or caregivers. There also exist smart pills[5] that contain specifically designed ingestible sensors (approved by both the U.S. Food and Drug Administration and CE marked in the E.U.) that activate by

---

[2] http://www.gartner.com/newsroom/id/3008917.

[3] https://www.smartbin.com/.

[4] https://adheretech.com/.

[5] http://www.proteus.com/.

contact with people stomaches at the time of ingestion and communicate with a matching sensor placed in a patch worn by the patient. The patch automatically logs the number, type and time when medications are taken, together with body vital signs (e.g. heart rate, body position, etc.). All these data are then shared, via Bluetooth, with the patient mobile device through a specific app that stores the data on a cloud service accessible to the patient and his physician. It is thus possible to reduce costs and save time by letting smart objects do tasks that can be easily accomplished by machines, not to mention that the large set of collected data might be analyzed to gather new insights on patient health-care.

Retail Industry. The IoT retail market size is expected to reach \$54 billion by 2022 according to a report by Grand View Research, Inc. Better customer experience, more efficient and secure supply chain and the development of new channels and revenue streams are among the main benefits that smart retail industry can bring. For instance, sensors can be used to track customers? behaviors in order to better organize products placements; RFID can be used to track products in the supply chain [17] and to update in real time inventories information from off-the-shelves products; smart price tags can be used to change, in real-time, the product price based on demands, sales, etc.; smart codes can give customers more information about products, and sensors can be used to automate many functions that are manually performed [18].

Smart Factory. The smart factory market size is expected to reach \$75 billion by 2020. In a Smart Factory [19], the manufacturing solutions exploit flexible and adaptive production processes, where the actors are equipped with enough computing and communication capabilities to give them an ability to act independently, without direct human intervention. For example, BMW has developed a tracking system based on RFIDs to enhance motor production and client customization. An RFID tag is attached to each engine as an unique identifier at the beginning of the assembly line and read at turn-points in the line to decide which way the engine should go (*e.g.*, lift or work station). Moreover, the tag brings along information about the customization of that specific car body, so that it is fast to recover and check information such as car color, internal details and door number. This brings to higher levels of automation, but also to optimizations in reducing unnecessary labor and waste of resources. The benefits could also go beyond the actual production of the goods. For instance, in a food supply chain scenario, IoT can enhance the whole process, from farms to processing plants, from processing plants to stores and from stores to consumers [17].

Although at first sight the above examples may look like a successful realization of IoT technologies, to a closer look they are just single IoT applications and do not represent a complete IoT scenario. Indeed, examples also showed one of the main problems that limits a successful employment of IoT technologies: the lack of interoperability between objects of the same scenario. For instance, a smart city is likely to have several different sub-networks (e.g., one for the sensors of the waste management system, one for the parking facilities, one for pollution measurement, etc.), each one working independently very well and suitable to provide an IoT service, but unable to interact with each other. Therefore, it is difficult to create a smart city. Indeed, there might be cities using many IoT applications, but these can not be labeled as complete smart cities. The current IoT scenario reminds the networking scenario of the 70s, composed of many networks (e.g., milnet, nsf-net, cs-net, etc.) unable to communicate within each other. Another example is what is happening in the health-care scenario: we have many companies each building their successful IoT ecosystem, but these systems only communicate within themselves and do not interact among each other. Once again, this reminds the scenario of the 70s, when each computer company developed its own operating system that was unfortunately unable to interact with the others. The fragmented scenario of the 70s was virtually unified by the standardization of protocols and services provided by the Internet and the Web. As discussed in the following section, likely, it is necessary to follow a similar path to make the IoT a successful scenario.

3   Open Issues and Future Directions

The IoT might open a wide new world of opportunities to offer new services to users, in many different forms, but for an actual large-scale employment it is still necessary to address some important open issues, including the ones related to interoperability, security and privacy, and devising new business models.

3.1   Interoperability

IoT objects and devices are produced by different vendors, have different technical characteristics and specifications (*e.g.*, smartphones are very different from simple RFID tags), use different communication protocols (Zigbee, Bluetooth, Bluetooth Low Energy, Wi-Fi, GSM, 3G and LTE, just to name few), and are often integrated with other heterogeneous sources of information. This heterogeneity is a big issue: on the one side, producers that want to invest do not have clear indications on standards to adopt when developing IoT products and do not know for how long their products will last on the IoT market; on the other side, users who want to buy IoT products do not know for how long these will be compatible with the upcoming IoT scenario.

Open standards seem to be the right answer to these problems, as they can give clear guidelines to create a competitive environment for companies to deliver quality products. The IEEE Standards Association (IEEE-SA) already started a process to develop open standards for the IoT[6] and even some private companies (*e.g.*, AllSeen Alliance) are contributing (and asking for contribution) to create open source frameworks to design common standards so that different devices might communicate between themselves, regardless of their brand, category and technical equipment. Needless to say, once open standards are defined, producers should be enforced to apply these standards (*e.g.*, identifying appropriate SLA, Service Level Agreements, for each service) in order to make human users trust new services offered through the IoT.

---

[6] http://standards.ieee.org/innovate/iot/projects.html.

In addition, the traditional Internet architecture needs to be revised to match the IoT challenges, both at low and high level. One main reason is the tremendous number of objects willing to connect to the Internet: 2010 has seen the surpass of the number of objects connected to the Internet over the earth's human population [8] and we have to expect that the former number is going to increase terrifically in the near future. Thus, we also have to expect a great increase of the traffic on the Internet, incurring into possible delays and in an increase of bandwidth request. Therefore, to allow IoT scalability, IPv6 and new generation of communication protocols (e.g., 5G is to provide speed between 10–800 Gbps, compared to the current technology 4G with speed of 2–1000 Mbps) seem to be mandatory.

There are also issues of interoperability at the platform level, concerning the need of integrating raw data coming from IoT objects with static and historical data stored in databases or accessible through Web services. For instance, let us consider a smart city control center that offers various cutting-edge services such as smart parking and dashboard view [20]. To this end, it is necessary to integrate heterogeneous information coming, for instance, from On Board Units and/or smartphones and multi-sensor weather stations together with official data available on Web sites, predictions on weather and traffic, tube schedules, etc. Indeed, information integration has been recognized as a key (and costly) challenge faced by large organizations today [21]. It is also well understood that information integration is not a single problem but, rather, a collection of interrelated problems that are addressed under the umbrella of architectures and unified data models. These problems include extracting and cleaning data from the sources, transforming data from the sources into data conforming with the unified format, and answering queries over the unified format. A possible answer to these problems is the dataspace paradigm [22], an emerging approach in the information integration agenda. In a dataspace, data coexist while the actual integration efforts are faced when needed. This paradigm might represent a good answer to the problem of interoperability for IoT because of the high level of heterogeneity of the involved information sources and the need of a large scale deployment. To this end, open source platforms might be used to facilitate the development of IoT applications through plug-in services for push/pull data connection and integrated view creation and maintenance.

3.2   Security and Privacy

One of the main advantages of IoT is the possibility to gather large sets of data that, properly analyzed, give information that can be used to provide better services. However (and again), issues arise: being connected to the Internet (and often unattended), objects are possible target to a wide range of security attacks that can lead to data leakage and/or data manipulation. Some recent examples of security issues include: a smart doorbell receiving the video feed from someone else house, people taking unauthorized control of the security system of specific buildings (e.g., houses, banks, factories, etc.), attackers compromising on-line car systems and stopping/speeding up cars with malicious intent. If customer are expected to use IoT technology and products, they must be assured that no accidental and/or malicious behavior might loose, steal or manipulate their data.

In the IoT scenario, security solutions cannot be limited to the single object or device, but they must be end-to-end solutions, going from the application level to the object level and vice-versa. Again, the heterogeneity of IoT interacting objects further complicates matters as different objects require different security levels (*e.g.*, fitness wearables vs. health care applications). Given such an extremely heterogeneous and vulnerable scenario, it is fundamental to provide security solutions at least for the following problems: *authentication* (any object involved in a communication must be clearly and uniquely identified); *confidentiality* (data must be secure and available only to authorized entities); *integrity* (data must not be altered by anyone when traveling from one point to another, or while stored in some database); *fault-tolerance* (even in the presence of a fault, security services must be continuously provided).

In addition to security, privacy plays an important role. Consider for instance the case of a person wearing a smart wrist collecting data such as heart rate, blood pressure, etc. One can imagine that the customer expects these data to be used to improve his/her personal performances or for self-usage check ups, but surely not that these data might become available (without his/her allowance) to his/her health insurance and used to tune the insurance policy cost or even to deny the policy. In the Internet scenario, consumers are becoming more and more aware that data are now trading currencies for services (let's just think at Gmail or Facebook), and, since most of the collected data are personal and sensitive, users are increasingly interested in their privacy [23,24]; the lack of clarity about who has access to data may limit the growth of the IoT scenario. Possible solutions to these privacy issues are new policies reassuring customers that data do not concern individuals but aggregates, clarifying the use of data, for how long these data are stored, and who has access to them.

3.3 Business

The lack of clear, widely accepted and successful business models, of use cases and of return of investment examples are slowing down the adoption of the IoT [25].

Although there are some early players that successfully invested in IoT (e.g., companies in the fitness and/or smart home scenarios), most of the companies are still thinking whether to enter or not in the IoT, because the scenario has characteristics that limit the development of a solid business model. According to [26], there are three main reasons that limit the design of a generic and successful IoT business model: (i) diversity of objects, (ii) immaturity of innovation, and (iii) unstructured ecosystem. The diversity of objects and the immaturity of innovation cause the employment of several different proprietary platforms and end-to-end IoT solutions, whereas the unstructured ecosystem causes doubts to investors because the scenario is too chaotic, just like the Internet was in the mid-90s.

The solution to these problems is closely dependent on the solution of the problems highlighted above. In particular, it is fundamental to first address the problems related to interoperability and security, as this would make available IoT communication standards and IoT end-to-end security solutions. These solutions could be the building blocks on which to build solid business models for the IoT scenario.

4 Conclusions

The interest around the IoT scenario is enormous, billions of objects/devices are being connected to the Internet to create the biggest network we have never seen, opening the possibility to create a new world of services in extremely different fields of application that can be offered to users by using the information that these devices can gather. Examples of how these smart objects can change the way we live and/or we work are written everywhere, from technological blogs to mass-media newspapers. Since it's been many years since media began talking about the wonders of IoT technologies, in this paper we tried to figure out if the IoT scenario is science fiction or a real revolution. We observed a very fragmented scenario that might compromise the successful employment of IoT: proliferation of communication technologies, absence of end-to-end security solutions and of solid business models that are able to guarantee a profitable return of investments. We also observed, by looking at some IoT examples, the benefits of IoT technologies, and we are positive about the fact that IoT may improve citizens life quality. Finally, since we are deeply convinced that a real employment of IoT passes through the unification (either virtual or not) of the fragmented scenario, we proposed some guidelines that move the IoT towards this direction.

References

1. Mahmoud, R., Yousuf, T., Aloul, F., Zualkernan, I.: Internet of things (IoT) security: current status, challenges and prospective measures. In: 2015 10th International Conference for Internet Technology and Secured Transactions (ICITST), pp. 336–341, December 2015
2. Bellavista, P., Cardone, G., Corradi, A., Foschini, L.: Convergence of MANET and WSN in IoT urban scenarios. IEEE Sens. J. **13**(10), 3558–3567 (2013)
3. Islam, S.M.R., Kwak, D., Kabir, M.H., Hossain, M., Kwak, K.S.: The internet of things for health care: a comprehensive survey. IEEE Access **3**, 678–708 (2015)
4. Zanella, A., Bui, N., Castellani, A., Vangelista, L., Zorzi, M.: Internet of things for smart cities. IEEE Internet Things J. **1**(1), 22–32 (2014)
5. Roccetti, M., Ferretti, S., Palazzi, C., Salomoni, P., Furini, M.: Riding the web evolution: from egoism to altruism. In: 2008 5th IEEE Consumer Communications and Networking Conference, pp. 1123–1127, January 2008
6. Ferretti, S., Furini, M., Palazzi, C.E., Roccetti, M., Salomoni, P.: WWW recycling for a better world. Commun. ACM **53**(4), 139–143 (2010)

7. Montangero, M., Furini, M.: TRank: ranking Twitter users according to specific topics. In: 2015 12th Annual IEEE Consumer Communications and Networking Conference (CCNC), pp. 767–772, January 2015
8. Al-Fuqaha, A., Guizani, M., Mohammadi, M., Aledhari, M., Ayyash, M.: Internet of things: a survey on enabling technologies, protocols, and applications. IEEE Commun. Surv. Tutor. **17**(4), 2347–2376 (2015)
9. Atzori, L., Iera, A., Morabito, G.: The internet of things: a survey. Comput. Netw. **54**(15), 2787–2805 (2010)
10. Bononi, L., Donatiello, L., Furini, M.: Real-time traffic in ad-hoc sensor networks. In: Proceedings of IEEE International Conference on Communications (ICC), pp. 1–5 (2009)
11. Donatiello, L., Furini, M.: Ad hoc networks: a protocol for supporting QoS applications. In: Proceedings of the 17th International Parallel and Distributed Processing Symposium (IPDPS 2003), April 2003
12. Manyika, J., Chui, M., Bughin, J., Dobbs, R., Bisson, P., Marrs, A.: Disruptive technologies: advances that will transform life, business, and the global economy. Technical report (2013)
13. Davis, R.: The internet of things. European Parliamentary Research, May 2015
14. Smart home market by product, security and access control, HVAC, entertainment, home healthcare and smart kitchen, software and service and geography - global forecast to 2022. Technical report (2016). marketsandmarkets.com
15. Alam, M., Reaz, B., Ali, M.: A review of smart homes - past, present, and future. IEEE Trans. Syst. Man Cybern. **42**(6), 1190–1203 (2012)
16. Internet of things (IoT) in smart cities market by solutions platform application - global forecast to 2020. Technical report (2016). marketsandmarkets.com
17. Zhao, X., Fan, H., Zhu, H., Fu, Z., Fu, H.: The design of the Internet of things solution for food supply chain. In: International Conference on Education, Management, Information and Medicine (2015)
18. Furini, M., Pitzalis, C.: Smart cart: when food enters the IoT scenario. In: Mandler, B., et al. (eds.) IoT360 2015. LNICSSITE, vol. 169, pp. 284–289. Springer, Cham (2016). doi:10.1007/978-3-319-47063-4_29
19. Katalinic, B., Radziwon, A., Bilberg, A., Bogers, M., Madsen, E.S.: International symposium on intelligent manufacturing and automation, 2013 the smart factory: exploring adaptive and flexible manufacturing solutions. Procedia Eng. **69**, 1184–1190 (2014)
20. Carafoli, L., Mandreoli, F., Martoglia, R., Penzo, W.: A data management middleware for ITS services in smart cities. J. UCS **22**(2), 228–246 (2016)
21. Bernstein, P.A., Haas, L.M.: Information integration in the enterprise. Commun. ACM **51**(9), 72–79 (2008)
22. Franklin, M.J., Halevy, A.Y., Maier, D.: A first tutorial on dataspaces. PVLDB **1**(2), 1516–1517 (2008)
23. Furini, M., Tamanini, V.: Location privacy and public metadata in social media platforms: attitudes, behaviors and opinions. Multimedia Tools Appl. **74**(21), 9795–9825 (2015)
24. Furini, M.: Users behavior in location-aware services: digital natives vs digital immigrants. In: Advances in Human-Computer Interaction (2014)
25. Laya, A., Bratu, V.-L., Markendahl, J.: Who is investing in machine-to-machine communications? In: Proceedings of the ITS Conference (2013)
26. Westerlund, M., Leminen, S., Rajahonka, M.: Designing business models for the internet of things. Technol. Innov. Manag. Rev. **4**, 5–14 (2014)

Design and Evaluation of an ICT Platform for Cognitive Stimulation of Alzheimer's Disease Patients

Andrea Caroppo[1](✉), Alessandro Leone[1], Pietro Siciliano[1],
Daniele Sancarlo[2], Grazia D'Onofrio[2], Antonio Greco[2],
Gianfranco Borrelli[3], Paolo Casacci[3], and Massimo Pistoia[3]

[1] Institute for Microelectronics and Microsystems,
National Research Council of Italy,
Via Monteroni, c/o Campus Università del Salento, Palazzina A3, Lecce, Italy
{andrea.caroppo,alessandro.leone,
pietro.siciliano}@le.imm.cnr.it
[2] Geriatric Unit and Laboratory of Gerontology and Geriatrics,
Department of Medical Sciences, IRCCS "Casa Sollievo della Sofferenza",
San Giovanni Rotondo, Italy
{d.sancarlo,g.donofrio,a.greco}@operapadrepio.it
[3] eResult s.r.l., Foggia, Italy
{gianfranco.borrelli,paolo.casacci,
massimo.pistoia}@eresult.it

Abstract. Cognitive Stimulation aims to improve cognitive skills and quality of life for people with dementia by helping to reduce the functional disability resulting from damage to the brain. Recent studies suggest that this kind of treatment is effective, but it is not yet possible to demonstrate that leads to changes in behavior or in the patient's lifestyle. The present work investigates the impact and the effectiveness of an information and communications technology platform able to allow the cognitive stimulation practice within a domestic environment. The platform is made up of a set-top-box connected to a TV monitor, a Microsoft Kinect sensor and a (optional) smart garment for clinical signs detection. Preliminary results, achieved after the tests performed on patients with mild to moderate Alzheimer, demonstrates that the aforementioned platform is a very useful tool able to increase the neuropsychiatric and cognitive state of the patient.

Keywords: ICT platform · Smart sensors · Cognitive stimulation · Rehabilitation practice · Alzheimer's disease

1 Introduction

Worldwide, 46.8 million people have dementia, and every year there are over 9.9 million new diagnosed cases [1], with an increase of the economic impact and cost of the 35.4% from 2010. Alzheimer's disease (AD) is the most common form of dementia [2] and represents one of the major causes of disability, dependency, burden and stress

© ICST Institute for Computer Sciences, Social Informatics and Telecommunications Engineering 2017
O. Gaggi et al. (Eds.): GOODTECHS 2016, LNICST 195, pp. 106–115, 2017.
DOI: 10.1007/978-3-319-61949-1_12

of caregivers increasing institutionalization among older people worldwide [3]. Currently, there is no effective disease-modifying cure and treatment is directed mainly to manage the symptoms of dementia [4].

The limited efficacy of drug therapy and the plasticity of the human brain are the two most important reasons that explain the growing interest in non-pharmacological intervention for dementia patients. Among possible cognition-focused interventions for people with AD, the importance of Cognitive Stimulation (CS) is highlighted by several scientific works [5–7]. In addition, a recent study showed that an integrated treatment (it lasted about six months) that consists in subjecting patients to CS and to rivastigmine transdermal patch improves the emotional and cognitive behavioural aspects and, at the same time, reduces the mortality risk [8].

Recently there have been many advances in the healthcare area, mainly with the help of Information and Communication Technologies (ICT) solutions; in particular, the researchers focused their activities towards the design and implementation of enabling solutions which first must be effective from a cost point of view.

The development of a low-cost platform that integrates both CS modules and homecare services could be very effective in order to select a more appropriate medical therapy. Analyzing recent research studies, it is clear that the use of new technologies is widely accepted by the elderly, even if within the age group 65 or over the skill level in the use of ICT instruments is very low. In the field of healthcare, cognitive training and stimulation have been faced in the past years through a large number of ICT technologies [9–11]. For example, virtual reality offers training environments in which human cognitive and functional performance can be accurately assessed and rehabilitated [12, 13]. On the other hand, augmented reality provides safer and more intuitive interaction techniques allowing interaction with 3D objects in real world [14, 15]. In this scenario, social communication channels (natural speech, para-language, etc.) are not blocked, breaking down mental barriers applying such a technology to specific problems or disabilities. New solutions for cognitive assistance based on touch system have been implemented: in the field of CS; for example, commercial products like Nintendo's Brain Age and Big Brain Academy have been tuned as educational tools helping to slow the decline of AD [16, 17]. More recently, the large diffusion of interaction devices enabling body movements to control systems have been investigated, with specific focus on ICT technologies for natural interaction. Microsoft Kinect is the state-of-the-art [18] as 3D device for body movements acquisition and gesture recognition and the effects of this kind of technology for rehabilitation purposes is widely investigated [19, 20].

In this work, a novel ICT platform has been designed with the aim to support different kind of patients during the multi-domain stimulation practice without the presence of medical staff or caregiver. The rest of the paper is organized as follows. Section 2 introduces the ICT platform describing some specifics of the hardware devices used for the interaction with the system. Moreover, in the same section, some details about the software architecture and specifications relating the CS practice are reported. In Sect. 3 the effectiveness and impact of the ICT platform in AD patients is evaluated through numerical results obtained in the preliminary tests performed on actual patients. Finally, conclusive considerations are presented in Sect. 4.

2 Materials and Methods

The developed ICT platform provides a system for CS at home through the use of Natural User Interfaces (NUI), giving the opportunity to perform the practice without the presence of medical staff or caregiver. Analyzing the implemented solution from this point of view, it turns out to be completely different and innovative compared to existing systems [21]. This innovative aspect is amplified by the integration of a software module that permits to customize the therapeutic session (compound by sequences of exercises) according to the residual abilities and skills of the end-users. The platform integrates the following hardware components: (a) an embedded PC equipped with an Intel Core i5 processor, (b) a monitor TV with a dimension equal to 42 inches or greater, (c) a commercial and low-cost 3D sensor (Microsft Kinect©) able to track the human skeleton and to recognize the gestures through the SDK freely distributed by Microsoft, (d) a smart garment that integrates an accelerometer and different textile electrodes for the extraction of several clinical parameters, such as heart rate, breath rate and energy expenditure (Fig. 1).

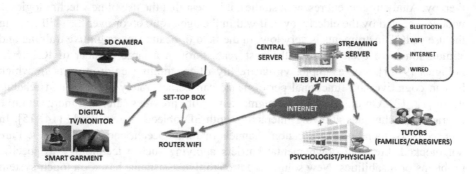

Fig. 1. ICT platform architecture overview

Moreover, a further innovative aspect developed in this ICT platform concerns the implementation of a software module for a real-time streaming of video data that are acquired during the execution of a therapeutic session. The module also records the video streaming, allowing the caregiver/physician the post-verification of correct CS practice from a remote location, such as the medical office. In this way, the psychologist or the physician has the opportunity to communicate with the observed patient during the exercise (highlighting for example errors in the execution of specific tasks) and to continuously monitor the progress or decline of their patients. Consequently, they have the ability to monitor multiple patients simultaneously. Whenever a CS session ends, a data synchronization is performed between a local database and a remote database (further details are given in Sect. 2.3) Finally, an ad-hoc multi-modal messaging procedure (SMS, Mobile App, e-mail, etc.) is performed. The data of the therapeutic session that are considered more important are sent to the physician/caregiver allowing an immediate check of the performance through an easy-to-use Graphical User Interface (GUI), available via Web on the Central Server.

2.1   Multi-sensor Devices as Enabling Technology

The core of the platform is represented by the sensor-based architecture that permits the natural interaction of the end-user with the system. Microsoft Kinect (Fig. 2a) is a motion sensing input device that allows users to interact intuitively and without any intermediary device with a Graphical User Interface (GUI) using body parts. From the working principle point of view, Kinect is a structured light scanner, meaning that it projects an infrared pattern that is then read by an infrared camera. After, the 3D information is reconstructed from the distortion of the pattern and this results in a depth channel which is made available through an Application Programmer's Interface (API) - Microsoft's 'Kinect for Windows SDK' [18]. The API was used to interface with its skeletal tracking software, providing an estimate for the position of 20 anatomical landmarks (2 of whom are used for hands tracking in the present platform) at a frequency of 30 Hz and spatial and depth resolution of 640 × 480 pixels.

Moreover, during the CS practice, a continuous monitoring of main clinical signs is obtained through a Wearable Wellness System (WWS) commercialized by Smartex [22]. The system integrates a sensorized garment equipped with textile electrodes and an electronic device (named SEW) dedicated to the acquisition, the processing and the storage of the data. The physiological parameters collected during the execution of the therapy (Heart Rate and Breath Rate) are analysed offline by the clinician in order to evaluate the level of psycho-emotive stress and the level of fatigue of the patients involved in CS practice (Fig. 2b).

Fig. 2. (a) Kinect 3d sensor device for human part detection and gesture recognition, (b) smart garment and electronic device (SEW) for the acquisition, processing and storing of physiological parameters

2.2   Cognitive Stimulation Practice Details

The CS program is composed by sequences of exercises appropriately tuned by the physician or psychologist. Each exercise belongs to a category, bringing out specific cognitive activities according to guidelines of the state-of-the-art international evaluation scales for AD (e.g., Mini Mental State Examination - MMSE [23]). An innovative feature of the platform deals with the opportunity to customize each exercise on the basis of the severity of cognitive impairment and residual skills of the target. For this purpose, during the setting procedure, few input parameters need to be defined a-priori (e.g., execution time, maximum numbers of allowed errors, movement sensitivity).

From the taxonomic point of view, the following categories of exercises have been implemented: temporal orientation, personnel guidance, topographical memory, visual memory, hearing attention, visual attention, categorization and verbal fluency. Figure 3 shows the GUI of some CS exercises.

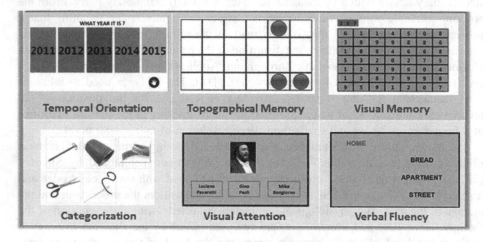

Fig. 3. Some example of exercise categories with related GUI

The design of the therapy can be remotely performed, thanks to a web application that allows physician to configure all the exercises based on the patient's residual abilities and related performance (see Sect. 2.3). In this way, the GUI related to a specific exercise could be different for each patient, for example the number of items displayed, the number of aids or the execution time may vary from the user's remaining abilities. In order to obtain an appropriate video rendering of every exercise, the ICT platform integrates an additional software module able to arrange the interfaces of each exercise independently from the display device (PC monitor, TV). The render of graphics objects integrated in the exercises has been designed according to the principles of usability, ergonomics and acceptability, as reported in ISO/IEC 2001a regulation [24] and through an extensive literature search, expert opinion and user experience.

2.3   Central and Home Server

The central platform is based on eResult's Omniacare, a multi-functional hardware and software system, specifically developed for the remote monitoring and assistance of frail users. The central platform's software architecture is modular: each element realizes some specific functions, as to be able to dynamically adapt to a variety of situations and environments. The system allows exploitation of more or less functionalities in a seamless way, by using specific elements, while the overall system keeps running.

Omniacare is based on a Central Server – Home Server concept. The Central Server is the main element of the system. User profiles, device configurations and all system data reside on the Central Server. It also provides the web interface that operators and therapists use to interact with the system, in order to customize exercises and therapy for patients. Configurations can be done on the Central Server by physicians only, to avoid unauthorized modifications by the users or caregivers. The Home Server and other devices periodically synchronize data and download configurations from and to the Central Server. It is endowed with the following robust inner characteristics: Hierarchical data structure; Web-based user interface; Advanced data navigation, display and search; Extensive data export functionalities; Granular user privilege management; Structured system event management; Information traceability. An example of the Graphical User Interface available on the Central Server is shown in the figure below (Fig. 4).

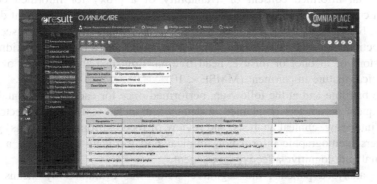

Fig. 4. Central server interface

The Home Server (HS) launches and controls the exercises, but also acts as a gateway that interfaces with detection sensors and external devices managing all of the diverse communication protocols. The HS collects data from the devices and provides configuration data exchange to proper manage them. The HS also consolidates and conditions data and sends them to the Central Server, according to the established rules and timing, while at the same time providing warning or alerts in case of a detected anomaly. The Home Server interface is shown below (Fig. 5).

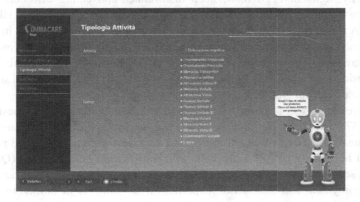

Fig. 5. Home server interface

3   Experimental Results

3.1   Impact of the CS Practice in AD Patients

The practical assessment of CS practice was performed in the period September 2013–February 2014; the study was conducted following the guidelines for Good Clinical Practice and the Declaration of Helsinki (DoH) that is the World Medical Association (WMA) best-known policy statement. The inclusion criteria adopted for the selection of patients were: (1) diagnosis of Dementia according to the National Institute on Aging-Alzheimer's Association (NIAAA) criteria [25]; (2) age ≥ 65 years; (3) ability to provide an informed consent or availability of a proxy for informed consent. Exclusion criteria were: presence of great comorbidity, tumours and different diseases that might be causally associated with psychological feature impairment (ascertained blood infections, vitamin b12 deficiency, anaemia, disorders of the thyroid, kidneys, or liver), history of alcohol or misuse, head trauma, drug use and presence of severe psychological feature impairment (MMSE < 10).

At the baseline and at the follow-up, performed once for each experimental stage, the subsequent parameters (explained in details within the text) were collected by a scientific interview, clinical analysis, and review of records from the patients' general practitioners: demographic information, clinical and medicine history and an entire dimensional and cognitive-affective assessment.

In the analysed patients, the cognitive status was evaluated by means of the Mini-Mental State Examination (MMSE), Babcock Story Recall Test (BSRT) [26], Verbal Fluency (VF) [27], Attentional Matrices (AM) [28] and Copying of Geometric Figures (CGF) [29].

Dementia was diagnosed by the Diagnostic and Statistical Manual of Mental Disorders – 5 Edition (DMS 5) criteria [30]. Diagnoses of possible/probable AD were made according to the NIAAA criteria and supported by neuroimaging evidence (CT scan and/or NMR).

Neuropsychiatric symptoms was evaluated with the Neuropsychiatric Inventory (NPI) [31] together with the subsequent twelve domains: hallucinations, delusions, depression mood, apathy, anxiety, euphoria, disinhibition, irritability/lability, aberrant motor activity, agitation/aggression, sleep disturbance and eating disorder. Emotive standing was evaluated using the Hamilton Rating Scale for Depression (HDRS-21) [32]. A CGA was carried out using assessment instruments widely employed in geriatric practice. Functional status was evaluated by activities of daily living (ADL) index [33], and by instrumental activities of daily living (IADL) scale [34]. Comorbidity was examined using the Cumulative Illness Rating Scale (CIRS) [35]. Nutritional status was explored with the Mini Nutritional Assessment (MNA) [36].

Cognitive status was screened by the Short Portable Mental Status Questionnaire (SPMSQ) [37]. The Exton-Smith Scale (ESS) was used to assess the risk of developing pressure sores [38]. The instrument to be used to assess the quality of life and satisfaction will be Quality of Life Enjoyment and Satisfaction questionnaire (Q-LES-Q) [39]. It's a self-report measure designed to simply acquire sensitive measures of the degree of enjoyment and satisfaction experienced by subjects in numerous areas of daily functioning.

Medication use was outlined in line with the Anatomical medicine Chemical Classification code system, and also the number of medicine utilized by patients was recorded. Social aspects such as family composition, home service, and institutionalization were also considered.

3.2 Pilot Results

The pilot study has included six patients enrolled in 3 completely different sites. Every patients have an initial program of six exercises for session with parameters established on the premise of the primary rehabilitation check. Analyzing the user responses, the amount of exercises (and related parameters) were raised or reduced respectively. All the patients enrolled showed the same good acceptability to the use of the ICT platform as measured through the employment of subjective feed-back. All patients have terminated the study and no drop-out were registered. The sensorized shirt was used to better set-up the system during the primary rehabilitation check meanwhile in the domestic environment the use of this instrument was not possible. After experimental period, the end users showed an improvement of 1.3% on the Rey-15, of 1.2% on the BSRT, of 10.4% on the MMSE score, of 2.5% on the VF, of 12.64% on the AM and 1.3% on the CGF. In addition, the end users showed an improvement of 13.2% on the NPI score, of 11.78% on the NPI-D (subscale of NPI that assesses the distress of the caregiver) score and 24.5% on the HDRS-21 score. The most marked improvement was achieved at Q-LES-Q score (47.89%), whereas the results obtained in correspondence of the CGA domains showed no differences. From the statistical point of view the results obtained may not be very reliable and this is more evident in correspondence of specific indexes used for cognitive evaluation of patients; however, it is important to note that the trends are promising and encourage to experience CS treatment through the proposed ICT platform on a greater number of patients.

4 Conclusion

The main purpose of the present work is to describe and to evaluate an ICT platform designed for autonomous CS practice within a domestic environment. The pilot results, even if referred to a limited number of patients, have shown that the use of the described platform improves the cognitive, affective, neuropsychiatric state, and the quality of life and the satisfaction of the patients.

The most important advantage emphasized by the end-users is related to the possibility of performing the CS treatment remaining in their own homes, and consequently keeping their safety and independence. Moreover, thanks to the platform architecture, the patients can avoid to move to a health care facility center that often can cause a lot of anxiety. Last but not least, the platform integrates monitoring and assistance modules from remote locations, facilitating the work of caregivers/ physicians.

Acknowledgments. This work was carried out within the project "ACTIVE AGEING AT HOME" funded by the Italian Ministry of Education, Universities and Research, within the National Operational Programme for "Research and Competitiveness" 2007–2013.

References

1. World Health Organization: Dementia: a public health priority (2012). http://apps.who.int/iris/bitstream/10665/75263/1/9789241564458_eng.pdf?ua=1. Accessed July 2016
2. Cummings, J.L.: Alzheimer's disease. N. Engl. J. Med. **351**, 56–67 (2004)
3. Schultz, R., Williamson, G.H.: A 2-year longitudinal study of depression among Alzheimer's caregivers. Psychol. Aging **6**, 569–578 (1991)
4. Atri, A.: Effective pharmacological management of Alzheimer's disease. Am. J. Manag. Care **17**, S346–S355 (2011)
5. Clare, L., Woods, R.T.: Cognitive rehabilitation in dementia. In: Neuropsychologistical Rehabilitation, pp. 193–196. Psychology Press Ltd. (2001)
6. Neal, M., Briggs, M.: Validation therapy for dementia, no. 2. The Cochrane Library, Chichester (2004). (Cochrane Review)
7. Clare, L., Woods, R.T., Moniz Cook, E.D., Orrel, M., Spector, A.: Cognitive rehabilitation in Alzheimer's disease. Aging Clin. Exp. Res. **18**, 141–143 (2006)
8. D'Onofrio, G., et al.: A pilot randomized controlled trial evaluating an integrated treatment of rivastigmine transdermal patch and cognitive stimulation in patients with Alzheimer's disease. Int. J. Geriatr. Psychiatry **30**(9), 965–975 (2015)
9. Richard, E., Billaudeau, V., Richard, P., Gaudin, G.: Augmented reality for rehabilitation of cognitive disable children: a preliminary study. In: Virtual Rehabilitation, pp. 102–108 (2007)
10. Standen, P., Brown, D.: Virtual reality and its role in removing the barriers that turn cognitive impairments into intellectual disability. Virtual Reality **10**(3), 241–252 (2006)
11. Taylor, M.J.D., McCormick, D., Impson, R., Shawis, T., Griffin, M.: Activity-promoting gaming systems in exercise and rehabilitation. J. Rehabil. Res. **248**(10), 1171–1186 (2011)
12. Wang, M., Reid, D.: Using the virtual reality-cognitive rehabilitation approach to improve contextual processing in children with autism. Sci. World J. **2013**, 716890 (2013). doi:10.1155/2013/716890
13. Larson, E.B., Feigon, M., Gagliardo, P., Dvorkin, A.Y.: Virtual reality and cognitive rehabilitation: a review of current outcome research. NeuroRehabilitation **34**(4), 759–772 (2014)
14. Azuma, R., Baillot, Y., Behringer, R., Feiner, S., Julier, S., MacIntyre, B.: Recent advances in augmented reality. IEEE Comput. Graph. Appl. **21**(6), 34–47 (2001)
15. Azuma, R.: A survey of augmented reality. Presence: Teleoper. Virtual Environ. **6**(4), 355–385 (1997)
16. Nacke, L.E., Nacke, A., Lindley, C.A.: Brain training for silver aged gamers: effects of age and game form on effectiveness, self-assessment, and gameplay. Cyberpsychol. Behav. **12**(5), 493–499 (2009)
17. Imbeault, F., Bouchard, B., Bouzouane, A.: Serious games in cognitive training for Alzheimer's patients. In: IEEE International Conference on Serious Games and Applications for Health, pp. 122–129 (2011)
18. https://developer.microsoft.com/en-us/windows/kinect. Accessed July 2016

19. Da Gama, A., Chaves, T., Figueiredo, L., Teichrieb, V.: Improving motor rehabilitation process through a natural interaction based system using kinect sensor. In: Proceedings of IEEE Symposium on 3D User Interfaces, pp. 145–146 (2012)
20. Lange, B., Chang, C.Y., Suma, E., Newman, B., Rizzo, A.S., Bolas, M.: Development and evaluation of low cost game based balance rehabilitation tool using the Microsoft Kinect sensor. In: 33rd IEEE International Conference on Engineering in Medicine and Biology Society (2011)
21. Solana, J., et al.: PREVIRNEC, a new platform for cognitive tele-rehabilitation. In: Third International Conference on Advanced Cognitive Technologies and Applications (2011)
22. http://www.smartex.it/index.php/en/products/wearable-wellness-system.   Accessed   June 2016
23. Folstein, M.F., Folstein, S.E., McHugh, P.R.: Mini-mental state: a practical method for grading the cognitive state of patients for the clinician. J. Psychiatr. Res. **12**(3), 189–198 (1975)
24. ISO/IEC: International Standard ISO/IEC 9126-1. Software Engineering - Product Quality - Part 1: Quality Model. International Organization for Standardization/International Electrotechnical Commision, Geneva (2001)
25. McKhann, G.M., et al.: The diagnosis of dementia due to Alzheimer's disease: recommendations from the national institute on aging-Alzheimer's association workgroups on diagnostic guidelines for Alzheimer's disease. Alzh. Dement. **7**, 263–269 (2011)
26. Babcock, H., Levy, L.: Test and manual of directions; the revised examination for the measurement of efficiency of mental functioning. In: Stoelting Test and manual of directions; the revised examination for the measurement of efficiency of mental functioning, Wood Dalc, IL, US, 41 p. (1940)
27. Spinnler, H., Tognoni, G.: Standardizzazione e taratura italiana di test neuropsicologici. Ital. J. Neurol. Sci. **8**(Suppl), 1–120 (1987)
28. Rey, A.: L'examen clinique en psychologie. Presses Universitaires de France, Paris (1964)
29. Lezak, H.M., Howieson, D., Bigler, E., Tranel, D.: Neuropsychological Assessment. Oxford University Press, New York (2012)
30. Arrigoni, G., De Renzi, E.: Constructional apraxia and hemispheric locus of lesion. Cortex **1**(2), 170–197 (1964)
31. Cummings, J.L., et al.: The neuropsychiatric inventory: comprehensive assessment of psychopathology in dementia. Neurology **44**, 2308–2314 (1994)
32. Hamilton, M.: A rating scale for depression. J. Neurol. Neurosurg. Psychiatry **23**, 56–62 (1960)
33. Katz, S., et al.: Progress in the development of an index of ADL. Gerontologist **10**, 20–30 (1970)
34. Lawton, M.P., Brody, E.M.: Assessment of older people: self-maintaining and instrumental activities of daily living. Gerontologist **9**, 179–186 (1969)
35. Parmelee, P.A., Thuras, P.D., Katz, I.R., Lawton, M.P.: Validation of the cumulative illness rating scale in a geriatric residential population. J. Am. Geriatr. Soc. **43**, 130–137 (1995)
36. Vellas, B., et al.: The Mini Nutritional Assessment (MNA) and its use in grading the nutritional state of elderly patients. Nutrition **15**, 116–122 (1999)
37. Pfeiffer, E.: A short portable mental status questionnaire for the assessment of organic brain deficit in elderly patients. J. Am. Geriatr. Soc. **23**, 433–441 (1975)
38. Bliss, M.R., McLaren, R., Exton-Smith, A.N.: Mattresses for preventing pressure sores in geriatric patients. Mon. Bull. Minist. Health Public Health Lab. Serv. **25**, 238–268 (1966)
39. Endicott, J., Nee, J., Harrison, W., Blumenthal, R.: Quality of life enjoyment and satisfaction questionnaire. Psychopharmacol. Bull. **29**(2), 321–326 (1993)

Android-Based Liveness Detection for Access Control in Smart Homes

Susanna Spinsante(✉), Laura Montanini, Veronica Bartolucci, Manola Ricciuti, and Ennio Gambi

Dipartimento di Ingegneria dell'Informazione,
Universita' Politecnica delle Marche, 60131 Ancona, Italy
s.spinsante@univpm.it
http://www.tlc.dii.univpm.it

Abstract. In the domain of smart homes, technologies for personal safety and security play a prominent role. This paper presents a low-complexity Android application designed for mobile and embedded devices, that exploits the on-board camera to easily capture two images of the subject, and processes them to discriminate a true 3D and live face from a 2D one. The liveness detection based on such a discrimination provides anti-spoofing capabilities to secure access control based on face recognition. The results obtained are satisfactory even in different ambient light conditions, and further improvements are being developed to deal with low precision image acquisition.

Keywords: Liveness detection · Spoofing · Face recognition · Android · Stereo vision

1 Introduction

The Smart Home (SH) domain encompasses a huge variety of technologies, applications, and services, aimed at providing intelligence to an environment in which people spend most of their lifetime. Intelligent capabilities in SH aim at improving the quality of life of the resident people, by facilitating routine operations, and anticipating the users' needs, by learning and understanding their behaviours. Pervasive sensing plays a fundamental role in SH, as well as wireless technologies enabling the connection among heterogeneous devices, and creating the conditions for new integrated functionalities [1]. Among them, personal safety and security play a critical role [2], and many different devices and applications have been developed to address these needs. At the same time, however, regardless of how safe individual devices are or claim to be, new vulnerabilities may arise when different hardware devices are networked and set up to be controlled remotely.

Personal safety involves several aspects of the home security. Among them, the most important concerns the detection of alarming events, such as flooding,

© ICST Institute for Computer Sciences, Social Informatics and Telecommunications Engineering 2017
O. Gaggi et al. (Eds.): GOODTECHS 2016, LNICST 195, pp. 116–124, 2017.
DOI: 10.1007/978-3-319-61949-1_13

gas and smoke leaks. Systems able to detect these events allow the user to be warned in time, promptly intervene and avoid potentially dangerous situations. Access control is another key point when dealing with security. Intrusion detection systems are becoming gradually more common. They exploit different technologies in order to detect the presence of unauthorized people at home. Most common technologies include magnetic sensors on doors and windows, motion sensors and cameras. Anyway, in this field, to distinguish between authorized and unauthorized subjects represents a primary objective.

Face recognition [3], one of the most successful image analysis and understanding applications, is a long-established research area that recently became extremely popular in consumer applications, thanks to advances in electronics and sensor technologies, that make high quality image sensors available in commercial devices, at a reasonable cost. Although extremely reliable methods for biometric personal identification exist, based on iris [4] or retinal scans [5], or fingerprint analysis [6], they still have to gain widespread acceptance by the general consumers.

In this paper, we address the design of a low-complexity Android-based application for liveness detection, based on image processing techniques, to be implemented in embedded Android platforms for video entry-phones. The aim of the project is to counteract face spoofing, one of the prominent threats to face recognition systems. The developed application focuses on the idea of discriminating a 2D face image, as a picture, from a real 3D face belonging to a live subject. The stereo vision technique is exploited, followed by the creation of a so-called *disparity map* in which, through different colors, the different areas of the image captured by the camera are highlighted, based on their relative distance from the camera itself. This way, the proposed application will discriminate a picture from a live face, according to the chromatic properties of the disparity graph output by the algorithm. A software library, named *BoofCV* [7], is used to implement the algorithm in a portable Android application.

The paper is organized as follows: Sect. 2 shortly presents the basic concepts upon which the application design has been conceived. The design of the Android mobile application is presented in Sect. 4, whereas Sect. 5 presents the experimental results obtained testing the application in real conditions. Finally, Sect. 6 concludes the paper.

2 Basic Concepts

For the human brain, binding an identity to a face is an automated and immediate task, despite its complexity. However, it is virtually impossible to reduce this operation to a search for objective parameters, that instead are essential to form the basis of an efficient biometric system. From a biometric point of view, we must consider that many factors can make it difficult to recognize a face, such as the different lighting conditions, the different facial expressions that a subject can take on, or the rotation of the face, the subject's age, physical radical changes, as well as the presence of obstructions, such as glasses, facial hair, or hair, covering part of the face. Despite these issues, algorithms that allow to obtain satisfactory results of personal identification have been proposed in the literature [8–10]. Nevertheless, some critical aspects have emerged recently, such as the resistance to external attack and, particularly, to spoofing. Anti-spoofing techniques applied to face recognition shall be unobtrusive, user-friendly, fast, low cost and well performing, e.g. able to avoid both false negative and false positive identifications.

Anti-spoofing, liveness detection and vitality detection are equivalent terms used in the literature to describe the same concept, that is: any technique aimed at verifying if the captured biometric information belongs to a live subject, or to an artificial and synthetic copy of him/her. As stated by Galbally et al. in [11], these techniques may be classified into three groups:

- sensor-level techniques: exploiting specific sensors in order to identify particular living traits (blood pressure, facial thermogram, etc.);
- feature-level techniques: in which the biometric data are acquired via a standard sensor and the distinction between fake and real faces is software-based;
- score-level techniques: much less common than the others, and focused on the study of biometric systems at a score-level.

The choice among one of the three groups should always balance advantages and disadvantages. Typically, hardware-based techniques have the best performance since they extract information directly from the human body. Nevertheless, they are quite intrusive and expensive. Conversely, the score-level techniques have limited performance, while maintaining low costs and intrusiveness. Among them, a compromise solution is represented by the feature-level group: it combines sufficient performance with low cost and less intrusiveness.

In the proposed application, the liveness detection problem is approximated as a problem of discriminating 2D from 3D objects, i.e. a picture of a face from a real face, exploiting a standard RGB camera. This is obtained basically by resorting to the stereo vision concept, according to which by comparing the images of the same subject captured from two different perspectives, the 3D information may be extracted, analysing the relative positions of the same elements in the two captured images. Since the application exploits a standard sensor and all the features are extracted by image processing, the technique used can be classified as a feature-level technique.

The robustness of the liveness detection process is then increased through a number of intermediate verification steps:

- check if the subject's nose is the element of the face at the shortest distance from the camera;
- check if different areas captured by the sensor (like nose and eyes, or face and background) are located at different distances from it;
- check if expected areas, like the face, the nose or the eyes, can be located in both the captured images;
- check if some kind of involuntary eye movements is detected.

3   Stereo Vision

The term stereo computer vision refers to the extraction of 3D information from digital images. By comparing the information captured from two different points of view, the 3D information can be extracted by examining the relative positions of objects in the two shots. Traditionally, in stereo vision, two different views of a scene are captured by horizontally disposed cameras: this mode is inspired by the binocular human visual system.

The problem of converting 2D information in 3D can be reduced substantially in two sub-problems: correspondence and reconstruction. The correspondence problem consists in identifying matched points in the images such that there are no ambiguities. In fact, ambiguous correspondences lead to different interpretations of the scene.

Figure 1 shows two simplified models of reality in order to better understand the concepts behind the stereo vision problem. In Fig. 1(a), two points P and Q on the same line of sight of the left image plane have been considered. Thanks to epipolar geometry the correspondence issue can be easily addressed. In fact, the epipolar constraint states that the projection of points P and Q in the right image plane must belong to the same line (dotted line) of their projection in the left side. The search in the space of corresponding points can then be narrowed from a 2D to a 1D search.

As regards the reconstruction, once the matching points have been identified, it is necessary to calculate their disparity. Referring to Fig. 1(b), the disparity can be defined as follows:

$$d = x_r - x_l. \tag{1}$$

It represents the difference between the x coordinate of the two corresponding points and allows to calculate the depth. In fact, through some simple steps, it is possible to obtain the relationship between the disparity d and the depth Z:

$$\frac{x_l}{f} = \frac{X}{Z} \ , \ \frac{x_r}{f} = \frac{X+b}{Z}$$

$$d = x_r - x_l = \frac{f(X+b)}{Z} - \frac{fX}{Z}, \tag{2}$$

whence:

$$d = \frac{fb}{Z}. \tag{3}$$

Therefore, the disparity of a point is proportional to focal length f and baseline b, and inversely proportional to its depth. Since f and b are constant over the whole image, a disparity map provides a direct encoding of the scene depth.

4   Design of the Android Mobile Application

A first version of the software application for liveness detection has been designed in Java language, for a desktop execution, exploiting the availability of the

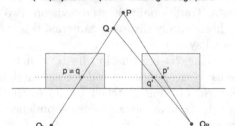

Legend:

O_L optical center for left camera
O_R optical center for right camera
p   projection of point P in the left image plane
q   projection of point Q in the left image plane
p'   projection of point P in the right image plane
q'   projection of point P in the right image plane

(a) Epipolar constraint for correspondence: matches for p and q in the right plane must lie on the epipolar line (dotted line)

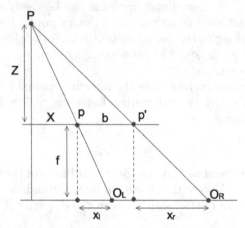

(b) A simplified model of reality in the top-view perspective

Fig. 1. Graphic representations of the stereo vision concepts

BoofCV libraries for stereo vision. Later, in order to get a portable code for Android devices, the *OpenBeans* library has been used. Using the camera sensor embedded in almost all the current mobile devices (smartphones), the application needs a couple of images gathered from two different perspectives (left and right), and processes them according to Sect. 2, to output a point-cloud of the detected subject. It denotes if a live (3D), or a fake (2D) picture, has been processed. The stereo vision implies a number of pre-requisites the captured images need to satisfy, such as: any image distortion due to the capturing sensor shall be compensated, in order to get pinhole camera - like images; each

image in the couple shall be rectified, to be comparable. To this aim, two fundamental operations must be performed before starting the stereo matching and
reconstruction processes: camera calibration and image rectification.

Calibration is a process for estimating the camera's intrinsic and extrinsic
parameters. The first concern the internal characteristics of the camera, such
as focal length or parameters of lenses distortion, while the extrinsic parameters describe the spatial position and orientation of the camera, i.e. the relative
translations and rotations between the two images. The knowledge of the intrinsic parameters is an essential first step for the 3D reconstruction, because it
enables the derivation of the scene structure in the space and removes the distortion of the lens, which leads to optical errors, degrading the accuracy. The
BoofCV library provides a calibration feature. To calculate the parameters it
is possible to use planar chessboards. Figure 2 shows a sample subset of the
chessboard grids used to calibrate the device camera in our experiments.

Fig. 2. Sample subset of calibration chessboards

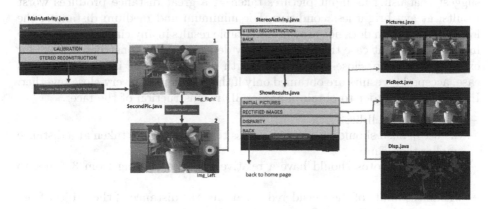

Fig. 3. Global flow diagram of the application steps

The image rectification is required when the considered image planes are not
coplanar: thanks to this operation the images become coplanar, and the following
procedures (matching and reconstruction) will be faster and more efficient, since
they will run on a single dimension, as mentioned in Sect. 3.

In summary, three main steps are executed by the application: the camera
calibration step; the rectification of the two images; the stereo matching between
features belonging to the captured images, and, finally, the output point-cloud
generation.

A global sketch of the different steps executed by the Android application is given in Fig. 3. The final image generated by the app features a single dominating color, which denotes a condition in which the input pictures are not associated to a live subject's face.

5 Experimental Results

In order to verify the proper functioning of the adopted method, several preliminary tests have been performed using a desktop PC. The objective of such tests is to identify the optimal resolution value which allows to correctly reconstruct the image. In fact, as the resolution increases, computational problems (processing time) increase or calibration inaccuracies appear. Test results show that the best resolution value is 0.3 megapixels. By using this value, the results are obtained in a very short time (about one second) and a correct calibration process is ensured. As already stated, this is a fundamental operation to properly carry out the stereo reconstruction.

Additional factors influencing the results are:

- the subject distance from the camera;
- the relative distance between the two pictures;
- the brightness.

For each of them, three different conditions have been considered, as shown in Table 1, and every possible combination of them has been considered. Results suggest that using as input pictures taken at a great distance produces worst results, at any brightness condition. For minimum and medium distances, the low-light condition does not provide acceptable results in any circumstance, while in the normal light case the face is entirely detected and reconstructed, both for extremely close-up, close-up and half-length photos. For the intense brightness case, acceptable results are obtained only if the two shots are very close together. In summary, in order to obtain a proper 3D reconstruction of the face:

- it should be well lit;
- the use of flash should be avoided, unless the two shots are taken at a distance smaller than 5 mm;
- the pair of photos should have a relative distance varying from 3–5 mm to 15 mm;
- within the limits of the considered situations, the distance of the subject from the camera is indifferent for a correct result.

After preliminary tests, the Android application has been tested on different devices (Samsung Galaxy S3, S5 and S6, LG G4, Huawei P8 Lite), equipped with diverse Android OS versions. The app execution runs smooth, if the device has at least 1 GB RAM available, but in any case it is necessary to downscale the camera resolution by a factor of at least 8, to enable a real-time processing of the captured images.

Also in this case, despite the not full precision of the acquisition process, the mobile application is able to discriminate faces shown in pictures (spoof) from live ones. Figure 4 summarizes some of the results obtained from lab experiments.

Table 1. Summary of the situations envisaged in the test phase, for each analysed factor.

Factor	Possible conditions	Description
Distance between subject and camera	Extreme close-up photos	The pictures contain just part of the face and neck
	Close-up photos	The pictures contain not only face and neck, but also the shoulders
	Half-length photos	The picture is cut at chest level
Distance between the two pictures	Minimum distance	The photos are almost coincident and the distance between the two shots is about 3–5 mm
	Medium distance	There is a slight shift between the two pictures (~15 mm)
	Great distance	The two pictures are far apart more than 30 mm
Brightness	Minimum brightness	The subject is illuminated by a low light (for example an abatjour)
	Medium brightness	The subject is illuminated by a common warm light bulb
	Intense brightness	The subject is illuminated by a common, warm light bulb and in addiction by a flash

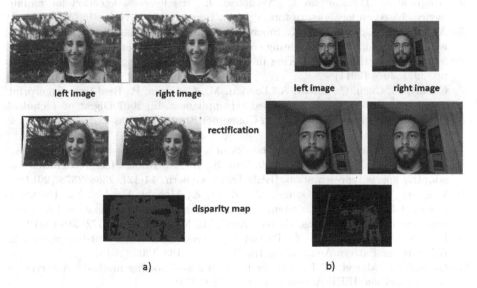

Fig. 4. Output of the liveness detection mobile app in the case of: (a) spoofed face images, (b) live and complex face image. The output disparity map in (b) clearly features the face profile distinguishable from the background.

6   Conclusion

The Android application for mobile and embedded devices presented in this paper demonstrates the feasibility of a real-time liveness detection process, which implements anti-spoofing by detecting the 2D or 3D nature of the captured face images. The application requires initial calibration of the device camera, and suffers from limitations due to possible imperfections in the image capturing process, however, it shows very promising results. Further developments are currently ongoing to increase the robustness of the application and test it on a larger variety of real-life conditions.

References

1. Spinsante, S., Cippitelli, E., Santis, A., Gambi, E., Gasparrini, S., Montanini, L., Raffaeli, L.: Multimodal interaction in a elderly-friendly smart home: a case study. In: Agüero, R., Zinner, T., Goleva, R., Timm-Giel, A., Tran-Gia, P. (eds.) MONAMI 2014. LNICSSITE, vol. 141, pp. 373–386. Springer, Cham (2015). doi:10.1007/978-3-319-16292-8_27
2. Ur, B., Jung, J., Schechter, S.: The current state of access control for smart devices in homes. In: Proceedings of Workshop on Home Usable Privacy and Security (HUPS) 24–26 July 2013, Newcastle, UK, pp. 1–6 (2013)
3. Zhao, W.Y., Chellappa, R.: Image-Based Face Recognition: Issues and Methods. Image Recognition and Classification, pp. 375–402 (2002). (Edited by B. Javidi, M. Dekker)
4. Gragnaniello, D., Sansone, C., Verdoliva, L.: Iris liveness detection for mobile devices based on local descriptors. Pattern Recogn. Lett. **57**(1), 81–87 (2015)
5. Azemin, M.Z.C., Kumar, D.K., Sugavaneswaran, L., Krishnan, S.: Supervised retinal biometrics in different lighting conditions. In: 2011 Annual International Conference of the IEEE Engineering in Medicine and Biology Society, Boston, MA, pp. 3971–3974 (2011)
6. Callaly, F., Cucu, C., Cucos, A., Leyden, M., Corcoran, P.: Real-time fingerprint analysis & authentication for embedded appliances. In: 2007 Digest of Technical Papers International Conference on Consumer Electronics, Las Vegas, NV, pp. 1–2 (2007)
7. BoofCV Software Library. http://boofcv.org/index.php?title=Download
8. Wang, J., Lu, C., Wang, M., Li, P., Yan, S., Hu, X.: Robust face recognition via adaptive sparse representation. IEEE Trans. Cybern. **44**(12), 2368–2378 (2014)
9. Wagner, A., Wright, J., Ganesh, A., Zhou, Z., Mobahi, H., Ma, Y.: Toward a practical face recognition system: robust alignment and illumination by sparse representation. IEEE Trans. Pattern Anal. Mach. Intell. **34**(2), 372–386 (2012)
10. Liao, S., Jain, A.K., Li, S.Z.: Partial face recognition: alignment-free approach. IEEE Trans. Pattern Anal. Mach. Intell. **35**(5), 1193–1205 (2013)
11. Galbally, J., Marcel, S., Fierrez, J.: Biometric antispoofing methods: a survey in face recognition. IEEE Access **2**, 1530–1552 (2014)

Smartphones as Multipurpose Intelligent Objects for AAL: Two Case Studies

Susanna Spinsante[1]([✉]), Laura Montanini[1], Ennio Gambi[1],
Lambros Lambrinos[2], Fábio Pereira[3], Nuno Pombo[3,4], and Nuno Garcia[3,4]

[1] Dipartimento di Ingegneria dell'Informazione,
Universita' Politecnica delle Marche, 60131 Ancona, Italy
s.spinsante@univpm.it
[2] Cyprus University of Technology, Limassol, Cyprus
[3] Department of Informatics, Universidade da Beira Interior,
6200-001 Covilhã, Portugal
[4] Instituto de Telecomunicações (Telecommunications Institute),
Universidade da Beira Interior, 6200-001 Covilhã, Portugal
http://www.tlc.dii.univpm.it

Abstract. The increasing adoption of smartphones among older adults, especially in most developed countries, suggests they can be used not only for personal communications, but also in the framework of Active and Assisted Living solutions. This paper addresses two case studies in which a smartphone, when equipped with a proper software application, may operate as an inactivity monitor, and a drug management assistant, respectively. Activity monitoring is carried out by targeting the user's interaction with the smartphone related to incoming, outgoing, and lost calls. In the latter case, an application processes images of drugs boxes captured by the smartphone camera, to automatically recognize the name of the drug, and inform the user about the corresponding prescription. Experimental results show this kind of approach is technically feasible and may provide satisfactory performance through a very easy interaction, thus supporting improved medication adherence by patients.

Keywords: Ambient assisted living · Mobile device · Activity monitoring · Drug management

1 Introduction

Several studies have shown the effectiveness and benefits of using mobile devices, such as tablets or smartphones, in Active and Assisted Living (AAL) applications, and in certain specific diseases treatment [1–3]. Mobile devices have the advantage of being intuitive, computationally powerful, personal, provided with high-resolution screens, rich of sensors (e.g. cameras, accelerometers and geo-positioning systems) and wireless interfaces (e.g. NFC, WiFi, Bluetooth, etc.), and portable, thanks to reduced size and weight. The personal nature of mobile

© ICST Institute for Computer Sciences, Social Informatics and Telecommunications Engineering 2017
O. Gaggi et al. (Eds.): GOODTECHS 2016, LNICST 195, pp. 125–134, 2017.
DOI: 10.1007/978-3-319-61949-1_14

phones suggests they are well suited for pervasive computing, but the data they are able to collect and process could be beneficially used in a wide range of context-aware applications, to automatically identify user's habits and provide structured knowledge [4].

Advances in smartphone applications technology, and their mass adoption, make these mobile devices an unprecedented vehicle to promote positive changes in users' habits, from reducing sedentary behaviors, to improving dietary choices and stimulating cognitive functionalities. The simple user-smartphone interaction that takes place when using the smartphone to communicate (i.e. to make calls or send messages) makes it possible to monitor different conditions, such as user's prolonged inactivity.

In [5], the feasibility of using smartphones for rheumatic diseases self-management interventions is widely discussed, while other studies, such as [6], show the benefits of using mobile devices, when dealing with people under treatment for addiction to drugs or alcohol. Self-monitoring of pain [7], and dietary intake to promote weight loss, are other possibilities of exploiting mobile devices in the healthcare arena. Just to mention an example, experimental results indicate that food records completed using digital tools are more acceptable to young women, than traditional paper-based methods, yet equally accurate [8]. Nevertheless, ICT-based solutions are sometimes inadequate for elderly or technologically inexperienced users. In fact, when designing a system for the self-management of health care or health status monitoring, a user-friendly interaction is essential, especially considering that the people who need it most, usually are affected by impairments or not familiar with technology [9]. In this paper, two examples of use of smartphones as intelligent multipurpose objects in AAL are presented.

The first case study relies in a software application that allows to use a smartphone as a personal assistant for inactivity detection, based on a multiple threshold analysis including incoming, outgoing, and lost calls. This way, the application may assess the behavior of a user (either a chronic disease patient or an old person) based on their interaction with the smartphone. The use of smartphones to monitor and stimulate physical activity has gained a great attention within the workplace context, as a tool to avoid prolonged sedentary behaviors by workers in modern workplaces [10], which may have dramatic impacts on their health conditions [11]. In this paper, a more general purpose inactivity detection application is addressed, which may be used in a home environment too.

In the second case study, a software application enabling the use of a smartphone as a personal assistant for drugs and therapy management is presented, which exploits the built-in camera of the device to capture a picture of the drug box, and processes the picture to automatically recognize the drug name and show details about it. This way, the specific information about the drug, such as active ingredients, intended purpose, method of use, dosage, contraindications, interactions and side effects, may be retrieved in a fast and easy way, by taking a picture of the package. The system also allows to check whether or not a drug is part of the user's therapy, by displaying required dosage and intake schedule.

The paper is organized as follows: Sect. 2 summarizes the relevant state-of-the-art in the use of smartphones as intelligent devices for personal assistance in AAL. The two use cases are discussed, in Sects. 3 and 4, respectively. Section 5 discusses the related experimental results, and finally Sect. 6 concludes the paper.

2 Background

Several applications aimed at monitoring how a smartphone is used are available from popular online repositories. The Apple (iTunes) mobile app store and Google Play mobile app store were searched for inactivity detection apps. The following search terms were used: *web browsing monitoring, incoming calls monitoring, incoming calls registering, incoming calls dashboard, incoming calls, logging, outgoing call, lost calls monitoring, SMS activity, SMS reporting,* and *SMS logging.* We excluded apps that were designed for call recording, SMS broadcasting and virus protection. In addition, data were collected using store description and the developer's website, including app name, functions, and developer information. Each app store was analyzed separately, as some apps were found in both mobile app stores. In line with this, the search terms yielded a total of 101 and 1058 unique apps, in the iTunes and Google Play app store, respectively. A total of 111 apps met the inclusion criteria, out of which 4 apps were available in iTunes, whereas 107 in the Google Play store. Finally, the included apps were segmented as presented in Table 1. In fact, the concept of inactivity may be observed from multiple and complementary perspectives, such as: web browsing monitoring, incoming, outgoing, and lost calls monitoring, and SMS activity monitoring. The web browsing monitoring aims to collect information about the Internet usage by capturing several parameters, such as time spent at each site, sites visited, and bandwidth consumed. Similarly, calls monitoring aims to obtain information on the phone activity in terms of time-stamp and contact of all the incoming, outgoing, and lost calls. Finally, the SMS activity aims to collect information about all the text messages issued or received by the user.

Table 1. Number of apps by topic.

Topic	iTunes	Google play
Web browsing monitoring	0	99
Incoming calls monitoring/registering/dashboard/logging	29	239
Outgoing calls	0	20
Lost calls monitoring	17	250
SMS activity/reporting/logging	55	450
	101	1058

The design of applications and systems for automatic visual recognition of drug boxes is still an open area, despite some proposals and ideas can be found in the literature. Typically, this kind of solutions is conceived to support impaired users, in order to improve their adherence to medication, reduce risks related to errors, and facilitate drug assumption. Benjamim et al. in [12] propose a system based on visual features matching applied to a captured picture of a drug box, to detect it and play audio files providing the user with information about dosage, indications and contraindications of the medication. Visually impaired subjects are supported in taking the right medicine at the time indicated in advance by the doctor. This system relies on a laptop and a connected web camera, to catch pictures of the drug boxes, and performs image processing by using a software developed for a Windows-based machine. Our proposal relies on the use of smartphones, avoiding the need for a personal computer at home and a web camera. This also facilitates image capturing, as the preview of the captured image is shown on the device screen, and it is easy to properly point the device with respect to the box, thanks to the reduced size and weight of the mobile device itself. In [13], an automated inspection system based on computer vision is presented, to inspect prescription drugs with press-through package (PTP). The system is designed to support pharmacists and decrease the rate of errors. This proposal targets different users from those we are interested in, who at home, are deemed not familiar with technology, and require very easy-to-use tools and intuitive interfaces. Yu et al. in [14] address a very complex issue, i.e. single pill recognition using imprint information. This is a quite tricky task, due to the huge variety of pill sizes, shapes, colors, and imprints. In the system herein presented, the drug boxes are subjected to automatic identification, not the single pills.

3   Inactivity Detection Application

At the current development stage, the proposed application for inactivity moni-toring features a complete processing engine, i.e. the set of methods to perform inactivity detection, including calls monitoring, alarm notifications, and contacts management in terms of user's preferences contact short list.

As depicted in Fig. 1, the application is persistent in the background, which means after the smartphone's boot, the app is automatically launched in back-ground mode (1. Start app). However, the user may access the application by selecting its icon from the list of installed applications. Since the application is launched, it triggers two main processes such as: the inactivity detection function (2), and the main menu navigator (3).

The inactivity detection is a cyclic service processed by the app, and it is defined by the following algorithm:

1. Start Hour is obtained from mean of the first incoming or outgoing call on the previous n days;
2. End Hour is obtained from mean of the last incoming or outgoing call on the previous n days;
3. The sleep period is defined as [Start Hour, End Hour];

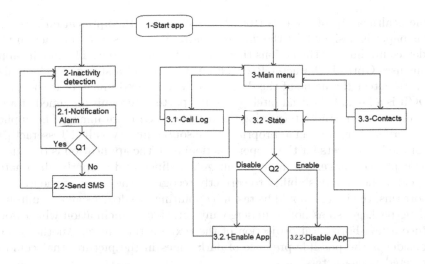

Fig. 1. Workflow of the inactivity detection app.

4. The awake period is defined as $[0...24] \notin [\text{Start Hour, End Hour}]$;
5. Maximum interval between calls, including incoming, outgoing calls on the previous n days, is obtained;
6. *if* awake period is *True* and (Current date-time) - (Last call (incoming, or outgoing) date-time) > Maximum interval between calls, *then* Inactivity trigger;
   otherwise
7. *if* the number of consecutive t lost calls is achieved *then* Inactivity trigger.

The *inactivity trigger* means that the user is asked to press a confirmation button in the app (Q1). If this does not happen, the app sends a short message (SMS) to the preferred contact on the user's defined short list (2.2.). The t is a dynamic threshold defined by the user, and may vary from 0 to 100, meaning a percentage of lost calls over all the incoming and outgoing calls.

On the one hand, the app allows Create, Read, Update, and Delete (CRUD) operations on a user's defined contact list (3.3.). On the other hand, the app provides its status information (3.2.) including: daily mean incoming/outgoing calls, sleep period, maximum interval among calls, and app state. In addition, the user may explicitly enable (3.2.1.) or disable (3.2.2.) the app when it is disabled or enabled, respectively (Q2). Finally, a call log (3.1.) is provided including the time-stamp and contact number related with the incoming, outgoing, and lost calls.

4   Drugs Management Application

Both in the literature and in the market there are many ICT-based solutions that allow to obtain drug reference and prescribing material, but they are designed for the healthcare professionals [15]. On the contrary, the application presented in this paper is designed for the final end-users: it enables easy interaction with the device minimising the actions that need to be carried out. The mobile applications uses Optical Character Recognition (OCR) and a string matching algorithm, to detect the name of the drug from the captured image of its box.

OCR is a field of artificial intelligence and pattern recognition aimed at automatically decoding and interpreting the text depicted in an image. The application described here uses an appropriate open source library, called Tesseract [16]. One of the key aspects for the proper functioning of the application is the quality of the captured image: the more the image is defined and properly illuminated, the greater the system's ability to correctly recognize the name of the drug. To support this, the image should be taken by pointing the device camera in front of the drug package, so as not to undergo any rotation or inclination which would produce a non-horizontal projection of the text on the image. Another aspect to consider is the possible presence of dark edges in the picture, that could be interpreted as characters.

In order to ensure adequate performance from the OCR, and avoid the need of taking into account all the previous requirements at the same time, a computer vision library to pre-process and correct the captured image, is exploited. Through well known line detection algorithms, the main lines of the image have been identified. Many of them correspond to the box's edge, this way it is possible to calculate its orientation and rectify the picture so that the drug's name becomes perfectly horizontal.

Once the text is detected from the straightened image, an algorithm able to identify the most likely word (i.e. the correct one) is necessary. For this purpose, error correction and string matching techniques have been evaluated. There are several string matching algorithms designed for word processing, database querying, and search engine implementation. Among them, the Levenshtein algorithm, a well-known process used to determine similarity between two strings, is used [17]. The returned result is called Levenshtein distance, or edit distance, and represents the number of characters to be changed to achieve equality between the strings being compared. Edit operations can either be insertions, deletions, or substitutions of characters. For example, the edit distance between "horse" and "house" is 1.

5   Experimental Results

The application for automatic recognition of drug boxes includes algorithms to perform image acquisition, pre-processing, text recognition, string matching, and data visualization.

According to a typical use case, when the user takes a picture of the drug package, the pre-processing algorithm detects the right orientation and rectifies the image. The rotated picture is fed into the OCR engine that outputs a text. This text could match exactly the real name of the drug, or could differ from it, due to errors in the OCR processing. The text provided by the OCR engine is compared to the name of all the drugs included in the Italian Drug Index, and based on the minimization of the Levenshtein distance computed by the algorithm, the most likely matching name is returned. At this point, the application sends a request to a server to obtain the details of that specific medicine. If it is included in the user's therapy, in addition to indications and contraindications, also the information on specific times and doses of assumptions defined for the user are shown.

As previously mentioned, Tesseract can not correctly recognize the text when the image provided as input is not properly illuminated, contains dark edges or is rotated with respect to the text. In Table 2, the outcome of tests performed in the laboratory environment in different conditions are shown. The text extracted by the OCR algorithm contains more errors when the image features an angled text, rather than the presence of a complex background, or dark borders. The strong misalignment case is certainly the most unfavorable situation for the application, because the system has not been able to recognize the text. This problem has been solved by introducing orientation recognition and picture rectification capabilities. Fig. 3 shows the OCR results for both the normal image, and the straightened one. Nevertheless, since Tesseract returns a string that does not correspond perfectly to the text in the image, the introduction of the Levenshtein algorithm has been fundamental to the proper functioning of the application, identifying within a file containing the names of more than 6,000 drugs, the most likely one. The complete application has been tested using four different drug boxes (see Fig. 4) in bright light conditions. Results are shown in Table 3.

Table 2. Tests performed on the same drug box in different conditions (see Fig. 2) without pre-processing and string matching algorithms, using an Android device equipped with built-in camera featuring 16 megapixels resolution.

Picture	Condition	Results
Figure 2(a)	Aligned picture, low light	94% chars detected, drug name partially recognized
Figure 2(b)	Slightly misaligned picture, normal light	100% chars detected, drug name correctly recognized
Figure 2(c)	Strongly misaligned picture, normal light	0% chars detected
Figure 2(d)	Dark edges in the picture	98% chars detected, drug name correctly recognized

The first line refers to a drug whose name is written in gold color (see Fig. 4(a)), it does not facilitate the detection of the text, however, more than half times the recognition has been successful. The second line refers instead to a drug whose box is very colorful and the text is underlined (see Fig. 4(b)); this prevents the proper recognition of the drug name, while the term "vitamin" reported under the name is recognized correctly, causing misunderstandings in

(a) Aligned picture

(b) Slightly misaligned picture

(c) Strongly misaligned picture

(d) Dark edges

Fig. 2. Pictures of the same drug box in different conditions related to Table 2.

OCR output:
m AmusCxo nominano l
Odluh www M manu

OCR output:
I f Diclofenac EG v
ATCMOMBOS commssn
Didofenoc Sod co P gmg
o a

Fig. 3. An example of OCR outputs for both normal and stretched pictures.

Table 3. Tests performed on 4 different drug boxes (see Fig. 4): for each drug, the success, failure, and misunderstanding percentages, and the number of performed tests are shown.

Drug	Success	Misunderstanding	Failure	Tests num.
Drug 1	53.85%	46.15%	0%	13
Drug 2	23.07%	38.46%	38.46%	13
Drug 3	84.61%	7.69%	7.69%	13
Drug 4	100%	0%	0%	13

the drug identification from the list of names. Graphics of the last two boxes, shown in Figs. 4(c) and (d), is very simple, thus, as expected, the results are highly positive.

Further tests are foreseen to evaluate the usability and acceptability of the proposed system by the target users, particularly the elderly in a real life scenario.

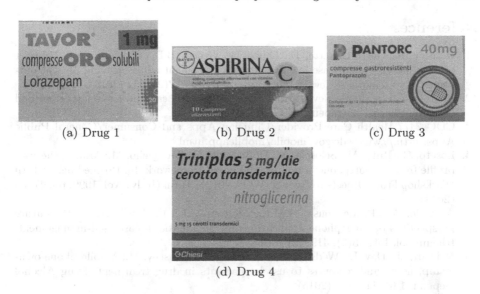

(a) Drug 1   (b) Drug 2   (c) Drug 3

(d) Drug 4

Fig. 4. Drug packages related to Table 3.

6   Conclusion

Well-being and good physical health are commonly associated to an active lifestyle, that also means being able to maintain stable social relationships and contacts with a specific group of fellows and relatives. As a consequence, the way a modern communication device such as a smartphone is used, to make calls or send messages, may reveal information on the activity or inactivity degree of the owner. This is a very hot topic in the Active and Assisted Living domain, and the application presented in this paper showed it is possible to unobtrusively gather information on the user's inactivity, by simply collecting data from the smartphone usage, through a simple though effective threshold-based algorithm.

Consistently with the increasing use of smartphones even among older adults, the number of apps aimed at supporting the user in organizing and taking their medications is also growing, across the dominant smartphone platforms. Most of them rely on a proactive behavior of the user, who is requested to interact with the device by answering questions or feeding data on medication assumption events. The application for drugs management presented in this paper adopts a different approach, that aims at minimizing or even avoiding the need for the user to input data or interact with the device, by resorting to the automatic processing and recognition of the drug box, through a picture captured by the smartphone camera. Despite some challenging issues that may occur, due to the way the picture is taken or to environmental conditions, the experimental results showed the technical feasibility of the approach, which is going to be complemented by future tests on usability in real-life conditions.

References

1. Hamine, S., Gerth-Guyette, E., Faulx, D., Green, B.B., Ginsburg, A.S.: Impact of mHealth chronic disease management on treatment adherence and patient outcomes: a systematic review. J. Med. Internet Res. **17**(2), e52 (2015)
2. Ventola, C.L.: Mobile devices and apps for health care professionals: uses and benefits. Pharm. Therapeut. **39**(5), 356 (2014)
3. CDC 24/7 Health Care Provider/Clinician Apps and Consumer/General Public Apps. http://www.cdc.gov/mobile/mobileapp.html
4. Loseto, G., Ruta, M., Scioscia, F., Di Sciascio, E., Mongiello, M.: Mining the user profile from a smartphone: a multimodal agent framework. In: Proceedings of 14th Workshop From Objects to Agents (WOA 2013), Turin (Italy), vol. 1099, pp. 47–53 (2013)
5. Azevedo, A.R.P., de Sousa, H.M.L., Monteiro, J.A.F., Lima, A.R.N.P.: Future perspectives of smartphone applications for rheumatic diseases self-management. Rheumatol. Int. **35**(3), 419–431 (2015)
6. Milward, J., Day, E., Wadsworth, E., Strang, J., Lynskey, M.: Mobile phone ownership, usage and readiness to use by patients in drug treatment. Drug Alcohol Depend. **146**, 111–115 (2015)
7. Pombo, N., Garcia, N., Bousson, K., Spinsante, S., Chorbev, I.: Pain assessment-can it be done with a computerised system? A systematic review and meta-analysis. Int. J. Environ. Res. Publ. Health **13**, 415 (2016)
8. Hutchesson, M.J., Rollo, M.E., Callister, R., Collins, C.E.: Self-monitoring of dietary intake by young women: online food records completed on computer or smartphone are as accurate as paper-based food records but more acceptable. J. Acad. Nutr. Diet. **115**(1), 87–94 (2015)
9. Spinsante, S., Cippitelli, E., Santis, A., Gambi, E., Gasparrini, S., Montanini, L., Raffaeli, L.: Multimodal interaction in a elderly-friendly smart home: a case study. In: Agüero, R., Zinner, T., Goleva, R., Timm-Giel, A., Tran-Gia, P. (eds.) MONAMI 2014. LNICSSITE, vol. 141, pp. 373–386. Springer, Cham (2015). doi:10. 1007/978-3-319-16292-8_27
10. Spinsante, S., Angelici, A., Lundström, J., Espinilla, M., Cleland, I., Nugent, C.: A mobile application for easy design and testing of algorithms to monitor physical activity in the workplace. Hindawi Mob. Inf. Syst. J. (in press)
11. Chau, J.Y., Daley, M., Dunn, S., Srinivasan, A., Do, A., Bauman, A.E., van der Ploeg, H.P.: The effectiveness of sit-stand workstations for changing office workers' sitting time: results from the Stand@Work randomized controlled trial pilot. Int. J. Behav. Nutr. Phys. Act. **11**, 127 (2014)
12. Benjamim, X.C., Gomes, R.B., Burlamaqui, A.F., Gonalves, L.M.G.: Visual identification of medicine boxes using features matching. In: Proceedings of 2012 IEEE VECIMS, pp. 43–47 (2012)
13. Morimoto, M., Murai, T.: A visual inspection system for prescription drugs in press-through package. In: Proceeding of 2014 World Automation Congress (2014)
14. Yu, J., Chen, Z., Kamata, S.I.: Pill recognition using imprint information by two-step sampling distance sets. In: Proc. ICPR 2014, pp. 3156–3161 (2014)
15. Haffey, F., Brady, R.R., Maxwell, S.: Smartphone apps to support hospital prescribing and pharmacology education: a review of current provision. Br. J. Clin. Pharmacol. **77**(1), 31–38 (2014)
16. Smith, R.: An overview of the Tesseract OCR engine (2007)
17. Levenshtein, V.I.: Binary codes capable of correcting deletions, insertions and reversals. In: Soviet Physics Doklady, vol. 10 (1966)

An Analysis of Ego Network Communities and Temporal a Affinity for Online Social Networks

Andrea De Salve, Barbara Guidi$^{(\boxtimes)}$, and Laura Ricci

Department of Computer Science, University of Pisa, Pisa, Italy
{desalve,guidi,laura.ricci}@unipi.it

Abstract. The wide diffusion of Online Social Networks (OSNs) presents several advantages, like the definition of simple tools for information sharing and spreading. However, OSNs present also some drawbacks, one of the most important one is the problem of privacy disclosures. Distributed Online Social Networks (DOSNs), which decentralize the control of the social network, have been recently proposed to overcome these issues. The decentralization of the control has issued several challenges, one of the main ones is guaranteeing data availability without relying on a central server. To define users' data allocation strategies, the knowledge of the structure of the ego network and of the user' temporal behaviour is required. Unfortunately, the lack of real datasets limits the research in this field. The goal of this paper is the study of the behaviour of users in a real social network in order to define proper strategies to allocate the users' data on the DOSN nodes. In particular, we present an analysis of the temporal affinity and of the social communities based on a real Facebook dataset.

Keywords: P2P social networks · DOSN · Data availability · Temporal affinity · Community detection

1 Introduction

Online Social Networks (OSNs) have created a new way of interaction and communication among people. An OSN [3] is an online platform that provides services for a user to build a public profile and to establish connection between users. OSNs are almost always based on centralized structures which have intrinsic drawbacks including scalability and privacy [7]. Privacy is probably the most studied issue because social networks have become the main channel of privacy disclosure. These drawbacks have led researchers to investigate alternative solutions, such as distributed approaches. A Distributed Online Social Network (DOSN) [7] is an online social network implemented on a distributed platform, such as a network of trusted servers, P2P systems or an opportunistic network. Decentralization has several consequences, in particular in term of privacy. In

© ICST Institute for Computer Sciences, Social Informatics and Telecommunications Engineering 2017
O. Gaggi et al. (Eds.): GOODTECHS 2016, LNICST 195, pp. 135–144, 2017.
DOI: 10.1007/978-3-319-61949-1_15

fact, no central entity exists that decides or changes the terms of service. However, since the social data is stored on the hosts of the users, its availability depends on the online behaviour of the users. This is a major problem in DOSNs because users' behaviour has a high fluctuation that can lead to data becoming unavailable or lost. Replication is one of the most popular approaches to manage this problem. Replica of user's profiles may be stored on nodes of the distributed systems to improve data availability, but at the same time, it introduces the problem of consistency and the problem of minimizing the number of replicas.

The study of good selection policies for the election of replica nodes with particular attention to the number of replicas has recently gained momentum. These mechanisms must allocate data on the users' nodes so to maximize the availability of the social data. Existing solutions may consider exclusively friend nodes, a set of trusted nodes among the friends, or random nodes; and existing selection policies may be based on information on both the duration and the distribution of online availability of nodes and on the ability of the replica to serve the requests for data replicated on it.

The main goal of this paper is to present a twofold study of a Facebook data set. First, we extend the analysis proposed in our previous work [8] regarding the temporal behaviour of users by considering the global ego network structure. As a second step, we introduce a first study of the communities present in the ego networks of the users. At the best of our knowledge, this is the first analysis of this kind, in this research field. The analysis may detect the nodes of the users which belong to more than one community and that may act as a "hubs", able to serve accesses to the replica they store for many nodes of the ego network.

The rest of the paper is organized as follow. Section 2 describes the related work. Section 3 introduces the problem of data availability in DOSNs. Section 4 describes our twofold work on temporal affinity and community detection. Section 5 investigates the result of our analysis. Finally, Sect. 6 draws the main conclusions.

2   Related Work

During the last years, several DOSNs have been proposed. The first important proposal is Diaspora [1], which consists of a federated network of servers. On one hand, Diaspora represents the first example of a real distributed social network, on the other hand, its main drawback is the scalability, due to its architecture not fully distributed.

Other proposals exploit a full distributed architecture often implemented by P2P systems. LifeSocial [11] is a P2P OSN focused on the privacy issue, where user information is stored by exploiting a DHT and it presents an approach where all OSN functionalities are realized by plug-ins.

PeerSon [4] is a distributed infrastructure for social networks whose focus is related to security and privacy concerns. It proposes a two-tier architecture where the first tier is a Distributed Hash Table (DHT) and the second tier consists of the nodes representing users. The idea is to use the DHT to find the necessary information for users connecting directly to the target nodes. This approach comes without a replication scheme and stores offline messages on the DHT (OpenDHT in the prototype implementation). All users' content is encrypted.

As concern the data availability problem, only few proposals have addressed this issue. Safebook [6] addresses privacy in OSNs by using a three-tiers architecture where data are stored in a particular social overlay named "Matryoshka". Matryoshkas are concentric rings of peers around each users peer that provide trusted data storage and obscure communication through indirection. Super-Nova [16] is an architecture for a DOSN that solves the availability issue by relying on super-peers that provide highly available storage. DiDuSoNet [12] is a P2P DOSN focused on the data availability problem which uses, as SafeBook, a particular overlay based on trusted connections to store data. Other specific solutions are presented in [14], where authors propose a replication strategy based on storing the replicas of users profiles only on a set of trusted proxies.

3   Data Availability in DOSN

The problem of Data Availability has been mainly studied in the area of P2P networks [2,13], for instance work on P2P storage systems date back to the OceanStore [13] initiative to achieve archival storage using end-user resources.

Recently, the problem has been studied also in the context of DOSNs. Most current approaches for DOSNs rely to external storages, such as private servers or cloud. Among DOSNs, only few approaches, such as PeerSoN [4], DiDuSoNet [12], and Safebook [6] do not rely on external storage. In detail, they exploit social relations between users to decide where data has to be stored. The rationale behind this strategy is that social friends are natural candidates for replicating the data of a user, as they are interested in his/her data. In particular, the solution proposed in [12] leverages the properties related to a friendship relationship (such as trust, strength, or types of the friendship) to guide the data storage.

However, taking into account only the friendship relations and their properties is not enough to ensure to each user the availability of his/her data, at any time. Indeed, geographical proximity between users is one of the most significant factor that make the formation of a friendship (and communities) possible. As result, the majority of the user's friends live geographically close to each other and time-zone differences are negligible since users are connected during the daylight hours and disconnected during the sleeping time (i.e. at night). Consequently, taking into account the temporal behavior of users is crucial when trying to maximize data availability.

In this work we are interested in studying the temporal affinity between Facebook users and their friends by considering a well-known social network structure: the ego network [10], which is the network constituted by a user (*the ego*), his/her direct friends (*the alters*) and the social ties occurring between them.

4   An Analysis of Facebook's Ego Networks: Temporal Affinities and Communities Structure

We evaluate a real dataset gathered by *SocialCircles!*, a Facebook application deeply described in [8]. At the best of our knowledge, our dataset is the only one which contains structural and temporal information about users.

We sampled 337 registered egos and their friends every 8 min for 10 consecutive days (from Tuesday 3 June 2014 to Friday 13 June). Using this methodology we were able to access the temporal status of 308 registered users and of their friends (for a total of 95.578 users). For the purpose of clarity, we will refer to ego nodes to indicate these 308 users. We consider the availability trace of each user to determine the start of a session and its termination. More specifically, time starts at the beginning of time s_0 and it is segmented in a subsequent time periods (*time slots*).

4.1   Temporal Affinity

With the term *Temporal Affinity* we refer to the phenomena of users having the same temporal behaviour, i.e. the probability that they are online in the same interval of time. In more detail, considering the ego network of an ego E, we study how similar is the temporal behaviour of E with respect to his/her the alters. To analyse the temporal affinity, we use a specific *presence array* of 2001 entries (one for each temporal slot in our dataset) for each couple ego-alter. Each slot refers to 8 min and it contains a value: 1 if the user is online in this slot, 0 otherwise. Since our goal is to understand how the temporal behaviour of users can affect the data availability in DOSNs and considering that there are particular day periods when users tend to be offline (e.g. during the night), we propose two different metrics for the Temporal Affinity:

- *Daily Temporal Affinity (DTA)*, which exploits all the 2001 temporal slots;
- *Nighttime Temporal Affinity (NTA)*, which considers a subset of nighttime slots.

The availability of each user is represented by an availability vector of fixed size. We evaluate the temporal affinity using the cosine similarity metrics.

To evaluate the NTA, we need to define when an ego can be considered active during the night (i.e. from 12:00 midnight to 06:00 a.m.) of a day i. An ego is *nighttime* during the night of the day i if and only if it has been online for at least 15 temporal slots. We define a *k-nighttime* ego an ego which has been nighttime for k nights and a *nighttime alter* as an alter which is online for the 95% in the same nighttime slots of a *k-nighttime* ego. The *nighttime affinity coefficient* is defined as the average number of nighttime alters of a *k-nighttime* ego.

4.2   Community Detection

Community structure is considered to be a significant property of social networks. Numerous techniques have been developed for both efficient and effective community detection. A user usually has connections to several social groups like family, friends, and colleagues. Further, the number of communities an individual can belong to is actually unlimited because a person can simultaneously take part in as many groups as he/she wishes [17].

To discover communities in the ego networks, we decide to use the Label Propagation (LP) [15], implemented by DEMON [5], which defines rules to spread labels in the network so that nodes labeled with the same colour form a community. DEMON is suitable for a distributed implementation and it can be easily adapted to any kind of network, dense or sparse.

We define a new index, the *k-overlapping index*, *KOI*, to evaluate the overlapping of communities. The index is defined as follow: for each ego network *EN* including a set CS of communities, for each alter $a \in EN$, we compute the number of communities $\in$ CS, the alter a belongs to and detect alters that appear in at least k communities. We compare this value with the total number of nodes in the ego network. Formally, the index is defined in the Eq. 1.

$$KOI(EN, k) = \frac{|V^1|}{|V|} \quad (1)$$

where V is the set of alters nodes of the ego network EN and V^1 is the set of alters of EN which belong to, at least, k communities.

On the basis of the KOI index, we can detect alters which belong to a significant set of communities and are, therefore, suitable to host and spread replicated data. On the other way round, the allocation strategy must take into account that, since each user device has a limited amount of memory, allocation can causes a huge amount of load on a single node belonging to a lerge set of communities, because it could be chosen by a large set of friends to replicate data.

5   Evaluation

In this section we describe the evaluation of the temporal affinity and of the communities belonging to an ego network.

5.1   Temporal Affinity

The first analysis concerns the evaluation of the Daily Temporal Affinity, referenced as DTA. As explained in [8], a user can be online, offline or in a idle state. We decide to consider the online state, and we do not distinguish the idle and offline state into the presence array so that both of them are represented by the value 0, in the presence array.

About the 80% of the couple ego-alter has a low similarity, as depicted in Fig. 1. This low value is influenced by the online behaviour of each ego. A little set of couples (less than 5%) show medium/high values of similarity. These results confirm our previous analysis on Dunbar-based ego networks where users present

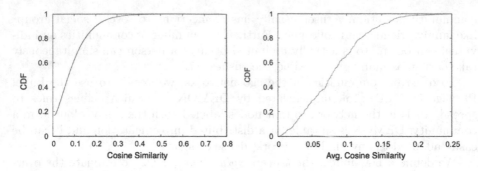

Fig. 1. The cosine similarity and the average value for the *daily temporal affinity*

a high similarity only with trusted nodes. In fact, extending the temporal affinity analysis to the ego networks, the result is similar.

The second step concerns the analysis of the ego networks to find the Nighttime Temporal Affinity, indicated with NTA through the *Temporal Affinity index* introduced in Sect. 4. For the evaluation, we consider both the online and the idle state, and we vary the parameter k which defines the k-nighttime ego. Notice that when an ego present a high NTA with a set of distinct alters means that tie strength between the ego and these alters is strong.

For the evaluation, we use two indexes: *fixed indexes*, when the night is divided into 38 slots from about the 03.00 A.M. to the 08.00 A.M. and *variable indexes*, when the night is defined by the slots containing less than 10000 users.

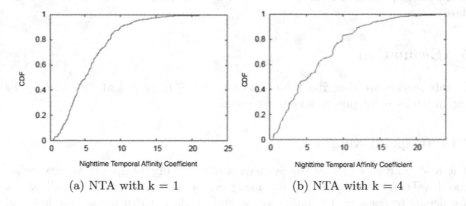

(a) NTA with k = 1   (b) NTA with k = 4

Fig. 2. NTA with fixed indexes, by varying the number of nights k

Analyzing the NTA we notice that less than 10% of egos can be considered nighttime. This value is drastically reduced when the constraints of the number of nights needed to be nighttime increase.

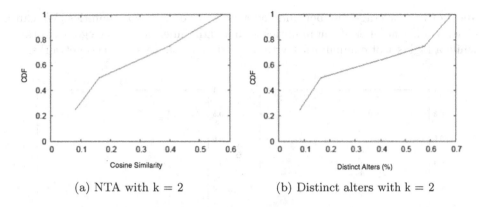

(a) NTA with k = 2   (b) Distinct alters with k = 2

Fig. 3. Variable indexes with k equals to 2

For example, if we consider an ego network of 400 nodes, the number of alters which contribute to the NTA is less than 40 considering the state online and idle and this number decreases when we consider only the online state (less than 10). This results tends to confirm the Dunbar's result about social circles [9] showing that the number of nodes which we interact with is very low if compared with the total number of alters.

5.2 Community Detection

Our goal is to identify, in each ego network, a group of users which are densely connected among them. We have considered the ego network EN of each of the 337 registered users and we have executed DEMON on EN to compute the number of communities in EN. As expected, the dataset has revealed the typical structure of the social network, including groups of nodes which are strongly interconnected between them (high cluster coefficient).

Table 1. Analysis of the communities.

Ego network size	Avg. number of communities	Avg. community size
0–199	43	44.01
200–299	53	65.1
300–399	51	87.71
400–499	49	103.02
500–699	48	141.03
700–899	29	175.51
900–2999	28	342.75

Table 1 shows the characteristics of the detected communities with respect to the size of the corresponding ego network. We show the size of an ego network and both the average number and the average size of its communities. We can observe a low number of communities with a high dimension in big ego networks, while a high set of communities with a low dimension, in small ego networks.

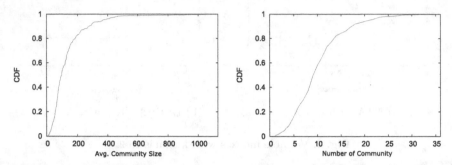

(a) CDF of the Average Community Size   (b) CDF of the number of Community

Fig. 4. Community detection: an analysis

Figure 4 depicts the CDF of the community size and of the number of communities. About the 80% of communities has less than 250 nodes. The ego networks show a complex structure and about 80% of them has a number of communities less than 15 (Fig. 4(b)). This information is important when we consider the goal of our analysis. In fact, it permits us to estimate the number of replicas which can be allocated for the ego's data. Another interesting analysis evaluates the overlapping of communities. We exploit the *k-overlapping index* defined in Sect. 4 to evaluate, for each ego, the number of communities an alter belongs to. To choose the value k, we consider the average number of communities an ego node could have, as shown in Fig. 4(b), varying k from 2 to 5.

Figure 5 shows the communities overlapping evaluation. Communities present a considerable overlap, also when we consider increasing values of k. This means that ego networks have a set of nodes which belong to more than 2 communities, these nodes represent a bridge between different communities and are central in the ego network. In detail, when we consider the two bounds of k (Fig. 5(a) and (d)), we can clearly notice that low values of the KOI index for k equals to 5, but the increase of k is not proportional to the decrease of the index.

The properties of detected communities define for us a guideline for the definition of a strategy for allocating the users' data replica in the ego network. A suitable node to store replicas of the user's data may be chosen among the set of nodes which belong to more than one community. A user paired with one of these nodes has direct friendship connections with many other nodes of the ego network and may guarantee a good coverage of the ego network. On the other hand, a clever allocation has to take into account also the problem of load balancing, because nodes belonging to a set of communities could be affected by a huge load.

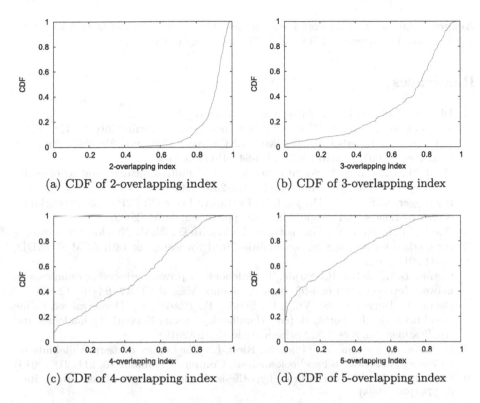

(a) CDF of 2-overlapping index   (b) CDF of 3-overlapping index

(c) CDF of 4-overlapping index   (d) CDF of 5-overlapping index

Fig. 5. Communit overlapping through the k-overlapping index

6 Conclusion and Future Works

This paper has analysed the temporal behaviour of users and the communities of a real OSN to understand how these issues can affect the data availability in DOSN. We have noticed that egos have not a similar behaviour by considering their ego network and only a subset of nodes are good candidate to store replicas of profiles, by confirming the results obtained in [8] The analysis has reported interesting results when the temporal affinity has been evaluated during the night. Furthermore, we have investigated the communities in the ego networks and shown that they are heterogeneous in term of structure and size. We found that ego networks are characterized by a low number of communities, which does not depend from the ego network size and that there is an high level of overlapping of these communities. These results can be used to support a proper data allocation strategy, for example by using the number of overlapping communities as parameter of the selection strategy. We plan to extend our work in several directions. First, we will extend our study to the investigation of dynamic communities, i.e. communities detected by considering each time slot separately. We plan also to define a good strategy to select the nodes to store data replica.

Acknowledgement. This work has been funded by the project *Big Data, Social Mining and Risk Management* (PRA_2016_15), University of Pisa.

References

1. Diaspora Website. https://diasporafoundation.org/
2. Bhagwan, R., Savage, S., Voelker, G.M.: Understanding availability. In: Kaashoek, M.F., Stoica, I. (eds.) IPTPS 2003. LNCS, vol. 2735, pp. 256–267. Springer, Heidelberg (2003). doi:10.1007/978-3-540-45172-3_24
3. Boyd, D., Ellison, N.B.: Social network sites: definition, history, and scholarship. J. Comput.-Mediat. Commun. **13**(1), 210–230 (2007)
4. Buchegger, S., Schiberg, D., Vu, L.H., Datta, A.: PeerSoN: P2P social networking - early experiences and insights. In: SNS, pp. 46–52. ACM (2009)
5. Coscia, M., Rossetti, G., Giannotti, F., Pedreschi, D.: DEMON: a local-first discovery method for overlapping communities. In: Proceedings of 18th ACM SIGKDD, KDD 2012 (2012)
6. Cutillo, L.A., Molva, R., Strufe, T.: Safebook: a privacy preserving online social network leveraging on real-life trust. Commun. Mag. IEEE **47**, 94–101 (2009)
7. Datta, A., Buchegger, S., Vu, L.H., Strufe, T., Rzadca, K.: Decentralized online social networks. In: Furht, B. (ed.) Handbook of Social Network Technologies and Applications, pp. 349–378. Springer, Heidelberg (2010)
8. De Salve, A., Dondio, M., Guidi, B., Ricci, L.: The impact of users availability on on-line ego networks: a Facebook analysis. Comput. Commun. **73**, 211–218 (2016)
9. Dunbar, R.I.M.: The social brain hypothesis. Evol. Anthropol.: Issues, News Rev. **6**, 178–190 (1998)
10. Everett, M.G., Borgatti, S.P.: Ego network betweenness. Soc. Netw. **27**, 31–38 (2005)
11. Graffi, K., Gross, C., Stingl, D., Hartung, D., Kovacevic, A., Steinmetz, R.: LifeSocial.KOM: a secure and P2P-based solution for online social networks. In: IEEE CCNC (2011)
12. Guidi, B., Amft, T., De Salve, A., Graffi, K., Ricci, L.: Didusonet: a p2p architecture for distributed dunbar-based social networks. Peer-to-Peer Netw. Appl. **9**, 1–18 (2015)
13. Kubiatowicz, J., Bindel, D., Chen, Y., Czerwinski, S., Eaton, P., Geels, D., Gummadi, R., Rhea, S., Weatherspoon, H., Weimer, W., et al.: Oceanstore: an architecture for global-scale persistent storage. ACM SIGPLAN Not. **35**(11), 190–201 (2000)
14. Narendula, R., Papaioannou, T.G., Aberer, K.: A decentralized online social network with efficient user-driven replication. In: 2012 International Conference on Privacy, Security, Risk and Trust (PASSAT), and 2012 International Confernece on Social Computing (SocialCom), pp. 166–175. IEEE (2012)
15. Raghavan, U.N., Albert, R., Kumara, S.: Near linear time algorithm to detect community structures in large-scale networks. Phys. Rev. E **76**, 036106 (2007)
16. Sharma, R., Datta, A.: SuperNova: super-peers based architecture for decentralized online social networks. CoRR abs/1105.0074 (2011)
17. Xie, J., Kelley, S., Szymanski, B.K.: Overlapping community detection in networks: the state-of-the-art and comparative study. ACM Comput. Surv. **45**(4), 43 (2013)

Computer Vision for the Blind: A Comparison of Face Detectors in a Relevant Scenario

Marco De Marco, Gianfranco Fenu, Eric Medvet,
and Felice Andrea Pellegrino$^{(\boxtimes)}$

Department of Engineering and Architecture, University of Trieste, Trieste, Italy
marco.de.marco.ts@gmail.com, {fenu,emedvet,fapellegrino}@units.it

Abstract. Motivated by the aim of developing a vision-based system
to assist the social interaction of blind persons, the performance of some
face detectors are evaluated. The detectors are applied to manually annotated video sequences acquired by blind persons with a glass-mounted
camera and a necklace-mounted one. The sequences are relevant to the
specific application and demonstrate to be challenging for all the considered detectors. A further analysis is performed to reveal how the performance is affected by some features such as occlusion, rotations, size and
position of the face within the frame.

Keywords: Face detection · Video sequences · Blindness · Comparison

1   Introduction and Related Work

In recent years, many contributions have been proposed as "smart" assistants
for blind people, with the aim to assist them in the everyday life and in the
social interaction. Some of that proposals are based on remote volunteers [1],
or on smart devices, as canes [2] or mobile phones [3]. Concerning visual-based
smart devices, a challenge consists in building First Person Vision (FPV) systems which can improve the social interactions of visually impaired persons [4]:
for instance, such systems should discover the number, the identity, and the
emotional state of people around the visually impaired person and communicate
that information to him/her. In facts, the *face detection* is the first, essential step
of such information flow. Many different approaches have been proposed in the
literature, with the aim to detect human faces in images or in still video frames,
for different purposes (tracking, recognition, surveillance, safety, human-machine
interaction, etc.). The reader may refer to the recent survey [5] and to the references therein to have an overview on this topic. A very debated theme, regarding
face detection algorithms, concerns how to compare the performances of different face detection algorithms and how to build proper benchmark datasets (see
for instance [6]).

With the aim to offer a benchmark platform for FPV systems assisting blind
people, recently a particular video dataset has been collected [7]. An *ad hoc*

© ICST Institute for Computer Sciences, Social Informatics and Telecommunications Engineering 2017
O. Gaggi et al. (Eds.): GOODTECHS 2016, LNICST 195, pp. 145–154, 2017.
DOI: 10.1007/978-3-319-61949-1_16

dataset is needed when a FPV system, or simply a face detection and recognition algorithm, has to be tested for applying in assisting blind people, due some specific features of blind people behavior (for instance mannerism [8]) that are responsible of disturbances and effects (such as blur, rapidly varying light conditions, occlusions [9]) normally not present in standard video dataset for face detection bench-marking.

Taking into account such features, is it possible to apply a standard face detector to the videos of that specific dataset? What are the performances of well known face detectors, if installed on a wearable smart device, used by a visually impaired person? The present paper deals with this topic, comparing the performances of some classical and some very recent face detectors, applied on the videos introduced in [7] and analyzing the results. In particular, the structure of the paper is as follows: the dataset is described in Sect. 2, then in Sect. 3 the face detectors are briefly presented. Section 4 is focusing on the comparison protocol and on the benchmark results, while in Sect. 5 some remarks and considerations are reported.

2   Dataset

For evaluating the performance of the face detectors, four video sequences have been employed, belonging to the dataset [7]. The mentioned dataset has been acquired specifically for providing realistic sequences for the considered application. More precisely, the sequences have been acquired by a blind person by means of two wearable cameras. Two commercial devices have been used, namely a pair of sunglasses equipped with a camera (*SportXtreme OverLook Gx-9*), and a *Polaroid CUBE* camera, held by a short necklace. The glasses-mounted camera has a resolution of 1280 px × 720 px and field of view of 135°; the resolution of the necklace-mounted camera is 1920 px × 1080 px and its field of view is 124°. Four video sequences, acquired using the different devices in different places (a university library, a coffee shop, an office, the neighborhood of a bus stop) have been selected and manually annotated. The data of the selected sequences, that contain a total of 3699 faces in 1728 frames, are summarized in Table 1.

Table 1. Salient information on the selected sequences.

Name	Resolution	Camera	Location	# frames	# faces
Coffee-shop	1280 × 720	GX9	Indoor	361	809
Library	1280 × 720	GX9	Indoor	361	1074
Office	1920 × 1080	CUBE	Indoor	558	206
Bus-stop	1920 × 1080	CUBE	Outdoor	448	1610

Inspecting the whole dataset some observations can be made [7]:

- faces can be partially occluded, mainly because there is no visual feedback during acquisition;
- the wide angles introduce distortion;
- the scene conditions are very different in the different contexts, and can change abruptly with time, especially the illumination conditions;
- sudden, fast and wide subjective movements occur, especially in the sequences acquired with the glass mounted camera.

As far as the annotation is concerned, each face has been annotated by tracing a rectangle (referred to as *bounding box* in the following). The rectangle is vertically delimited by chin and forehead (normal hairline, independent of the actual presence of hair in the subject), and horizontally delimited by the ears or, for rotated faces, one ear and the opposite foremost point between the tip of the nose and the profile of the cheek. The presence of significant yaw (possibly also with pitch and roll contributions) was denoted by a dedicated flag, set if the farthest eye was not clearly visible. A further flag was set if the face was partially occluded. Beyond the rectangle, the positions of the centers of the two eyes and of the mouth were also annotated. Faces whose resulting bounding box longest size was less than 20 px long were not annotated.

In the following we point out some features of the annotated faces that will be used in Sect. 4 for a sensitivity analysis:

- normalized bounding box area (NBBA): the ratio between the bounding box area and the frame area;
- normalized distance of the bounding box from the center of the image (NDFC): distance between bounding box center and frame center, divided by the frame circumcircle radius;
- roll angle: the roll angle is estimated as the angle between the x-axis of the frame and the line passing through the eyes;
- root mean square contrast (RMSC) within the bounding box [10], given by $\sqrt{\frac{1}{\#B} \sum_B \left(I_{ij} - \bar{I}\right)^2}$ where I_{ij} is the intensity of the i-th j-th pixel of the bounding box B, $\bar{I}$ is the average intensity of the bounding box and $\#B$ denotes the number of pixel within the bounding box;
- lateral/non-lateral flag (L/NL): a face is labeled as *lateral* when the farthest eye is not clearly distinguishable due to the rotation oh the head w.r.t. the point of view;
- occluded/non-occluded (O/NO): a face is labeled as *occluded* when it is partially occluded.

Each sequence may be characterized by the distribution of the above features related to the faces annotated in the sequence. For space reason, we do not report the distribution of all the features for each sequence. Instead, we fixed a reasonable threshold τ for each of the numeric features (NBBA, NDFC, Roll, and RMSC) and show in Table 2 the percentage of the annotated faces having, for the given feature, a value *below* the threshold: the threshold values (shown in the table) have been chosen manually by looking to the histograms of the occurrences and assuming a bi-modal underlying distribution. For categorical features (L/NL and O/NO), Table 2 shows instead the percentage of annotated faces in which the features assumes the ideal value (non-lateral and non-occluded, respectively) from the point of view of the face detection task.

Table 2. Percentage of annotated faces having a given feature value below the chosen threshold (for numeric features) or equal to the ideal value (for categorical features).

	NBBA	NDFC	Roll	RMSC	L/NL	O/NO
Threshold τ	0.01	0.33	15	0.15	–	–
Coffee-shop	80.34	26.94	86.47	72.93	47.23	76.14
Library	98.13	14.71	67.26	17.51	77.23	98.17
Office	37.86	20.87	95.32	43.69	91.26	92.23
Bus-stop	88.50	52.98	96.58	75.53	94.04	95.71
All sequences	86.70	34.39	87.01	56.34	78.7	92.06

3   Detectors

Viola-Jones. The Viola-Jones face detector is well-known and is based on a cascade of simple classifiers. The features are Haar-like and easily computed by means of the integral image [11]. Among the several existing implementations we used the one provided by the Matlab Computer Vision Toolbox.

GMS Vision. Google has developed a framework for object detection, integrated within its Google Mobile Service (GMS)[1]. The vision package offers a face detector and a bar-code reader. Because of the limitations imposed by Google about the use of Google Mobile Service, the integration of the face detector GMS Vision within the testing framework was not possible. As a workaround, an Android application was created using an Android emulator environment. Unfortunately Vision libraries available with the Google Mobile Service, do not allow to process a video stream from a file but only from the camera. To overcome this limitation, the OpenCV frame grabber was employed for extracting frames from the video to be analyzed.

NPD. The Normalized Pixel Difference (NPD) algorithm [12], is based on the difference to sum ratio between couples of pixels, and uses a decision tree for the learning. A Matlab implementation has been made available by the authors[2].

---

[1] https://developers.google.com.
[2] http://www.openpr.org.cn/index.php/107-NPD-Face-Detector/View-details.html.

PICO. Pixel intensity comparison is also used in the PICO algorithm [13]. Hence the features are fast to compute and scale independent. The classifier is a random forest with binary decision trees. The full source code has been made available by the authors[3].

Face-Id. Face-Id [14] is a face detection framework based on deep learning. It has been developed using Torch Tensor Framework, Lua and C++ languages. The source code was provided by the authors.

Visage. We used the demo-version of the Face Detect component that belongs to Visage SDK[4]. It is a commercial product that performs the face detection by identifying the facial features in facial images containing one or more human faces. For each detected face it returns the 2D and 3D head pose, 2D and 3D coordinates of facial feature points (chin tip, nose tip, lip corners, etc.), ignored in the present study.

4 Comparison

4.1 Protocol

The above face detectors have been applied to the selected sequences by setting all the parameters to their default values.

Given the output of a detector for a sequence and the corresponding ground truth data, the number of True Positive (TP), False Positive (FP), and False Negative (FN) are determined through the following 3 steps:

1. Calculate the Intersection to Union Areas Ratio (IUAR) index for each pair of a ground truth object and a detection belonging to the same frame of the sequence. For a detection d_i and a ground truth object g_j, $\text{IUAR}(d_i, g_j) = \frac{\text{area}(d_i \cup g_j)}{\text{area}(d_i \cup g_j)}$.
2. Find the best match between ground truth and detections, using Hungarian Algorithm [15]: the best match is the one having the highest cumulative IUAR index.
3. Consider as a True Positive a detection for which the IUAR of the best match is > 0.5, as a False Positive a detection for which the IUAR of the best match is ≤ 0.5, and as a False Negative a ground truth object which is not the best match of any detection.
4. Set TP, FP, and FN, to the counts of True Positives, False Positives, and False Negatives within the sequence.

Given TP, FP, FN, and the number of frames n_f in the sequence, we express the performance of the detector applied to that sequence in terms of three indexes: *precision*, computed as $\frac{\text{TP}}{\text{TP+FP}}$, *recall*, computed as $\frac{\text{TP}}{\text{TP+FN}}$, and *false*

---

[3] https://github.com/nenadmarkus/pico.
[4] https://visagetechnologies.com/products-and-services/visagesdk/.

positive per frame (FPPF), computed as $\frac{FP}{n_f}$. Precision and recall are indexes commonly used for assessing the effectiveness in information retrieval tasks, but have also be used in tasks related to computer vision (e.g., image segmentation [16]). The latter index, FPPF, is particularly relevant for the application. Indeed, since the aim of the devised vision-based system is to assist the social interaction of blind persons, it must deliver information "continuously" in time. The number of false detections per frame indicates how frequently, on average, the delivered information is not correct.

4.2   Results and Discussion

Table 3 shows the performance for each method and for each sequence, and the average across all the sequences.

It is clear by inspecting Table 3 that all the face detectors perform poorly in the considered sequences. The best result seems to be achieved by NPD on the sequence Bus-stop (a recall of 0.747, a precision of 0.687, and 1.221 false positive per frame)—interestingly, this is the only outdoor video sequence. In all the other cases either the precision or the recall are well below 0.5. It is clear that some detectors, in particular GMS and Face-Id are tuned to avoid false positives (resulting in relatively high precision but low or very low recall) and some other such as Viola-Jones are tuned to avoid false negative (leading to high FPPF). Table 3 shows that the best average recall (0.513) is achieved by Viola-Jones, that leads however to the worst FPFM. The best precision is achieved by Face-Id that leads to the worst recall. The detectors that seem to be tuned halfway between the extrema (such as NPD, resulting in a recall of 0.489 and a precision of 0.376), still do not exhibit a satisfactory performance.

In order to gain deeper insights, we plotted the Receiver operating characteristic (ROC) curves for the detectors PICO and NPD, which are shown in Fig. 1 for each of the four sequences. We chose these methods because they provide, along with each detection, a confidence value which can be used to further refine the outcome of the frame processing by discarding the detected objects for which the confidence is low—the other 4 methods do not provide such an information. Figure 1 confirms the results of Table 3 and highlights the obvious trade-off between recall and FPPF.

From results shown in Table 3 and Fig. 1, it can be argued that the sequences under examinations are particularly challenging. Hence we performed a sensitivity analysis of the performance with respect to some features of the annotated faces that can possibly explain the poor performance of all the detector. The results of the sensitivity analysis are reported in Table 4, in terms of the average recall achieved by different methods computed on annotated faces having the feature value below or above the reference threshold τ (for numeric features, see Table 2) or equal to a given value (for categorical features).

Regarding the NBBA, it can be observed that some detectors perform better with bigger faces, some the opposite. This is easily explained by the default

Table 3. Precision, recall and false positive per frame for the six face detectors and each of the four sequences.

Method	Sequence	Precision	Recall	FPPF
Viola-Jones	Coffee-shop	0.129	0.367	5.543
	Library	0.140	0.267	4.867
	Office	0.031	0.709	8.197
	Bus-stop	0.222	0.725	9.158
	Average	0.132	0.513	7.196
GMS	Coffee-shop	0.364	0.015	0.058
	Library	1.000	0.004	0.000
	Office	0.387	0.141	0.082
	Bus-stop	0.202	0.020	0.290
	Average	0.284	0.021	0.114
NPD	Coffee-shop	0.228	0.305	2.319
	Library	0.159	0.222	3.504
	Office	0.256	0.583	0.625
	Bus-stop	0.687	0.747	1.221
	Average	0.376	0.489	1.735
PICO	Coffee-shop	0.337	0.121	0.535
	Library	0.030	0.003	0.266
	Office	0.538	0.413	0.131
	Bus-stop	0.202	0.020	0.290
	Average	0.589	0.160	0.238
Face-Id	Coffee-shop	0.143	0.001	0.017
	Library	0.889	0.007	0.003
	Office	–	0.0	0.0
	Bus-stop	1.000	0.001	0.000
	Average	0.611	0.003	0.004
Visage	Coffee-shop	0.043	0.002	0.125
	Library	0.045	0.001	0.058
	Office	0.137	0.068	0.158
	Bus-stop	0.072	0.006	0.286
	Average	0.087	0.007	0.163

parameters of each detector[5]. Concerning L/NL, the table shows that all the detectors perform better with non-lateral faces and this is not a surprise, as well

---

[5] We did not change the default parameters on purpose, for two reasons: first, some detectors have fixed parameters and second, the choice of default parameters made by the authors of the detector may reflect a compromise between various aspects of performance that we are not aware of.

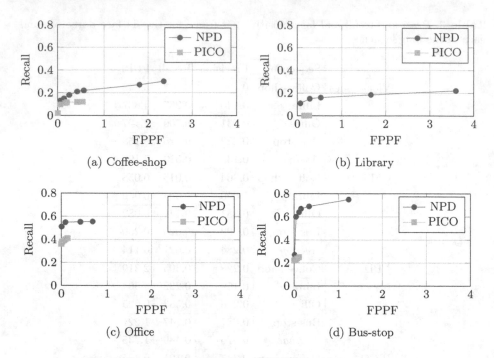

Fig. 1. ROC curves of PICO and NPD for the four sequences.

as the results obtained for O/NO and Roll, that show that all the detectors perform better with non-occluded faces and with low in-plane rotation (roll angle).

On the contrary, results concerning RMSC and NDFC deserve some comments. Regarding the sensitivity to the RMS contrast, Table 2 shows that the detectors can be divided into two groups: NPD, PICO and Viola-Jones exhibit rather small sensitivity to the contrast, while the remaining detectors perform more poorly at low contrast. A possible explanation is that NPD, PICO, and Viola-Jones are based on ad hoc features consisting of differences of intensity values that are either normalized (NPD), or computed over a normalized candidate window (Viola-Jones) or simply, contribute to the decision function based on the difference sign only; in all the three cases, however, contrast insensitivity is incorporated in the detector, at the level of features. We do not know the details of the other detectors, but we conjecture that none of them is based on contrast-insensitive features.

As far as the normalized distance from center (NDFC) is considered, Table 2 shows that all the detectors perform better with off-center faces. This is surprising because off-center faces undergo major distortions due to wide angle optics and one would expect the opposite result. By looking to the sequences, one may argue that this result is due to the different size of the faces close to the center w.r.t. that far from the center. However, since the detectors have a diverse behavior w.r.t. the size of the faces (see results for NBBA), that explanation

Table 4. Influence of faces features on recall: average recall achieved by different methods computed on annotated faces having the feature value below or above the reference threshold τ (for numeric features, see Table 2) or equal to a given value (for categorical features).

Method	NBBA		NDFC		Roll		RMSC		L/NL		O/NO	
	$< \tau$	$\geq \tau$	$< \tau$	$\geq \tau$	$< \tau$	$\geq \tau$	$< \tau$	$\geq \tau$	NL	L	NO	O
Face-Id	0.001	0.001	0.001	0.002	0.001	0.000	0.000	0.002	0.001	0.001	0.002	0.000
GMS	0.006	0.039	0.004	0.041	0.041	0.002	0.006	0.039	0.044	0.001	0.043	0.002
NPD	0.304	0.160	0.122	0.342	0.443	0.009	0.277	0.188	0.441	0.024	0.441	0.023
PICO	0.054	0.143	0.046	0.151	0.190	0.005	0.093	0.104	0.196	0.001	0.187	0.010
Viola-Jones	0.364	0.149	0.148	0.366	0.491	0.004	0.325	0.189	0.486	0.027	0.475	0.038
Visage	0.002	0.018	0.002	0.018	0.019	0.000	0.003	0.017	0.019	0.001	0.020	0.000

must be rejected. We plan to investigate this point in future work, by considering the co-distribution of the NDFC and other features, such as lateral/non-lateral, occluded/non-occluded, roll angle and other (for instance, the sharpness of the bounding box).

5 Conclusions and Future Work

We considered the problem of FPV systems for the improvement of social interactions of visually impaired persons and, in particular, the task of face detection on video sequences captured by devices worn by the blind person. We evaluated the effectiveness of six face detectors on a set of four sequences which have been captured purposely basing on the considered application: the video sequences exhibit specific disturbances and effects related to the acquisition machinery and scenario. We systematically took into account those disturbances and effects by defining a set of six quantitative features on which we based a sensitivity analysis of the face detectors effectiveness.

Our comparative experimental evaluation shows that the considered detectors perform poorly in the considered application, with figures suggesting that their usage would be hardly practical in the general task of detecting all faces in the frame. Indeed, a possible future expansion of the present study consists in considering a more specific application: for instance, the detection of faces of persons who are approaching the visually impaired user, or of persons who are actively interacting with the user as a premise for a subsequent facial expression recognition.

Acknowledgment. This work has been supported by the University of Trieste - Finanziamento di Ateneo per progetti di ricerca scientifica - FRA 2014, and by a private donation in memory of Angelo Soranzo (1939–2012).

References

1. Online: Be my eyes. http://www.bemyeyes.org
2. Jin, Y., Kim, J., Kim, B., Mallipeddi, R., Lee, M.: Smart cane: face recognition system for blind. In: Proceedings of 3rd International Conference on Human-Agent Interaction, HAI 2015, pp. 145–148. ACM, New York (2015)
3. Chaudhry, S., Chandra, R.: Design of a mobile face recognition system for visually impaired persons. CoRR abs/1502.00756 (2015)
4. Carrato, S., Fenu, G., Medvet, E., Mumolo, E., Pellegrino, F.A., Ramponi, G.: Towards more natural social interactions of visually impaired persons. In: Battiato, S., Blanc-Talon, J., Gallo, G., Philips, W., Popescu, D., Scheunders, P. (eds.) ACIVS 2015. LNCS, vol. 9386, pp. 729–740. Springer, Cham (2015). doi:10.1007/978-3-319-25903-1_63
5. Zafeiriou, S., Zhang, C., Zhang, Z.: A survey on face detection in the wild: past, present and future. Comput. Vis. Image Underst. **138**, 1–24 (2015)
6. Hsu, G.S., Chu, T.Y.: A framework for making face detection benchmark databases. IEEE Trans. Circuits Syst. Video Technol. **24**(2), 230–241 (2014)
7. Carrato, S., Marsi, S., Medvet, E., Pellegrino, F.A., Ramponi, G., Vittori, M.: Computer vision for the blind: a dataset for experiments on face detection and recognition. In: Proceedings of 39th International Convention on Information and Communication Technology, Electronics and Microelectronics, pp. 1479–1484. Mipro Croatian Society, Opatija (2016)
8. Fazzi, E., Lanners, J., Danova, S., Ferrarri-Ginevra, O., Gheza, C., Luparia, A., Balottin, U., Lanzi, G.: Stereotyped behaviours in blind children. Brain Dev. **21**(8), 522–528 (1999)
9. Bonetto, M., Carrato, S., Fenu, G., Medvet, E., Mumolo, E., Pellegrino, F.A., Ramponi, G.: Image processing issues in a social assistive system for the blind. In: 2015 9th International Symposium on Image and Signal Processing and Analysis (ISPA), pp. 216–221. IEEE (2015)
10. Frazor, R.A., Geisler, W.S.: Local luminance and contrast in natural images. Vis. Res. **46**(10), 1585–1598 (2006)
11. Viola, P., Jones, M.J.: Robust real-time face detection. Int. J. Comput. Vis. **57**(2), 137–154 (2004)
12. Liao, S., Jain, A.K., Li, S.Z.: A fast and accurate unconstrained face detector. IEEE Trans. Pattern Anal. Mach. Intell. **38**(2), 211–223 (2016)
13. Markuš, N., Frljak, M., Pandžić, I.S., Ahlberg, J., Forchheimer, R.: Object detection with pixel intensity comparisons organized in decision trees (2013). arXiv preprint arXiv:1305.4537
14. Dundar, A., Jin, J., Martini, B., Culurciello, E.: Embedded streaming deep neural networks accelerator with applications. IEEE Trans. Neural Netw. Learn. Syst. (2016, to appear)
15. Kuhn, H.W.: The Hungarian method for the assignment problem. Nav. Res. Logist. Q. **2**(1–2), 83–97 (1955)
16. Fenu, G., Jain, N., Medvet, E., Pellegrino, F.A., Pilutti Namer, M.: On the assessment of segmentation methods for images of mosaics. In: Proceedings of 10th International Conference on Computer Vision Theory and Applications (VISIGRAPP 2015), pp. 130–137 (2015)

A Serious Games System for the Analysis and the Development of Visual Skills in Children with CVI

A Pilot Study with Kindergarten Children

Ombretta Gaggi[1,3](✉), Teresa Maria Sgaramella[2,3], Laura Nota[2,3], Margherita Bortoluzzi[2,3], and Sara Santilli[2,3]

[1] Department of Mathematics, Padua, Italy
ombretta.gaggi@unipd.it
[2] Department of Philosphy, Sociology, Education and Applied Psychology, Padua, Italy
{teresamaria.sgaramella,laura.nota}@unipd.it,
margherita.bortoluzzi89@gmail.com,
santilli.sara@gmail
[3] Centro di Ateneo Disabilità Riabilitazione e Integrazione, Università degli Studi di Padova, Padua, Italy

Abstract. The development of visual skills is crucial in sustaining an adaptive cognitive and social development in children. The paper describes the result of a pilot study, involving a group of 4 years old children, with a set of serious games to improve the assessment and rehabilitation process in children with CVI. The system uses an eye tracker system to correctly measure the performances of the child and his/her capability to watch and touch a moving object at the same time and to perform ab cognitive visual decision making.

Keywords: Serious games based assessment · Rehabilitation

1 Introduction

The development of visual skills is crucial in sustaining an adaptive cognitive and social development in children. Cerebral Visual Impairment (CVI) is the leading cause of visual impairment in western countries. It is crucial then to develop procedures and activities effective in involving children in an early assessment and in the rehabilitation process. In this paper we will describe a set of serious games, with a particular emphasis on the *HelpMe!* game, created to improve the assessment and rehabilitation process in children with CVI.

Cerebral Visual Impairment (CVI), also known as Cortical Visual Impairment, is a disability that entails a visual deficit, due to a brain damage [13]. People affected by this disability need that an object is moving to be able to see it; they have a reduced ocular field and ocular delay, and find it difficult to understand complex images. Moreover, they are not able to see and touch an object at the same time: they usually watch the

O. Gaggi et al. (Eds.): GOODTECHS 2016, LNICST 195, pp. 155–165, 2017.
DOI: 10.1007/978-3-319-61949-1_17

object first, and then they try to touch it, often losing eye contact. A child affected by CVI can experience all (or a set of) these difficulties, with different level of severity. Additionally, psychological literature has shown that the development of visual skills is crucial not only for the independent movement in the environment but also both for a positive social and cognitive development [8, 12, 15].

The use of a serious game with this kind of children allows to obtain as much attention as possible from them, since they have fun, but it is very important that the game interface is fluid to adapt itself to different situations: the child can then play the game using different devices, e.g., a tablet, a computer with or without a touch monitor, etc. Moreover, the game must work even in absence of the network connection and must be configurable to adapt itself to any child with different difficulties. Finally, the game must evolve together with the improvement of the child.

Given the particular target of users, there are two main issues which should be addressed in order to increase the effectiveness of the system. First of all, the choice of an interactive modality is very important. As shown by Forlines and colleagues, the touch interfaces are a more ecological paradigm for children; indeed, they interact with the screen as they would interact with a real object [6]. For this reason, the interaction method preferred for the children interface component is a touch interface, to better involve the children to the game and naturalize the interaction with it, through a tablet or a touch monitor.

Secondly, the system integrates an eye tracker system to correctly measure the performances of the child and his/her capability to watch and touch a moving object at the same time and to perform a cognitive visual decision making.

In this paper we will describe the system and a set of three serious games developed to train and assess children affected by CVI. An initial development of the system can be found in [2]. At that time, we developed a prototype which has not been tested with children. In this paper we begin the test phase of the system involving a group of normally developing children in the study in order test the feasibility of the games and the effort needed in the learning process. Additionally, different levels of difficulty and processes were taken into account together with the recording of different performance indices to be used as baseline in the rehabilitation program against which to measure the effectiveness of the system in the habilitation/rehabilitation process.

The aim of this study was then to test the system using several tasks with a group of normally developing children; to test the adaptability of the system to various children characteristics. This will help setting the level of difficulty and sensitivity to address different clinical issues before using it in the assessment of visual skills in children with CVI and in training their ability to watch, touch and move an object at the same time, their visual problem solving skills.

The paper is organized as follows: Sect. 2 discusses background with related works, Sect. 3 describes the three serious games and Sect. 4 provides some details about system development and architecture. In Sect. 5, a pilot study with kindergarten children is described. Finally, Sect. 6 presents conclusions and directions of research studies.

2 Background

Serious games, i.e., games or applications developed not only for fun, but to propose, under a game, exercises helpful in developing particular skills of the user, have been developed in several different contexts and applications are known for example in the military field, in the governmental field and also in the education field [11].

Serious games are becoming very important also in clinical setting both for professionals, to train or to simulate real-life experiences, and for patients, for instance, to hide rehabilitation and rehabilitation exercises under a game. Esteban et al. developed a system to combine 3D computer simulation to the learning process for new doctors, to teach them particular procedures [5].

Several studies show the goodness of the usage of serious games with children. De Bortoli and Gaggi showed how a visual acuity test can be hidden under a much more interesting game, with the consequence that children pay much more attention and the diagnosis is more accurate [3]. Other authors [4, 7] showed that non-expensive equipment and serious games can open opportunities for home rehabilitation, reducing the *drop-out-from-therapy* phenomenon, and improving the effectiveness of rehabilitation programs. This is the case for instance, of children with CVI.

An early assessment and intervention can increase the possibility for children with CVI to drastically reduce the effects of this deficit [10]. A good diagnosis can be achieved only with the total collaboration and attention of the patient, but test exercises (like Lea symbols) are extremely boring and children usually do not pay much attention the answers they give. So, the diagnosis may become inaccurate.

Serious game can support effectively the diagnostic as well as the rehabilitation process. Campana has shown that, in children with CVI, simple iPad games which did not address specific goals (i.e., *Bubbles Magic*), but presenting words or pictures and playing different sounds on the device, are effective in orienting attention to the tablet and to what happens on the screen [1].

Tap-n-see Zoo is a game specific for children with CVI where a teddy bear moves on the screen and a sound is heard by the child when he/she taps on it. In order to use this system to track the development or improvement in visual skills, there is the need to integrate the serious game with an eye-tracker system to record the child's eyes movement during the rehabilitation program and to better measure his/her improvements. We developed this improvement in our system and we also propose a game to train a specific skill: the *problem*-solving capabilities of the child.

3 The Serious Games Activities

Our system proposed three serious games which consisted in different interactive situations through which the typical development and assessment of visual abilities in children is conducted. During the execution indices related to eye movements, accuracy, response time and completion task time, are collected and later analyzed.

A. *Where is Nemo going?* This is the first situation proposed, which we use to calibrate the eye tracker. Participants are asked to look to the goldfish Nemo, which move though 5 points on the screen. This step allows also the participant to practice with the system. Eye movements across different quadrants of the visual field are stimulated in the child since Nemo is placed in the four corners and its midpoint.

B Where is Peppa/George going? With this game, we ask children to orient their attention. Children must follow a stimulus, a cartoon character chosen according to participant gender, which is moving on the screen. The situation stimulates eye movements and attention shift across different quadrants of the visual field.

C. Help me! The Santa Claus's assistant. Children are trained in more complex visual processing requiring cognitive decision making. The location of the game is the North Pole, in particular at Santa Claus' laboratory. Participants are asked to help Santa Klaus in a long lasting task, that is preparing in advance the bags of Christmas presents. Pictures of objects belonging to three different target semantic categories (animals, vehicles and clothing) are used together with objects belonging to other categories (intruders) taking into account the age of acquisition and the organization of the semantic lexicon at children's age. Each level of the game has a different set of target semantic objects, e.g., "musical instruments", "clothes for dolls", "cars" and so on, each of which is composed by a set of different images that show objects belonging to that particular semantic category.

Participants are then required to orient the attention and focus on an object; to discriminate between target images (i.e., images that belong to the target category) and intruders, and make a cognitive decision putting the firsts into Santa Claus' sack, and throwing out of the screen the other ones. Figure 1(a) depicts the game interface dedicated to the children. Eye and touch movements are recorded by the system and showed to the doctor (see Fig. 1(b)).

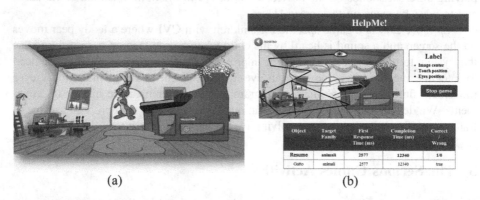

(a)   (b)

Fig. 1. (a) Screenshot of the child interface of the game '*Help me! The Santa Claus's assistant*'; (b) Screenshot of the doctor interface of the game '*Help me! The Santa Claus's assistant*'.

To avoid that the child becomes more interested on the background image instead of the objects presented on the screen, the background image was made as easier as possible, avoiding a large use of details.

Each level is described inside the system by a target category, the number of target images and intruders which compose that level and the maximum amount of time (in seconds) the child can use to give an answer. Every level is organized with a sequence of images, both target and intruders, organized according to a specific pattern previously established.

Orienting sounds and audio are also used to guide the child during the game, i.e., to give the first instructions, to tell the child which is the target family coming next, to provide live feedback about his behavior and choices, etc.

If the child fails to discriminate one of the images of a particular set of pictures, the child is asked to repeat the actions. After three failures in the same level, the game moves to the next sequence.

4 The System: Architecture and Implementation Issues

The system used here was initially presented in [2] and goes under a process of adjustments and improvements. We report here the main issue and we refer to [2] for detail information.

The design of the system architecture has been deeply influenced by the need of being used in very different scenarios, e.g., kindergarten, doctor's offices, children' house, and has to transform its user interfaces gracefully, in order to adapt itself to the different characteristics of each environment and to remain usable by all the children with any kind of devices. As an example, the system should work even in absence of Internet connectivity which is necessary only to send to the server the information stored during the rehabilitation made at home. The server receives this information, saves them and calculates an evaluation of each exercise. All the information are stored in the database to provide to the doctor the possibility to watch a simulation of the rehabilitation program performed by the user and his/her progress

However, the system does not need to provide all its features in all situations, but it must be robust in case some components are lacking e.g., even if the eye tracker is not available when a child is at home, the system must provide the possibility to play the game even with the child computer or tablet. In this case the system will record only the touch interactions of the child and not the movement of the eyes.

For this reason, the system has been structured in four different components, following a client-server architecture. In particular, our system includes:

1. a server, which manages, synchronizes and stores data produced from the other components;
2. an eye-tracker system that produces information relative to eyes position;
3. the user interface for the children, i.e., a component responsible to present the game and manage child interactions (see Fig. 1 (a));
4. the user interface for the doctor, i.e., a component which is able to present data collected on the child performances (see Fig. 1(b)). Moreover, it gives to the doctor the possibility to change the game behavior to better adapt it to a specific patient.

All the components have been developed as much independent as possible, so that they can be removed, or replaced in the future. This is particular important both to adapt the system to particular situations, e.g., the absence of the eye tracker system or if the child uses a tablet instead of a computer to perform his/her rehabilitation exercises, and to allow an easy reconfiguration of the system. As an example, we substitute the original open source eye tracker system used in [2] with the professional Eye Tribe Tracker Pro[1] without the need to change the anything in the other components. Moreover, all components can reside, all together, in the same computer: as an example we used a Microsoft Surface 4, 4 GB RAM, Inter Core i5, with an additional external monitor, during our pilot study. We need the external monitor since we need to interface, one for the doctor and one for the child.

Two specific components, one for the child to play the game, and one for the doctor to manage the game settings and to provide online information about children behavior, manage the user interface. To better involve the children to the game and naturalize the interaction with it, we use a touch interface. However, it is possible to interact with a mouse if a touch device is not available.

To address portability, the game and the child interface must be usable on any device. For this reason, the application has been developed as a Rich Internet Application (RIA), a web application that works with lots of data elaborated both by the client and the server, exchanged in an asynchronous way, with a look and feel similar to desktop application.

We developed our application using the new HTML5 standard, which is nowadays widely supported and that does not require to download a specific plugin and offers two important features which improve portability of the system: local storage and cache manifest. When a cache manifest file is associated to an HTML page, the browser reads this files and downloads all the files listed in its cache, that are all the files necessary to provide the requested page. In this way, we have a performance improvement (the browser does not need to download all the file every time) and the browser can provide the application even without Internet connectivity.

The client-server communication is based on a simple protocol of packets exchanging encoded into the JSON format. The protocol has been developed using Web Socket API, a new feature of HTML5 which allows to defines a new communication protocol that creates a full-duplex single socket connection between server and client [9].

The WebSocket protocol is implemented, at client side, by the browser. At the server side we implemented the server component using Java 7, using a Java implementation of the server which supported the last specification of the WebSocket protocol and handshake.

The usage of the WebSocket protocol provides several improvements in real-time application performances. Firstly, it reduces the amount of overhead introduced in each information packet, reducing the throughput necessary to send all the packets. Secondly, it reduces latency, because after the initial handshake between the client and the server, every time the server has new data for the client it can send it immediately, without waiting for a new request from the client (like the polling technique). Moreover, WebSocket allows to provide to the doctor a real-time feedback about the behavior of the child, with information packets sent every 40 ms (limited by

---

[1] https://theeyetribe.com/.

eye-tracker performances). Figure 1 (b) shows the doctor interface: the server receives, records and sends to the doctor client the movements of the image (the red line), of the user touch (the light green line) and of the gaze (the black line) along the time. In this way, the doctor is able to watch what is happening on the child side, viewing where the child is touching, how he/she is moving the image on the screen, and where he/she is watching. Furthermore, we provide several summary information about child choices and interaction with the game.

Our system is also able to store data about patients' exercise for further consultation by doctors. The doctor can consult data during the child exercises or offline, for further analysis. For each session game an XML file stores information about the used device, the screen size, etc. Information about the image position on the screen, the touch interaction of the child and where the eyes are watching on the screen are stored into three different text files, in which each entry, i.e., a packet, follows the pattern $<\Delta T$; $left;$ $top>$ where ΔT is the timestamp, and $left$ and top contains the left position and the top position of the recorded element (the touch position, the center of the image or where the eyes are watching) on the screen. Even the exercises settings used by the doctor for each child are stored in the server with an XML file (every child has his own settings associated), providing the possibility to the doctor to use several times the same exercise with the same child, avoiding him to insert every time the same settings (this is particular important for performances analysis for the doctor).

The application has been successfully tested with Chrome from version 14.0, Firefox from version 11.0, Safari from version 5.0 and Opera from version 12.0.

An important issue that our system has to deal with is the synchronization of the components. As we will see in the next section, data about children exercises are measured in milliseconds. Therefore, if system components are distributed in different computers, it is very important to synchronize information coming from eye-tracker and child interface.

Therefore, the main task of the server is to synchronize and store this information during the session game, in order to avoid loss of data, so to define a common initial time zero shared by all the components.

Due to the natural difference between clocks in different autonomous computers, the starting time for the game and the eye-tracking software will be different. But this different times have to represent the same UCT time, in order to start their operation at the same moment. In this way, if two packets have the same ΔT, i.e. the offset from the beginning of the game, the information provided are relative to the same moment. The algorithm used to synchronize the starting times for all the components is based on the work by Sichitiu and Veerarittiphan [14]. This synchronization step usually requires less than a minute and must be performed only once for each component, the first time it is connected to the system.

5   A Pilot Study with Kindergarten Children

A pilot study was carried out involving 20 children whose age ranged from 4 years to 4 years and 10 months, who attended a Nursery School in the city of Padova. None of the participants presented developmental issues.

Table 1. Analysis of Pearson's correlations between indices recorded in the game

MEANS	1	2	3	4	5	6	7	8	9	10	11	12
1.Animals Target Response Time	-	.893**	.485*	.625**	.304	.212	.566**	.252	.304	.645**	.455*	.540*
2. Animals Intruder Target Response Time		-	.619**	.880**	.652**	.258	.765**	.289	.134	.321	.648**	.235
3. Animals Target Completion Time			-	.680**	.534*	.562**	.541*	.635**	.504*	0.041	.866**	.471*
4. Animals Intruder Completion Time				-	.714**	.548*	.738**	.644**	.167	.149	.840**	.169
5. Vehicles Target Response Time					1	.537	.591**	.637**	.444*	.213	.672**	.281
6.Vehicles Intruder Response Time						-	.514*	.746**	.501*	0.37	.583**	.550*
7. Vehicles Target Completion Time							-	.567***	.175	.222	.649**	.284
8. Vehicles Intruder Completion Time								-	.568**	.227	.748**	.498**
9. Clothing Target Response Time									-	.715**	.467*	.813**
10. Clothing Intruder Response Time										-	.530*	.938**
11. Clothing Target Completion Time											-	.283
12. Clothing Intruder Completion Time												-

Procedure The activity was proposed to children individually and articulated in a session lasting about 45–50 min. It was carried out in the reading room of the kindergarten. The activity required the presence of two operators dedicated respectively to the equipment and children characteristics (e.g., tallness and distance from the screen), task instruction and analysis of the recorded responses.

Results The correct answers, response and completion times recorded in the '*Help me! Santa Claus's assistant*' game have been analyzed insofar they are relevant for the issues addressed here: response time refers to the time needed to touch the picture appeared on the screen (either target or intruder), while the completion time refers to the time needed to put the object in Santa's sack or to take it out of the screen.

The performance recorded evidence that the majority of participants is capable of correctly executing the game on the first run, with a percentage of correct answers equal to or higher than 90%. The remaining 10% of participants correctly complete the game within the third presentation.

Analysis of Pearson's correlations between indices recorded in the game (see Table 1) highlights significant positive correlations between the response time and the completion time of the task for each category. More specifically a positive relationship was found between the time required to direct the attention and initiate the response and the time needed to take and carry out the semantic decision.

Response times recorded for each semantic category suggest specific decision-making patterns for the different categories in response activation and completion times (see Table 2).

Table 2. Means and standard deviations of response and completion time respectively for target items and intruders, in the semantic categorization task (*Santa Claus' assistant* task).

	RESPONSE TIMES		COMPLETION TIMES	
	M	DS	M	DS
ANIMALS – target	6006,42	4733,921	9759,02	5815,76
ANIMALS – intruder	6109,80	3386,81	9548,83	10203,97
VEHICLES – target	3148,90	2229,05	5752,00	5446,14
VEHICLES – intruder	6750,00	9318,25	9780,00	9725,55
CLOTHING – target	2481,97	2037,00	4210,17	2469,62
CLOTHING – intruder	1684,00	897,40	5493,67	1385,16

In particular, results from t-tests show that to decide that a stimulus does not belong to the semantic category (intruder) requires a longer time than deciding that a stimulus (target) belongs to a specific category, namely animals (t = −5.85, df 19, p = .001), vehicles (t = 2.831, df 19, p = .01) or clothing (t = −3.257, df 19, p = .004).

6 Conclusions and Future Directions

The aim of the study was twofold, i.e., to test the system with a group of normally developing children and the adaptability of the system to the variability of children characteristics before using in the clinical setting. Moreover, we want to test the adequacy and sensitivity of a set of games with increasing difficulty in the assessment of the ability to watch, touch and move an object at the same time, to test their visual problem solving skills.

As regards the content and the information gathered from the games, there are some relevant conclusions which are preliminarily suggested by the study.

First of all, the proposed tasks are well accepted and agreeable to participants. As highlighted by the accuracy level, the games are very easy to understand in 4 years old children, who can deal with them flawlessly. When a difficulty occurs, children easily learn how to correctly execute them. As regards the information gathered from the serious game 'Help me!' data collected underlines its usefulness in analyzing two distinct, but related, levels of visual processing; analyzing a more complex cognitive processing of visual information and decision making in children.

This test suggested us some procedural and methodological issue for the use with CVI children. In order to maximize the effectiveness, it is important to properly prepare the setting for an effective performance: child sitting and instrumentation, position of the chair, audio adequacy, and it is important to provide repeated feedback throughout the games.

Moreover, initial tests with children affected by CVI have provided good results in terms of acceptability of the system, so, given that, these games are intended for a long period of rehabilitation, we are currently developing the system to be accessible from the Internet, providing a specific user-dedicated interface, so that the user can be trained at home, thus reducing the *drop-out-from-therapy* phenomenon.

References

1. Campana, L.: iPad apps for children with visual impairments. In: Proceedings of CTEVH (2012)
2. Ciman, M., Gaggi, O., Nota, L., Pinello, L., Riparelli, N., Sgaramella, T.M.: HelpMe!: a serious game for rehabilitation of children affected by CVI. In: WEBIST, pp. 257–262 (2013)
3. De Bortoli, A., Gaggi, O.: PlayWithEyes: a new way to test children eyes. In: Proceedings of SeGAH 2011, pp. 1–4 (2011)
4. Di Loreto, I., Gouaich, A.: Mixed reality serious games: the therapist perspective. In: Proceedings of SeGAH 2011, pp. 1–10 (2011)
5. Esteban, G., Fernandez, C., Matellan, V., Gonzalo, J.: Computer surgery 3D simulations for a new teaching-learning model. In: Proceedings of 1st SeGAH 2011, pp. 1–4 (2011)
6. Forlines, C., Wigdor, D., Shen, C., Balakrishnan, R.: Direct-touch vs. mouse input for tabletop displays. In: Proceedings of ACM CHI 2007, pp. 647–656 (2007)

7. Gaggi, O., Galiazzo, G., Palazzi, C., Facoetti, A., Franceschini, S.: A serious game for predicting the risk of developmental dyslexia in pre-readers children. In: Proceedings of ICCCN 2012, pp. 1–5 (2012)
8. Galway, T.M., Metsala, J.L.: Social cognition and its relation to psychosocial adjustment in children with nonverbal learning disabilities. J. Learn. Disabil. 44(1), 33–49 (2011)
9. IETF, Internet Engineering Task Force. The websocket protocol, RFC 6455 (2012)
10. Malkowicz, D., Myers, G., Leisman, G.: Rehabilitation of cortical visual impairment in children. Int. J. Neurosci. 116(9), 1015–1033 (2006)
11. Michael, D.R., Chen, S.: Serious games: games that educate, train and inform. Thomson Course Technology, 1st edition (2006)
12. Odom, S.L., Chandler, L.K., Ostrosky, M., McConnell, S.R., Reaney, S.: Fading teacher prompts and peer initiation interventions for young children with disabilities. J. Appl. Behav. Anal. 25(2), 307–317 (1992)
13. Roman-Lantzy, C.: Cortical Visual Impairment: An Approach to Assessment and Intervention, 1st edn. American Foundation for the Blind, New York (2007)
14. Sichitiu, M., Veerarittiphan, C.: Simple, accurate time synchronization for wireless sensor networks. In: Proceedings of IEEE WCNC 2003, pp. 1266–1273 (2003)
15. van Nieuwenhuijzen, M., Vriens, A., Scheepmaker, M., Smit, M., Porton, E.: The development of a diagnostic instrument to measure social information processing in children with mild to borderline intellectual disabilities. Res. Dev. Disab. 32(1), 358–370 (2011)

Voice Controlled Quiz for People with Hearing Impairment

Goran Bujas[1]([⊠]), Luka Bonetti[2], Zeljka Car[1], and Marin Vukovic[1]

[1] Faculty of Electrical Engineering and Computing, University of Zagreb,
Unska 3, Zagreb, Croatia
{goran.bujas, zeljka.car, marin.vukovic}@fer.hr
[2] Faculty of Education and Rehabilitation Sciences, University of Zagreb,
Zagreb, Croatia
luka.bonetti@erf.hr

Abstract. Persons with complex communication needs have difficulties in production and/or understanding of oral and/or written language. Software applications have great potential in speech rehabilitation, especially when providing visual feedback of the produced voice to users thus enabling better rehabilitation and increased user motivation. This paper presents software application for people with hearing impairment that has a form of voice controlled quiz with visual feedback of the users' input voice frequency. The proposed application is evaluated through a case study of using it as an input for on-line application for hearing-aid evaluation.

Keywords: Biofeedback · Hearing impairment · Voice controlled quiz · Complex communication needs

1 Introduction

Complex communication needs is a term referring to significant speech, language, motor and/or cognitive impairments which restrict person's ability to participate independently in society. Persons with complex communication needs are not able to communicate temporarily or permanently by using speech that is the basic mean of communication between people. They also have difficulties in production and/or understanding of oral and/or written language. They are of different ages, abilities, social status, nationality, etc.

Software solutions managed by voice have great potential in speech rehabilitation of people with complex communication needs. Proper selection of design and development technology could result in software applications that will motivate users, especially children, during rehabilitation.

In this paper we present software application for people with hearing impairment that uses biofeedback during rehabilitation. Biofeedback can be tactile or visual and software applications are most suitable for providing visual feedback. In the presented application, we analyse the user's voice frequency in real time and show its level as a bar on smartphone interface. By lowering or raising voice frequency the user selects answers to questions ("Yes", "No" and "Don't know") which can then be used as an

© ICST Institute for Computer Sciences, Social Informatics and Telecommunications Engineering 2017
O. Gaggi et al. (Eds.): GOODTECHS 2016, LNICST 195, pp. 166–175, 2017.
DOI: 10.1007/978-3-319-61949-1_18

input to various other applications such as quizzes. This functionality provides visual feedback of the input frequency to users, thus giving them the ability of better control of the produced frequency. Furthermore, answering questions in this manner can be entertaining which motivates the users for practicing their voice frequency output while using the proposed application.

The rest of the paper is organized as follows. Section 2 explains the multidisciplinary research background and an existing need for software applications managed by voice that could be used in rehabilitation of hearing impairment. The rehabilitation science findings that biofeedback significantly affects the production of standard speech and can improve rehabilitation process is explained in Sect. 3 and presents a motivation for developing the presented software solution. Software prototype and used technologies are presented in Sect. 4. Section 5 gives a case-study of using developed prototype with on-line application for hearing-aid evaluation. Finally, we conclude the paper with future research directions in Sect. 6.

2 Research Background

One of the main achievements of EU funded research[1] was establishment of multidisciplinary Competence Network for Innovative Services for Persons with Complex Communication Needs. The Competence Network has been established to provide a framework for its members to cooperate in education, research, development and innovation, joint applications for projects and establishing a dialogue with European and national government bodies and agencies responsible for the development of an inclusive society. Competence network members are University of Zagreb and University of Osijek faculties in the fields of electrical engineering and computing, education and rehabilitation, psychology and graphic arts. Also the members are parental and professional non-governmental associations, polyclinic for consultative health protection of persons with problems of speech communication and several hi-tech and software SMEs.

Scientists and professionals closely collaborate with persons with complex communication needs and their parents and caretakers, collect and analyse their needs and try to find innovative solutions based on information and communication technology and Design for All concept. The multidisciplinary research is focused on the:

- Innovative web and mobile applications for Alternative and Augmentative Communication (AAC)
- Web and Mobile Prototypes for communication and education
- Accessibility analysis of software solutions and emerging mobile devices
- Accessible native User Interfaces (UIs) and AAC service dynamic content adaptation.

---

[1] ICT Competence Network for Innovative Services for Persons with Complex Communication Needs "(ICT-AAC)" 03/2013 - 03/2015, http://www.ict-aac.hr/projekt/index.php/en/.

The research is under way for more than seven years and there is a portfolio of about 20 web, Android and iOS applications that are free and can be downloaded from Stores or Competence Network Web site.

The multidisciplinary research presented in this paper is part of Competence Network ICT-AAC activities and described research background.

3 Related Work and Benefits of Using Biofeedback

Control of voice production in speech rehabilitation of children with hearing impairment (HI children) is traditionally treated by visual or tactile feedback – i.e. biofeedback treatment [1]. Compromised hearing and auditory feedback significantly affects the production of standard speech. Therefore, speech training of HI children is often facilitated with visual representation of the essential characteristics of speech signals.

Treatments that are based on these foundations have a positive impact on learning of correct speech production [2], and are especially supported by development of software applications allowing graphical representation of speech movements in real time. Such biofeedback applications are attractive and stimulating, making clinical atmosphere more relaxing and accessible to HI children, allow clearer instructions from the therapists, and in general provide more effective training of voice and speech production [3].

Visual presentation of articulators' movement complements to some extent parts of speech signals that are filtered by hearing impairment. This association between the complementary auditory-visual input and speech production has already been noted at the beginning of the last century [4]. According to the acoustic theory of speech production, acoustic patterns of speech signals are received through hearing, processed and organized as internal experience maps [5].

However, they can deviate from the standard if the acoustic patterns of speech are not appropriately adopted, which is exactly the case with hearing impairment. The results of incorrect mapping due to improper auditory input can be various coexisting articulation and prosodic deviations from standard speech [6].

In addition to articulation errors negatively affecting speech intelligibility, voice pitch and intensity control are also important for speech intelligibility, as well as for positive experience in communication with a person with hearing impairment [7]. Visual feedback can provide a HI child with acoustic and physiological information necessary to control the invisible and complicated respiratory-phonation processes in the background of speech prosody [8]. This information would otherwise remain partially or completely unavailable due to the limitations of discrete hearing discriminatory skills that provide auditory feedback and allow the production of speech.

A HI child who learns to speak can compare his/her production efforts with the given model by tracking visual information, which gives objective feedback on the accuracy of their prosody and/or pronunciation [9].

Several studies that have examined the option of applying visual biofeedback in speech training for HI children proved that electropalatography [9, 10] and software technology of voice-games can have a positive effect on training results and duration [11–15].

Specifically in the case of prosodic skills, it has been shown that computer games that provide visual feedback about acoustic characteristics of phonation can help HI children develop more standard vocal skills, i.e. to achieve better coordination of breathing and phonation, better control of the voice pitch and its variation in speech, better control of intonation, speech intensity, voiced-voiceless contrast, as well as better control of accent and speech tempo. Therefore, it is not surprising that the market already recognizes several biofeedback software solutions, especially for the training of voice skills – a segment of speech production most suitable for their implementation. However, the most important advantage of these biofeedback solutions in clinical sense is in their creativity and innovation, user friendliness and high level of personalization. It is therefore appropriate to continuously offer new software solutions, which can be extended with improvements in speech signal processing as well as graphic and acoustic improvements. This was the goal behind creation of the presented Voice Controlled Quiz.

During prototype development the existing voice management solutions were analysed: Pah! game [16] in which the course of the game depends on the volume of the input sound, therefore it can provide good practice for controlling the voice intensity. Although it can be used in rehabilitation, this game was not primary developed as rehabilitation application.

Magic Voice [17] was created by certified speech and language pathologists to promote improved speech and language. It allows users, primary children, to initiate and move animated scenes using the power of their voice. The application is developed only for iOS devices.

Tiga Talk [18] is speech rehabilitation game and help children to learn how to make 23 core phonetic sounds through voice-controlled games that can improve speech clarity and articulation. It is developed for iOS devices only.

4 Voice Controlled Quiz

In this section we present an application designed for Android smartphones that is controlled by user voice frequency.

The Quiz is designed as a biofeedback tool for vocal training of individuals with hearing impairments. It is implemented as an Android application to be used with smartphones and tablet computers. It features interactive graphics that provide feedback to the users and is controlled by continuous phonation into the device microphone. The phonation is adapted according to the levels of desired pitch, controlled and overviewed by a speech rehabilitation therapist. The application recognizes the desired pitch levels and transforms them into visual representation, thus providing feedback to the user in real time. As the main idea of the bio-feedback is to provide a visual change on the device screen as the results of the change in phonation, such graphic information can be used to support the training of coordination and exhalation, phonation, average pitch and even intensity of voice and their changes in speech.

The idea of the application is to use voice frequency for answering any type of questions with simple answers – "yes", "no" and "don't know". Frequency in lower range produced by the user will select "yes" as an answer, middle range frequency will result in "don't know" while frequency in high range will be considered as a "no". The frequency ranges can be configured in terms of both central frequency and the upper and lower frequency definition (range of each answer). Configuring central frequency moves all the required answer ranges along the complete frequency range, thus giving the users the possibility to personalize the application to their basic voice frequency. Without this option, the application would be applicable only for certain groups of users with same or similar voice frequencies. Furthermore, definition of range boundaries, i.e. upper and lower boundaries for each answer, gives the users the ability to practice more generally (using larger ranges) and to fine-tune and focus on the desired frequencies (using smaller ranges).

The application uses TarsosDSP library [19] to perform pitch detection. TarsosDSP is a Java library for audio processing that implements several pitch estimation algorithms. The application enables selection of the following parameters:

- pitch estimation algorithm (used for evaluation)
- the lowest pitch value to be recognized
- the highest pitch value to be recognized
- ranges between each answer
- timeout, defining how long should the user hold a certain pitch in order to be selected as an answer within certain range

Pitch estimation algorithm estimates user's pitch represented in Hertz (Hz). As each person has different frequency range, application has to adapt to particular user by setting lowest and highest pitch. Users can choose between the following algorithms available through TarsosDSP library:

- Fast YIN algorithm (FFT_YIN) implemented by Matthias Mauch, Queen Mary University, London.
- YIN algorithm described in [20]
- McLeod Pitch Method algorithm (MPM) described in paper [21]
- Dynamic wavelet algorithm described in [22]
- Average Magnitude Difference algorithm (AMDF) implemented by Eder Souza and adapted for particular need of TarsosDPS library.

For evaluation purposes, we used Fast YIN which proved to be acceptable for the given purpose. However, in further evaluation we plan to examine the differences in performance between the available algorithms to see whether another algorithm will yield better recognition than the Fast YIN.

Figure 1 shows application interface. Selection scale is on the left with answers indicated by colours. Timeout gauge is in the middle and boxes indicating selected answers are on the right of the interface. Interface also contains text area with information about user input values and calculated pitch ranges for particular answer, on the right hand side of Fig. 1. This was added for evaluation purposes in order to detect how well the pitch is recognized.

Selection scale represents current user pitch. It is divided into seven areas, three of them (coloured in green, grey and red) representing accepted pitch values for particular answer. Accepted pitch values for particular answer are calculated depending on user inputted values for low and high pitch. The bottom edge of the selection scale has low

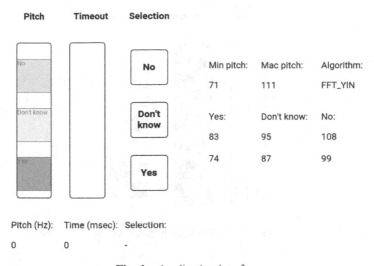

Fig. 1. Application interface

pitch value selected by the user. Top edge of the selection scale has high pitch value selected by the user. Accepted pitch values for particular answer are calculated within these limits.

Timeout scale in the middle represents amount of time necessary for selection to take effect. When user levels his voice within the limits of accepted pitch values for particular answer, the time starts to countdown. After the timeout expires, the answer is selected and is marked so by highlighting the answer in the Selection column.

As the user produces a sound, current pitch value is marked on the pitch scale. Text area on the right with reflects currently measured pitch value. As the user pitch oscillates so does the marker on the selection scale. User has to keep his pitch within the limits of accepted pitch values for particular answer for the amount of time necessary for selection to take effect, defined by timeout.

If the user pitch falls under acceptable levels or goes above acceptable levels the countdown restarts. To be able to select one of the answers a user has to retain his pitch level within the limits of accepted pitch values for particular answer for a defined amount of time (200 ms for evaluation purposes). After countdown time expires selection is made and answer box changes accordingly. An example of positive answer is presented on Fig. 2, with indicators of current pitch and timeout (blue bars).

By using timeout and graphical representation of the user's input pitch in the presented application, we encourage users to try and hold a certain pitch for a defined period of time. This is important as it encourages users to produce a constant pitch for a period of time, which is an important feature in speech production. By gradually narrowing answers' frequency ranges and extending timeout for answer selection, the users can become more and more focused on producing a desired frequency necessary for better speech performance.

Pitch   Timeout   Selection

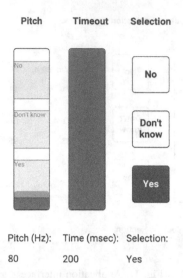

Pitch (Hz):   Time (msec): Selection:

80   200   Yes

Fig. 2. Positive answer selection and indication

5   Case Study: Using Voice Controlled Quiz with Application for Hearing-Aid Evaluation

As a case study, we used the voice-controlled quiz as an input for existing application used for hearing-aid evaluation. The hearing-aid evaluation application is a web application that was developed previously at the Department of Telecommunications in cooperation with Faculty of Education and Rehabilitation Sciences and is used for user evaluation of various hearing aids.

In short, the users are presented with a pre-recorded audio stories about various every-day topics (e.g. newspaper articles). The stories are grouped into three groups with regards to complexity of the phrases and sentences from the hearing perspective. Furthermore, a background noise is added to the pre-recorded story, with a certain variable percentage of loudness over the original story. There are several available background noise sounds from every-day, such as traffic, people talking, rain and similar. After the users listen to a story with added background noise, they are required to answer several selected questions regarding the story. The questions are presented in a form of a claim and the users have to select whether the claim is true ("yes"), false ("no") or state that they are not sure ("don't know"). The questions are used to evaluate how well did the users hear and generally understood the story despite the background noise. This can be used to evaluate the performance of hearing-aid the users are carrying and also track the users' performance over a period of time. Home screen of the hearing-aid evaluation application is shown on Fig. 3, where the users can select story difficulty level, background noise type and level, as well as the form of questions to show - text, voice or both.

Voice controlled quiz was used as an input for this application, enabling the users to respond to the presented questions by using their voice. This made answering more

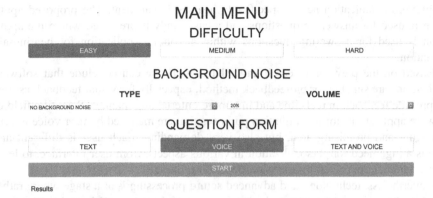

Fig. 3. Hearing-aid evaluation web application

entertaining to the users and encouraged them to focus more on their performance. For this purpose, the voice-controlled quiz application had to be adapted in a way that the user's selected answers triggered requests that were sent to the hearing-aid evaluation web application.

Initial evaluation was performed internally by ten users, mainly developers, students and faculty staff involved in the design and implementation of the application. Each answer that resulted from pitch was considered "selected" after a timeout expired, as explained in Sect. 4. Correct or incorrect selection was reported by the users, i.e. the users told us whether they wanted to select the answer or did the application failed to recognize the correct frequency range they wanted to achieve. In total, the users had to answer 15 questions in order to complete one evaluation iteration, which was mandated by the existing application for hearing–aid evaluation.

The initial results are promising since high majority of the users managed to select the answers successfully, with success rate at over 90% of the answers across all users. Furthermore, the use of voice controlled application gave the users an additional channel for answering questions and made the process more entertaining. Besides hearing-aid evaluation, the users got the ability to practice pitch production which may prove to be beneficial in the long term. However, further evaluation with external users of various backgrounds is required and will be performed in future work. We will observe two groups of users over a longer period of time and track their performance. The first group will be using standard click-based selection of correct answer and the second group will use Voice-controlled quiz application. We expect that the second group will be more motivated for using both applications and may gain benefits from practicing the desired pitch production.

6 Conclusion and Future Work

This paper presents a smartphone application that measures users' input voice frequency and displays the value in form of a bar. This is an example of visual feedback, a subset of biofeedback method that aims to provide better rehabilitation to people with complex communication needs, specifically hearing impairment. The proposed application is used for answering questions and a case study is presented where the application is used for answering questions within an online application for hearing-aid evaluation.

Based on the previous research and related work we can conclude that software applications are suitable for biofeedback method, especially for visual feedback as they can provide feedback in real-time and in a more entertaining manner. Scientific field of software applications for rehabilitation purposes that are managed by user voice is very interesting and promising area, but also very demanding. Each user is different and there is a high need for personalization in various aspects, from user interface, to level of entertainment expected by the user, depending on age.

Nevertheless, technology and advanced sound processing is at a stage where rather complex analysis can be performed even from a web browser and in real time, which will enable more and more sophisticated solutions for the purpose of speech rehabilitation.

Our future work will be focused at analysing different algorithms for sound processing in order to detect whether some users might yield better results when using different algorithms. Furthermore, we will examine the possibilities of applying machine learning methods in order to achieve automated personalization of voice controlled solutions and reduce the need to manually select the recognition boundaries.

Acknowledgement. This work has been fully supported by Croatian Science Foundation under the project 8065 "Human-centric Communications in Smart Networks".

References

1. Ling, D.L.: Speech and the Hearing-Impaired Child: Theory and Practice. Alexander Graham Bell Association for the Deaf, Washington (1976)
2. Öster, A.-M.: Clinical applications of computer-based speech training for children with hearing impairment. Department of Speech, Music and Hearing, KTH Stockholm, Stockholm (1996)
3. Tye-Murray, N.: Foundations of Aural Rehabilitation: Children, Adults, and Their Family Members, 2nd edn. Thompson Learning - Delmar Learning, Singular Publishing Group, New York (2004)
4. Liberman, A.M., Cooper, F.S., Shankweiler, D.P., Studdert-Kennedy, M.: Perception of the speech code. Psychol. Rev. **74**, 431–461 (1967)
5. Stevens, K.N.: Toward a model for lexical access based on acoustic landmarks and distinctive features. J. Acoust. Soc. Am. **111**, 1872–1891 (2002)
6. Bonetti, L.: Prediktori razumljivosti govora osoba s oštećenjem sluha. Doctoral thesis, University of Zagreb (2008)
7. Abberton, E.: Voice quality of deaf speakers. In: Kent, R.D., Ball, M.J. (eds.) Voice quality measurement, Singular Publishing Group, San Diego (2000)
8. Crawford, E.E.: Acoustic signals as visual biofeedback in the speech training of hearing impaired children, Department of Communication Disorders, University of Cantebury (2007)

9. Dagenais, P.A., Citz-Crosby, P., Fletcher, S.G., McCutcheon, M.J.: Comparing abilities of children with profound hearing impairments to learn consonants using electropalatography or traditional aural-oral techniques. J. Speech Hear. Res. **37**, 687–699 (1994)

10. Pantelemidou, V., Herman, R., Thomas, J.: Efficacy of speech intervention using electropalatography with a cochlear implant user. Clin. Linguist. Phonetics **17**(4–5), 383–392 (2003)

11. Ertmer, D.J., Maki, J.E.: A comparison of speech training methods with deaf adolescents: Spectrographic versus noninstrumental instruction. J. Speech Lang. Hear. Res. **43**(6), 1509–1523 (2000)

12. Massaro, W., Light, J.: Using visible speech for training perception and production of speech for hard of hearing individuals. Department of Psychology, University of California, Santa Cruz, CA 95064 USA (2004)

13. Ryalls, J., Le Dorze, G., Boulanger, H., Laroche, B.: Speech therapy for lowering vocal fundamental frequency in two adolescents with hearing impairments: a comparison with and without SpeechViewer. Volta Rev. **97**(4), 243–250 (1995)

14. Pratt, S.R., Heintzelmann, A.T., Deming, S.E.: The efficacy of using the IBM SpeechViewer vowel accuracy module to treat young children with hearing impairment. J. Speech Hear. Res. **36**(5), 1063–1074 (1993)

15. Shuster, L.I., Ruscello, D.M., Smith, K.D.: Evoking [r] using visual feedback. Am. J. Speech-Lang. Pathol. **1**(3), 29–34 (1992)

16. Taguri, Y.: About PAH! http://ahhhpah.com/. Accessed July 2016

17. Magic Voice. http://pocketslp.com/our-apps/magic-voice/. Accessed July 2016

18. Tiga Talk Speech Therapy Games. http://tigatalk.com/app/. Accessed July 2016

19. TarsosDSP library, https://github.com/JorenSix/TarsosDSP. Accessed July 2016

20. de Cheveigné, A., Kawahara, H.: YIN, a fundamental frequency estimator for speech and music. J. Acoust. Soc. Amer. (JASA) **111**(4), 1917–1930 (2002)

21. McLeod, P., Wyvill, G.: A smarter way to find pitch. In: Proceedings of the International Computer Music Conference, Barcelona, Spain, pp. 138–141, 5–9 September 2005

22. Larson, E.; Maddox, R.: Real-time time-domain pitch tracking using wavelets. In: Proceedings of the University of Illinois at Urbana Champaign Research Experience for Undergraduates Program, Champaign, IL, USA, 3 August 2005

Data Dissemination in a Wireless Video Surveillance Platform for Elderly Monitoring: Implementation and Experiments

Anis Harfouche[1], Saadi Boudjit[2(✉)], and Azeddine Beghdadi[2]

[1] ESI – Ecole nationale Supérieure d'Informatique, 16309 El Harrach, Algiers, Algeria
ba_harfouche@esi.dz
[2] Université Paris 13, Laboratoire de Traitement et Transport de l'Information L2TI,
99 Av J-Baptiste Clément, 93430 Villetaneuse, France
{boudjit,beghdadi}@univ-paris13.fr

Abstract. Nowadays, the number of elderly people keeps growing and represents a non negligible part of the global population in the world. Consequently, healthcare and monitoring expenses destined to them become more and more important. Indeed, receiving ageing people in dedicated infrastructures with qualified staff costs a lot of money either for them and for governments. Also, a large number of elderly prefer continue to live in their own houses rather than joining those healthcare centers. However, they could be subject to domestic accidents and the latters are often detected after a while. This work aims to setup a efficient wireless video surveillance system to help elderly people who need a permanent assistance while they prefer still living in their houses. Our main objective is to early detect and transmit via Internet any abnormal behavior or domestic accident to assistance services. For this, small cameras embedded on wireless home deployed sensors have been considered. Moreover, a simple and lightweight routing protocol for an optimized data transmission have been proposed. The whole system was implemented on an Arduino based platform on which a set of experiments were conducted.

Keywords: Wireless Sensor Networks (WSNs) · Wireless Multimedia Sensors (WMSs) · Network routing protocols · Platforms · Health databases

1 Introduction

The average age of the population tends to increase and the number of people requiring more or less home intensive monitoring is not small. Indeed, 8.2% of global population in the world are beyond 65 years old [1]. Hence, platforms for remote monitoring of elders may be of interest at different levels. First, it would allow ageing people to stay home which may have an important impact on

© ICST Institute for Computer Sciences, Social Informatics and Telecommunications Engineering 2017
O. Gaggi et al. (Eds.): GOODTECHS 2016, LNICST 195, pp. 176–185, 2017.
DOI: 10.1007/978-3-319-61949-1_19

their state of mind, a very important element in case of recovery or chronic diseases. Secondly, those platforms are cost effective and use either Bluetooth [2] or ZigBee [3] based radio transmissions to exchange data. In most cases, however, ZigBee is preferred because of its low energy consumption due to the possibility to put the radio in the sleep mode. As depicted in Fig. 1, such platforms are usually composed of sensors with embedded cameras and coordinators called sinks which collect pictures from the network and transmit them to remote databases servers. Sinks are generally linked to a computer or a smartphone/PDA that offer them different transmission technologies for Internet access (WiFi/4G). Pictures on these databases servers can be accessed through simple browsers to allow monitoring staff to have a continuous view of elders environments.

This paper presents our platform details that can be deployed in a common house, permitting the monitoring of several areas (rooms, kitchen, garden, ...) at the same time, by using small non-intrusive devices which route collected data towards sinks. The paper is organized as follows. In Sect. 2, we will present and discuss some previous works related to remote monitoring through WSNs in general and WMSNs in particular. In Sect. 3, we will give more details about our own contribution and some of its key parts. The implementation details of the proposed architecture are presented in Sect. 4. Section 5 concludes the paper and highlights some improvements that can be brought to our contribution as long as future planned works and perspectives.

2 Related Work

Several works on remote monitoring have been proposed in the literature either for health purposes or for safety checking especially for a specific category of persons as elders. The majority of them use scalar sensors embedded on those persons or setted in their environment to collect simple measures as temperature, heartbeat, blood sugar or brain activity. In Oslo University Hospital, researchers implemented and tested a Biomedical Wireless Sensor Network (BWSN) [4] where they integrated six different types of sensors; Wireless Pressure Transducer, DigiVent Pulmonary Air Leakage, CardioPatch ECG sensor, Medical UWB-IR radar, Heart Monitoring Accelerometer, SpO2 & Temperature sensors. Patients which got these sensors could keep a good mobility and met a shorter hospital stay period than usually with this procedure.

In [5,6], a system prototypes that provide distance healthcare at home have been proposed. These systems automatically measure and collect home and body parameters and transmit them to a central server through a public network. The central server analyses retrieved data to form reports about elder's activity and health state, and in case of emergency, automatically sends an alarm to assistance services through voice phone calls, SMS or E-mails.

However, works where monitoring platforms use multimedia aspect are fewer. In [7], the architecture of a monitoring platform based on WMSN is proposed. The monitored persons are equipped with smartphones to be localized by a program agent and the latter sends the localisation to image, sound and depth based sensors deployed in the environment. The sensors start to track the persons and send data back to the agent. The agent uses machine learning techniques based on usual behavior of those persons to detect any abnormal behavior and launches alerts destined to monitoring staff. For the best of our knowledge no complete implementation of this platform has been made. Moreover, the use and processing of machine learning techniques need a non negligible period of time which will impact the real time aspect of the platform.

Another platform proposed in [8] allows to detect some basic events by making images processing at sensor level. Two consecutive images are compared in order to identify a simple behavior. For example, the sensor is able to detect the event of leaving a room by first noticing nobody in front of the door in a picture followed by a picture with a person in door step and finally a last picture with nobody in front of the door. Obviously, these kind of platforms may be useful only for detecting simple events and would meet more difficulties with more complex events as human falls.

3   Our Contribution

For our solution, we considered the scenario of ageing people living in a house with several areas. For this scenario, several sensors are deployed to maintain a good coverage of all the areas where these people can be and the deployed sensors meet low mobility during network's lifetime. Moreover, we considered a multi-hop sink rooted tree topology for data transmission. Indeed, due to radio range restrictions imposed by ZigBee technology, some sensors may be too far from the sink for a direct data transmission. Therefore, we have proposed a multi-hop routing algorithm which gives the possibility to remote nodes without direct links with the sink to transmit their data to the latter through multi-hop. The general architecture of the proposed system is presented in Fig. 1. Sensor nodes exchange data with the sink which has in addition to its ZigBee interface, a WiFi interface for Internet access without the need for a PC or a PDA. Information about taken pictures are stored in a remote database server and the pictures themselves are stored in a remote file server. This allows the web application we developed, to answer requests coming from end users asking for last pictures related to a specific monitored person. The web application gets information about stored pictures from the database server and then, requests them from the file server. Due to sensor's low calculating capabilities, we are not proposing any image processing made on sensors level. Any processing on pictures can be done at servers level which offer greater processing abilities.

3.1   Data Exchange Within the Network

To take advantage of the static aspect of the nodes within the network, our routing algorithm doesn't use generic 'Hello' and 'Topology control' packets to maintain the topology as it is the case in common routing algorithms for ad hoc networks: CTP [9], MintRoute [10] or MultiHopLQI [11]. The discovery of the

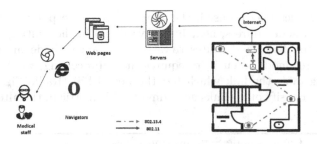

Fig. 1. General platform architecture

whole topology is realized at the initialization phase made at the beginning of the platform deployment. This may help to save network bandwidth and reduce its energy consumption. We propose a sink driven routing protocol to build a sink-rooted tree topology of the network. The sink is the only node that identifies all camera nodes present in the network and it is responsible of sending requests periodically to each camera node in order to ask for a picture. Each camera node has only a local view of the topology which helps it to route data coming from neighborhood towards the sink and requests coming from the sink towards other camera nodes (Fig. 2).

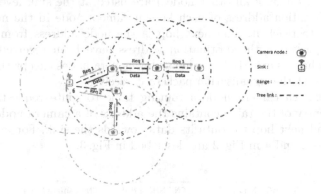

Fig. 2. Example of a tree topology

When camera nodes get launched for the first time, they start to broadcast signed signalisation packets to join the network. This first phase is called Signalisation Phase and it's pseudo-code is given in Algorithm 1. When a camera node receives a signalisation packet from an unknown source, it records the source address of the packet and the one of the node the packet have been relayed from (next hop to the source), then it broadcasts the packet itself. If it receives, however, a signalisation packet generated by an already known source but relayed by a different next hop node, it stores the source address and the new next hop address in an alternate table that would be useful in case of old next hop node failure. Two modes may be used, the simplest one is to put the first received couple (camera node address, next hop towards it) in the routing table and to store other later discovered routes towards this camera node in the alternate table. A smarter mode, even if it requires more processing, would be to keep in the routing table the link which has the best RSSI (Radio Signal Strength Indicator) and classify other links according to this metric in the alternate table.

Algorithm 1. Camera node Signalisation Phase

1: While (Signalisation Timer)
2:      Broadcast signalisation
3:      **if** (Received signalisation packet)
4:      **# source node & relay node refer to the packet**
5:          **if** (Unknown source node)
6:              Add_route(source node, relay node)
7:          **elseif** (Unknown (source node, new relay node))
8:              Add_alternate(source node, new relay node)
9:          relay node = me
10:         Broadcast the packet

After a period of time, all camera nodes which are not isolated from the network (out of range of all other nodes) are listed at the sink level. The sink keeps the destination address of each known camera node in the network and the next hop to reach it. The next hop is the node address from which the signalisation packet of the destination address have been received. The sink signalisation phase is exactly the same as for camera nodes except that the sink doesn't broadcast the signalisation packets it receives.

We use at each camera node a routing table to route requests and data packets. An entry of the table contains the address of a camera node, next hop to reach it and next hop to route its data towards the sink. For example, the tables of nodes 2 and 4 in Fig. 2 are described in Fig. 3.

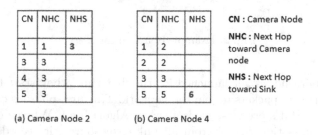

CN	NHC	NHS
1	1	3
3	3	
4	3	
5	3	

CN	NHC	NHS
1	2	
2	2	
3	3	
5	5	6

CN : Camera Node

NHC : Next Hop toward Camera node

NHS : Next Hop toward Sink

(a) Camera Node 2   (b) Camera Node 4

Fig. 3. Routing tables

First and second fields of each entry of the table are filled during Signalisation Phase, third field is filled when a sink request is received. A similar table is used at the sink with only the first and second fields, the third being useless.

At the end of the Signalisation Phase, a second phase called Collection Phase begins. The sink starts to periodically send, in a Round Robin order, unicast requests to camera nodes it has recorded in the first phase to ask for pictures. The pseudo-code of this phase is given in Algorithm 2. This technique is a very simple way to avoid additional delays generated by packets losses due to channel multiple access. Indeed, the sink is responsible of organizing data production in the network, which avert getting several data sources transmitting at the same time.

Algorithm 2. Sink Collection Phase

1: **if** (Cycle Timer Expires)
2:    **foreach:** CN in RoutingTable
3:       Send request to CN
4:       Wait for data from CN
5:       **if** (receiving data)
6:          **while** (receiving data)
7:             Concatenate in SD file
8:          Upload file's data to database
9:          Upload file to FTP server
10:      **elseif** (timer expires)
11:         **if** (NbRetransmissions reached)
12:            **if** (alternate route exists)
13:               Swap it to routingTable
14:            **else**
15:               Retransmit request packet
16:               Go to 5

At the reception of a request packet, a node verifies if it is addressed to it. If it isn't, it records the address of the node from which it got the request, this one will be the next hop towards the sink for data packets coming from the camera node specified as destination address in the request packet. Then, this intermediate node forwards the request packet to the next hop it has recorded during Signalisation Phase towards the destination camera node. When receiving a request packet addressed to it, a camera node takes a picture and starts to send data packets to sink via the node it got the request packet from. This way, request packet and data packets follow the same route (in opposite directions) for each camera node. The pseudo-code of this process is given in Algorithm 3.

If the sink (respec. a camera node) generates (respec. forwards) a request without getting back data after a period of time, it retransmits the request packet. If after several attempts no data packet is received, it suspects a failure of the next hop. If a route towards the same destination camera node is found in the alternate table, it replaces the one in the routing table and get deleted from the alternate table. If no alternate route is found, the request packet is locally dropped. In Fig. 4, we give an example of the backup scenario at sink level in case of failure of the node 3 in Fig. 2.

Algorithm 3. Packet Processing at Camera Node

```
1:  if (Received packet via a relay node)
2:    switch (packet type)
3:    Request:
4:      # Source & relay & destination refer to the packet
5:      if(destination == me)
6:        Take snapshot
7:        Send fragments to the source via relay node
8:      else
9:        NHS = relay in routingTable where CN == destination
10:       Forward request to NHC in routingTable where CN == destination
11:       if (timer expires)
12:         if (NbRetransmissions reached)
13:           if (alternate route exists)
14:             Swap it to routingTable
15:         else
16:           Retransmit request packet
17:           Go to 11
18:    Data:
19:      Forward to NHS in routingTable where CN == source
```

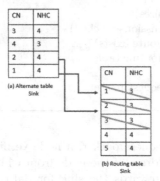

Fig. 4. Sink's routing and alternate tables

3.2 Picture's Remote Display

When the sink starts receiving data packets, it concatenates them in a picture file located in the MicroSD memory because of the lack of storage space in the memory of the node. The MicroSD acts like a buffer for the received pictures before being uploaded to remote servers. At the reception of all packets composing a picture, the sink which established a connexion to database and FTP servers at initialization phase, inserts into the database images table a novel entry where it specifies the identification of the camera node which captured the picture (ZigBee address in the network), the identification of the monitored person and the date/time of picture's capture. This 3-tuple identifies in a unique manner a picture as shown in Fig. 5. The second operation for the sink is to upload the picture to the FTP server.

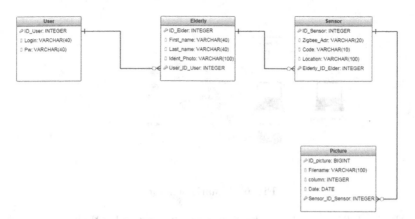

Fig. 5. Database scheme

When a user asks through a web application for pictures related to a specific person, a request is addressed to the database to get all file names of pictures related to this person. For each file name, the picture is retrieved from the FTP server and then displayed. The user can address more detailed requests by specifying an interval between two dates or by asking only for pictures of a specific area of the monitored structure.

4 Implementation

The sensors used in our platform are Arduinos Mega 2560 equipped with cameras. We used TTL Serial cameras and Wireless proto Shields with XBee S1 senders to handle ZigBee transmissions between camera nodes. It was possible for us to use a 32 bits long addresses for the nodes, however, due to the nature of the use case of our platform we opted for 16 bits addresses. The sink doesn't integrate a camera but has a Wireless WiFi Shield to connect to an access point and upload collected data into servers. This shield contains a MicroSD slot which is used by the sink to store a picture while the fragments composing it are being received. When a picture is fully received, the sink transmits its information to remote database and then uploads it into remote FTP server. We have used three servers, a MySQL database server V5.7 to store information about end-users accounts, monitored persons as long as received pictures and sensors details. A FileZilla server V0.9.49 used to store photos of monitored persons and pictures sent by sensors. Finally, a JEE based web application running on an Apache Tomcat V8.0 server. The web application communicates with FTP and database servers to retrieve pictures and information asked for by the end-user. We tried several scenarios for our network topology to retrieve pictures from nodes up to three hops far from the sink as in Fig. 6. We used a WiFi LAN to access to remote servers which were running on a laptop. The web browser to access to the web application was used on an end-user laptop. Finally, a smartphone was used as an access point.

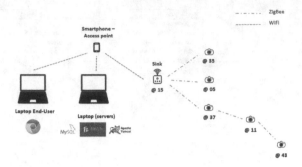

Fig. 6. Scenario scheme

At the initialization phase, the sink connects to the LAN through the access point and creates a connexion with the remote database and FTP servers. After the signalisation phase which runs for 2 min, it starts to receive data from camera nodes and to upload it to the servers. We didn't implement yet node's failure detection scheme based on alternate tables. The sink detects a non responding node if it doesn't receive data from it after a period of time following a request transmission, after what, a new request is then retransmitted.

Using NTP to keep a continuous correct time at Arduino level needs too frequent refresh and, hence, consumes more energy. In order to still be able to have the time and the date where pictures have been taken, we use a Python script at servers level to change the file name of a picture to insert time and date of its reception at the server. It also exchanges the ID of the sensor in the file name with an abbreviation of its location, which is more meaningful for the end-user.

5   Conclusion and Future Works

In this paper, we first proposed a routing algorithm for images collection in a WMSN adapted to a specific case of use which is elders monitoring in domestic areas. Then we implemented our algorithm in a generic platform based on Arduino Mega 2560 multimedia sensors. The presented solution may be seen as an alternative for regular monitoring platforms based on fixed cameras. It may offer some advantages compared to the latter in terms of mobility, simplicity of network expansion and thus covered area, and continuity of service compared to fixed cameras in case of energy breakdown (power cut off).

Finally, we have identified several ideas which could improve our platform in our future works. First, the implementation at server level of an automatic scheme for abnormal behavior detection and alert generation such as elderly falls. We will also be working on empirical studies to determine the best size of picture frames transmitted within the network to achieve the best delivery time. It would also be interesting to consider the use of scalar sensors as long as multimedia sensors; the two types being complementary for a global health and safety monitoring.

References

1. World population in 2013. http://www.worldometers.info/fr/population-mondiale/#age. Accessed June 2016
2. Bluetooth Technology - Bluetooth Special Interest Group (SIG). www.bluetooth.com
3. Zigbee Alliance - 802.15.4 Standard. www.zigbee.org
4. Eirik, N., et al.: Biomedical Wireless Sensor Network, Phase II. http://www.imatis.com/imatis/wireless-sensor-healthcarehomecare_files/BWSN%20II%20Technical%20Project%20Report_March2010.pdf. Accessed June 2016
5. Townsend, K.: Recent advances and future trends on low power wireless systems for medical applications. In: 2005 Proceedings of Fifth International Workshop on System-on-Chip for Real-Time Applications, pp. 476–478 (2005)
6. Boudra, H.: Un prototype de systeme de telesurveillance medicale base sur les capteurs et les reseaux de capteurs sans fil (2014)
7. Jin, S.-Y., Jeong, Y.-S., et al.: An intelligent multi-sensor surveillance system for elderly care. Smart CR 2(4), 296–307 (2012)
8. Al-Marakeby, A.: Camera-based wireless sensor networks for E-Health. Adv. Res. Comput. Commun. Eng. 2, 4757–4761 (2013)
9. Fonseca, R., Gnawali, O., et al.: The collection tree protocol (CTP). TinyOS TEP 123, 2 (2006)
10. Woo, A., Tong, T., et al.: Taming the underlying challenges of reliable multihop routing in sensor networks. In: Proceedings of the 1st international conference on Embedded networked sensor systems. ACM (2003)
11. Tolle, G., Levis, P., Buoadonna, P., Woo, A., Polastre, J.: MultiHopLQI protocol (2007)

A Situation Aware Information Infrastructure (SAI^2) Framework

Angelos K. Marnerides[1]([✉]), Dimitrios P. Pezaros[2], Joemon Jose[2],
Andreas U. Mauthe[1], and David Hutchison[1]

[1] InfoLab21, School of Computing and Communications,
Lancaster University, Lancaster, UK
{angelos.marnerides,a.mauthe,d.hutchison}@lancaster.ac.uk
[2] School of Computing Science, University of Glasgow, Glasgow, UK
{dimitrios.pezaros,joemon.jose}@glasgow.ac.uk

Abstract. Computer network infrastructures constitute the critical backbone of every socio-economic ICT system. Consequently, they are becoming increasingly mission-critical in our society since they provide always-on services for many everyday applications (e.g., Cloud Data Centres), safety-critical operations (e.g., Air Traffic Control networks), critical manufacturing services (e.g., Utility networks and Industrial Control Systems), and critical real-time services (e.g., Financial Trading Systems). The resilience and ability of such systems to remain operational in the face of threats is therefore paramount; this needs to be done by taking remedial action and intelligently reshaping their resources. At the same time, current communication architectures do not allow for such informed and adaptive provisioning. In this paper, we introduce the concepts, principles and current research activities related to a new Situation Aware Information Infrastructure (SAI^2) framework being developed for next generation ICT environments.

Keywords: Situation awareness · Network resilience · Security · Computer networks

1 Introduction

Undoubtedly, the adequate functionality of todays' society relies heavily on the efficiency and performance of services deployed by mission-critical socio-economic ICT systems that operate over networked infrastructures. With the rapid emergence of new areas such as the IoT, it is anticipated that future mission-critical as well as everyday end-user applications will essentially require intelligent and autonomic principles to be adhered to by the underlying networked infrastructures. Such properties will enable future underlying networked infrastructures to deploy the necessary intelligence to dynamically self-protect and self-manage their own operation, hence improve their resilience and resource provisioning.

© ICST Institute for Computer Sciences, Social Informatics and Telecommunications Engineering 2017
O. Gaggi et al. (Eds.): GOODTECHS 2016, LNICST 195, pp. 186–194, 2017.
DOI: 10.1007/978-3-319-61949-1_20

However, current networked infrastructures do not provide the necessary mechanisms to systematically assess resilience natively through a generic framework, which consequently leads to monolithic solutions targeting only partially e.g., fault-tolerance, security, or survivability [2,3]. At the same time, cross-layer resilience schemes tend to insufficiently serve the application layer end-user QoS requirements since they architecturally fail to control and manage their various embedded protocols in a scalable manner [5]. Moreover, situation-awareness under a synergistic use of contextual and operational information has been partially applied in the context of resilience for explicit services and mobile networks but never in the context of mission-critical ICT environments that engage a number of diverse networked infrastructures and services [6].

In general, current communication architectures do not allow for such informed, adaptive and intelligent resource provisioning since there does not exist a generic resilience framework that considers the overall impact of simultaneous challenges manifest in several inter-dependent physical infrastructures. For instance, legacy strategies are bespoke and monolithic (e.g., static firewalls) since they are deployed to protect specific services over specific locations of the infrastructure, against specific and mostly known threats (e.g., signature-based intrusion detection) [6]. Furthermore, network provisioning mechanisms do not incorporate situation awareness or intelligence from the system's evolution to profile infrastructure-specific behaviour, nor do they harness any local or global context (e.g., prior network attack at another facility) which would aid proactive response to adversarial events. Current anomaly detection practices operate solely on aggregate context-agnostic statistical data over long timescales and are isolated from network control and provisioning algorithms (e.g., routing) [6].

Given the aforementioned limitations, this paper introduces the notion of a Situation Aware Information Infrastructure (SAI^2) framework that is currently an on-going collaborative effort between two UK academic institutions (Lancaster University and the University of Glasgow), driven by pragmatic requirements and input by four industrial partners (The UK National Air Traffic Service - NATS, Solarflare Communications, Jisc, and Airbus Group). The proposed architecture aims to detect and remediate resilience challenges by enabling a deeper understanding of the dynamic evolution of mission-critical ICT systems through harnessing and correlating diverse internal and external network context. In this context of operation, the overarching goal of SAI^2 is to create an adaptive, situation-aware information infrastructure for future mission-critical networked environments. Hence, a range of processes derived out of network resilience, anomaly detection, content-awareness, network instrumentation and measurement, information retrieval, and filtering and semantic processing are merged in order to vertically integrate data, information, measurement and control mechanisms from different layers of the communications stack.

The remainder of this paper is structured as follows: Sect. 2 introduces the SAI^2 conceptual framework, while Sects. 3 and 4 present two schemes where SAI^2 principles are applied. Finally, Sect. 5 summarizes and concludes this paper.

2 SAI^2 Framework

The main hypothesis underpinning the development of SAI^2 is that the legacy static provisioning of networked infrastructures will not be sustainable; this is because it is content and context-agnostic, and therefore cannot adapt at the onset of adversarial events. This is particularly amplified when one considers the growing trend in co-locating critical and commodity services over converged ICT (e.g., Cloud) environments and the consequent centralisation that constitutes the actual and meta-cost of infrastructure failures and outages simply not affordable.

Figure 1 illustrates the SAI^2 conceptual framework that enables the composition of situation awareness mechanisms from harnessing diverse data sources. In general, the main scientific and technical objectives behind this framework are:

- Development of new statistical techniques derived from machine learning, signal processing and information theory to profile normal network-wide behaviour and detect incidents from aggregating diverse and distributed operational data.
- Compose modelling methods that depend on content analysis in order to adequately map infrastructure-specific context.
- Construction of an always-on, instrumentation and measurement infrastructure.
- Development of network-wide situation-aware resilience mechanisms.

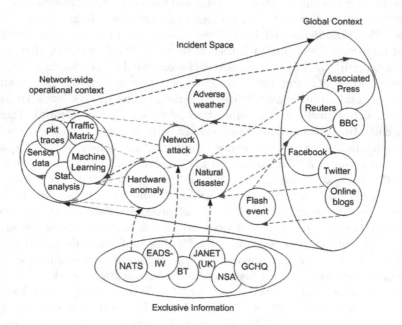

Fig. 1. The SAI^2 framework

Based on the above objectives, the on-going activities in SAI^2 have identified a number of use case studies in which situation-aware mechanisms are designed and developed(e.g., [1–3,7]). For the purpose of this paper we restrict ourselves to briefly describing two such studies in the following sections.

3   Arbitrary Packet Matching in Openflow for Enabling Situation Aware Applications

In its current form, OpenFlow [4], the *de facto* implementation of Software-Defined Networking (SDN), separates the network's control and data planes allowing a central controller to alter the match-action pipeline using a limited set of fields and actions. Even though SDN can in principle facilitate a programmable control plane capable of monitoring the network operation and of alerting the central controller at the onset of adversarial events, Openflow's inherent rigidity prevents the rapid introduction of custom data plane functionality that would enable the design of high-speed, in-band packet processing modules for, e.g., custom routing, telemetry, debugging, and security.

We argue that packet matching should be designed independently of any (control) protocol implementation, and allow the control plane to specify the matching process through a set of platform-independent instructions designed to match packets at every layer (rather than protocol version-specific and inflexible hard-coded match fields). Through such instruction set, the execution of the matching could be left as an implementation detail relying on software optimisations (such as Just In Time (JIT) compilation) or hardware acceleration using, e.g., FPGAs or ASICs.

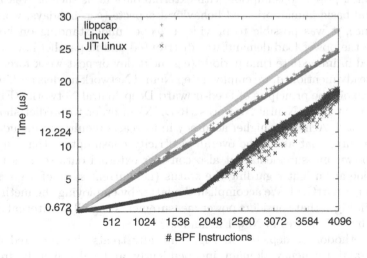

Fig. 2. Performance of different BPF engines

We have developed an arbitrary matching framework for OpenFlow switches based on the Berkeley Packet Filter (BPF) packet matching instruction set, and have defined a new OpenFlow eXtended Match field (OXM) to match packets using BPF at the switches [1]. We show that our proposed match scheme reduces the number of flow entries, allows matching on fields and protocols not supported by current OpenFlow, and mitigates the use of the SDN controller for the classification of packets unmatchable by the switch. Using diverse prototype and compiler implementations on a software switch platform, we have demonstrated the feasibility of BPF matching for line-rate processing, as shown in Fig. 2. We have further developed example programs that can be executed as part of this BPF-based arbitrary packet matching engine that include network telemetry (e.g., real-time packet size and inter-arrival time distributions computation), and lightweight (e.g., EWMA) anomaly detection that can form the basis (infrastructure-support) for natively resilient and self-managed networked environments. Such functionality is not possible using today's SDN/Openflow technology since packet matching rules are restricted to a protocol version-specific set, and do not allow for, e.g., arbitrary functionality, or even port range matching to be implemented.

4   Situation Awareness in the SmartGrid

A part of the activities within SAI^2 has placed a strong emphasis on composing solutions for the adequate profiling of power consumption in SmartGrids and further relating such measurements with diverse sources of information. In particular, we have developed and introduced short term power load forecasting schemes that rely on Deep Learning Neural Network models [8] and enable the correlation of power consumption with external data feeds such as weather conditions and basic human-oriented behavioral aspects (e.g. holidays, work hours etc.). Hence, it was possible to provide a deeper understanding on how, why and when the power load demand was distributed and in parallel how it will be distributed in immediate time periods (e.g. next day or next week forecast).

As already mentioned, we employ Deep Neural Network models and in particular we exploit the principles of Feed-froward Deep Neural Networks (FF-DNN) and Recurrent Deep Neural Networks (R-DNN) in order to predict short term electricity load. Achieving higher accuracy in forecasts requires to include all the related features that affect the overall electricity consumption that go beyond the raw power measurements but also consider external data sources that can also provide an insight regarding the status (i.e. current state of a given situation) of the SmartGrid. We accomplish the latter by employing the methodology depicted in Fig. 3 that considers power measurements as well as external datasets gathered by 6 US states in New England[1].

The methodology depicted in Fig. 3 initially treats the gathered data on the time and frequency domain independently and subsequently frequency

---

[1] ISO New England Dataset: http://www.iso-ne.com/isoexpress/web/reports/load-and-demand.

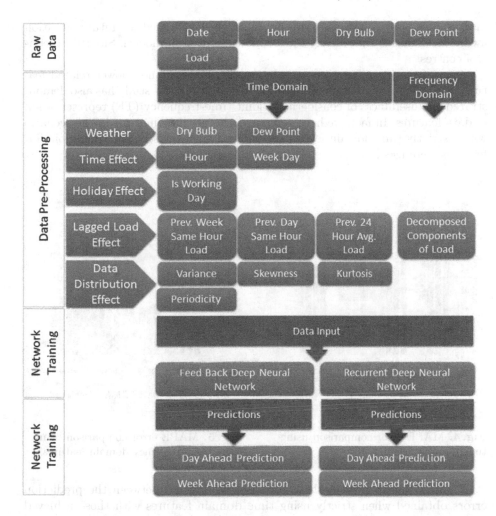

Fig. 3. Visual description of load prediction methodology

domain components are transformed back to the time domain. The resulted time-frequency (TF) features efficiently capture dominant effects i.e. weather, time, working and non-working days, lagged load and data distribution effects, thus providing an insight on the current and potential state of the SmartGrid. Nonetheless, due to the constantly changing environment, electricity consumption patterns of domestic as well as commercial users carry complex characteristics. Hence, these characteristics are analyzed in time and frequency domain where we compare the prediction performance of the utilized deep neural network models on the basis of the Root Mean Square Error (RMSE), Mean Average Error (MAE) and Mean Absolute Percentage Error (MAPE) error metrics. As we present in our recent work in [8], the results obtained with the presented methodology indicate least MAPE errors as compared to other existing models (e.g., [9]). Thus, they can be definitely considered for future situation aware mechanisms that ideally can be instrumented in modern SmartGrid control centres.

Apart from identifying the correlations between the non-power related features with the actual power consumption distribution, this study has also demonstrated the usefulness of considering a joint time-frequency (TF) representation of data features. In fact, we have compared the prediction errors in the scenario where strictly time domain features were used with the scenario where join TF features were used.

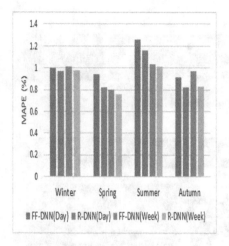

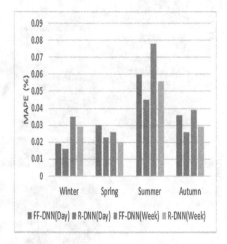

Fig. 4. MAPE error comparison using time domain features.

Fig. 5. MAPE error comparison using joint time-frequency domain features.

Figures 4 and 5 present the comparison conducted between the prediction errors obtained when strictly using time domain features with those achieved with the use of TF data metafeatures of the original raw datasets. The comparison was performed for predictions generated for the "next day" and "next week" power consumption from data sampled randomly in the various seasons (i.e. winter, autumn, spring and summer) of the year 2011 throughout all the 6 US states in New England, USA. As evidenced, the MAPE metric resulted to hold much smaller values in the scenario of using TF features rather than those obtained when time domain features were used. Thus, the prediction accuracy was much more improved.

In general, the contribution behind this work lies with the utilisation of a time-frequency (TF) feature selection procedure from the actual "raw" dataset that aids the regression procedure initiated by the use of Deep Neural Networks (DNNs). We show that the introduced scheme may adequately learn hidden patterns and accurately determine the short-term load consumption forecast by utilising a range of heterogeneous sources of input that relate not necessarily with the measurement of load itself but also with other parameters such as the effects of weather, time, holidays, lagged electricity load and its distribution over the period. Overall, our generated outcomes reveal that the synergistic use of TF feature analysis with DNNs enables to obtain higher accuracy by capturing dominant factors that affect electricity consumption patterns and can surely contribute significantly in the context of situation awareness for the recently introduced SmartGrid.

5 Conclusions

Situation awareness is acknowledged as a critical property in which next generation, mission-critical ICT environments are required to possess in order to confront the dynamic and unpredictable behaviour of their use as well as to maintain their overall resilience. In order to achieve situation awareness that will essentially offer societal and economical benefits, it is quite important to devise mechanisms that are not strictly dependent on the explicit properties of a given system but rather consider external and diverse sources of information. Therefore, in this paper we have briefly presented the main principles and some of the on-going activities conducted within the SAI^2 project. We have introduced the SAI^2 framework and initially described an SDN-based scheme that can aid towards the dynamic deployment of applications that can serve situation awareness. In addition, we have presented a use case study that aims on strengthening situation awareness in the SmartGrid scenario by exploiting the regression capabilities of Deep Neural Networks by harnessing diverse sources of information. We argue that the work reported herein can set concrete foundations towards the refinement of situation aware mechanisms and further establish a strong basis for future design of resilience mechanisms for next generation mission-critical ICT systems.

Acknowledgments. The work has been supported in part by the UK Engineering and Physical Sciences Research Council (EPSRC) grants EP/N033957/1, EP/L026015/1, and EP/L005255/1. The authors are grateful to Simon Jouet, Long Chen, Noor Shirazi, Steven Simpson and Ghulam Mohi Ud Din for their valuable input.

References

1. Jouet, S., Cziva, R., Pezaros, D.P.: Arbitrary packet matching in openflow. In: 16th IEEE International Conference on High Performance Switching and Routing (IEEE HPSR), Budapest, Hungary, 1–4 July 2015
2. Marnerides, A.K., Bhandari, A., Murthy, H., Mauthe, A.U.: A multilevel resilience framework for unified networked environments. In: 2015 IFIP/IEEE International Symposium on Integrated Network Management (IM), Ottawa, ON (2015)
3. Ariffin, M.A.M., Marnerides, A.K., Mauthe, A.U.: Multi-level resilience in networked environments: concepts & principles. In: IEEE CCNC 2017, Las Vegas, NV, USA (2017, to appear)
4. McKeown, N., Anderson, T., Balakrishnan, H., Parulkar, G., Peterson, L., Rexford, J., Shenker, S., Turner, J.: Openflow: enabling innovation in campus networks. In: ACM SIGCOMM, March 2008

5. Sterbenz, J., Hutchison, D., Cetinkaya, E., Jabbar, A., Rohrer, J., Schoeller, M., Smith, P.: Redundancy, diversity, and connectivity to achieve multilevel network resilience, survivability and disruption tolerance. J. Telecommun. Syst. **56**(1), 17–31 (2014)
6. Marnerides, A.K., Schaeffer-Filho, A., Mauthe, A.: Traffic anomaly diagnosis in Internet backbone networks: a survey. Comput. Netw. **73**, 224–243 (2014). http://dx.doi.org/10.1016/j.comnet.2014.08.007. ISSN 1389–1286
7. Watson, M.R., Shirazi, N., Marnerides, A.K., Mauthe, A., Hutchison, D.: Malware detection in cloud computing infrastructures. IEEE Trans. Dependable Secure Comput. **13**(2), 192–205 (2016)
8. Ud Din, G.M., Marnerides, A.K.: Short term power load forecasting using deep neural networks. In: IEEE International Conference on Computing, Networking and Communications (ICNC) 2017, Silicon Valley, USA, January 2017, to appear
9. Fan, S., Hyndman, R.J.: Short-term load forecasting based on a semi-parametric additive model. IEEE Trans. Power Syst. **27**(1), 134–141 (2012)

Delay Tolerant Networking
for the Socio-Economic Development
in Rural South Africa

Adriano Galati[1]([✉]), Aleksejs Sazonovs[1], Maria Olivares[1], Stefan Mangold[2],
and Thomas R. Gross[3]

[1] Disney Research Zurich, Stampfenbachstrasse 48, 8006 Zurich, Switzerland
adriano.galati@disneyresearch.com
[2] Lovefield Wireless, 3097 Liebefeld, Switzerland
[3] Department of Computer Science, ETH Zurich,
Universitätstrasse 6, 8092 Zurich, Switzerland

Abstract. Rural areas in economically developing regions often suffer from a slow and unreliable communication network infrastructure, which turns out to be a common bottleneck limiting access to content and services that promote economic growth. We report here how Delay Tolerant Networking (DTN) can serve micro-business opportunities in such challenged locations. A DTN field trial conducted in 2015 in rural South Africa is examined to evaluate DTN architectures to best enable content distribution in areas where affordable communication channels are not fully available. The use-case in the trial was the support of micro-entrepreneurs that had been given access to simple cinema-in-a-backpack kits (battery, mobile projector and WLAN connection, plus software) that opportunistically connect to a DTN in the area. The network enabled the micro-entrepreneurs to order, receive, and screen movies at locations in under-served regions and in addition to invent and to execute micro-business activities around the screenings. The digital content was distributed to the micro-entrepreneurs by means of a DTN network with mobile infostations (wireless DTN-enabled devices) mounted on public transportation vehicles (commuter buses). In this paper, we present a six-month long field deployment that was organized in partnership with local institutions. We discuss the technical implications and make recommendations to support a socio-economic development in the under-served regions of rural South Africa.

Keywords: Socio-economic development · Business models · Delay tolerant networks

1 Introduction

ICT is playing a significant role in achieving future sustainable development goals as the world moves faster and faster towards a digital society. ICT has been utilized in many recent economic development projects to improve the

© ICST Institute for Computer Sciences, Social Informatics and Telecommunications Engineering 2017
O. Gaggi et al. (Eds.): GOODTECHS 2016, LNICST 195, pp. 195–202, 2017.
DOI: 10.1007/978-3-319-61949-1_21

socio-economic status of rural populations in economically developing regions and drive economic development. The MOSAIC_2B project [11] aims to unleash opportunities for micro-entrepreneurs in rural areas of South Africa by providing them with entertainment and educational media content. Then these micro-entrepreneurs, equipped with a low-complexity cinema-in-a-backpack kit (see Fig. 1), can deliver educational and entertainment content in remote villages. We have designed the cinema-in-a-backpack kit that exploits the advantages of Delay Tolerant Networking [7] to create opportunities for entrepreneurial activity in South Africa. Internet access is mostly unavailable or often available only at exorbitant costs and therefore not affordable to populations in rural areas of developing regions. Particularly, in areas lacking affordable and continuous network connectivity a DTN infrastructure could facilitate technology-based micro-entrepreneurship because a DTN infrastructure is simple and low-cost. DTN is an architecture aimed at providing communication in situations where end-to-end connectivity is not available. To ease the development process of DTN applications, the DTN Research Group (DTNRG) [8] has defined an experimental network protocol for challenged networks. The protocol specification is described in detail in RFC5050 [6]. In our use case scenario, the content is distributed to micro-entrepreneurs by means of buses equipped with infostations, named MOSAIC network. Mobile infostations mounted on public buses deliver content to rural areas of South Africa without the support of telecom operators or any other network infrastructures. In this paper, which builds upon previous work [5,12], we discuss the six-month long field deployment and the MOSAIC network in Sect. 2 and describe the experimental setup in Sect. 3. We present initial results and implications in Sect. 4. Related work is outlined in Sect. 5. Finally, Sect. 6 concludes the paper.

Fig. 1. The cinema-in-a-backpack kit (left) to download media content at the bus depot in Siyabuswa, South Africa (right).

2   MOSAIC 2B Network Scenario

MOSAIC 2B is a research project aiming to provide business opportunities for micro-entrepreneurs living in rural South Africa by delivering multimedia content to them in a low cost manner. Since cellular data access is usually unavailable or expensive in rural areas, content delivery will be performed using DTN.

Multimedia content will be delivered by means of DTN-enabled mobile infostations. Infostations are battery-powered Wireless Local Area Network (WLAN)-enabled devices mounted in buses and bus depots We refer to the infostations placed in the bus depots as fixed infostations and the infostations placed in the buses as mobile infostations. Such infostations act as peers that broadcast the content. The multimedia contents are archived at the fixed infostation located at the main bus depot in the city of Pretoria, which is within a 3G/LTE covered area. Every day, such a fixed infostation fetches a list of contents requested by the micro-entrepreneurs from a server located in the Internet cloud, finds such requests in the local archive, and injects them in the DTN network. Micro-entrepreneurs are provided with a tablet which exposes a catalog of movies that are available to be ordered by sending an SMS to the MOSAIC_2B Control Unit (MCU) server in Pretoria. Content is sent from the fixed station in Pretoria, through mobile infostations mounted on buses, to the fixed infostations installed at the rural bus depots, by means of a DTN network. Namely, content is forwarded from one infostation to another as soon as they are in radio range with each other. We have identified three bus depots of the PUTCO bus transportation in Siyabuswa, Vlaklaagte, or Kwaggafontein, about 135 km north-east of Pretoria, which serve several rural communities. Usually, buses take commuters living in rural areas to the city of Pretoria early in the morning and the other way round in the evening. They travel for three hours in the morning and three hours in the evenings in predetermined paths. Thirteen local micro-entrepreneurs living in rural areas near Kwaggafontein, Vlaklaagte and Siyabuswa are equipped with the cinema in-a-backpack kit that allows them to download content from the final fixed infostation and screen it, e.g. in schools or villages, and in addition to invent and to execute micro-business activities around the screenings, e.g. selling candy, providing health-care related or public information, education, leisure games. Figure 1 (right) shows some micro-entrepreneurs downloading media content at the bus depot in Siyabuswa using their cinema-in-a-backpack kit. They run their own mobile cinema business within the surrounding communities during a period of about five months, during which we monitored their actions and collected valuable data, both from the network performance and the business activity.

3   Experimental Setup

Micro-entrepreneurs were assigned to a "rural" infostation based on their preference. At the beginning of the experiment, micro-entrepreneurs were asked which bus depot they prefer to go to download the content they order. Taking into account the preferred bus depot of each micro-entrepreneur, bus routes and their timetables, we set up each infostation with a static routing table. Buses are assigned to predefined routes and travel between two end-locations every day following a predetermined time-table. In this way, content is forwarded to mobile infostations traveling to the right bus depots. Two buses equipped with mobile infostations are assigned to each route to Kwaggafontein, Vlaklaagte and

Siyabuswa. We have deployed 10 infostations, six mobile (two for each route) and four fixed (one for each bus depot). Once movies are forwarded to the rural infostations, they are stored and a notification email is sent to the micro-entrepreneurs who ordered them. Besides, such an activity is logged to the MCU server via 3G, when available. Note that, we experienced 3G disruptions from time to time while logging infostation activity. Micro-entrepreneurs are allowed to go to the bus depot and download their content whenever they can. However, this approach might lead to memory saturation, resulting in loss of processing power and interruption of the infostation activity. Eventually, micro-entrepreneurs might decide to order a large number of movies and wait for all of them to arrive at the rural infostation, so as to fetch them all at once. Because of the low CPU speed (400 MHz) and the small internal memory space (32 MB RAM) of the computing devices, the amount of stored content in the external memory storage (64 GB USB flash drive) and the number of running processes impacts on the performance of the infostations. Therefore, network resources need to be carefully allocated. Based on the results presented in a previous study [12], and observations regarding contact durations and inter-contact times [4] between mobile and fixed infostations at the bus depots, we set up the mobile infostations with a time-to-live of three days and the external memory storage limit to 30 GB. After that limit, the performance of infostations drastically decreases. The mobile infostations are continuously in contact with the fixed infostations at the rural bus depots approximately from 8pm until 4am, while buses are on the sleeping grounds. They arrive at the main bus depot in Pretoria between 9am and 10am, after taking their passengers to town, and do not leave before 3pm. Once the content is forwarded to the fixed infostations at the rural bus depots, it will be erased after one day to free memory space. However, a back up of all the content is made available in the external memory storage in case the ordered movie is deleted before being delivered to the final recipient. We decided to place a back up of all the content at the fixed infostations in rural areas to avoid unexpected disruptions to compromise the business activity of the micro-entrepreneurs. Such settings are enough to prove the viability of delay tolerant networking to deliver media content to rural under-served regions in a low-cost manner. Thirteen micro-entrepreneurs are provided with a tablet which exposes a catalog of movies that are available to be ordered by simply sending a text message to the MCU server in Pretoria. A new catalog of movies is also delivered to micro-entrepreneurs via the MOSAIC network every two months and notified to them by email. We use encryption and audiowatermarking to ensure a certain level of security and to detect copyright violation. All of the movies are encrypted and audiowatermarks are embedded in the soundtrack. Content is decrypted once the payment is completed and erased from the tablet at the end of the experiment.

4   Performance Analysis

During the 6-month field trial we logged network activities. Because of several circumstances due to MCU glitches, delay with the allocation of buses and

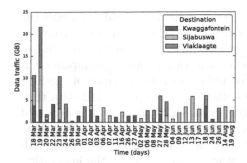

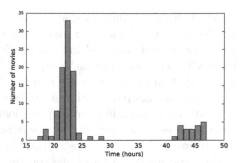

Fig. 2. Data sent by means of the MOSAIC network.

Fig. 3. Distribution of delivery time of movies sent from the fixed infostation in Pretoria to the fixed infostations at the remote bus depots.

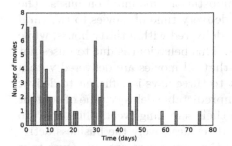

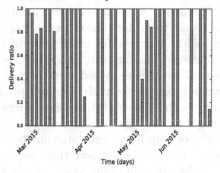

Fig. 4. Time elapsed between the order and the delivery of movies to micro-entrepreneurs.

Fig. 5. Daily delivery ratio of the amount of data sent from Pretoria to the rural bus depots (GBs).

bus drivers, time allocated to provide business and marketing trainings, as well as technical support to the micro-entrepreneurs, the experiment lasted about five months. During this time 109 movies were sent through the MOSAIC network. The fixed infostations logged information such as movies injected in the network, movie size, contact times between mobile and fixed infostations, and delivery of movies. Such information allows us to analyse the performance of the MOSAIC network and to estimate the contribution of such an infrastructure to support the mobile cinema business activity in rural areas. To evaluate the MOSAIC network we analyse the delivery ratio and delay of the ordered movies from the bus depot in Pretoria to the rural bus depots. Initially, we investigate whether the current set up can cope with the demand of movies from the micro-entrepreneurs. The plot in Fig. 2 shows the aggregated daily data transmission rate distinguishing between the three rural destinations, from the 18th of March until the 19th of August. Note that, the missing data in July and beginning of August was due to an interruption of the network activity caused by unexpected interruptions of the MCU server. Nonetheless, such disruption did not affected the micro-entrepreneurs' business activity as they could download the movies from the back up stored at each rural infostation. Another disruption, which prevented the fixed infostations from logging network activity via 3G to the MCU, was caused by an unexpected behaviour of the data consumption balancing system of the network operator. For unknown reasons, some of the SIM cards ran out of credit within a few hours after topping up (250 MB data traffic) without performing considerable logging activity. Such behaviour occurred several times, randomly, during the experiment, and affected some of the fixed infostations. The Fig. 2 shows a peak in the data traffic during the first month of the experiment. In particular, on the day with most requests the infostation was able to send approximately 21.6 GBs in total in a single day (March 19th), sending a maximum of 9.6 GBs to the Siyabuswa bus depot. Based on such initial results, and given that the setup can cope with the peak demand, we can argue that the DTN network can handle the daily requests of movies from the micro-entrepreneurs. As soon as content is bundled at the fixed infostation in Pretoria, it is ready to be forwarded to the mobile infostations mounted on buses. The plot in Fig. 3 shows the distribution of the delivery time of movies to the rural infostations. The majority of the movies are delivered within thirty hours, while a second batch is delivered after forty hours. This behaviour is due to buses not traveling during weekends. Figure 3 proves that all movies are delivered within two days and the expiration time-to-live set to three days is sufficient to deliver successfully the content. After all, long or unpredictable delivery time of content would not help micro-entrepreneurs to plan their screening events efficiently. To make sure that the delivery time does not affect negatively the business activity of the micro-entrepreneurs, we consider the time micro-entrepreneurs take before going to download their orders at the rural bus depots. Figure 4 shows the time elapsed between ordering and downloading movies to the tablet at the rural bus depots. The distribution in Fig. 4 shows that the big majority of micro-entrepreneurs go to get the ordered movies after three days, meaning that a two-day delay to deliver content to the rural bus depots is unlikely to cause frustration to them. Such a behaviour shows that the bus network is not a bottleneck for the micro-entrepreneurs' business activity. Note that, the movies downloaded the first day were ordered and injected in the MOSAIC network the first day of the experiment as demonstration to the micro-entrepreneurs. The plot in Fig. 5 presents the daily delivery ratio of the amount of data sent from Pretoria to the rural bus depots. In many cases, data is successfully delivered, with the exception of some days where the delivery ratio is zero. In this case, it is not possible to assert with certainty whether the network failed, for example to deliver movies, or there are logging issues due to 3G disconnections. This might be caused by 3G outages in rural areas. Here, the 3G coverage was often intermittent. In this case, a buffering mechanism for sending log messages should be implemented, that is, if the 3G network is unavailable the logs could be stored locally, and sent to the MCU when 3G connectivity is available. By excluding 3G network outages from the receiver side (when delivery ratio is zero), the DTN network expresses 95% delivery ratio. Nonetheless, if some movies are not delivered through the DTN network, a backup is available at the infostations, thus allowing micro-entrepreneurs to download them.

5 Related Work

Considerable work has been carried out by the scientific community to devise reliable routing strategies in DTNs [1–3]. Initial work focusing on rural environments in developing regions where buses connect a number of villages spread over a large area is conducted by [10]. Their common goal is to provide network access for delay tolerant applications such as e-mail and non-real time web browsing. DakNet [10] was one of the first projects to propose the use of an existing transport infrastructure to bring connectivity to developing regions in India and Cambodia at low cost. The MOSAIC 2B project is in a similar vein as DakNet. However, we make use of delay tolerant networking for transmission of larger amounts of data. Not only this, we use different equipment that we hope brings down the costs further. KioskNet [9] attempted to improve the service provided by rural kiosks in a low cost manner. These kiosks are a means to provide Internet connectivity at a low cost but technical problems led to unreliable service. In KioskNet, buses acted as ferries that carried data to and from kiosks to a gateway that had reliable Internet connection. Our approach is quite similar to KioskNet since we use buses as ferries and a DTN method of communication. However, we differ in the hardware and DTN software used and in the objective of delivering large amounts of media content to the end users.

6 Conclusions

In the MOSAIC 2B project we offer DTN as a technology that is uniquely suited to the challenge of providing network access to people in under-served regions. We present a 6-month long field deployment that provides communities in rural South Africa with cinema experience by equipping a small group of micro-entrepreneurs with the cinema-in-a-backpack kit and training them in the operation of a DTN-enabled micro-franchise. The DTN network performed efficiently in these settings, allowing cost-effective delivery of movies with acceptable delay. Despite some unexpected disruptions, the MOSAIC network performance was satisfactory and delivered 95% of the content within three days. The general flow of ordering, downloading and screening movies worked without any major issues. The quality of the equipment allowed the screenings of movies in these remote areas. In the future, we intend to analyze in more details the DTN-based micro-franchise model and the micro-entrepreneurs's business activity whose operations are enhanced by opportunistic networking.

Acknowledgment. The MOSAIC_2B project is partially funded by the EU FP7 framework program for research, technological development and demonstration under grant agreement no. 611796, as well as from the Department of Science and Technology South Africa under financial assistance agreement DST/CON 0227-0229/2013.

We thank Johannes Morgenroth and the team of Lars Wolf at Techn. Univ. Braunschweig, Germany, for providing support on their IBR-DTN. We thank the South African partners, Infusion, Epi-Use, the University of Pretoria, and the PUTCO transport corporation in Pretoria (South Africa) for their support in this project.

References

1. Jain, S., Fall, K., Patra, R.: Routing in a delay tolerant network. In: Proceedings of SIGCOMM 2004, Portland, Oregon, USA, pp. 145–158 (2004). ISBN: 1-58113-862-8
2. Yuan, Q., Cardei, I., Wu, J., Predict, R.: An efficient routing in disruption-tolerant networks. In: ACM MobiHoc (2009)
3. Nelson, S., Bakht, M., Kravets, R.: Encounter-based routing in DTNs. In: IEEE INFOCOM 2009, April 2009
4. Chaintreau, A., Hui, P., Crowcroft, J., Diot, C., Gass, R., Scott, J.: Impact of human mobility on the design of opportunistic forwarding algorithms. In: The Proceedings of the 25th IEEE International Conference on Computer Communications (INFOCOM 2006), pp. 1–13, Barcelona, Spain (2006)
5. Siby, S., Galati, A., Bourchas, T., Olivares, M., Mangold, S., Gross, T.R.: METhoD: a framework for the emulation of a delay tolerant network scenario for media-content distribution in under-served regions. In: The proceedings of the 24th IEEE International Conference on Computer Communications and Networks (ICCCN 2015), pp. 1–9 (2015)
6. Bundle Protocol Specification (2016). https://tools.ietf.org/html/rfc5050
7. Fall, K.: A delay-tolerant network architecture for challenged internets. In: Proceedings of the 2003 Conference on Applications, Technologies, Architectures, and Protocols for Computer Communications, SIGCOMM 2003, Karlsruhe, Germany, pp. 27–34 (2003). ISBN: 1-58113-735-4
8. Delay-Tolerant Networking Research Group (DTNRG) (2016). https://irtf.org/dtnrg
9. Guo, S., Falaki, M.H., Oliver, E.A., Ur Rahman, S., Seth, A., Zaharia, M.A., Keshav, S.: Very low-cost internet access using KioskNet. ACM Comput. Commun. Rev. **37**, 95–100 (2007)
10. Pentland, A., Fletcher, R., Hasson, A.: DakNet: rethinking connectivity in developing nations. IEEE Comput. Soc. **37**, 78–83 (2004)
11. MOSAIC 2B: Mobile Empowerment (2016). http://mobile-empowerment.org
12. Galati, A., Bourchas, T., Siby, S., Mangold, S.: System architecture for delay tolerant media distribution for Rural South Africa. In: ACM WiNTECH 2014, pp. 65–72 (2014)

Preserving Privacy in a P2P Social Network

Monica Mordonini, Agostino Poggi, and Michele Tomaiuolo(✉)

Department of Information Engineering, University of Parma, Parma, Italy
michele.tomaiuolo@unipr.it

Abstract. Building centralized social networking systems has many drawbacks, e.g., lack of privacy, lack of anonymity, risks of censorship, and operating costs. As it is discussed in this article, an alternative approach is possible. A prototype system, named Blogracy, has been realized as a micro-blogging social networking system, based on well-known P2P technologies, such as DHTs and BitTorrent. In particular, this article presents the security architecture of the system, which relies on a key-based identity system and a scheme for attribute-based content encryption, with multiple authorities. Moreover, some empirical results obtained in test operations over PlanetLab are presented, comparing plain and I2P anonymized communications.

Keywords: Social network · Peer-to-Peer · File sharing · Distributed hash table · Anonymity · Confidentiality · Key-based identity · Attribute-Based Encryption

1 Introduction

In parallel to their large success, online social networks are also raising significant alarms. Users are beginning to question the mechanisms and policies that are used to protect their privacy and freedom of expression. The clamor about the PRISM program and the release of classified documents by Edward Snowden have sensitized a larger audience towards those issues of current social networking applications [15]. Thus, in many cases an approach based on peer-to-peer (P2P) or distributed technologies can be desirable. Attacks to distributed and P2P social platforms are yet possible. However, analysing these kinds of attacks is not the focus of the article. A comprehensive list of such attacks and countermeasures is presented in [12].

Instead, this article will deal with the possibility to use schemes for targeted broadcasting in a P2P social networking application. Some experiences have been acquired thanks to Blogracy, a new P2P system for social networking. The system is modular in the approach to the core problems of (*i*) data availability and resilience to censorship, (*ii*) content authenticability, (*iii*) data confidentiality, (*iv*) network anonymity, and (*v*) semantic interoperability. All these aspects are kept as much orthogonal as possible in the system. The system has been implemented and tested on the PlanetLab infrastructure. For both its architecture

© ICST Institute for Computer Sciences, Social Informatics and Telecommunications Engineering 2017
O. Gaggi et al. (Eds.): GOODTECHS 2016, LNICST 195, pp. 203–212, 2017.
DOI: 10.1007/978-3-319-61949-1_22

and its level of implementation, to our knowledge it is quite unique. Blogracy is available as open source software (http://dev.blogracy.net/), thus it can be freely exploited for conducting further analysis and evaluations in the larger research area of distributed social platforms, exploring alternative architectural choices and implementations along each axis.

The rest of the article is organized in two main section: Sect. 2 presents background information about Attribute-Based Encryption (ABE) schemes and some related work about the realization of distributed social networking applications; then, Sect. 3 presents the security architecture of Blogracy and some experimental results obtained after its realization, in particular about the costs of network anonymization. Eventually, some concluding remarks are reported.

2   Background: ABE Schemes and Distributed Social Networks

In social networking and micro-blogging applications, it is often desirable to make some content available to a restricted audience, only. Access may be limited to the members of a circle of personal acquaintances, or authorized subscribers of a news channel. In some sense, this problem of confidentiality is similar to the case of broadcasting with DRM over an untrusted medium in general. Exploiting traditional public key cryptography and multicast group key management, it is possible to deliver a secret session key to intended recipients of confidential messages. This requires to rekey users periodically.

A recently emerging approach is to publish content, possibly on an insecure medium, in a form which can be decrypted only by users with proper attributes, as required by the content publisher's policy. In these Attribute-Based Encryption (ABE) schemes, in the general case the attribute authority is considered as a separate abstract entity. In fact, it may be an autonomous entity, and thus there is a third party ownership of the cryptosystem. Alternatively, the attribute authority may coincide with either the encryptor agent or the decryptor agent, creating a targeted broadcast [13], or a duty delegation scenario, respectively [20]. Those various alternatives are represented in Fig. 1. In particular, this work will focus on the targeted broadcast scenario (encryptor as owner).

2.1   Multi-authority ABE Schemes

The basic ABE schemes leave some open issues, especially with regard to the presence of many different Attribute Authorities (AAs). In fact, some practical use cases require that many different attributes can be defined in the network by different authorities, potentially corresponding to each single user. This regards the particular case of Blogracy, but also other generic P2P platforms for content distribution.

Chase [6] advanced one of the first proposals for a distributed CP-ABE scheme. In this scheme, all authorities are managed centrally by a trusted master authority. Attribute authorities can issue secret attribute keys autonomously.

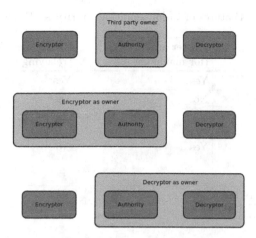

Fig. 1. Three scenarios for attribute authority ownership in ABE.

However, the addition of an attribute authority requires rekeying all users. A scheme proposed by Chase and Chow [7] removes the requirement for a central authority. However, it still relies on a pre-determined set of attribute author-ities, which in fact need to coordinate during the setup phase for generating the distributed function. Müller et al. [21] propose another distributed exten-sion of the CP-ABE scheme. Differently from Bethencourt et al. [4], they intro-duce algorithms for generating public and secret attribute keys, to be executed autonomously by some attribute authority. However, a central master authority is required to manage attribute authorities and users, to avoid possible collusion attacks. Lewko and Waters [17] describe a system where each node can act as an attribute authority, without any need for mutual trust or a master authority. An access policy can include attributes defined by different authorities. Secret attribute keys assigned to users still need to be distinguished, to avoid collusion threats. For this purpose, a hash of the users global identity is used. Unfortu-nately, this hash function is only modeled as an abstract random oracle, which is yet to be resolved to a concrete function. Wang et al. [24] describe a Hierarchical ABE (HABE) system. Basically, a root master authority empowers lower level attribute authorities, which can manage attributes and users at different levels, replicating the hierarchical structure of departments inside an organization. Wan et al. [23] propose a similar scheme named HASBE (Hierarchical Attribute Set Based Encryption). Lin et al. [19], instead, substitute the single central authority with a pre-defined set of attribute authorities, coordinating their operation dur-ing a setup phase. Anne et al. [2] propose a system which is quite similar to the previous one, using a secret sharing scheme. Table 1 summarizes the differences among the various proposals for Multi-Authority ABE.

Table 1. Features of various multi-authority ABE schemes.

System	Master authority (for managing AAs)	Pre-defined set of AAs (rekeying on changes)
Chase [6]	Yes	Yes
Chase and Chow [7] Lin et al. [19] Anne et al. [2]	No	Yes
Müller et al. [21] Wang et al. [24] Wan et al. [23]	Yes	No
Lewko and Waters [17]	No	No

2.2 Information Security in Distributed Social Networks

Various solutions are being proposed to overcome the centralized architecture of the most widespread social networking platforms. In particular, the following systems are designed according to a full-fledged P2P architecture. PeerSoN [5] is a system designed to provide encryption, decentralization and direct data exchange in the field of social networks, dealing with privacy and connectivity issues. Safebook [8] is based on a DHT and a network of socially close peers, defined Matryoshka. Peers in a user's Matryoshka are trusted and support the user by anonymizing communications and replicating content and profile information. Persona [3] is designed as a set of social networking services. For the confidentiality of users' profiles and data, it combines an ABE scheme with traditional cryptography, in such a way that a change in group membership requires widespread re-keying. LifeSocial [14] is a prototype developed over FreePastry for DHT indexing and PAST for data replication. Possibly, it is the more advanced system, with regards to implementation. For confidentiality, it uses a quite traditional encryption scheme. DiDuSoNet [16] is a multi-layered system, including (*i*) a lookup service based on a DHT and (*ii*) a Dunbar-based social overlay dealing with communication and storage of users' profiles. It exploits Dunbar's concept of tie-strength, thus reling on friend nodes with the highest level of intimacy [1].

Blogracy shares some architectural choices with the other distributed social networking systems that have been discussed above. It differs mainly in the adoption of an open and simple key-based identity system, and the use of interoperable protocols and widespread technologies, including OpenSocial, BitTorrent and Kademlia. It can be considered the first concrete attempt to cross the border between the application domains of file-sharing and social networking. Currently, it is one of the few systems which is freely available as a working prototype, as an open source project. Thus, it may represent an important resource for further analysis and testing in the whole research area of distributed social networks.

3   The Security Architecture of Blogracy

As discussed in the previous section, ABE schemes may be applied for targeted broadcasting (Fig. 1). In principle, they may also be useful in P2P systems, but some constraints remain about the need of a master authority, or some coordination mechanism among a predefined set of attribute authorities. The original ABE scheme has been adapted for use in Blogracy (http://www.blogracy.net/), a prototype P2P social network.

The architecture of the application is modular and is built around two basic components: (*i*) an underlying BitTorrent module for basic file sharing and DHT operations, exploiting an existing implementation, and (*ii*) an OpenSocial container, i.e., a module providing the services of the social platform to the local user, to be accessed through a web interface. For its basic operation, Blogracy exploits a P2P file-sharing mechanism and two logically separated DHTs [11]. Users in Blogracy have a profile and a semantically meaningful activity stream, which contains their actions in the system (e.g., add a post, tag a picture, comment a video). The first DHT (DHT1) associates the user's identifier with a reference to his social data. The user's social data is represented in a standard format, conforming to OpenSocial and ActivityStreams specifications (http://www.w3.org/wiki/Socialwg). It is encoded as a JSON file which contains all the elements described in OpenSocial Social API, including people, groups, activity streams, app data, albums, media items and messages, regarding a single user. All contained references, in the form of magnet-URIs, are keys of the second DHT (DHT2), which orchestrates the sharing of actual files, according to the BitTorrent protocol. In the following paragraphs, the security features realized in Blogracy over this extensible architecture will be described.

3.1   Identity and Authentication

Anonymity or pseudonymity are often a requirement of users of micro-blogging and other Internet applications. Nevertheless, user content needs to be verified for authenticity and integrity, properties which can be easily enforced by means of public-key cryptography and digital signatures. Usually, a public key is associated to a person or a legal entity through a certificate issued by a globally acknowledged authority. Instead, in Blogracy a user is represented directly though his own, locally generated, public key, according to a key-based identity scheme [18,22]. Thus, a user can reach other users only after obtaining their ID, i.e., the hash of their public key.

A signature scheme is used for attesting the authenticity of DHT entries, in particular the magnet-URIs used as values in the DHT1. The scheme is based on the JWS (JSON Web signature), which is currently an Internet Draft (http://tools.ietf.org/html/rfc7515). In fact, JWS is a quite practical specification, based on simple JSON objects and Base64 encoded strings. In particular, the header is a JSON object which specifies the cryptographic algorithms to use; the payload contains the signed message, which may be a JSON object or any byte sequence. Both the header and payload are encoded as Base64 strings, which are concatenated (separated though a dot). A signature is then calculated, encoded as a Base64 string, and concatenated to the previously obtained text. At the end of the process, the JWS is represented as a concatenation of the three Base64 strings (header, payload, signature), separated by two dots. The header JSON object in use by Blogracy currently refers to the quite usual SHA256withRSA algorithm, named HS256 in the specifications. The "kid" field is an identifier for the signing key: in Blogracy the user's main public key is numbered as 0. The hash of this public key is also the user's unique identifier. Additional signing keys, corresponding to different kid values, may be added in the user's profile (which is included in the file containing all the user's social data, as an OpenSocial Person object).

The payload, instead, is simply the magnet-URI for the updated user's social data file. Verifying a DHT entry is handy, since the signing key corresponding to a certain kid can be found easily into the user's profile and then it can be stored locally by the user's followers for faster access (each signing key must itself be signed by the user's main public key). This way, the authenticity of an entry can be verified and the typical pollution of keyword-based DHT indexes can be easily detected.

3.2   Attribute Authorities

For its privacy model, Blogracy adopts an Attribute-Based Encryption scheme. It uses attribute credentials for protecting access to sensible content, creating a sort of very flexible personal circles of contacts, i.e., parametrized roles to be assigned to users for granting a certain set of access rights. The encryption scheme is based on the CP-ABE protocol [4]. In the current security model of Blogracy, each user is considered an authority for his own groups of contacts, in a typical Targeted Broadcast scheme. Each user can thus grant attributes and authorizations to his own contacts, and attributes are intended as defined in a namespace local to that user, without possible overlappings. All currently available multi-authority schemes have been discarded, because they do not fit a completely distributed P2P context. In fact, according to the design of Blogracy, it is not possible to identify a globally trusted central authority, even if distributed over a limited number of entities.

Nevertheless, Blogracy permits operation in a multi-authority scenario, though indirectly. In fact, in Blogracy attributes are attested by means of signed certificates (or delegation chains), originated by locally trusted attribute authorities. This way, other authorities can be taken into account, by allowing a user to show some attribute certificates. If the user proves to be eligible and the remote authority is trusted for those attributes, the user is issued a local attribute key.

Since each user is also an attribute authority for accessing his own social activities, then all relevant information is stored directly into his own JSON file, containing all the user's social data. In particular, in the "people" section, a list of acknowledged users can be created, as OpenSocial Person objects, where each user can be associated with a particular private attribute key. Each private attribute key is generated by the local user, using his own local master key MK

and a set of attributes S to associate with the acknowledged user. To keep the generated attribute key confidential, it is encrypted used the public key of the remote user. Additionally, the social data file of a user also contains his own public parameters (the PK data, according to the ABE scheme). Currently, encrypted data and plaintext data (SK and PK, respectively, according the ABE scheme) are stored in the appData section of OpenSocial Person objects.

Assigned attributes serve to mark group membership, and thus some social activities may be disclosed only to a certain set of groups. This is obtained by encrypting sensible social data, according to the desired policy. In Blogracy, an access policy for a resource is essentially a list of groups which are authorized for access. In fact, each object in the social data file can be encrypted according to a different policy; otherwise, it is kept as a plaintext JSON object.

3.3 Network Anonymity

Blogracy doesn't require users to expose their real identity and offers instead a pseudonimity mechanism based on public keys. However, anonymity is an issue also at the lower network level. In fact, if communications among users are based on direct connections, or file locations are expressed as plain network addresses, these can be easily associated with a particular person or entity. Various network technologies are being developed, which promise to guarantee a certain level of anonymity for their users, disguising their real network location. One of the best known is Tor (http://www.torproject.org/), but other similar networks are also available, which in fact may be more adequate for an application based on file sharing techniques.

In particular, I2P (http://geti2p.net/) is a anonymizing P2P overlay network, implementing a protocol similar to Tor. Since the I2P architecture is more distributed and focused on darknet-type services, it welcomes file sharing applications running inside the network (and thus separated from the larger communities operating on the plain Internet). Instead, Tor discourages the use of file sharing applications for not overloading its own outproxies. The operation of Blogracy over I2P requires the creation of a number of tunnels at each participant (router), determining their length, i.e., how many hops each tunnel should use. Thus security and latency can be balanced according to the needs of a particular application. Moreover, when used over I2P, BitTorrent clients do not support any Distributed Database, so they require a tracker to operate over I2P.

3.4 Experimental Results

In order to validate the feasibility of our approach, both simulations and performance tests were performed, as described in [11]. The evaluation confirmed our confidence about the realizability of a completely distributed social network, in the case of users with a sufficient number of followers and few relatively stable nodes. About the problem of data availability against the typical P2P node churn, we have discussed the results of some simulations in [11]. I particular, the average notification delays are quite severe in the case of few followers, without stable nodes. However, when a user has more than 100–150 followers, the delays are negligible with just 5–10% of stable nodes. Thus, some aid has to be provided to newly joined users, in the form of resource hosting by other users, in addition to the small group of followers.

For testing the actual functioning of the system, twelve instances of Blogracy were executed over different remote nodes of PlanetLab Europe. For simplicity and consistency, the nodes were arranged in a small fully connected social network (i.e., each node follows all the others). Over this testbed, the pushing mechanism was verified. It is a direct form of communication, which nodes use most often. It allows a source node to notify its followers in a timely and effective way about the availability of update in the local social data file. Since it occurs directly between interested nodes (those participating in a swarm) it is virtually instantaneous [11].

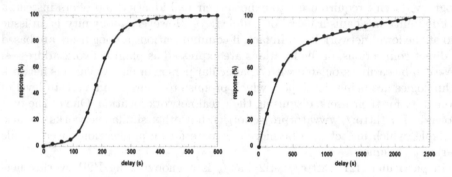

Fig. 2. Cumulative distribution of the notification delay in the reception of messages over the PlanetLab testbed; the polling cycle, repeated every two minutes, accounts on average for one minute. The first graph shows the case of normal Internet communications. The second graph shows the case of communications over I2P.

The polling mechanism was also verified. It involves sending various queries overs the DHT, downloading a torrent file and finally passing through download queues, before receiving the latest messages. It is worth noting that in a real system, this mechanism would be used only at the node startup, for receiving interesting activities produced when it was offline. Afterwards, push notifications would be more effective. In the tests, the polling cycle was set at two minutes, i.e., the availability of new messages from a certain source node was checked every two minutes. Probably, the more interesting result is the delay in the reception of new messages at follower nodes. The delays shown in the first graph of Fig. 2 are those concretely measured. In this setting, 90% of messages are received in 4.5 min. However, the measured times include a delay due to the polling cycle, which on average accounts for 1 min. Thus, in the mean delay of 4.5 min, 3.5 min are effectively due to DHT and BitTorrent download mechanisms. Analogous tests were finally conducted to evaluate the effectiveness of actually running a distributed social network on top of I2P. In this case, an additional node was configured to host a tracker service on I2P. The cumulative distribution of measured delays is shown in the second graph of Fig. 2. The reception of 90% of messages requires around 20 min. With respect to direct connections, delays increase roughly by a factor of 4. It is possible that results could be improved slightly through finer setup, reducing the length of tunnels (and thus the level of anonymity). Results are in accordance with more extensive performance tests conducted over I2P [9].

4 Conclusion

This research work was aimed at studying a possible application of well-known P2P technologies, such as DHTs and BitTorrent, in the new domain of distributed social networking. In fact, although the primitives offered by those technologies were created with other goals in mind, however, they could be effectively adapted for Blogracy, a novel P2P micro-blogging and social networking system. Its main features are: (*i*) data availability and resilience to censorship, (*ii*) content authenticability, (*iii*) data confidentiality, (*iv*) network anonymity, and (*iv*) semantic interoperability. In particular, the security architecture of Blogracy has been presented, including its key-based identity system, a scheme for attribute-based content encryption with multiple authorities, and the option for network anonymization over I2P. In fact, the main aspects are kept as much orthogonal as possible in the system. Thus, it can also serve as a testbed for conducting further analysis and evaluations in the larger research area of distributed social platform, exploring alternative architectural choices and implementations along each axis. Moreover, some simulation results for notification delays and some empirical results obtained in test operations over PlanetLab have been presented. In particular, a quantitative comparison of plain and I2P anonymized communications has demonstrated that the latter implies much slower operations.

References

1. Amft, T., Guidi, B., Graffi, K., Ricci, L.: Frodo: friendly routing over dunbar-based overlays. In: 2015 IEEE 40th Conference on Local Computer Networks (LCN), pp. 356–364. IEEE (2015)
2. Anne, V.K., Praveen, G., Ramesh, N., Kurra, R.R.: Extension of MA-ABE for better data security in cloud. Int. J. Comput. Sci. Technol. (IJCST) 3(1–1), A-419 (2012)
3. Baden, R., Bender, A., Spring, N., Bhattacharjee, B., Starin, D.: Persona: an online social network with user-defined privacy. ACM SIGCOMM Comput. Commun. Rev. 39(4), 135–146 (2009)
4. Bethencourt, J., Sahai, A., Waters, B.: Ciphertext-policy attribute-based encryption. In: 2007 IEEE Symposium on Security and Privacy (SP 2007), pp. 321–334. IEEE (2007)
5. Buchegger, S., Schiöberg, D., Vu, L., Datta, A.: Peerson: P2P social networking: early experiences and insights. In: Proceedings of the Second ACM EuroSys Workshop on Social Network Systems, pp. 46–52. ACM (2009)

6. Chase, M.: Multi-authority attribute based encryption. In: Vadhan, S.P. (ed.) TCC 2007. LNCS, vol. 4392, pp. 515–534. Springer, Heidelberg (2007). doi:10.1007/978-3-540-70936-7_28

7. Chase, M., Chow, S.: Improving privacy and security in multi-authority attribute-based encryption. In: Proceedings of the 16th ACM Conference on Computer and Communications Security, pp. 121–130. ACM (2009)

8. Cutillo, L., Molva, R., Strufe, T.: Safebook: a privacy-preserving online social network leveraging on real-life trust. IEEE Commun. Mag. 95 (2009)

9. Ehlert, M.: I2P usability vs. tor usability a bandwidth and latency comparison. In: Seminar Report, Humboldt University of Berlin (2011)

10. Falkner, J., Piatek, M., John, J.P., Krishnamurthy, A., Anderson, T.: Profiling a million user DHT. In: Proceedings of the 7th ACM SIGCOMM Conference on Internet Measurement, pp. 129–134. ACM (2007)

11. Franchi, E., Poggi, A., Tomaiuolo, M.: Blogracy: a peer-to-peer social network. Int. J. Distrib. Syst. Technol. (IJDST) 7(2), 37–56 (2016)

12. Franchi, E., Tomaiuolo, M.: Distributed social platforms for confidentiality and resilience. In: Social Network Engineering for Secure Web Data and Services, p. 114 (2013)

13. Goyal, V., Pandey, O., Sahai, A., Waters, B.: Attribute-based encryption for fine-grained access control of encrypted data. In: Proceedings of the 13th ACM Conference on Computer and Communications Security, pp. 89–98. ACM (2006)

14. Graffi, K., Groß, C., Mukherjee, P., Kovacevic, A., Steinmetz, R.: Lifesocial.kom: a P2P-based platform for secure online social networks. In: 2010 IEEE Tenth International Conference on Peer-to-Peer Computing (P2P), pp. 1–2. IEEE (2010)

15. Greene, M.: Where has privacy gone? How surveillance programs threaten expectations of privacy. J. Marshall J. Info. Tech. Privacy L. 30, 795 (2014). John Marshall J. Inf. Technol. Privacy Law 30(4), 5 (2014)

16. Guidi, B., Amft, T., De Salve, A., Graffi, K., Ricci, L.: Didusonet: a P2P architecture for distributed dunbar-based social networks. Peer-to-Peer Netw. Appl. 1–18 (2015)

17. Lewko, A., Waters, B.: Decentralizing attribute-based encryption. In: Paterson, K.G. (ed.) EUROCRYPT 2011. LNCS, vol. 6632, pp. 568–588. Springer, Heidelberg (2011). doi:10.1007/978-3-642-20465-4_31

18. Li, N.: Local names in SPKI/SDSI. In: Proceedings of 13th IEEE Computer Security Foundations Workshop, CSFW-13. IEEE Computer Society (2000)

19. Lin, H., Cao, Z., Liang, X., Shao, J.: Secure threshold multi authority attribute based encryption without a central authority. Inf. Sci. 180(13), 2618–2632 (2010)

20. Muijnck-Hughes, J.: Json Web Signature (JWS). Radboud University Nijmegen, Nijmegen (2011)

21. Müller, S., Katzenbeisser, S., Eckert, C.: On multi-authority ciphertext-policy attribute-based encryption. Bull. Korean Math. Soc. 46(4), 803–819 (2009)

22. Tomaiuolo, M.: Trust management and delegation for the administration of web services. In: Organizational, Legal, and Technological Dimensions of Information System Administration, pp. 18–37 (2014)

23. Wan, Z., Liu, J., Deng, R.H.: Hasbe: a hierarchical attribute-based solution for flexible and scalable access control in cloud computing. IEEE Trans. Inf. Forensics Secur. 7(2), 743–754 (2012)

24. Wang, G., Liu, Q., Wu, J., Guo, M.: Hierarchical attribute-based encryption and scalable user revocation for sharing data in cloud servers. Comput. Secur. 30(5), 320–331 (2011)

A Heuristic Path Planning Approach for UAVs Integrating Tracking Support Through Terrestrial Wireless Networks

Mustapha Bekhti[1], Nadjib Achir[1(✉)], Khaled Boussetta[1,2],
and Marwen Abdennebi[1]

[1] Université Paris 13, Sorbonne Paris Cité – L2TI (EA 4303), Villetaneuse, France
{bekhti.mustapha,nadjib.achir,khaled.boussetta,
marwen.abdennebi}@univ-paris13.fr
[2] INRIA URBANET, INSA Lyon, 69621 Villeurbanne, France

Abstract. In this paper we propose a new approach based on a heuristic search for UAVs path planning with terrestrial wireless network tracking. In a previous work we proposed and exact solution based on an integer linear formulation of the problem. Unfortunately, the exact resolution is limited by the computation complexity. In this case, we propose in this paper a new approach based on a heuristic search. More precisely, a heuristic adaptive scheme based on Dijkstra algorithm is proposed to yield a simple but effective and fast solution. In addition, the proposed solution can cover a large area and generate a set of optimum and near optimum paths according to the drone battery capacities. Finally, the simulation results show that the drone tracking is sustainable even in noisy wireless network environment.

1 Introduction

For decades, Unmanned Aerial Vehicles (UAVs) are widely used in modern warfare for surveillance, reconnaissance, sensing, battle damage assessment and attacking. The benefits of UAVs include reduced costs and no warfighter risk. Recently, technological advances in micro controllers, sensors, and batteries have dramatically increased their utility and versatility and yet, a new horizon is open for civilian uses. This began with limited aerial patrols of the nation's borders, observation and aerial mapping, disaster response including search and support to rescuers, sports event coverage and law enforcement. Although the market is almost nonexistent today, this is most likely in the civil field that drones are expected to play the largest role. Recently, those flying machines have also been destined to the commercial market and have gained much attention. In fact, a forthcoming plans for commercial drone use have been recently announced by a number of companies around the world such, Amazon, Wallmart, DHL, and Zookal which are investing in mini drones development for variety of tasks, including freight and package delivery to consumers. The introduction of drones in civil applications raises new challenges to the government authorities in charge

© ICST Institute for Computer Sciences, Social Informatics and Telecommunications Engineering 2017
O. Gaggi et al. (Eds.): GOODTECHS 2016, LNICST 195, pp. 213–223, 2017.
DOI: 10.1007/978-3-319-61949-1_23

of flight security and air traffic management which have to balance safety and public concerns against potential economic benefit (Fig. 1).

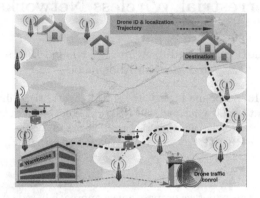

Fig. 1. Drone package delivery

By virtue of their small size, mini drones are difficult to be detected and to track. In this frame, the European Parliament adopted a resolution on the use of drones, which requires Member States to implement various regulations to ensure the safety of the airspace and to ensure the privacy of citizens threatened by the use of these flying machines. Through this resolution, it is considered that regardless of their sizes, the question of identifying is essential, and emphasizes the need to provide appropriate solutions in terms of locating and tracking. In other words, this new report aims to ensure the traceability of all UAVs, but also operators and owners as a sine qua non-conditions for any use.

It is obvious that path planning is one of the most crucial tasks for mission definition and management of the aircraft and it will also be an important requirement for UAVs that has autonomous flight capabilities [1]. The operational problem that this work address is enabling the government authorities in charge of flight safety to identify, locate and to track drones. Usually the area is large and the detection and localization time to find the UAV is the critical parameter that should be minimized. To this end and in order to make this possible, we present in this paper a newly approach based on the exploitation of the available wireless network coverage. This approach relies on a powerful interaction, or collaboration between the UAVs and the operators. Cooperation in such environment implies that the drone periodically send his identification, localization, speed and other information to the remote operators through the available wireless networks. The solution we aim to present provide or inform of the optimum and the near optimum paths that the drone should follow to ensure a reliable communication and high packet delivery rate depending on its battery autonomy.

In our previous work [2], we formulated the problem as an Integer Linear Problem. Moreover, we expressed in an analytic manner the packet loss rate of tracking messages depending on the UAV location and the wireless network coverage. By solving the ILP problem using CPLEX, we were being able to analyze how the radio coverage as well as the threshold on the packet success rate, impact the number of possible solutions and the trajectory of the UAV. Unfortunately, due to the computational complexity the proposed approach was not able to provide a path planning solution for a large area. In addition, the packet success rate was computed by considering only the radio channel and without any MAC layer operations.

Our current investigations focus on the complexity issue raised for larger size of the area A. For the drone path planning, a heuristic adaptive scheme based on Dijkstra algorithm is presented to cope with the problem of scalability. The flight path of drone is optimized in order to improve its connectivity to the available terrestrial wireless network and consequently its localization, identification and tracking. Moreover, the solution is proposed to yield a simple but effective and fast solution and tested under a more realistic scenario characterized with a noisy environment.

2   State of the Art

Path planning for a kinematic system issues has been widely studied and have been addressed using different approaches and techniques. Thus, several approaches exist for computing paths given some input variables of the environment and in general, the two most popular techniques are deterministic, heuristic-based algorithms [3–5] and probabilistic, randomized algorithms [6,7]. The choice of the algorithm to use depends on the type of problem to be solved. Although, the robotic bibliography on this subject is very rich, it's not the case for the UAV's one.

For the autonomous flight of drones, path planning is one of the most crucial and important issues to solve. Nowadays, the application of UAV is extending from high-altitude flight to very low-altitude, where the impact of the terrain, the environment and the air traffic will be the keys factor to be considered to avoid collision [8]. However, we do not aim to provide an exhaustive list but we will be content to provide the most relevant work related to the path planning regarding to the nature of the objectives, problems formalization and resolving methods.

The author in [9] presented a framework to compute the minimum cost cooperative route between a heterogeneous package delivery team composed of a truck and micro drones. They abstracted the problem on a graph and formulate the issue as a discrete optimal path planning problem. In the same context of heterogeneous teams, the authors in [10] presented a path planning problem involving an UAV and a ground vehicle for intelligence, surveillance and reconnaissance missions. The addressed problem is similar to the ring-star problem and the hierarchical ring network problem.

On the other hand, the authors in [8,11] presented three dimensional path planning solution for unmanned aerial vehicles. The first solution is based on interfered fluid dynamic system, while the second approach uses linear programming where obstacle avoidance and target tracking are linearized to generate a linear programming model in relative velocity space. Dealing with adversarial environments, the authors in [12,13] presented solutions for unmanned aerial vehicles path planning in uncertain an adversarial environment in sight to reach a given target, while maximizing the safety of the drone. They proposed a path planning algorithm based on threats probability map, which can be built from a priori surveillance data and from a mechanism based on a model predictive control.

Another important work is [14], which contains concise summaries and focused on dynamic problems and discussed a family of heuristic algorithms for path planning in real-world scenarios such as A*, D*, ARA* and AD*. Finally, it is worth mentioning the research done by [15] that can be considered one of the few papers dealing with path planning strategies destined for a based UAVs network. The authors compared deterministic and probabilistic path planning strategies for autonomous drones to explore a given area with obstacles and to provide an overview image. The results showed that although the deterministic approach could provide a solution it requires more knowledge and time to generate a plan. However, the probabilistic approaches are flexible and adaptive.

To the best of our knowledge, none of the above works have investigated UAV path planning problem assuming that UAV uses terrestrial wireless networks to transmit its locations.

3   Path Planning Problem Formulation

3.1   Problem Statement and System Description

In this paper, we are considering a package delivery services using UAVs. Basically, a UAV has to deliver a package from a depot to a predetermined destination or consumer. In this frame, the system is modeled as 2D area A without any obstacle. The projection of the flying area is represented by a rectangular with length of x_{max} and a width of y_{max}. We suppose that the drone D_{rone} keeps the same altitude h from the starting point O to the destination D. A set of wireless receivers or Base stations $BS = \{BS_1, BS_2, ...BS_n\}$ is deployed randomly at different altitudes in order to provide a wireless access infrastructure. In addition, we assume a partially noisy environment with the existence of a certain number of noise nodes $N_{oise} = \{N_{N1}, N_{N2}, ...N_{Nn}\}$ deployed within A and use the wireless infrastructure as an access network. We also consider that the drone has a limited flight autonomy Υ and equipped with a wireless interface in order to communicate with the other Base stations. The latter has a short sensing range compared to the size of the region of interest. Moreover, we consider that A is discretized into C hexagonal Area Units (AU) of the same dimension. The transition cost between two neighbor cells depicts certain reliability of communication, i.e. a certain probability that the communication is not interrupted and has a specified Packet Reception Rate PRR.

Our goal is to determine a path or a set of paths that optimize the drone localization and tracking using a wireless network, such as cellular or IEEE 802.11x technologies. For this purpose, we assume that after each period T drone generates a message of size D bits containing its identification, its position and speed. The on-board wireless interface tries to send each generated message to the remote UAV monitoring and controlling system via the BS while the jamming nodes attempt to exhaust and to overload the network by sending messages in a continuous and unpredictable manner to the BS. For that reason, a message can be corrupted or lost due to possible interference and collisions. The opportunity to transmit also depends on the radio coverage, the capacity of the related wireless technology and the drone's location.

The basic concept in building the probability map in this paper is different to the probability grid-based in our previous work. Thus, in this paper, the OMNeT++ 4.61 simulator and the INET framework were used to generate the Received Packet Rate and the signal-to-interference-plus-noise ratio $SINR$ maps. Thereby, for each cell C the Received Packet Rate RPR is computed as the proportion of received messages over generated ones and the values of the $SINR$.

3.2   Problem Formulation

In order to describe the proposed mathematical model that represents the optimum path planning problem, it is useful to introduce the following notations and definitions.

First, we model the problem with the help of a directed and valued graph G consisting of n hexagonal cells c, where the valuation of an arc is comprised between 0 and 1, indicating the packet error delivery on that arc. The unit cost for using the arc going from node i to node j is c_{ij}. The flow going that way is denoted by a binary variable x_{ij}

$$x_{ij} = \begin{cases} 1, & \text{if the drone moves from } AU\ i \text{ to } AU\ j \\ 0, & \text{otherwise.} \end{cases} \tag{1}$$

The cost of a path represents its reliability and it is set to the product of the RPR of each cell forming the resulted path.

$$Path_{cost} = \prod_{i=1}^{n} \prod_{j=1}^{n} RPR_{ij} * x_{ij} \tag{2}$$

As, the RPR_{ij} is comprised between $]0, 1]$, this means more we add a new cell to the path more the path cost is low. Thus, the mathematical formulation of the optimal drone path planning problem is reported as follows:

$$\text{minimize} \sum_{i \in A} \sum_{j \in A} c_{i,j} x_{ij} \tag{3}$$

and

$$\text{maximize} \prod_{i=1}^{n} \prod_{j=1}^{n} (PRR_{i,j}) x_{ij} \tag{4}$$

The objectives functions (3) and (4) represent respectively the distance or the delivery delay that should be minimized between the start point O and the destination D and the drone tracking possibility that should be maximized, by passing through cells with highest Received Packet Rate.

In addition to the last two objectives we add a last objective that aims to minimize the tracking time loss of the drone, by avoiding to pass through several adjacent cells with low RPR. Basically, we need to maximize a given cost function noted as f. For example, as illustrated in Fig. 2, if we have to choose between the paths a (0.9, 0.9, 0.9, 0.1, 0.1, 0.1) and b (0.9, 0.1, 0.9, 0.1, 0.9, 0.1) with the same distance and the same average packet delivery ratio, than the score function f has to privilege the solution b rather than a. The privilege of the solution b is motivated by the fact that we have less adjacent cells with low packet delivery probability. The main benefit of this choice is to have the communication rupture spaced out on the time rather than having a long time with no communication.

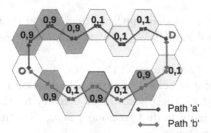

Fig. 2. Example of paths with the same cost

To this end, we need to analyze the cells data in terms of RPR values and their positions in the path by creating series of averages of different subsets of the full path. Basically, given K a path and the subset size equals to 2, the first element of the moving average is obtained by taking the average of the initial fixed subset of the number series. Then the subset is modified by shifting forward, excluding the first number of the series and including the next number following the original subset in the series. This creates a new subset of numbers $\overline{K}$, which is averaged. This kind of mathematical transformation is also used in the signal processing in order to mitigate the higher frequencies and to retain only the low frequencies or the contrary. The principle of moving averages is interesting, especially when it comes time to make predictions. Basically, this is about to calculate an average data based on the most recent results in order to create forecasts. Thus, it is assumed that the most recent data are more important or more meaningful than older data.

Let's consider $f(K)$ the score function and K is the path to analyze, where $K = \{RPR_1; RPR_2; ....RPR_n\}$ with RPR_1, $RPR_2,...$ RPR_n are the Received Packet Rate at the cells c_1, c_2, $...c_n$ constituting the given path k and $\overline{K} = \{\overline{K}_1; \overline{K}_2; ....\overline{K}_{n-1}\}$ where $\overline{K}_i = (RPR_i + RPR_{i+1})/2$. Finally, since the geometric average is less sensitive than the arithmetic average to the highest or lowest values of a series, we propose the following cost function:

$$f(K) = \sqrt[n-1]{\prod_{i=1}^{n-1} \overline{K}_i} \tag{5}$$

In addition to the last objectives we add a constraint related to the UAV's maximal flight distance:

$$\sum_{i \in A} \sum_{j \in A} c_{i,j} x_{ij} < \delta \tag{6}$$

where δ is the maximum distance that the UAV could perform, taking in account UAV autonomy, speed and package weight.

3.3 Path Computation

Different shortest path algorithms exist like A*, Dijkstra, Bellman-Ford and others. Our proposal is based and adapted from Dijkkstra algorithms. The latest is one of the most common and effective algorithms used to search the shortest path between two vertices in a graph in terms of distance. For our case, we adapt the Dijkstra algorithm to find the shortest path with high communication reliability and high packet reception.

Since we are dealing with probabilities, the best way to find the shortest path with high Received Packet Rate is to seek for a path where the product of the probabilities RPR_i of the visited cells that constitute a given path is maximized. This also guarantees that if each time a cell is added to a path, the product of the probabilities decreases.

In this case, our algorithm first starts by initializing the cost of the origin cell c_o to 1. The cost of the remaining cells is set to 0. Starting from the origin point, we built step by step a set of P marked cells. For each marked cell c_i, the cost is equal to the product of the Received Packet Rate probabilities of all predecessors cells. At each step, we select an unmarked vertex c_j whose cost is the highest among all vertexes not marked, then we mark c_j and we update from c_j the estimated costs of unmarked successors of c_j. We repeat until exhaustion unmarked vertices.

Based on the above algorithm, we also derived a set of near optimal paths. In fact, the solution was extended to compromise localization data delivery rates and distance between the starting point and the destination with the respect of the drone autonomy. To this end, if the length of the optimal path is greater than the drone autonomy or simply, the operator would to have multiple choice of short paths, then we re-execute the function above until we get the desired solution and for each execution we set the RPR of the cells of the obtained path to ϵ, where ϵ is a small non-null value. This allows us to generate a new path totally different from the previous one. All these paths can then be compared using the cost function f.

4 Results

In this section we evaluate our proposed algorithm to generate optimal and near optimal paths for a drone to deliver packages from a start point to a given destination. Two main objectives were fixed, first, to ensure a maximum tracking and localization time of the drone along with its flight while the second one was to minimize the length of the path in accordance with the drone flight autonomy and the capacity of its battery. Thus, we assess the algorithm in different scenarios. Using OMNET++ simulator, we generate the RPR map for a given altitude and in the presence of a given number of nodes using the wireless network. Basically, in order to increase the packet losses we can increase the altitude of the drone or the number of nodes acting as noisy nodes. In the following, we provide some results according to the simulation parameters summarized in the Table 1.

Table 1. Simulation parameters

Area	X = Y = 1000 m
AU radius (constant)	a = 5 m
BSs	10
Noise nodes	10, 20, 30, 40, 50
UAV altitude	60 m
D	200 bytes
P_t	20 dBm (100 mW)
Background noise power	−72 dBm
Path loss type	Two ray ground reflection
Antennas gains	Ge = Gr = 10 dBi
Carrier frequency	2.4 GHz

Figure 3a and b represents respectively the shortest path with highest RPR (optimal path) at 60 m of altitude with the presence of 20 and 50 noise nodes. Since the problem is new and there is no other similar algorithm in the literature, we compare the resulted paths to the shortest path using the well-known Dijkstra algorithm.

The set of paths illustrated in the Fig. 3c represents the near optimal paths calculated by our algorithm. As indicated in the Fig. 4, our proposed solution is able to provide other paths, called near optimal paths shorter than the optimal one but eventually with less important RPR. It is clear that even for the shortest near optimal path with a distance almost equal to the Dijkstra short path length, the RPR is even important. The relationship between path length and RPR is shown in Fig. 4. It proves the efficiency of our solution to find more than one optimal paths with different lengths and RPRs. More the path is longer more the RPR is important.

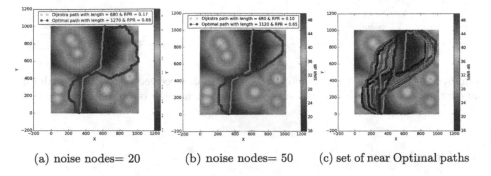

(a) noise nodes= 20   (b) noise nodes= 50   (c) set of near Optimal paths

Fig. 3. Optimal and near optimal paths, $h = 60\,\text{m}$

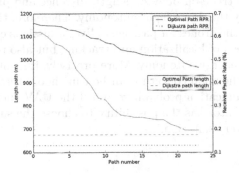

Fig. 4. Near Optimal paths with respective length and RPR

To understand more the impact of the noisy environment on the path length and quality, we varied the number of the nodes simulating the noisy environment, we fixed the drone altitude to 60 m and we measure the length of the optimal paths and their respective RPRs. If we increase the number of noise nodes, we gradually decrease the quality of the signal and subsequently the RPR and the path length decrease too as shown in the Figs. 5 and 6.

It's clear that bad quality of the signal and a noisy environment cause a low RPR; But how it can affect the path length? This can be explained as follows: with an excellent radio coverage, the drone tends to be attracted to the cells with higher SINR, which represent the BS locations. And as we go along with a bad or a noisy radio coverage, the drone tends to take the shortest path to its destination.

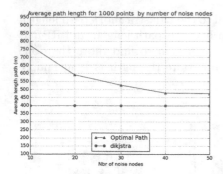
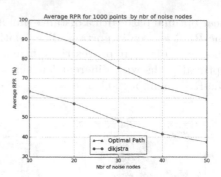

Fig. 5. Path lengths with different number of noise nodes, h = 60 m

Fig. 6. Received packets rate with different number of noise nodes, h = 60 m

5   Conclusion

In this paper, we propose a path planning algorithm for UAV. Our approach doesn't only generate one single optimal solution but a number of other near optimal paths with a trade-off between length distance and probability of localization determined by the drone flight autonomy. Therefore, the operator who is in charge of tracking the drones for package delivery missions can choose the best path suited to the need of localization and tracking but also to the capability of the UAV in terms of energy autonomy. More precisely, if identification, localization and tracking is the main concern than he can choose the longer path which insures a high communication probability and if the UAV energy autonomy is a priority than the operator has the possibility to choose the suitable path length according to the battery duration.

References

1. De Filippis, L., Guglieri, G.: Advanced Graph Search Algorithms for Path Planning of Flight Vehicles. INTECH Open Access Publisher, Rijeka (2012)
2. Bekhti, M., Abdennebi, M., Achir, N., et al.: Path planning of unmanned aerial vehicles with terrestrial wireless network tracking. In: 2016 Wireless Days (WD), pp. 1–6. IEEE (2016)
3. Hart, P.E., Nilsson, N.J., Raphael, B.: A formal basis for the heuristic determination of minimum cost paths. IEEE Trans. Syst. Sci. Cybern. **4**(2), 100–107 (1968)
4. Nilsson, N.J.: Principles of Artificial Intelligence. Morgan Kaufmann, Burlington (2014)
5. Podsedkowski, L., et al.: A new solution for path planning in partially known or unknown environment for nonholonomic mobile robots. Robot. Autonom. Syst. **34**(2), 145–152 (2001)
6. Kavraki, L.E., et al.: Probabilistic roadmaps for path planning in high-dimensional configuration spaces. IEEE Trans. Robot. Autom. **12**(4), 566–580 (1996)

7. LaValle, S.M., Kuffner, J.J.: Randomized kinodynamic planning. Int. J. Robot. Res. **20**(5), 378–400 (2001)
8. Wang, H., et al.: Three-dimensional path planning for unmanned aerial vehicle based on interfered fluid dynamic system. Chin. J. Aeronaut. **28**(1), 229–239 (2015)
9. Mathew, N., Smith, S.L., Waslander, S.L.: Planning paths for package delivery in heterogeneous multirobot teams. IEEE Trans. Autom. Sci. Eng. **12**(4), 1298–1308 (2015)
10. Manyam, S., Casbeer, D., Sundar, K.: Path Planning for Cooperative Routing of Air-Ground Vehicles. arXiv preprint arXiv:1605.09739 (2016)
11. Chen, Y., Han, J., Zhao, X.: Three-dimensional path planning for unmanned aerial vehicle based on linear programming. Robotica **30**(05), 773–781 (2012)
12. Jun, M., D'Andrea, R.: Path planning for unmanned aerial vehicles in uncertain and adversarial environment. In: Butenko, R., Murphey, R., Pardalos, P.M. (eds.) Cooperative Control: Models, Applications and Algorithms, pp. 95–110. Springer, Heidelberg (2002). doi:10.1007/978-1-4757-3758-5_6
13. Peng, X., Demin, X.: Intelligent online path planning for UAVs in adversarial environments. Int. J. Adv. Robot. Syst. **9**, 1–12 (2012)
14. Ferguson, D., Likhachev, M., Stentz, A.: A guide to heuristic-based path planning. In: Proceedings of the International Workshop on Planning Under Uncertainty for Autonomous Systems, International Conference on Automated Planning and Scheduling (ICAPS) (2005)
15. Yanmaz, E., et al.: On path planning strategies for networked unmanned aerial vehicles. In: 2011 IEEE Conference on Computer Communications Workshops (INFOCOM WKSHPS). IEEE (2011)

Object Detection and Spatial Coordinates Extraction Using a Monocular Camera for a Wheelchair Mounted Robotic Arm

Alessandro Palla$^{(\boxtimes)}$, Alessandro Frigerio, Gabriele Meoni, and Luca Fanucci

University of Pisa, Pisa, Italy
alessandro.palla@for.unipi.it, a.frigerio@studenti.unipi.it,
gabriele.meoni@ing.unipi.it, luca.fanucci@unipi.it

Abstract. In the last decades, smart power wheelchairs have being used by people with motor skill impairment in order to improve their autonomy, independence and quality of life. The most recent power wheelchairs feature many technological devices, such as laser scanners to provide automatic obstacle detection or robotic arms to perform simple operations like pick and place. However, if a motor skill impaired user was able to control a very complex robotic arm, paradoxically he would not need it. For that reason, in this paper we present an autonomous control system based on Computer Vision algorithms which allows the user to interact with buttons or elevator panels via a robotic arm in a simple and easy way. Scale-Invariant Feature Transform (SIFT) algorithm has been used to detect and track buttons. Objects detected by SIFT are mapped in a tridimensional reference system collected with Parallel and Tracking Mapping (PTAM) algorithm. Real word coordinates are obtained using a Maximum-Likelihood estimator, fusing the PTAM coordinates with distance information provided by a proximity sensor. The visual servoing algorithm has been developed in Robotic Operative System (ROS) Environment, in which the previous algorithms are implemented as different nodes. Performances have been analyzed in a test scenario, obtaining good results on the real position of the selected objects.

Keywords: Robotic arm · Power wheelchair · Visual Servoing · PBVS · Eye-in-hand · Computer Vision · SIFT · Features extraction · PTAM · ROS · Human machine interface · Assistive technology · Open-source

1 Introduction and State of the Art Presentation

Nowadays many people are affected by motor skill impairments and their number is constantly increasing. The cardinal causes are often various kinds of diseases associated with age, neurologic and muscular disorders like SMA (Spinal Muscular Atrophy), Muscular Dystrophy, Multiple Sclerosis and Duchenne Dystrophy or Cerebral Palsy, but there are many other reasons that can cause mobility impairments, for example injuries derived by a car/motorbike/work accident.

© ICST Institute for Computer Sciences, Social Informatics and Telecommunications Engineering 2017
O. Gaggi et al. (Eds.): GOODTECHS 2016, LNICST 195, pp. 224–232, 2017.
DOI: 10.1007/978-3-319-61949-1_24

The possibility of moving in an autonomous way gives individuals a remarkable physical and psychological sense of well-being. Electric-powered wheelchairs are often a suitable option for those who are unable to self-propel a manual wheelchair. These wheelchairs are available on the market in a wide variety of seat widths, depths and heights, and feature a number of armrest, leg rest and seating options.

Electric-powered wheelchairs are typically controlled by a joystick, but higher-end models offer a multitude of alternative control options such as proximity switches, sip-n-puff, head arrays, infrared switches and magnetic angle sensors just to name a few. This way they can be also used by people with severe motor skill impairments. Driving a power wheelchair is still a quite difficult task for people with low vision, visual field reduction, spasticity, tremors, or cognitive deficits. In order to give also to these people a higher degree of autonomy, and to lighten the duties of those who assist them, a large number of solutions have been studied by researchers since the 1980s, by using technologies originally developed for mobile robots to create the so called smart wheelchairs.

A smart wheelchair typically is a standard powered wheelchair with the addition of a set of sensors to collect environmental data and a computer unit to process them and to find obstacles and hazards. One of the first examples of autonomous wheelchairs is proposed in [1], where a wheelchair is equipped with sonars and a vision system to identify landmarks and correct the trajectory in a hallway.

Recently, more sophisticated systems also implement robotic arms for gesture emulation, such as interacting with objects like bottles, glasses, buttons etc. On the market there are just a few examples of Wheelchair Mounted Robotic Arm (WMRA) systems, such as:

   The Manus WMRA (Fig. 1a), manufactured by Exact Dynamics. This system, developed since the mid of 80s, entered in production at the beginning of the 90s and consists in a 6 DOF arm that can be programmed in a manner comparable to industrial robotic manipulators [2].
 - The Raptor WMRA (Fig. 1b), manufactured by Applied Resources. This manipulator is much simpler in respect of the Manus one. Indeed it has 4 DOF robotic arm that can be directly controlled with either a joystick or a 10-button controller [3]. Typically, the joystick that controls the manipulator arm is located on the armrest opposite to the input device that controls the steering of the power wheelchair.

Systems like the one presented in [3] require the user to manually control the arm position and move it to the desired place. Performing tasks that need high accuracy and precise gestures, such as button pressing, could be very hard for people with severe motor skill disability using this kind of control. For that reason, more autonoums solutions are usually preferred.

For example, in the work presented in [4] authors follow a very promising Eye-in-Hand approach designing a WMRA system. It consists in a 7-DoF wheelchair mounted robotic arm (WMRA) with a camera placed in the end-effector.

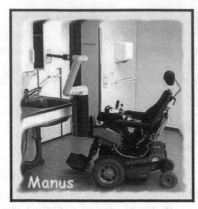

Fig. 1. Manus & Raptor robotic arm

The robotic arm control system uses an Image Based Visual Servoing (IBVS) approach described with a Speeded Up Robust local Features detection (SURF) algorithm in order to detect the features from the camera picture. In an IBVS system, the arm is controlled through information about the distance of the object from a desired position in the image plane, without the necessity of a pose estimation of the target.

Another example is presented in [5], in which a robotic arm is used to press a recognized buttons. In this experiment an IBVS system is implemented in a Raspberry Pi board, using a Raspberry Pi Camera module and a Touch Screen. From an user point of view, the control of the arm is very simple: the video captured by the camera is processed and showed on the screen and the user just have to select which button he wants to press with the robotic arm, then it will move autonomously to the target. Using a Linux based device and a monocular camera - implemented in mobile phones and tablets - increases the portability of the system, also leading to a low-cost, light and small solution. A simple setup like this will have although very reduced computational capability due to the performance of the involved board, which leads to limited computer vision performance.

In our work, we present a system to be used in a Position Based Visual Servoing (PBVS). The system setup is similar to [5], but a parallelization of the processing is possible thanks to the use of Robotic Operative System (ROS) environment, that allows to map different tasks into different "ROS nodes", increasing the computer vision performance and the quality of the control feedback. Differently from the IBVS approach, the PBVS controls the arm via real world coordinates, estimating the pose of the target, giving the arm control node accurate information about the position of the tracked objects.

2   System Description

Our project aims to help people with motor skill impairments to interact with the surrounding environment by performing simple gestures like pressing buttons, knocking on doors, etc. Among these tasks the most complex and computationally intensive is certainly an elevator panel interaction. In this situation the control system shall detect the buttons, track the selected one and control the arm in order to reach it. That is why in this project we focused mainly on this scenario.

The utilized hardware consists of:

- A 5 Degrees of Freedom (DOF) robotic arm
- A Raspberry Pi 3 Model B
- A Raspberry Camera Module V1.3
- A Linux Laptop
- A HCSR-04 Ultrasonic Proximity Sensor

The Raspberry Camera Module is a light camera capable of capturing video at up to 1080p at 30 fps. Thanks to its small dimensions it can be easily placed on the end effector of a robotic arm without interacting with the motor movements. The HCSR-04 proximity sensor is also connected to the Raspberry Pi 3 Board, using the GPIO port. This sensor provides a wide range of measurements, from 2 cm to 400 cm with an accuracy of 3 mm. In Fig. 2 we can see the complete setup of the Raspberry Pi module, which is connected via Wi-Fi to a Linux-based computer.

As previously described, the software architecture is developed in a ROS environment, both on the Raspberry Pi and on the Linux Workstation. The

Fig. 2. The Raspberry Pi Setup, including Camera Module and HCSR-04 sensor

Fig. 3. The robotic arm

Fig. 4. End effector and camera module

Raspberry board holds two ROS nodes, one controlling the camera and publishing video frames with a resolution of 640 × 480, the other polling the proximity sensor, calculating and publishing the object distance. The Workstation runs the ROS master node, the Computer Vision node, the Parallel Tracking and Mapping node and the Scale Extimation node. The information obtained by this system will be sent to the ROS robotic arm controller nodes, which will handle the Inverse Kinematics and the calculation of the arm's joints positions. Figure 3 shows the robotic arm used in this project, while Fig. 4 shows the end effector on which the camera module is mounted.

3   Computer Vision

The Computer Vision task consists in elaborating frames in order to detect the buttons' position in the robot reference frame. After the user selects one of them, the system shall track the selected button, calculating its position in real world

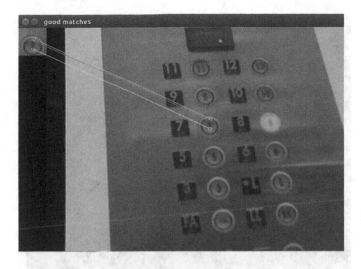

Fig. 5. SIFT extracted features matched to the ROI keypoints

coordinates, in order to provide them to the robotic arm controller in a Position Based Visual Servoing (PBVS) approach. In order to do this, we can separate the computer vision architecture into four different parts:

- Shape detection, in which buttons are detected through their shape;
- Features extraction, using the Scale-Invariant Feature Transform (SIFT) algorithm;
- Parallel Tracking and Mapping, to extract the 3D information out of a monocular camera video;
- Scale estimation and 3D reprojection of the tracked button.

The shape detection is processed via a prebuilt OpenCV function that provides circles centers and radiuses. SIFT algorithm is applied on a small Region of Interest (ROI) around the selected button. In the following frames, the Computer Vision node will extract SIFT features and match them to the ROI ones using Fast Library Approximate Nearest Neighbor (FLANN) [6], realizing the visual tracking of the button. Figure 5 shows extracted keypoints matched to the original button ones.

Parallel Tracking and Mapping [7] algorithm is used to generate a pointcloud of the environment seen by the camera, as shown in Fig. 6. However the information coming from PTAM is not sufficient to obtain real world dimensions since the pointcloud is scaled by an unknown λ scale factor. A Maximum-Likelihood Estimation method [8] is used to estimate λ, getting information from the PTAM pointcloud and the distance provided by an ultrasound proximity sensor.

In order to obtain the button 3D position we need to relate the detected button in the image plane to the pointcloud points. For that reason, it is necessary to project the pointcloud into the image plane, as shown in Fig. 7.

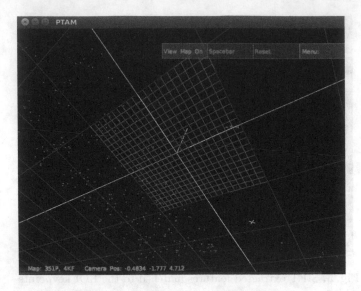

Fig. 6. Generated pointcloud by PTAM

In Eq. 1 is expressed the relationship between the two coordinate systems. The parameters f_x and f_y are the focal lengths of the camera, c_x and c_y are the optical centers. Those parameters are extracted via the OpenCV camera calibration routine.

$$\begin{cases} x_i = f_x * \dfrac{X_c}{Z_c} + c_x \\ y_i = f_y * \dfrac{Y_c}{Z_c} + c_y \end{cases} \tag{1}$$

In order to find the real world coordinates X_c, Y_c, Z_c, another equation is needed.

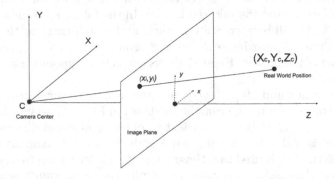

Fig. 7. Real world coordinates and image plane coordinates

The 3D points are projected to the camera plane and the points close to the target are selected. Then a plane is fitted between those points in the real world coordinate system with a Least Squares method.

The plane parameters a, b, c, d obtained from the previous step are used in Eq. 2

$$a * X_c + b * Y_c + c * Z_c + d = 0 \qquad (2)$$

The real world button position is finally calculated in Eq. 3 from Eqs. 1 and 2 using the obtained plane parameters and the camera optical center and focal lengths.

$$\begin{cases} X_c = \dfrac{(x_i - c_x) * Z_c}{f_x} \\ Y_c = \dfrac{(y_i - c_y) * Z_c}{f_y} \\ Z_c = -\dfrac{d}{a * \dfrac{x_i - c_x}{f_x} + b * \dfrac{y_i - c_y}{f_y} + c} \end{cases} \qquad (3)$$

4 Results

The system was tested in a controlled environment: the camera is positioned at a distance range of [18–50] cm. Figure 8 shows measurements taken on the principal camera axis. Table 1 shows the performance of the system in this situation.

Table 1. System performance on principal axis measurement

Min error	Max error	Std deviation	Mean absolute error	R^2
0.05 cm	0.95 cm	0.36 cm	0.31 cm	0.99%

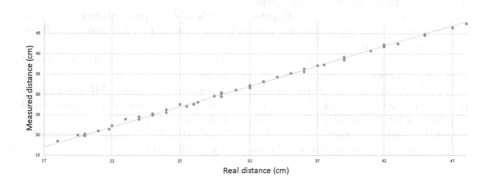

Fig. 8. Real vs. measured distance between end effector and object

5   Conclusion

In this paper we presented a system that calculates the real world coordinates of tracked objects in order to control a robotic arm with a PBVS approach.

The advantage of using a PBVS approach is to have accurate information of the 3D surroundings, allowing a simple implementation of the arm control algorithm to generate the arm movement trajectory. The use of the ROS environment leads to a modularity of the software architecture, making the implementation of new features possible without modifying the other ROS nodes. In addition, executing tasks in different nodes allows to split the calculations into different machines. Finally ROS and all the other softwares and libraries used are open source, and in combination with the Raspberry Pi and Camera Module, realize a low-cost and portable system, simplifying the algorithms implementation. In the next future the computer vision algorithm will be embedded into the robotic arm framework.

Acknowledgment. This research was supported by Fondazione Cassa di Risparmio di Lucca in the framework of the project "RIMEDIO: Il braccio Robotico Intelligente per Migliorare l'autonomia delle pErsone con DIsabilità mOtoria".

References

1. Madarasz, R.L., Heiny, L.C., Cromp, R.F., Mazur, N.M.: The design of an autonomous vehicle for the disabled. IEEE J. Robot. Autom. **2**(3), 117–126 (1986)
2. Eftring, H., Boschian, K.: Technical results from manus user trials. In: International Conference on Rehabilitation Robotics, ICORR 1999 (1999)
3. Hillman, M., Gammie, A.: The bath institute of medical engineering assistive robot. In: Proceedings of ICORR, vol. 94, pp. 211–212 (1994)
4. Elarbi-Boudihir, M., Al-Shalfan, K.A.: Eye-in-hand, eye-to-hand configuration for a WMRA control based on visual servoing. In: 2013 IEEE 11th International Workshop of Electronics, Control, Measurement, Signals and their Application to Mechatronics (ECMSM), pp. 1–6. IEEE (2013)
5. Palla, A., Frigerio, A., Sarti, L., Fanucci, L.: Embedded implementation of an eye-in-hand visual servoing control for a wheelchair mounted robotic arm. In: IEEE ICTS4eHealth (2016)
6. Muja, M., Lowe, D.G.: Scalable nearest neighbor algorithms for high dimensional data. IEEE Trans. Pattern Anal. Mach. Intell. **36** (2014)
7. Klein, G., Murray, D.: Parallel tracking and mapping for small AR workspaces. In: Proceedings of Sixth IEEE and ACM International Symposium on Mixed and Augmented Reality (ISMAR 2007), Nara, Japan, November 2007
8. Engel, J., Sturm, J., Cremers, D.: Scale-aware navigation of a low-cost quadrocopter with a monocular camera. Robot. Autonom. Syst. **62** (2014)

Segmentation of Mosaic Images Based on Deformable Models Using Genetic Algorithms

Alberto Bartoli, Gianfranco Fenu, Eric Medvet$^{(\boxtimes)}$, Felice Andrea Pellegrino, and Nicola Timeus

Department of Engineering and Architecture, University of Trieste, Trieste, Italy
emedvet@units.it

Abstract. Preservation and restoration of ancient mosaics is a crucial activity for the perpetuation of cultural heritage of many countries. Such an activity is usually based on manual procedures which are typically lengthy and costly. Digital imaging technologies have a great potential in this important application domain, from a number of points of view including smaller costs and much broader functionalities. In this work, we propose a mosaic-oriented image segmentation algorithm aimed at identifying automatically the tiles composing a mosaic based solely on an image of the mosaic itself. Our proposal consists of a *Genetic Algorithm*, in which we represent each candidate segmentation with a set of quadrangles whose shapes and positions are modified during an evolutionary search based on multi-objective optimization. We evaluate our proposal in detail on a set of real mosaics which differ in age and style. The results are highly promising and in line with the current state-of-the-art.

Keywords: Multi-objective optimization · Cultural heritage · Image processing

1 Introduction

A *mosaic* is a painting made with small pieces of stone, ceramic, glass or other similar materials of various shapes and colors (called *tiles* or *tessellae*) tied together by plaster or other binder to form geometrical or figurative decorative compositions. Mosaics have a long history, became widespread in ancient times and represent an essential component in the cultural heritage of many countries. Preservation and restoration of ancient mosaics is thus an important activity, usually requiring lengthy and costly procedures based on manual acquisition of the contour of each single tile over a semi-transparent paper superimposed to the mosaic.

Modern *digital imaging* technologies may be a great help in this respect, as tile contours could be collected much more quickly, more cheaply and more accurately with a suitable *image segmentation algorithm* applied to a digital image of the mosaic. In fact, a "digital model" of a mosaic may enable a full range of radically novel approaches and solutions in this area, ranging from

© ICST Institute for Computer Sciences, Social Informatics and Telecommunications Engineering 2017
O. Gaggi et al. (Eds.): GOODTECHS 2016, LNICST 195, pp. 233–242, 2017.
DOI: 10.1007/978-3-319-61949-1_25

analysis of the distribution in large mosaics of tile shapes or of *filler* between tiles, to construction of 3D models to be browsed and zoomed interactively.

To the best of our knowledge, there is only one mosaic-oriented segmentation algorithm that has been proposed in the literature [1]. The performance of the cited work has been assessed and compared to general purpose segmentation algorithms recently [2]. In this work, we propose and evaluate a novel mosaic-oriented image segmentation method. Our proposal consists of an evolutionary procedure based on a *Genetic Algorithm* (GA) [3, 4]. We represent each candidate segmentation as a fixed-size set of quadrangles and quantify its quality based on two indexes that can be calculated without knowing the ideal segmentation in advance. This property is essential in order to make our approach really practical. Such indexes assess the average color dissimilarity within each quadrangle (i.e., tile) and the average color similarity within adjacent quadrangles. We construct a set of different candidate segmentations and then modify such candidate segmentations stochastically for a predefined set of iterations, according to an evolutionary paradigm. We drive evolution with a multi-objective optimization algorithm aimed at minimizing the two indexes mentioned above and associated with each candidate segmentation.

We assess our proposal on 5 real mosaics which differ in age and style and have been used in [2]. We analyze the behavior of our proposal in different flavours, by varying the representation of a candidate segmentation, the criterion for choosing among the resulting candidate segmentations and the number of candidate segmentations. The results are highly promising and in line with the best result in the literature [1, 2].

2 Related Work

Image segmentation amounts to partitioning the pixels into groups according to some criterion, e.g., color similarity. Another, more difficult to evaluate, partitioning criterion consists in grouping pixels depending on the object they belong to. Image segmentation is one of the oldest and most extensively studied problems in Computer Vision, dating back to the early seventies [5]. A general overview can be found, for instance, in [6, 7].

One of the many possible approaches to image segmentation is based on *optimization*: the segmented image acts as the minimizer of a suitable objective function, depending on the original image and on the labeling of individual pixels in the segmented image itself. Choice of a suitable objective function is clearly crucial. Optimization-based segmentation methods may be classified depending on (i) the representation of the candidate solutions, and (ii) the optimization technique used for finding the minimizer.

The simplest representation for a candidate segmentation is a labeled image, i.e., a matrix containing the label assigned to each of the pixels. A more compact and widely employed kind of representation is based on *deformable models*. A taxonomy of deformable models in the context of optimization based image segmentation can be found in [8]. Roughly speaking, deformable models can be thought of as flexible shapes that can be placed over the image and suitably adapted to match the regions in it. There may be either a fixed or a variable number of models and they may be defined either implicitly (for instance by means of the level sets of a proper function [9]) or explicitly (for instance as polygons whose vertices are decision variables [10]).

Concerning the optimization technique, the approaches used in practice rely on an objective function that is not convex and thus may be characterized by many local extrema. Furthermore, the solution space (i.e., the set of all possible segmentations for a given image) is huge and cannot be exhaustively explored. These facts motivate the resort to metaheuristics [11], which can be partitioned in (i) trajectory methods, in which the search process can be seen as the evolution in discrete time of a dynamical system; and, (ii) population-based methods, which iteratively modify a set of candidate solutions thus the search process can be seen as the evolution in discrete time of a set of points in the solution space.

The method presented in this work is based on a particular kind of deformable models, i.e., parametrized convex polygons, and a population-based metaheuristic, i.e., GA. An extensive survey of optimization-based segmentation methods based on deformable models and metaheuristics is reported in [8], while a review of segmentation methods based on GA can be found in [12].

3 Our Method

We consider the problem of the segmentation of a mosaic image, i.e., assigning a label to each pixel of the image: adjacent pixels in the segmented image with the same label belong to the same *region*. Ideally, regions in a mosaic image which has been correctly segmented exactly correspond to mosaic tessellae.

Formally, we denote by S the segmentation method, i.e., a function which assigns a label $S(p)$ to each pixel p of the image I. We assume that the range of S includes a special value $\varnothing$ which should be assigned to pixels which do not belong to any mosaic tessella, but instead correspond to the *filler*, i.e., the cemented network between tessellae.

The quality of a segmentation of a mosaic image can be assessed objectively by comparing it against a manual labeling of that image [2]. In detail, let T_I be the *ground truth* for a mosaic image I and let $S(I)$ be the segmentation obtained by applying a method S to I. Three objective indexes can be computed to compare $S(I)$ against T_I, the average tile precision $\text{Prec}(S(I), T_I)$, the average tile recall $\text{Rec}(S(I), T_I)$, and the tile count error $\text{Count}(S(I), T_I)$:

$$\text{Prec}(S(I), T_I) = \frac{1}{|T_I|} \sum_{T \in T_I} \frac{\max_{R \in S(I)} |R \cap T|}{|R|} \tag{1}$$

$$\text{Rec}(S(I), T_I) = \frac{1}{|T_I|} \sum_{T \in T_I} \frac{\max_{R \in S(I)} |R \cap T|}{|T|} \tag{2}$$

$$\text{Count}(S(I), \mathcal{T}_I) = \frac{\text{abs}(|\mathcal{T}_I| - |S(I)|)}{|\mathcal{T}_I|} \qquad (3)$$

where $|R|$ is the number of pixels which belong to a region R and $|R \cap T|$ is the number of pixels which belong both to R and T. In an optimal segmentation, precision and recall are equal to 1 and the tile count error is equal to 0. The former two indexes may be summarized in the F-measure index, which is the harmonic mean of precision and recall.

The goal of this work is to propose a new segmentation method which improves the state-of-the-art on mosaic images segmentation. We propose to use GA for segmenting mosaic images: a population of individuals—i.e., candidate segmentations—is iteratively evolved trying to maximize their quality. In next sections, we describe how we represent a candidate segmentation $S(I)$ in the GA framework and how we assess it; finally, we discuss other general GA-related choices.

3.1   Solution Representation

A segmentation $S(I)$ is a set of regions of the image: since we are interested in segmenting mosaic images, regions should be able to describe mosaic tessellae, which, in general, are convex polygons, often with 4 vertexes. For this reason, we chose a representation which consists of a fixed-size set of convex quadrangles $S(I) = \{q_1, \ldots, q_n\}$, defined by means of their position within the image I and their size. We explored two variants: one in which each quadrangle q of $S(I)$ is a "rotated rectangle" and one in which each quadrangle q is a "rotated and deformed square".

More in detail, in the rectangle-based representation, each quadrangle is defined as $q^{(i)} = (\Delta x^{(i)}, \Delta y^{(i)}, w^{(i)}, h^{(i)}, \phi^{(i)})$ where $\Delta x^{(i)}$ and $\Delta y^{(i)}$ are the offsets of the rectangle center of gravity with respect to a fixed point $(x^{(i)}, y^{(i)})$ in the Cartesian coordinate system of the image, $w^{(i)}$ and $h^{(i)}$ are the rectangle width and height, and $\phi^{(i)}$ is the angle of rotation of the rectangle. The domain of each component of the rectangle-based representation is the same for each rectangle and depends on a parameter s whose value has to be determined before the segmentation of the image I: s represents the size in pixel of an ideal average squared tessella of the mosaic and can be roughly estimated by a human operator who inspects the mosaic image. In particular, $\Delta x^{(i)}, \Delta y^{(i)} \in \left[-\frac{1}{2}s, \frac{1}{2}s\right]$, $w^{(i)}, h^{(i)} \in \left[\frac{1}{2}s, 2s\right]$ and $\phi^{(i)} \in \left[-\frac{1}{2}\pi, \frac{1}{2}\pi\right]$, for each i. The number n of rectangles in the segmentation and the reference position $(x^{(i)}, y^{(i)})$ of each rectangle are determined using s, the width w_I, and height h_I of the input image I, as follows. First, we determine the number $n_w = \left\lfloor \frac{w_I}{s} \right\rfloor$ and $n_h = \left\lfloor \frac{h_I}{s} \right\rfloor$ of rectangles along the x and y axes of the image, respectively. Then, we set $n = n_w n_h$, $x^{(i)} = ((i-1) \bmod n_w) \frac{w_I}{s} + \frac{1}{2}s$, and $y^{(i)} = \left\lfloor \frac{i}{n_w} \right\rfloor \frac{h_I}{s} + \frac{1}{2}s$, where $i \bmod n_w$ is the remainder of the division between i and n_w, and $\left\lfloor \frac{i}{n_w} \right\rfloor$ is the floor value of $\frac{i}{n_w}$. In other words, given s, a grid of $n_w \times n_h$ square cells is built on the image I and each $(x^{(i)}, y^{(i)})$ is the center of a grid cell.

In the deformed-square-based representation, each quadrangle is defined as $q^{(i)} = (\Delta x^{(i)}, \Delta y^{(i)}, \Delta x_1^{(i)}, \Delta y_1^{(i)}, \ldots, \Delta x_4^{(i)}, \Delta y_4^{(i)}, \phi^{(i)})$ where $\Delta x^{(i)}$, $\Delta y^{(i)}$, and $\phi^{(i)}$ have the same meaning and domain as in the rectangle-based representation; similarly, the number n of quadrangles in the segmentation and their reference positions $(x^{(i)}, y^{(i)})$ are determined from s, w_I, h_I as described above. Concerning the other components, each pair $\Delta x_j^{(i)}, \Delta y_j^{(i)}$ represents the offsets of the jth quadrangle vertex with respect to the corresponding vertex of a square with the same center and with side size equal to s, before the rotation. We set a single domain for all those components which is $\left[-\frac{1}{4}s, \frac{1}{4}s\right]$, i.e., the actual position of each vertex of the quadrangle can be moved, in each direction, at most a quarter of side size away from its reference position. It can be proven that $\left[-\frac{1}{4}s, \frac{1}{4}s\right]$ is the largest domain for which the convexity for a quadrangle defined in this way is granted: despite the convexity of the region is not an intrinsic property of mosaic tessellae, we chose to impose this constraint because it allows a faster computation of aggregate features of pixels within the quadrangle, which is what we do for computing the fitness (see next section). By the way, our experience suggests that mosaic tessellae are in general convex.

3.2   Fitness Function

The quality of a candidate segmentation $S(I)$ can be expressed in terms of precision, recall, and count error. Those indexes can be computed only if a ground truth $\mathcal{T}_I$ is available for the image I. However, when segmenting a mosaic image in a real deployment, $\mathcal{T}_I$ is not available; hence, it follows that they cannot be used to drive the evolution.

In order to overcome this limitation, we use two other indexes as fitness: the *in-tile color dissimilarity* D_{in} and the *out-tile color dissimilarity* D_{out}. Intuitively, the former quantifies, for each region of the candidate segmentation, how different is the color among the region pixels; the latter quantifies, for each region, how different is the average color inside the region with respect to the average color of an external band around the region. If a region correctly superimposes a mosaic tessella on the image, the region in-tile color dissimilarity is low and the out-tile color dissimilarity is high. In order to drive the evolution considering the entire segmentation, D_{in} and D_{out} are the averages across all regions in $S(I)$:

$$D_{\text{in}} = \frac{1}{|S(I)|} \sum_{R \in S(I)} \left(\sigma_{L^*}^R + \sigma_{a^*}^R + \sigma_{b^*}^R \right)$$

$$D_{\text{out}} = \frac{1}{|S(I)|} \sum_{R \in S(I)} \sqrt{\left(\mu_{L^*}^R - \mu_{L^*}^{\bar{R} \backslash R} \right)^2 + \left(\mu_{a^*}^R - \mu_{a^*}^{\bar{R} \backslash R} \right)^2 + \left(\mu_{b^*}^R - \mu_{b^*}^{\bar{R} \backslash R} \right)^2}$$

where $\sigma_{L^*}^R$, $\sigma_{a^*}^R$, and $\sigma_{b^*}^R$ are the standard deviations of the L^*, a^* and b^* channel values of the pixels within the region R (in the CIE-Lab color space), $\mu_{L^*}^R$, $\mu_{a^*}^R$, and $\mu_{b^*}^R$ are the corresponding mean values, and $\bar{R}$ is a region which has the same center of gravity of R but is scaled by a factor $\beta = 1.2$—i.e., $\bar{R}$ is 20% larger than R, hence the out-tile color dissimilarity D_{out} is computed considering the impact on color of the region expansion.

It can be noted that the objectives deriving from the two indexes are not strictly anti-correlated by design. On the other hand, there is a region of the search space in which D_{in} does not improve and D_{out} does worsen, corresponding to regions slightly smaller than the actual tile. Indeed, we observed experimentally that this trade-off is beneficial to the overall evolution.

3.3   GA Parameters and Best Selection

We used NSGA-II [13] as the actual GA-based optimization algorithm. Concerning the genetic operators used to generate new offspring, we used three operators: crossover, uniform mutation, and Gaussian mutation, respectively applied with a probability of 0.8, 0.1, and 0.1.

The crossover operator works as follows: given two segmentations $S'(I)$ and $S''(i)$, a new segmentation $S(I)$ is generated such that the ith component of the jth region of $S(I)$ has one of the two values of the corresponding ith components in the jth regions of the parents $S'(I)$ and $S''(i)$, with equal probability. Note that, in this way, the value of each component in $S(I)$ is granted to stay within the proper domain.

The uniform and Gaussian mutation operators work as follows: given a segmentation $S'(I)$, a new segmentation $S(I)$ is generated such that the ith component of the jth region of $S(I)$ has the same value of the corresponding component in $S'(I)$ with probability $1 - \frac{2}{|S'(I)|n_c}$ and has a new randomly generated value with probability $\frac{2}{|S'(I)|n_c}$, where n_c is the number of components in the representation for each region (i.e., $n_c = 5$ in the rectangle-based representation and $n_c = 11$ in the deformed-square-representation). The new value is chosen according to a uniform distribution within the component domain by the uniform mutation operator, and with Gaussian distribution by the Gaussian mutation operator. For the latter, the mean is set to 0 and the standard deviation is equal to $\frac{1}{10}$ of the component domain width—we set this value after preliminary experimentation. Values mutated with the Gaussian mutation operator are checked and possibly adjusted to stay within their domain. Note that the number of regions in the segmentation is never affected by the genetic operators.

Concerning the criterion for selecting the best individual upon the last generation, i.e., the actual proposed segmentation $S(I)$ for the image I, we explored two options, based on the two fitness function components. Considering the subset of the population consisting of the individuals belonging to the first Pareto front, we choose as best (a) the individual with the lowest in-tile color dissimilarity D_{in}, or (b) the individual with the greatest out-tile color dissimilarity D_{out}.

4   Experimental Evaluation

We were interested in investigating the effectiveness of our proposed segmentation method in general and with respect to its main design choices: the solution representation (rectangle-based vs. deformed-square-based), the best individual selection criterion (min D_{in} vs. max D_{out}), and the population size n_{pop}.

To this end, we considered 5 mosaics which differ in age and style (see Fig. 1) and which have already been used in [2]. For all the 5 mosaic images, we obtained the corresponding ground truth segmentations.

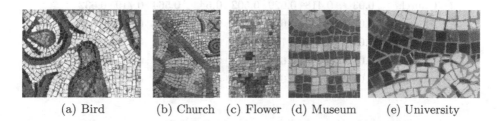

(a) Bird   (b) Church   (c) Flower   (d) Museum   (e) University

Fig. 1. The five mosaics of our experimental evaluation.

We performed several experiments: in each experiment, we applied our method to each mosaic image three times, by varying the random seed used in the evolutionary search. For each mosaic image, we set the parameter s—which represents the side length, in pixel, of an ideal squared tessella (see Sect. 3.1)—to $s = \sqrt{\frac{w_{img}h_{img}}{n_{img}}}$, where w_{img} and h_{img} are the width and height of the image, in pixels, and n_{img} is the number of tessellae in the corresponding grount truth segmentation.

Table 1 shows the main results of our experimentation obtained with $n_{pop} = 50$, deformed-square-based representation, and max D_{out} best selection criterion. The table shows the values, averaged across the three repetitions, of the objective quality indexes presented in Sect. 3: tile count error (Count), average tile precision (Prec), average tile recall (Rec), and F-measure (Fm). In order to provide a baseline, we also applied the state-of-the-art method, Tessella-oriented Segmentation (TOS) [1], to the same mosaics: concerning TOS, as suggested in [2], we set the main parameter α to the value which led to the best F-measure on each mosaic image—differently from our method, for which we used the same parameter values for all the mosaics.

The main finding of the results in Table 1 is that our method is, on the average, competitive with TOS. However, there is no clear winner between the two segmentation methods: the Count index is remarkably better for our method (0.03 vs. 0.33), whereas Fm is better for TOS (0.658 vs. 0.544). In general, hence, our method is better in capturing the number of tessellae, but is not particularly accurate in determining the boundaries of each tessella in the image.

A different point of view on the effectiveness of our method, beyond the analysis of objective indexes, is offered by Fig. 2, which shows two segmentations of the University mosaic image obtained with our method (Fig. 2a, in the variant of Table 1) and TOS (Fig. 2b). Again, a clear conclusion about the best method cannot be drawn. However, it can be seen that the polygon-based representation,

Table 1. Results of a selected variant of our method ($n_{pop} = 50$, deformed-square-based representation, and max D_{out} best selection criterion) compared to TOS [1].

Mosaic	Our method				TOS			
	Count	Prec	Rec	Fm	Count	Prec	Rec	Fm
Bird	0.01	0.411	0.659	0.506	0.03	0.528	0.817	0.642
Church	0.03	0.418	0.629	0.502	0.54	0.564	0.719	0.632
Flower	0.07	0.503	0.626	0.558	0.06	0.494	0.678	0.572
Museum	0.03	0.503	0.760	0.605	0.14	0.644	0.873	0.741
University	0.03	0.459	0.674	0.546	0.90	0.632	0.785	0.701
Average	0.03	0.459	0.669	0.544	0.33	0.572	0.774	0.658

which our method bases on, allows to obtain a segmentation in which pixels deemed to belong to a tessella are clearly distinguishable from pixels deemed to belong to the filler, the criterion being their belonging to a polygon. On the other hand, such discrimination is not possible based on the segmentation obtained with TOS, in which every pixel belongs to a single region and that region provides no information about its nature (filler vs. tessella).

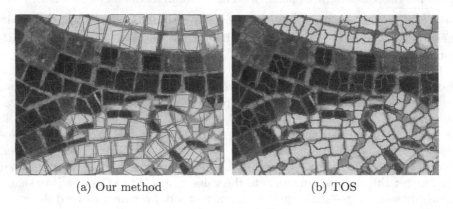

(a) Our method   (b) TOS

Fig. 2. Two segmentations of the University mosaic image obtained with our method (left) and TOS (right).

Tables 2 and 3 show how our main design choices affect the method effectiveness. The Count index is not shown in these tables since it depends only on s (which determines the number n of polygons in the segmentation) and is hence not affected by these design choices.

The impacts of different representations and best selection criteria are shown in Table 2. It can be seen that the representation slightly impacts on Fm: deformed-square-based representation scores 0.543, on average, vs. 0.539 with rectangle-based representation. Differently, the best selection criterion does not affect the average Fm, whereas it can be seen that it does impact on Prec and Rec (largest Prec with min D_{in} and largest Rec with min D_{out}): this finding is consistent with the nature of D_{in} and D_{out} which are intrinsically related to precision and recall, respectively.

Table 2. Precision, recall, and F-measure obtained with $n_{pop} = 50$, different representations and best selection criteria.

Mosaic	Rectangle max D_{out}			Deformed-square min D_{in}			Deformed-square max D_{out}		
	Prec	Rec	Fm	Prec	Rec	Fm	Prec	Rec	Fm
Bird	0.404	0.669	0.504	0.406	0.654	0.501	0.406	0.655	0.502
Church	0.408	0.635	0.497	0.419	0.630	0.503	0.419	0.632	0.504
Flower	0.492	0.630	0.553	0.509	0.621	0.559	0.506	0.624	0.559
Museum	0.529	0.734	0.615	0.525	0.722	0.608	0.518	0.730	0.606
University	0.440	0.652	0.526	0.474	0.643	0.546	0.470	0.653	0.546
Average	0.455	0.664	0.539	0.467	0.654	0.543	0.464	0.659	0.543

Finally, Table 3 shows how the population size n_{pop} affects the effectiveness of our method: we experimented with three values (20, 50, and 100). The results suggest that the choice of $n_{pop} = 50$ is good: a significant decrease in Fm is obtained by reducing n_{pop} to 20, whereas no significant improvement appears to be achievable by doubling the population size. Moreover, in the latter case, the time needed to perform a segmentation (fourth column of each group) roughly doubles.

Table 3. Precision, recall, F-measure, and elapsed time (in s) obtained with different population sizes, the deformed-square-based representation, and the max D_{out} best selection criterion.

Mosaic	$n_{pop} = 20$				$n_{pop} = 50$				$n_{pop} = 100$			
	Prec	Rec	Fm	Time	Prec	Rec	Fm	Time	Prec	Rec	Fm	Time
Bird	0.379	0.671	0.484	2554	0.406	0.655	0.502	4824	0.411	0.659	0.506	12507
Church	0.391	0.643	0.486	2937	0.419	0.632	0.504	7482	0.418	0.629	0.502	16254
Flower	0.480	0.636	0.547	1990	0.506	0.624	0.559	5117	0.503	0.626	0.558	12864
Museum	0.490	0.728	0.585	59	0.518	0.730	0.606	158	0.503	0.760	0.605	409
University	0.416	0.672	0.514	54	0.470	0.653	0.546	156	0.459	0.674	0.546	346
Average	0.431	0.670	0.523	1519	0.464	0.659	0.543	3548	0.459	0.669	0.544	8476

5   Concluding Remarks

We have proposed and evaluated experimentally a novel mosaic-oriented image segmentation method. The method is completely unsupervised, in the sense that does not require any ground truth, and is based on a GA which evolves a fixed-size set of candidate segmentations according to a multi-objective optimization algorithm. The performance indexes to be minimized during the search are a measure of the average color dissimilarity within each tile and of the average color similarity between adjacent tiles.

We have assessed our method on a set of real mosaics which differ in age and style, by using objective measures of segmentation quality (i.e., which require a ground truth associated with each pixel). The results are highly promising and in-line with the existing state-of-the-art.

We believe our method may still be improved and we plan to investigate, in particular, (a) a mechanism for taking into account the possible overlapping among regions of the candidate segmentation, (b) the possibility of varying the number of candidate tiles during a search dynamically, (c) the impact of suitable image preprocessing techniques on segmentation quality.

References

1. Benyoussef, L., Derrode, S.: Tessella-oriented segmentation and guidelines estimation of ancient mosaic images. J. Electron. Imaging **17**(4), 043014 (2008)
2. Fenu, G., Jain, N., Medvet, E., Pellegrino, F.A., Namer, M.P.: On the assessment of segmentation methods for images of mosaics. In: Proceedings of 10th International Conference on Computer Vision Theory and Applications, Institute for Systems and Technologies of Information, Control and Communication (2015)
3. Man, K.F., Tang, K.S., Kwong, S.: Genetic Algorithms: Concepts and Designs. Springer Science & Business Media, Heidelberg (2012)
4. Goldberg, D.E.: Genetic Algorithms. Pearson Education India, Delhi (2006)
5. Brice, C.R., Fennema, C.L.: Scene analysis using regions. Artif. Intell. **1**(3), 205–226 (1970)
6. Szeliski, R.: Computer Vision Algorithms and Applications. Springer, London (2011)
7. Forsyth, D.A., Ponce, J.: Computer Vision: A Modern Approach. Prentice Hall, Upper Saddle River (2003)
8. Mesejo, P., Ibáñez, O., Cordón, O., Cagnoni, S.: A survey on image segmentation using metaheuristic-based deformable models: state of the art and critical analysis. Appl. Soft Comput. **44**, 1–29 (2016)
9. Sethian, J.A.: Level Set Methods and Fast Marching Methods: Evolving Interfaces in Computational Geometry, Fluid Mechanics, Computer Vision, and Materials Science, vol. 3. Cambridge University Press, Cambridge (1999)
10. Kass, M., Witkin, A., Terzopoulos, D.: Snakes: active contour models. Int. J. Comput. Vis. **1**(4), 321–331 (1988)
11. Glover, F.W., Kochenberger, G.A.: Handbook of Metaheuristics, vol. 57. Springer Science & Business Media, Heidelberg (2006)
12. Maulik, U.: Medical image segmentation using genetic algorithms. IEEE Trans. Inf Technol. Biomed. **13**(2), 166–173 (2009)
13. Deb, K., Agrawal, S., Pratap, A., Meyarivan, T.: A fast elitist non-dominated sorting genetic algorithm for multi-objective optimization: NSGA-II. In: Schoenauer, M., Deb, K., Rudolph, G., Yao, X., Lutton, E., Merelo, J.J., Schwefel, H.-P. (eds.) PPSN 2000. LNCS, vol. 1917, pp. 849–858. Springer, Heidelberg (2000). doi:10. 1007/3-540-45356-3_83

On the Retweet Decay of the Evolutionary Retweet Graph

Giambattista Amati[1], Simone Angelini[1], Francesca Capri[2], Giorgio Gambosi[2], Gianluca Rossi[2], and Paola Vocca[3(✉)]

[1] Fondazione Ugo Bordoni, Rome, Italy
{gba,sangelini}@fub.it
[2] University of Rome Tor Vergata, Rome, Italy
francesca.capri.ext@mise.gov.it,
{giorgio.gambosi,gianluca.rossi}@uniroma2.it
[3] University of Tuscia, Viterbo, Italy
vocca@unitus.it

Abstract. Topological and structural properties of social networks, like Twitter, is of a major importance in order to understand the nature of user activities, for example how information propagates or how to identify influencing accounts. A deeper analysis of these properties may have a crucial impact on the design of new applications and of existing ones.

In a social network there are different relations among nodes that can be defined and analyzed by keeping track of how the generated links evolve over time. So far, all evolutionary studies analyze the graph in a *cumulative way*, that is, once a link is inserted in a graph it is never eliminated [9,12]. However, in social networks like Twitter interactions are more volatile, and after a period of life they should die.

In this paper, we consider the *Retweet Graph*, where links are generated by the retweet action made by an user. The life of a tweet is limited in time, and it spans from the time it is generated, to the last time it is retweeted. To take into account the dynamics of Twitter users, we consider a model in which, when a tweet expires, we delete all the edges representing the retweet action relative to this tweet and all users corresponding to involved nodes become inactive, unless they are alive with respect to a different retweeting activity. In particular, we define a new version of the usual Retweet Graph, the *Dynamic Retweet Graph (DRG)*: when a tweet has been retweeted for the last time all the edges related to this tweet are deleted. This allows to model the decay of tweet relevance in Twitter. To evaluate the structural properties of a DRG, we consider three different Twitter streams, derived by monitoring the Twitter flow on three different contexts: two of them are based on a specific event (the 2015 Black Friday and the 2015 World Series) while the third is the Firehose of the whole Twitter stream, filtered by the Italian language.

We study the differences between the DRG graphs and the corresponding cumulative ones by comparing standard metrics for social networks, such as average distance, clustering coefficient, in-degree and out-degree distributions. The analysis shows an important difference

© ICST Institute for Computer Sciences, Social Informatics and Telecommunications Engineering 2017
O. Gaggi et al. (Eds.): GOODTECHS 2016, LNICST 195, pp. 243–253, 2017.
DOI: 10.1007/978-3-319-61949-1_26

between the cumulative graphs and the corresponding DRGs, both on the way they grow, and on the way the observed measures evolve.

Keywords: Graph analysis · Social media · Twitter graph · Retweet graph · Graph dynamics

1   Introduction

The analysis of the topological characteristics of graphs derived from social community systems has a remarkable significance either to derive social properties (the degree of separation, the community detection, the degree distribution, etc.) or to analyze the information flow (how data spread over the network, which are the authoritative users, etc.). Twitter is largely dissimilar to other kind of social networks mainly because all information is open to everyone. On the contrary, on Facebook users adopt very restricted privacy policies and accessibility is only once a friendship relation is established. Additionally, Twitter lets users act freely, e.g. by retweeting posts, following or mentioning any account, and such interactions among accounts result in different kinds of networks [1].

The most studied relationship is the follower/following one, also known as the *Follow Graph*, and is obtained by yielding a directed edge from a vertex a to a vertex b when a follows b. However, it is an almost static form of relation characterized by a small effective diameter (the 90% of reachable pairs have a minimum distance less than this value), a non-power-law in-degree distribution (the followers distribution), and low reciprocity, which overall marks a deviation from known features of other social networks [8]. More generally, the follow graph shows structural properties of both a social and an information network [13].

The follow graph has also been studied in [7] in order to identify authoritative accounts.

The Twitter dataset is prohibitive to crawl on a huge scale because of the very restrictive policy of Twitter's API, therefore the analysis of the follow graph is impractical, and, moreover, it cannot be used to fully describe user interests, because the follow graph does not contain temporal or text information [13].

A different kind of network induced by Twitterverse is the *Retweet Graph*. A Retweet Graph is described as a directed graph, where nodes are accounts and edges between nodes are when one retweets the second. Studies on the retweet graph can be found in [2,4,6,15,16].

The graph representation of a social network is frequently used to assess the temporal evolution of the network, and there are several mathematical models that predict the growth and the trends evolution [4,15,18]. In these models the graph representing the social network is considered in a cumulative way, that is once an edge or a vertex is inserted it is never eliminated, even when the relation or the account they represent does not exist anymore (e.g. the two accounts terminate the following/follower relationship, the retweeted tweet is obsolete, etc.). Whilst this assumption may be still plausible in the case of the following/follower relationship, which is inherently static because, the deletion of a following/follower link takes place less often, and thus a cumulative evolutionary graph model may be reasonable, it is largely unrealistic when considering more dynamic relations as the retweeting one.

In this paper, in order to take into consideration the dynamics of the Twitterverse, we introduce a variant of the retweet graph, that is, the *Dynamic Retweet Graph (DRG, for short)*. The graph is built as follows: when a tweet is retweeted for the last time, all edges associated to this tweet are removed. This assumption would model the expiration of a tweet in Twitter.

The DRG behavior is tested against three distinct Twitter collections, derived by monitoring the activities in three distinctive contexts: two collections refer to a specific event (*event driven*), that is, they are derived by filtering the Twitter stream using a set of words related to these specific events (the first one refers to the 2015 Black Friday whilst the second the 2015 World Series); the third one is the whole Italian Twitter stream, filtered by the Italian language, denoted *Italian Firehose*. To derive the Italian Twitter Firehose we use a list of the most frequently used Italian stop words and the Twitter native selection function for languages.

We observed the evolution of the DRGs for two months and compute the basic structural measures that are normally used to evaluate social networks. Then we compare results on DRGs with their corresponding cumulative graphs [2], in terms of clustering coefficient, in-degree and out-degree distributions, average distance.

Results point out a substantial difference between the DRGs and the relative cumulative graphs both on how they grow and the way the structural measures evolve. Only the Italian Firehose shows a similar behavior of the cumulative and the dynamic graph, whilst for the event driven graphs some properties show different trends. In particular, in the case of the Italian Firehose retweet graph the sizes of the edges and vertices sets and the considered measures do not show discontinuity in their growth, while the event driven graphs show a skewed distribution and reach a predictably saturation point at end of the event. The measures for the firehose retweet graph are more similar to a social network, such as Facebook, than to an information network, whilst the event driven retweet graphs is the opposite.

The study of the temporal evolution of the retweet graphs is a preliminary work in order to better understand the nature of Twitter, how trends evolve over time, to detect both authoritative and spamming accounts, and to derive a suitable mathematical evolutionary model of Twitter communities.

1.1 Related Work

A large literature on the evolution of Twitter [8,13] compare Twitter to other social networks, or analyze the evolution over time of the Twitter social graph in order to model topic trends [5,17] or model just the twitter network [5,14,15,17, 18]. One of the open problem is to assess the social nature of Twitter, whether it is more a social network than a social media, or is both showing a double nature of the Twitterverse [8,13]. On the other hand, the evolutionary behavior of Twitter is mostly studied for trends analysis. News streams in Twitter, as well as in many other news media, show a star-like shape [5]. This shape is shown by means of a dataset gathered on Twitter during the Iranian election on the 2009 [17], reflecting the tendency that flows spread widely and not deeply. Starting from the Superstar model, that represents the condensation phenomenon occurring in the largest component of a retweet graph [4], a evolutionary mathematical model for the retweet graph based on the density distribution of edges, and the density of the largest connected component [14,15]. Finally, a classification method allows to rapidly identify categories of trends by means of different triggers that starts trends, through [18].

2   Graph Construction and Evolution

A DRG $G = (V, E, \ell)$ is a graph where the vertex set V is made of Twitter accounts and a direct edge $(a, b) \in E$ exists if and only if a has retweeted at least one tweet of b, that can be itself already a retweet. Since an user a may retweet many tweets of b we maintain them distinct labeling the edge (a, b) with the id of the original tweet and the timestamp on which this retweet occurs. Labels are represented with a list $\ell(e)$ associated to each edge $e = (a, b)$, consisting of pairs (i, t) where i is the id of a tweet and t is the timestamp in which a retweets i from b. The pairs of $\ell(e)$ are sorted for timestamps in non-decreasing order.

Starting from the information represented, for each tweet i we define the *date of birth* denoted by $\mathrm{dob}(i)$, as the timestamp of the first retweet of i. Dually, the *date of death* of i, denoted $\mathrm{dod}(i)$, is the timestamp of the last retweet of i. In a formal way,

$$\mathrm{dob}(i) = \min_{e \in E}\{t : (i, t) \in \ell(e)\}$$

and

$$\mathrm{dod}(i) = \max_{e \in E}\{t : (i, t) \in \ell(e)\}.$$

Therefore, a tweet i is *alive at time* t if and only if $\mathrm{dob}(i) \leq t \leq \mathrm{dod}(i)$.

A node $v \in V$ is *alive at time* t if and only if there is a tweet connecting the node v that is alive.

With the above definitions we can derive a sequence of DRG graphs G_t based on time variation. Let $V_t \subseteq V$ be the set of alive nodes of V at time t. The graph $G_t = (V_t, E_t)$ at time t is a subgraph of G, when E_t all edges e are relative to alive tweets. For simplicity, we give an example. If G is the retweet graph (see the left side of Fig. 1) then G_{20} coincides with G since the tweets with labels 1 or 2 are alive before the timestamp 20, according to periods in the left part of Fig. 1. Differently, E_{35} contains only edges (c, a) and (a, b).

We set a 4 hours interval in our experiments, that is the series of DRGs are $(G_{t_i})_{i \geq 0}$ and $t_{i+1} - t_i = 4$.

In order to compare results with the corresponding cumulative graphs we use the same data sets as in paper [2]. Among the three different collections, two are *event driven*, that is filtered by using a set of words specifying two events,

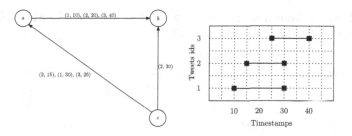

Fig. 1. On the left, a retweet graph with edges labeled with $\langle i, t \rangle$. On the right, a the life-time interval are represented.

the 2015 Black Friday and the 2015 World Series; the last is the whole Italian Twitter stream, also called the *Italian Firehose*. We filtered by the most frequent Italian stop-words and by the Twitter native selection function for languages. Table 1 shows the sizes of the cumulative retwet graphs of the three collections.

Table 1. Dimensions of the three cumulative graphs

	Black friday	World series	Italian firehose
Vertices	2.7e+06	4.74e+05	2.541739e+06
Edges	3.9e+06	8.4e+05	1.3708317e+07
Tweets/edges	2.603	2.3	5.45
Tweets/vertices	3.66	4	29.4

Figure 2 describes the dimensional evolution of the three graphs over the observation.

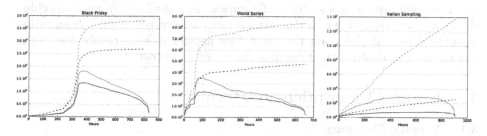

Fig. 2. Vertex number (blue) and edge number (green) of the Italian Firehose, World Series, and Black Friday as a function of hours. Solid lines represent the trend of the DGR, dashed lines represent the trend of the cumulative graphs

Figure 3 shows that the graphs densify over time, having the size edge set growing more than the node set. A densification law for edges with respect the number of nodes, known as *Densification Power Law (DPL)* also holds for all DRG graphs and follows a power-law [10,11].

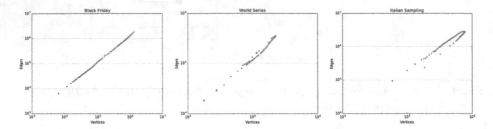

Fig. 3. Densification Power Law holds for all three DRG graphs (Black Friday coefficient = 1.06, World Series coefficient = 1.18, Italian Firehose coefficient = 1.32). The color change from green to red in accordance with the timestamp growth. When approaching the end of the stream the edge number decay is more rapid than node number decay in the case of the Italian Firehose.

Note that the event-driven graphs and the Firehose graph evolve differently: the event-driven graphs rapidly grow near the event time and afterward they have a gradual decline. On the contrary, we note that the Twitter Italian Firehose DRG graph has a slower growth and a more rapid decline, maybe due to the border effect. The DPL shows that the Firehose retweet graph behaves two ways (green line and red line): with the green line it increases, and, afterwards, with the red line it declines abruptly reaching the very last timestamp.

For what concern the event-driven graphs, the rapid growth near the event can be easily established with the growing interest for the event itself. Moreover, the slow decline suggests the diminished interest.

Concerning the Firehose graph, the increase and the decline is because of "border effects". Beginning from empty graph G_0, we have a sequence of increasing sizes before reaching a stable configuration. In a similar way, while reaching the final state G_{final} in which the graph is again empty, the stable configuration starts to decay. At this point the curve does not decrease vertically due to the fact the date of death is the final time the tweet is retweeted.

3   Measures Description and Trends

3.1   Average Distance

The average distance $Avg(G)$ is defined as follows:

$$Avg(G) = \frac{\sum_{d \geq 1} d \cdot \text{number of pair of vertices at distance} \quad d}{\text{number of connected pairs of vertices}}$$

Figure 4a shows the evolution of the average distances. Again, the event-driven graphs are different to the Firehose graph. In this last graph the average distance

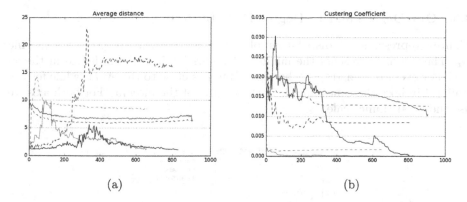

Fig. 4. Trend of the average distance (a) and cluster coefficient (b) in the three observed retweet graphs: Black Friday in blue; World Series in green and Italian Firehose in red. The DRGs are represented with solid lines and the corresponding cumulative graphs with dashed lines.

is almost constant while in the event driven case we have a climax in proximity of the event.

The Italian Firehose has the same distance tendency and average distance as the corresponding cumulative graph. On the contrary, event-driven DRG graphs arc unstable and both growth and decay are very steep having reached a peak and that they do no longer converge. Moreover, the average distance value is much smaller than the corresponding cumulative graphs. On the contrary, event-driven DRG graphs are very unstable and the growth and the decay are very rapid reaching a peek and they do not converge. In addition, the average distance magnitude of event-driven DRG graphs is much smaller than the corresponding cumulative graphs.

3.2   Clustering Coefficient

Figure 4b shows the global clustering coefficient trend. Barrat and Weigt [3] introduced the global clustering coefficient in the physical and mathematical context as largely used in social sciences. Clustering coefficient correlates to the probability of obtaining a triangle of connections from two consecutive connecting edges, in other words, the clustering coefficient is the probability that a friend of your friend is likely to be your friend. Mathematically:

$$C = \frac{3 \times \text{number of triangles in the network}}{\text{number of paths of length 2}}$$

The Italian Firehose DRG's clustering coefficient is similar to that of the cumulative graph. Black Friday's DRG is different to the cumulative retweet graph, but the World Series has the DRG and the cumulative graphs following a similar trend. This is mainly because the observation of the World series event begun when it was already started.

3.3   Out-Degree and In-Degree Distributions

Figure 5 represents the distribution of the in-degrees with respect to a specific G_t. The y-axis represents the number of nodes having the in-degree in the x-axis. For event driven graphs, the timestamp t is close to the event, while for the Italian Firehose the timestamp is in the middle of the interval. For both axis we use the logarithmic scale.

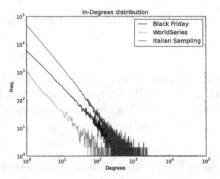

Fig. 5. The in-degrees distribution of a DRG at a specific timestamp.

From Fig. 5 it follows that the in-degrees distributions of all the three graphs attain a power-law distribution. The same trend can be observed both with different time-stamps and for the out-degree distribution, whose plots are not reported here for lack of space. Figure 6 reports the trend of the power-law exponents of the in- and out- degrees distribution.

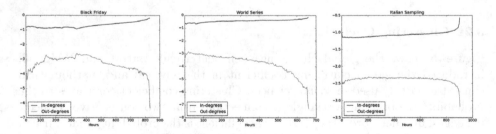

Fig. 6. Power-law exponents of the out-degrees (green) and of the in-degrees (blue) distributions of the World Series, Black Friday and Italian Firehose as functions of hours. (Color figure online)

4   Discussion and Conclusions

There are well known properties that actual graphs fulfil, which include heavy tails for the out-degree and in-degree distribution, shrinking average distance and diameters, and the Densification Power Law (DPL) [10,11]. The retweet graphs of all collections fulfill all these properties [2]. In this paper, we have analyzed the tweet lifetime and its natural temporal decay, by considering only the subgraphs (DRG) that remain active during the stream, and, thus, by cutting off those elements (accounts and interactions) in the graph that become obsolete in the whole network. The analysis performed shows a substantial difference in the evolution for the two classes of graphs: the event driven (both the Black Friday and the World series) and the Italian Firehose. It is interesting to note that for the Italian Firehose, which can be seen as the superposition of a sequence of event-based subgraphs, the DRGs evolution has the same structural properties of the cumulative graph. Moreover, in the case of the average distance and of the clustering coefficient no change occurs, which substantiates that the Firehose is indeed the result of the union of different communities induced by different event-driven streams. On the contrary, for the event-based graphs we have a border effect on all structural metrics, all growing and decaying in a similar way, and reaching a climax in the middle of their lifetime interval with a value much smaller than the values of their corresponding cumulative graphs. Additionally, all the structural properties valid for the cumulative graphs, with the exception of the Densification Power Law and Degree Power Laws, do not hold for the DRGs. In fact, the average distance and the clustering coefficient tend to converge super-linearly. Note that, from the analysis performed, the model proposed (DRG) better captures the different evolutionary behavior of the two kinds of retweet graphs (event-driven and the firehose). In fact, in [2], the topological measures on the cumulative retweet graphs without taking into account the edges decay, do not show a substantial difference. Additionally, the generative models proposed in literature [4,14,15] fail in representing the edges decay in the event-driven retweet graphs. Hence, a promising future research direction is to define a tighter mathematical model.

Acknowledgments. This work was conducted in the Laboratory of Big Data of ISCOM-MISE (Institute of communication of the Italian Ministry for Economic Development). Francesca Capri was supported by a grant of ISCOM-MISE.

References

1. Amati, G., Angelini, S., Bianchi, M., Fusco, G., Gambosi, G., Gaudino, G., Marcone, G., Rossi, G., Vocca, P.: Moving beyond the Twitter follow graph. In: Proceedings of the International Conference on Knowledge Discovery and Information Retrieval, KDIR 2015, part of the 7th International Joint Conference on Knowledge Discovery, Knowledge Engineering and Knowledge Management (IC3K 2015), Lisbon, Portugal, 12–14 November 2015, vol. 1, pp. 612–619 (2015)

2. Amati, G., Angelini, S., Capri, F., Gambosi, G., Rossi, G., Vocca, P.: Twitter temporal evolution analysis: comparing event and topic driven retweet graphs. In: Proceedings of the International Conference on Big Data Analytics, Data Mining and Computational Intelligence, BIGDACI 2016, Funchal, Madeira, Portugal, 2–4 July 2016, vol. 1 (2016)

3. Barrat, A., Weigt, M.: On the properties of small-world network models. Eur. Phys. J. B-Condens. Matter Complex Syst. **13**(3), 547–560 (2000)

4. Shankar Bhamidi, J., Steele, M., Zaman, T., et al.: Twitter event networks and the superstar model. Ann. Appl. Probab. **25**(5), 2462–2502 (2015)

5. Bhattacharya, D., Ram, S.: Sharing news articles using 140 characters: a diffusion analysis on Twitter. In: 2012 IEEE/ACM International Conference on Advances in Social Networks Analysis and Mining (ASONAM), pp. 966–971. IEEE (2012)

6. Bild, D.R., Liu, Y., Dick, R.P., Mao, Z.M.: Aggregate characterization of user behavior in Twitter and analysis of the retweet graph. ACM Trans. Internet Technol. **15**(1), 4 (2015)

7. Java, A., Song, X., Finin, T., Tseng, B.: Why we Twitter: understanding microblogging usage and communities. In: Proceedings of the 9th WebKDD and 1st SNA-KDD 2007 Workshop on Web Mining and Social Network Analysis, WebKDD/SNA-KDD 2007, pp. 56–65. ACM, New York (2007)

8. Kwak, H., Lee, C., Park, H., Moon, S.: What is Twitter, a social network or a news media? In: Proceedings of the 19th International Conference on World Wide Web, WWW 2010, pp. 591–600. ACM, New York (2010)

9. Leskovec, J., Chakrabarti, D., Kleinberg, J., Faloutsos, C., Ghahramani, Z.: Kronecker graphs: an approach to modeling networks. J. Mach. Learn. Res. **11**, 985–1042 (2010)

10. Leskovec, J., Kleinberg, J., Faloutsos, C.: Graphs over time: densification laws, shrinking diameters and possible explanations. In: Proceedings of the Eleventh ACM SIGKDD International Conference on Knowledge Discovery in Data Mining, KDD 2005, pp. 177–187. ACM, New York (2005)

11. Leskovec, J., Kleinberg, J., Faloutsos, C.: Graph evolution: densification and shrinking diameters. ACM Trans. Knowl. Discov. Data **1**(1), 2 (2007)

12. Leskovec, J., Chakrabarti, D., Kleinberg, J., Faloutsos, C.: Realistic, mathematically tractable graph generation and evolution, using kronecker multiplication. In: Jorge, A.M., Torgo, L., Brazdil, P., Camacho, R., Gama, J. (eds.) PKDD 2005. LNCS, vol. 3721, pp. 133–145. Springer, Heidelberg (2005). doi:10.1007/11564126_17

13. Myers, S.A., Sharma, A., Gupta, P., Lin, J.: Information network or social network?: the structure of the twitter follow graph. In: Proceedings of the Companion Publication of the 23rd International Conference on World Wide Web Companion, WWW Companion 2014, Republic and Canton of Geneva, Switzerland, pp. 493–498. International World Wide Web Conferences Steering Committee (2014)

14. ten Thij, M., Bhulai, S., Kampstra, P.: Circadian patterns in Twitter. In: Data Analytics, pp. 12–17 (2014)

15. ten Thij, M., Ouboter, T., Worm, D., Litvak, N., Berg, H., Bhulai, S.: Modelling of trends in Twitter using retweet graph dynamics. In: Bonato, A., Graham, F.C., Pralat, P. (eds.) WAW 2014. LNCS, vol. 8882, pp. 132–147. Springer, Cham (2014). doi:10.1007/978-3-319-13123-8_11

16. Yang, M.-C., Lee, J.-T., Lee, S.-W., Rim, H.-C.: Finding interesting posts in Twitter based on retweet graph analysis. In: Proceedings of the 35th International ACM SIGIR Conference on Research and Development in Information Retrieval, SIGIR 2012, pp. 1073–1074. ACM, New York (2012)

17. Zhou, Z., Bandari, R., Kong, J., Qian, H., Roychowdhury, V.: Information resonance on Twitter: watching Iran. In: Proceedings of the First Workshop on Social Media Analytics, pp. 123–131. ACM (2010)
18. Zubiaga, A., Spina, D., Martinez, R., Fresno, V.: Real-time classification of Twitter trends. J. Assoc. Inf. Sci. Technol. **66**(3), 462–473 (2015)

Maps for Easy Paths (MEP): Enriching Maps with Accessible Paths Using MEP Traces

Sara Comai(✉), Emanuele De Bernardi, Matteo Matteucci,
and Fabio Salice

Politecnico di Milano, Piazza L da Vinci, 32, 20133 Milan, Italy
{sara.comai, emanuele.debernardi, matteo.matteucci,
fabio.salice}@polimi.it

Abstract. MEP (Maps for Easy Paths) is a project for the enrichment of geographical maps with information about accessibility of urban pedestrian pathways, targeted at people with mobility problems and, in particular, with motor impairments. In this paper we describe the application to collect data along the paths travelled by target people and show experimental results.

Keywords: City accessibility · Path reconstruction · Mobility impairments · Mobile application

1 Introduction

According to World Health Organization about 15% of the world's population has some form of disability and traveling through cities is one of the main concerns for people with mobility impairments [12]. Some help could come from an adaptive navigating system capable of considering their needs and taking into account the (mapped) accessibility of urban routes. Nevertheless, mapping accessible paths in a sustainable way is still an open challenge. The most cumbersome activity in providing an enriched map with accessibility information is gathering such information through field surveys, which is typically done manually by users or volunteers.

Maps for Easy Paths (MEP) is an ongoing project [8] aiming to overcome the limitations of current collaborative approaches in mapping accessible routes by easing the surveying effort through the collection of motion data from sensors commonly available in mobile devices. The accessibility of city routes, e.g., sidewalks, walkways, etc., is defined through the active contribution and participation of the target users, which include people with permanent or temporary motor disabilities and, possibly, also active citizens.

To ease target users and volunteers in data collection, we developed a mobile application called *MEP Traces* to automatically store mobile sensors data (e.g., positions estimated from GNSS satellites, motion sensors data, etc.) when users travel through the city: they just need to start the app at the beginning of their journey and stop it when they arrive. The underlying idea is that the route travelled by a person with disability, i.e., the target user of the MEP project, can be considered *accessible* also for other persons having the same (or a lower) type of disability. More in general, we

© ICST Institute for Computer Sciences, Social Informatics and Telecommunications Engineering 2017
O. Gaggi et al. (Eds.): GOODTECHS 2016, LNICST 195, pp. 254–263, 2017.
DOI: 10.1007/978-3-319-61949-1_27

assume that a path taken mostly by people with disabilities can be perceived as a friendlier route; this allows us to automatically identify *accessible paths* without the need of an ad-hoc field survey simply because the traveler who captures the data has been register to have some specific sort of disability.

After reporting related works in Sect. 2, in Sect. 3 we describe the MEP project and in particular MEP Traces and the overall process to extract the accessible paths. In Sect. 4 experimental results of a survey done in Cernobbio (Como, Italy) are reported, while in Sect. 5 conclusions are drawn and future works are described.

2 Related Works

Several collaborative projects proposed in the literature aim to improve city accessibility, through the Web or, more recently, through smartphones/tablets applications, as surveyed in [3]. Different types of barriers, but also of facilitators, have been identified and classified in several studies: such classifications are at the basis of our analysis for the collection of data about accessibility of city pedestrian pathways.

Considering the status of Web/Android/iOS applications available to the public, almost all of them focus on accessibility of points of interest (e.g., museums, restaurants, etc.). Only some of available apps include also information about condition of sidewalks and pedestrian crosswalks, or about the presence of cobblestones, curb ramps, and street lighting, such as RotaAccesivel [10], Comuni per tutti [4] and Mapability [7]. These proposals are very general and try to address all the disabilities. However, the collection of data is quite heavy, being mainly manual.

In the literature, solutions for the identification of accessible paths and sidewalk conditions have been considered only by few approaches, like, e.g., [2, 6, 9, 11]. Cardonha et al. [2] adopted an approach, in part, similar to MEP: the *Breadcrumb* application was developed to periodically capture a sequence of measurements based on the device geo-location (i.e., longitude and latitude) without any need for user intervention. To enhance the quality of the collected data, *Breadcrumb* applies a simple moving average of the last 10 estimates of the velocity of the device to identify slowdowns as obstacles. Compared to *Breadcrumb*, in our approach we try to extract as much as information as possible from the available sensors fusing the GNSS with the inertial data in order to reconstruct the exact path of the user, supposed to be accessible, besides trying to infer the presence of obstacles from motion data, as explained in Sect. 3.3.

Karimi et al. [6] propose a routing module which tracks the shuttles available in the main campus of the University of Pittsburgh and, given an accessibility map built manually, they provide turn-by-turn directions distinguishing among sidewalks along a street, along a building, and crosswalks along a building. Also [9] collects GPS data to determine the users' trajectories and provides an algorithm to determine an accessible path between two locations for users with a certain disability: however, to the best of our knowledge, only a prototype has been produced. Finally, also [11] consider sidewalks, by providing a mobile application to capture pictures and upload data about some observable aspects of sidewalk conditions such as holes, presence of steps, etc.

3   MEP Traces and Path Reconstruction

In the MEP project we adopted a user-centered design approach involving target users from the early phases of the project being them the main actors of the data collection besides being the beneficiaries of the collected data.

3.1   Requirements of the Application

Users' requirements were collected with focus groups involving both manual and electric wheelchair users, as well as elderly people with mobility issues. The main requirements that emerged from the focus groups include: easiness in using the app, interactive interfaces, easy to click and to understand icons and interactive buttons. With respect to this last point some of the wheelchair users of the focus group had finger movement limitations, for example when performing zoom in and out or in typing with digital keyboards: simple single click commands are therefore required.

Regarding the information to be collected along the pathways, and therefore to show on the map, they highlighted that they would prefer an app telling them the *accessible* paths to follow, and that they would not like to hear about obstacles. Among possible accessible elements they are interested in accessible toilets, transportation stops, and parking lots, as well as any building or point of interest of the city. In this project we have mainly focused on the paths and on the algorithms for their reconstruction.

In case of obstacles, it should be possible to signal them together with pictures that may give a better idea of the obstacle for the specific disability; simple and not-long-to-fill obstacles' evaluation forms should be offered by the application. Finally, personalized maps according to typical disabilities (e.g., manual vs. electric wheelchair) should be provided: the collected data should therefore take into account also the users' characteristics, so that, for example, a path travelled by a user requiring step-free accessibility can be considered accessible also for users able to climb low curbs.

The whole mapping process should take into account the different kinds of users: not only the interface should be suitable for users with motor impairments, but also processing algorithms should take into account mobility problems: in particular, when using sensor fusion techniques, they should be suitable for data collected on wheelchairs and cannot exploit step detection or similar techniques to improve the reconstruction of the path.

3.2   Data Collection and Processing Overview

Figure 1 describes the process for the collection of paths data and for their reconstruction: when a user starts a route, s/he activates an app called MEP-Traces to collect along the whole path data needed to its reconstruction. Such data include GNSS positions estimates (at present, GPS and GLONASS), motion sensors data (e.g., accelerometer, gyroscope, etc.) and, possibly, images; all the data are stored on the

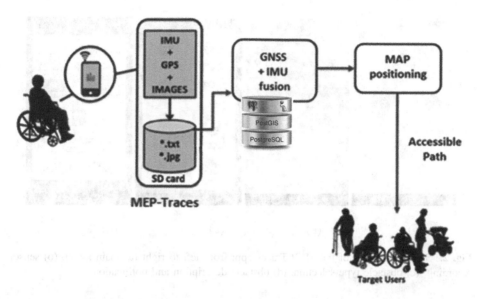

Fig. 1. Overview of the (accessible) path computation process

device SD-card and then uploaded on the server in a PostGIS database for further processing. On the server, since the accuracy in positioning of GNSS data is quite low for mobile device GNSS receivers, we fuse GNSS positions with motion data to provide a better estimate of the path, especially in those parts of the route where GNSS satellites are not visible; the output is an accessible path, which is then positioned in a geographical map.

3.3 MEP-Traces Application

MEP-Traces is the Android application for the collection of data from common hardware sensors like GNSS, accelerometer, magnetometer, gyroscope, and barometer, embedded in the current generation of smartphones and tablets. Data are collected simultaneously, at the highest possible frequency, and locally stored in the mobile device SD-card.

Figure 2 shows some snapshots of our Android prototype: after registration, it provides a simple menu to start the recording of the route, manage user's profile, send collected data, and exit the application. The main task of MEP-Traces is to track the user with motor impairments while s/he is travelling with the idea of mapping only accessible paths. Nevertheless, while the application runs and records all the sensors data, it is possible to signal obstacles (e.g., stairs, slopes, etc.) that can be then used for further analysis or refinements of the collected traces; moreover, it is possible to enrich maps also with accessible elements (e.g., parking lots for disabled people, accessible transport, etc.).

Some information, like available memory, and battery level can also be checked. This is used to warn the user when critical levels are reached, and to promptly save the

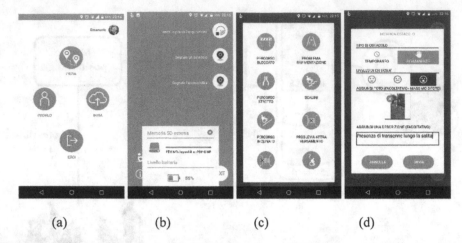

(a)   (b)   (c)   (d)

Fig. 2. Some snapshots of the MEP Traces app; from left to right (a) main menu, (b) sensor recording, (c) obstacle type selection, (d) obstacle description and notification.

acquisitions not to miss important data for processing. Obstacles can be notified with a simple click among predefined obstacle types: then, some characteristics, like the type (temporary or permanent) and the criticality level (low, medium, high), can be specified. Optionally, some pictures and a description can be included.

The application has been developed to dynamically recognize all the motion sensors in the device (e.g., step detector, orientation, proximity, rotation vector, etc.), but only accelerometer, gyroscope and magnetic field sensors are acquired by default. To retrieve the device position, the GPS sensor is used. The application automatically starts the sensor monitoring as soon as the GPS geo-location is obtained. For each acquisition phase, a specific folder is created, to store the files containing all the information of the sensors changes during the movement. Collected data need to be explicitly sent by the user to the server for further processing and sharing. Before sending them, we minimize the upload effort compressing each acquisition folder. The upload operation is forced with a connection between the device and our server over WiFi using the SFTP (SSH File Transfer Protocol), as in Fig. 3. During this task, the acquisition uploaded correctly to the server (after a client/server check) is automatically deleted from the mobile device while the upload proceeds.

3.4   Path Reconstruction

Data collected with the MEP-Traces application are used by the MEP-Fusion engine to reconstruct the path followed by MEP-Traces users. The approach used in the reconstruction is based on the fusion of information coming from multiple sensors to overcome issues related to the poor quality of the mobile sensors: indeed, the GPS and the internal Inertial Measurement Unit of the mobile device could single-handedly provide an absolute position and orientation for the device, but measurement noise produces inaccurate results.

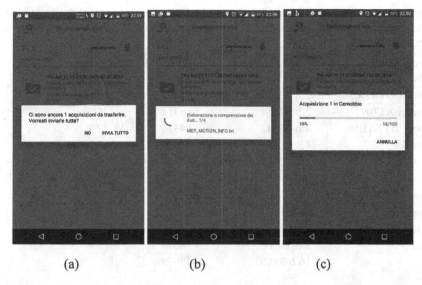

(a)   (b)   (c)

Fig. 3. MEP-Traces upload interface example: from left to right (a) automatic selection of all the acquisitions, (b) data compression, (c) connection and uploading task

Being the application targeted to users with disabilities, including those with motor impairments, methods often used to track pedestrian movements using mobile devices, which are based on step detection, are ineffective. For this reason, our solution is based on (and extends) the ROAMFREE sensor fusion library [5]. ROAMFREE, which stands for Robust Odometry Applying Multisensor Fusion to Reduce Estimation Errors, is a framework developed at the Artificial Intelligence and Robotics lab of Politecnico di Milano originally designed to fuse measurements coming from an arbitrary number of sensors, including images, in order to determinate the position and orientation of a mobile robot. Details of the approach can be found in [1]. Since the ROAMFREE library is able to reconstruct the trajectory using the absolute reference frame of the GNSS and the orientation provided by the Earth magnetic field recorded by the magnetometer, the device during the route can be held freely by the user. However, a swinging device, produces less accurate results.

4 Experimental Results

The experimental activity done in Cernobbio (Como, Italy) consisted in two days of acquisition, with MEP-Traces installed on different Android smartphones and tablets (used devices are listed in Table 1). The collected GPS data are graphically shown in Fig. 4. In the left-hand side picture, data are represented over a cartographic map using different colors, one for each device; only a portion of the city is included in the picture. In the right-hand side picture, the whole amount of collected GPS sensor data made in Cernobbio (Como, Italy) with all devices is shown.

Table 1. Average battery consumption for each device in using MEP-Traces during the experiments in Cernobbio (Como, Italy) with total acquisition time and the total length (in meters).

Android device	Acquisition time	Walk [m]	Average 1 h battery consumption
Samsung GT-I9505	1 h 13' 54"	3792	3%
Motorola XT1092	2 h 07' 54"	6312	16%
Huawei MT7-TL10	4 h 43' 42"	14314	7%
Nexus 5	42' 31"	1862	3%
Motorola XT1092	2 h 10' 47"	6730	5%
Nexus 7 2013	20' 55"	971	5%
Nexus 7 2013	1 h 33' 20"	1070	24%
Nexus 7 2012	06' 08"	152	2%
Samsung GT-I9070	2 h 22' 45"	3796	15%
Nexus 5	1 h 16' 06"	4074	5%
	16 h 38' 02"	43073	

Fig. 4. GPS data collected in Cernobbio (Como, Italy) with MEP Traces, two different views

To evaluate the quality of the acquisitions of mobile devices, the collected GPS data have been compared with the data of a high-cost geodetic device – in our case a Leica GPS 1200 receiver. Figure 5 shows the acquisitions for the same path of the geodetic device (in black) and the low cost GNSS receiver of a Google Nexus 6P GPS sensor (in purple); you can notice how it is affected by a lot of noise. To provide a better estimation of the correct path, we have already fused our GPS data with the motion sensors data.

During the acquisition along the routes, some obstacles have been notified with the application. Figure 6 shows some details of obstacle visualizations.

The average battery consumption of MEP-Traces has also been computed for each device. The application is designed to run in background trying to use the minimal Android system resources, allowing the user to do any other task (e.g., calls, receiving sms and emails, using the internet, etc.). Table 1 shows the total acquisition time and the total length of the walked path (expressed in meters).

Fig. 5. Details of two different acquisitions with a geodetic device – Leica GPS 1200 receiver (black route) and a low cost GNSS receiver - Nexus 6P (purple route). (Color figure online)

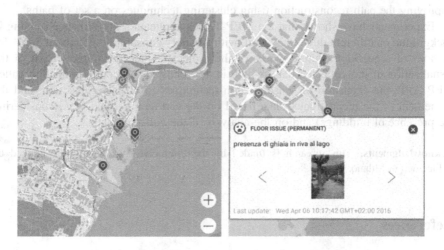

Fig. 6. Barriers signaled in Cernobbio (Como, Italy) with MEP Traces

A total acquisition time of 16 h 38′ 02″ was done, reaching about 43 km as the total length of the walked path. The battery consumption of MEP-Traces has also been computed considering one hour of acquisition: the battery consumption of the application is about 5–6% in one hour. For some devices (omitted from our computation) we used power banks: in such cases the battery consumption was 0%.

All the acquisitions were taken with the application running in background. In order to consider a common user in a daily device usage, mobile data connection was enabled. Most of the used devices were personal devices, therefore the consumption may be affected also by other applications running on them. Several factors may affect the results of the battery consumption and for personal devices it is difficult to have homogeneous conditions. Indeed, results may depend also by the Android OS version installed on the device, the Linux Kernel version and its optimization, the hardware device composition like CPU and RAM, the read/write SD-card speed, etc. However, since the applications are thought to be used by any user with any Android device, these data can be considered as approximations of possible behaviors.

5 Conclusions and Future Work

In this paper we have described the results of data acquisitions done in Cernobbio (Como, Italy) for the MEP (Maps for Easy Path) project. The tools developed for the project have been illustrated and in particular the app MEP-Traces has been described in more detail: it retrieves raw GNSS data from low cost GPS sensor installed on commercial mobile devices, together with other sensor data like accelerometer, magnetometer etc. Then the entire path is reconstructed. Each reconstructed path is associated with the user's profile (e.g., wheelchair type, requirements like "no-step", etc.), to build accessible paths for different users' types. Consistency and reliability of the collected data can be increased if more users trace the same routes. At this aim, we are improving the path reconstruction using clustering techniques on a set of paths.

Experiments have shown that the MEP-Traces application performance running in background on different devices is good, with a battery consumption of about 5–6% for an hour of acquisition. Future works of the project include the improvement of the visualization of the collected data, which is the focus of a second application called MEP APP; the extension of sensor fusion techniques to obstacle detection; and the refinement of the reconstructed data based on the cartography data (e.g., considering the presence of buildings) and on the analysis of the collected data.

Acknowledgments. This research is funded by the Polisocial Award program, granted by Politecnico di Milano, Italy.

References

1. Bardaro, G., Vali, A., Comai, S., Matteucci, M.: Accessible urban routes reconstruction by fusing mobile sensors data. In: 13th International Conference on Advances in Mobile Computing & Multimedia (MoMM2015), Bruxelles, Belgium, December 2015
2. Cardonha, C., Gallo, D., Avegliano, P., Herrmann, R., Koch, F., Borger, S.: A crowdsourcing platform for the construction of accessibility maps. In: Proceedings of the 10th International Cross-Disciplinary Conference on Web Accessibility, W4A 2013, pp. 26:1–26:4. ACM (2013)
3. Comai, S., Kayange, D., Mangiarotti, R., Matteucci, M., Ugur Yavuz, S., Valentini, F.: Mapping city accessibility: review and analysis. In: Proceedings 13th International Conference on Advancing Assistive Technology and eAccessibility for People with Disabilities (AAATE 2015), Budapest, Hungary (2015)
4. Comuni per tutti, 25 July 2016. http://www.comunipertutti.it/maps/
5. Cucci, D.A., Matteucci, M.: On the development of a generic multi-sensor fusion framework for robust odometry estimation. J. Softw. Eng. Robot. **5**(1), 48–62 (2014)

6. Karimi, H.A., Zhang, L., Benner, J.G.: Personalized accessibility maps (PAMs) for communities with special needs. In: Liang, S.H.L., Wang, X., Claramunt, C. (eds.) W2GIS 2013. LNCS, vol. 7820, pp. 199–213. Springer, Heidelberg (2013). doi:10.1007/978-3-642-37087-8_15
7. Mapability, 25 July 2016. http://www.mapability.org
8. MEP Project, 25 July 2016. http://mep5x1000.wix.com/mepapp
9. Palazzi, C.E., et al.: Path 2.0: a participatory system for the generation of accessible routes. In: ICME, pp. 1707–1711 (2010)
10. Rota Accesivel, 25 July 2016. https://itunes.apple.com/it/app/ibm-rota-acessivel/id6447129 74?mt=8
11. Shigeno, K., et al.: Citizen sensing for collaborative construction of accessibility maps. In: Proceedings of the 10th International Cross-Disciplinary Conference on Web Accessibility, p. 24 (2013)
12. USCensus: Mobility is Most Common Disability Among Older Americans, Census Bureau Reports. United Census Bureau (2014). http://www.census.gov/newsroom/press-releascs/2014/cb14-218.html

A Review of Websites and Mobile Applications for People with Autism Spectrum Disorders: Towards Shared Guidelines

Antonina Dattolo[1] and Flaminia L. Luccio[2(✉)]

[1] SASWEB Lab, DIMF, University of Udine, Gorizia, Italy
antonina.dattolo@uniud.it
[2] DAIS, Università Ca' Foscari Venezia, Venezia, Italy
luccio@unive.it

Abstract. Many studies show the effective positive impact of using computer technologies to support the lives of users with autism spectrum disorders (ASD), for simplifying interaction with other people, for organising daily activities, for improving relation with family and friends. Despite that, only a restricted part of the current websites is accessible for people with ASD. In this paper, we discuss a set of guidelines that should be followed by designers while developing websites or mobile applications for users with ASD. We review many of the existing websites and applications in order to check which comply with all, or parts of these guidelines. We finally highlight current common limitations and address new challenging research directions.

Keywords: Information and communication technology · Mobile applications · Websites · Autism spectrum disorders

1 Introduction

The wide spread of Information and Communication Technologies (ICT) and the increasing use of mobile devices, as smartphones or tablets, have changed the life of people with disabilities and in particular with Autism Spectrum Disorders (ASD), i.e., with disorders mainly related to impairments in social and communication interactions. Although users with ASD are different one from another, they generally show good abilities in using computer technologies. Thus, using them in a proper way, can become a very powerful interaction tool.

In this paper, we are interested in discussing the guidelines for developing accessible websites and mobile applications for users with ASD, and to identify typical limitations of existing tools. With this aim, in the first part of this paper, after an introduction to the autism spectrum disorder (Sect. 2), we will discuss, compare and summarise existing guidelines already present in the literature that we approve (Sect. 3). In the second part, we will analyse existing websites and mobile applications and compare them, in order to highlight which of them comply with all or parts of the guidelines (Sect. 4). We will finally discuss, which,

© ICST Institute for Computer Sciences, Social Informatics and Telecommunications Engineering 2017
O. Gaggi et al. (Eds.): GOODTECHS 2016, LNICST 195, pp. 264–273, 2017.
DOI: 10.1007/978-3-319-61949-1_28

in our opinion, are the future trends in the development of usable and accessible technologies for users with ASD (Sect. 5).

2 The Autism Spectrum Disorder

The Autism Spectrum Disorders is defined by the American Psychiatric Association as a neuro-developmental disorder with persistent impairments in social communication and social interaction, and restricted, repetitive patterns of behavior, interests, or activities [37].

The *incidence* of this disorder is not negligible. In [38], the authors present an interesting study on worldwide available data that estimates at the date of 2010 the number of people with ASD as 1 out of 132. The study finds no evidence of a change in prevalence for ASD between 1990 and 2010, although there are some small changes depending on regional origins. A more recent study conducted in 2012 among 346,978 children aged 8 years in 11 different cities of the United States, shows a general evidence of one child in 68 with ASD.

Each person with ASD is different, this is where the term "spectrum disorder" comes from. The areas which are most affected are: social interaction, social imagination, and social communication. Regarding *social interaction*, typically, people with ASD tend to isolate themselves showing no interest in other people, do not have a good eye contact, try to avoid physical contacts, have problems processing their own emotions and the ones of people around them. Their *social imagination* is limited: They tend to avoid symbolic games, tend to repeat the same game or even movements over and over (hand flapping, spinning or waving objects, etc.), get frustrated when something changes in their daily routine. Finally, they often show impairments in *social communication*. These impairments are often related to language delays or, in some cases, to the complete lack of verbal communication. People with ASD have also problems understanding instructions, gestures and so on. Finally, they often show *limited attention*, i.e., they are able to concentrate on tasks for a limited amount of time, and have also *Sensory Processing Disorders* (SPD), i.e., have problems processing information from the five senses, from the vestibular system, and/or the positional sense [52].

Modern therapies propose very different approaches (which are out of the scope of this paper), however, it is widely known that people with ASD usually present good visual abilities, such as visual memory, i.e., are able to represent concepts by sequence of images [46]. Thus, to support these individuals many of the proposed therapies rely on the use of photographs, images, flowcharts, cartoons, checklists, etc. What we will be concentrating on in this paper, is the use of technology to support all the therapies, and in particular, the use of images as a very powerful communication tool. In particular, to support communication interventions, often speech therapies are also sustained by Augmentative and Alternative Communication (AAC) techniques, which are based on the use of symbols or images as a method for communicating [53]. The most common AAC approach is the Picture Exchange Communication System (PECS): users communicate needs and requests by exchanging pictures with their partners; these pictures are laminated and stored in a special book that has to be carried around [32]. Another AAC technique is, e.g., the sign language, which can be very effective, but however requires the partners to be trained, and thus restricts the communication to a limited set of individuals. An evolution of AAC techniques relies on the use of different computer devices such as tablets, smartphones, etc. These new tools allow to increase number of stored images, have limited physical size, and can thus be carried out everywhere.

3   Website and Application Accessibility Guidelines

Many studies show the effective positive impact of using computer technologies to support the lives of users with ASD, for simplifying interaction with other people, for organizing daily activities, for improving relation with family and friends [39,51]. Moreover, users with ASD show a positive attitude towards computer technologies due to the predictability of the interaction - in contrast to normal day-to-day interaction with other people - and due to the perfectability of the tool, that may induce repetitive behaviours, usually preferred by this set of users. Thus, ICTs are powerful tools for improving their learning process [49].

The set of available computer technologies is very wide, since it ranges from virtual reality, to robotics, multitouch interfaces, websites, Web apps, affective computing. These tools are often customizable with respect to the different users' abilities, and thus targeted to the different skills. We here focus only on websites and (mobile) applications.

Accessibility makes users with a wide range of abilities able to perceive, operate, interact and understand a user interface [35]. The target users might have physical (visual, auditory, etc.), cognitive or neurological disabilities, might be children or elderly people. Accessibility has always been a big concern for websites and app developers, however, it is often neglected during the development phase mainly due to the lack of knowledge by the developers, and also to the extra costs it introduces. This is in contrast with the statement declared during the 2016 United Nations Convention on the Rights of Persons with Disabilities (CRPD), that access to information technologies has to be considered a basic human right [28].

Moving towards this direction, in 2012 the W3C [29,35] has created a new task force group, called Cognitive and Learning Disabilities Accessibility Task Force (COGA), whose aim is to propose accessibility guidelines for Web accessibility for people with cognitive or neuronal disabilities [36]. The COGA group, together with the Protocols and Formats Working Group, and the Web Content Accessibility Guidelines Working Group, has published in 2016 some interesting general guidelines for the development of websites for users with Cognitive and Learning Disabilities [48]: They are too generic, and not directly targeted to users with ASD, which typically show other specific problems such as limited attention, sensory hypersensitiveness, limited text comprehension, etc. They can be a good starting point, but more specific targeted issues should be taken into account, together with further guidelines that apply to more general computer applications.

In the last years some work have been devoted to the definition of guidelines for people with cognitive disabilities [34,39,40,42,45,48,51]. However, while dealing with users with ASD with cognitive disabilities, more specific features have to be added to the general ones. Thus, starting from the international standard reference model of WCAG 1.0 and WCAG 2.0 [29], other practical and operative guidelines have been proposed [30,33,34,39,40,42,45,50,51]. Note that in general, while developing a website, or an application, it is a good idea to include an accessibility specialist in the team so to design and then evaluate the results of the design in a proper way [50].

We studied current literature, comparing the shared (and not) guidelines, and we present, in Table 1, the guidelines we approve, divided in four macro-areas: graphical layout, structure and navigation, user and language (indicated respectively by G1-G6, N1-N3, U1-U3, L1-L2).

Table 1. Accessibility guidelines for users with ASD

G1	The general design and the structure should be simple, clear and predictable, secondary content that distracts the user should be avoided
G2	The content should be predictable and should provide feedbacks
G3	Pictures should be copiously used together with redundant representation of information
G4	Pictures can be drawings, photographs, symbolic images, should be easy to understand, should not go in the background, should be in a sharp focus
G5	Background sounds, moving text, blinking images and horizontal scrolling should be avoided
G6	The text should go with pictures. It should be clear, simple, and short (at most one sentence on a line); should be in a big font (14), in plain Sans-serif style (e.g., Verdana), in a mild color. Headings and titles should be used
N1	Navigation should be consistent and similar in every page/section
N2	The website and every applications should have a simple and logical structure, the user should be able to easily navigate inside
N3	Add navigation information and navigation buttons at the top and the bottom of the page. In case of webpages the navigation inside the site should be limited by three clicks
U1	Allow customisation
U2	Try to engage the user
U3	Make adaptive the interaction with users, considering their interaction history, their preferences, requests, and needs
L1	The language should be simple and precise
L2	Acronyms and abbreviations, non-literal text, and jargon should not be used

The accuracy of *graphical layout* is useful to simplify the interaction: layout and content should be predictable. A critical issue is the choice among images, photographs, and symbolic pictures. What kind of pictures should be included close to the text? A recent paper [54] presents the first study to use eye-tracking technology with a set of adult users with ASD, in order to evaluate text documents with specific features, and it provides specific guidelines for creating accessible text for autism. The text was combined with photographs and symbols. The outcome of the study is that autistic users prefer texts that are paired with images, moreover, both photographs or symbols seem to work well. Note however, that the study was done on a set of adult autistic users without developmental delays. As the authors suggest, this result might be different with children, since the symbolic understanding users with ASD arrives later in their lives compared to neurotypical users.

The study of [42] suggests that for children with developmental delays photographs seem to be more understandable. Other issues are the copious use of pictures and of redundant representation to simplify the concepts absorption. Moreover, pictures should not be used when they are non-relevant or too abstract to help the text comprehension. The *structure and the navigation* should be usable and logic, while the *user* should give space to adaptive personalisation: currently, customisation is applied; engagement is a very important issue. Adaptivity is an open challenge. In order to engage users, in [42] the authors add to the design of a dedicated website some games. These games have resulted into a deep engagement between the users with ASD and the site. On the other hand, [50] introduces the concept of participatory design of user interfaces, i.e., users with ASD highly benefit of personalised interfaces. In this direction interesting results are presented in [42,47], and also in [44], were the authors discuss a participatory design process experimented with four children with autism, to develop their own smart object. The aim and the obtained results were to go beyond functional limitations and to engage the children with ideas, desires and problems. Finally, the use of the *language* should be simple and precise: it is well known that people with ASD literally interpret the text content, and have problems understanding metaphors and abstract sentences.

4   Websites and Dedicated Applications for Users with ASD: A Systematic Comparison

In this section we present a systematic comparison among accessible websites and dedicated applications for people with ASD, and we analyse which and to which extent they follow the guidelines presented in the previous section.

Dedicated Websites for Users with ASD. We have done an extensive search in the Web for sites whose authors have claimed to follow different accessibility standards (e.g., are compliant with W3C standards for HTML and CSS, can be displayed correctly in current browsers. etc.). Although this search is not exhaustive, we have noticed that most of these sites are of autism associations and autism conferences, and are mainly directed to researchers, parents or adults with autism. In next Tables 2 and 3, we refer to all the points mentioned in

Sect. 3. For lack of space, we refer to them as G1 up to G6 for the 6 points of the Graphical Layout; N1 to N3 for the 3 points of the Structure and Navigation; U1 and U2 for the Users, and finally L1 and L2 for the Language. Since **none** of the websites and apps satisfy U3, we avoid to insert this point in our analysis. The outcome can be ● (the guideline has been respected), ○ (no), or ◐ (in part).

Table 2. Implementation of the accessibility guidelines in the current websites.

Websites	G1	G2	G3	G4	G5	G6	N1	N2	N3	U1	U2	L1	L2
[7,8,11]	○	○	○	●	●	○	●	●	○	◐	○	◐	○
[3,13,16]	○	○	○	●	●	◐	●	●	○	◐	○	◐	○
[14,15,25]	○	○	○	●	○	○	●	●	○	●	○	◐	○
[21,22]	○	○	◐	●	●	○	●	●	○	●	○	◐	○
[5,10,18,24]	○	○	◐	●	●	◐	●	●	○	●	○	◐	●
[26]	●	◐	●	●	○	●	●	●	●	●	●	◐	●
[1,17]	●	●	●	◐	●	◐	●	●	●	●	○	●	●
[4,9]	●	●	●	●	●	◐	●	●	●	●	○	●	●
[42]	●	●	●	◐	●	●	●	●	●	◐	●	●	●

Table 3. Implementation of accessibility guidelines in the current apps.

App	G1	G2	G3	G4	G5	G6	N1	N2	N3	U1	U2	L1	L2
[27]	◐	◐	●	◐	○	○	◐	○	○	◐	●	●	●
[12]	●	●	●	◐	●	◐	●	○	○	◐	●	●	●
[2]	◐	◐	●	◐	●	●	●	●	●	◐	◐	●	●
[19]	◐	◐	●	●	◐	◐	○	◐	◐	◐	○	●	●
[20]	◐	◐	◐	◐	●	◐	◐	●	◐	◐	●	●	●
[6]	◐	◐	●	●	●	◐	◐	○	◐	○	○	●	●
[41]	●	●	●	●	●	●	●	●	●	◐	◐	●	●

While navigating on the sites we have noticed that some of them have similar features, so we have grouped them together. In all these works, we have seen that navigation is consistent, however not very simple. The language is simple in some sections but others connect to many links outside and provide too much information. There is a lot of secondary content inside some pages, and this content is not simple, and there are no feedbacks. [5,10,18,21,22,24] contain many pictures, but not the other sites, the same holds for the text that is short only in [3,5,10,13,16,18,23,24]. [14,15,25] contain some moving text. [7,8,11] lack of images, the general design is not very simple. [3,13,16] have few more images. [26] contains many pictures and tries to engage the user with pictures and videos. [1,17] follow most of the guidelines, but what they really lack of is the engagement of the user. The sites contain lots of information, in some parts the text is too long, and is accessible for users with ASD which are high functioning, able to read and to communicate. [4,9] respect the graphical layout specifications, however in different parts the text is too long. Navigation is coherent however more buttons and navigation information in the bottom would help. There is no user engagement. The sites mentioned in [42] were designed to follow all the guidelines above presented (except for $U3$). They are the first example of websites explicitly dedicated to users with ASD that independently want to choose their own touring activity close to a specific city (in particular, Rieti and Venice). The sites only lack of adaptivity, and of dynamical customisation of style attributes, on the other hand the users may independently choose different navigational paths depending on their own interests. To engage the user the authors have added games and videos. The sites were tested on a set of users with ASD that have shown their great appreciation.

Thus, to conclude, with the exception of [42], all the websites we have analysed seem to be directed to users which are adults and high functioning (i.e., to users with mild cognitive disabilities), and not to children. Moreover, most of the sites lack of engagement, and all of them of adaptivity.

Dedicated Applications for Users with ASD. Mobile applications represent an important opportunity for users with ASD, as they take advantage of the modality of interactions, like touch screen, and the manageability of the device. Evidence suggests that children with ASD are more engaged and verbal during their use. However, there is a proliferation of commercially available apps, which range from free to very expensive tools: unfortunately this leaves very little room for quality control and the large majority of apps lack any foundation in theory or research evaluation [43]. Obviously, this is a big risk for a vulnerable part of the population.

Table 3 summarises, for a set of current mobile apps, the implementation of the previously listed accessibility guidelines.

A set of apps by *Touch Autism* [27] (like *Social Stories Creator and Library*, *Turn Taker*, *Puzzle Spelling Words*, and others) present some relevant limitations, mainly located in the areas of graphical layout and navigation: for example, *Puzzle Spelling Words* uses an improbable font, starts using a background sound without evident control (it may be interrupted only by the settings panel), does not offer support at the navigation (there are neither navigation buttons, nor exit/pause buttons). In addition, only one set puzzle is free (Playground), while all the others require a payment. *Findme* [12] has been designed at the University of Edinburgh to help children improve their causal and attentions skills. It respects the major part of guidelines, but it does not offer navigation support. The navigation is more complete in the set of *Apps for Autism* by EdNinja [2]: it is possible open a simple visual menu. However, the use of these apps appears to be complex. *Niki Apps* [19] is based a set of apps based on AAC techniques: the apps present different graphical layouts, navigation modalities and styles. The navigation presents some limitations (there are some parts of the app in which it is difficult find the exit); however, it is possible to draw a sketch but it is not clear where is the saved image and in which way it could be used. Belonging to the same AAC category are the Proloquo apps [20]: *Proloquo4Text* and *Proloquo2Go*. These apps have been created for people who cannot speak, not specifically for people with ASD; they appear too rich of images and content, in contrast with an essential layout. *Autism iHelp Apps* [6] are vocabulary teaching aids developed by parents of a child with Autism and a speech-language pathologist. There are a set of apps: *Same and different; Opposites; Colors;* etc. They are simple to use and propose concrete pictures, but have some limitations: the navigation is linear and is not possible to return back; the end of an activity is not predictable; and an activity is not reproducible in the same way. Finally, an interesting prototype of mobile app for ASD people is *Volo* [41]; based on AAC techniques, it uses zz-structures, which are hyper-orthogonal, non-hierarchical structures for storing, linking and manipulating data. Summarising, we note that most of the apps provide tools for editing and adding new and eventually personal data, but important limitations involve the process of customisation (often difficult to realise), the user engagement and mainly the lack of user adaptivity.

Some apps use sketched images, other real pictures, most of them provide the user with an initial set of pictures and allow the import of new images from a personal computer, a camera, etc. (see, e.g., [19,27]). Another feature is the possibility of adding *sounds*, which can be synthetic or natural (see, e.g., [31]), or can also be recorded (see, e.g., [19]). Some apps allow the creation of *calendars*: the daily routine might be organised in sequence of actions which describe the activities of the day in a fixed temporal order.

Differently from websites, the apps are conceived for children and they address general issues, not always specifically for people with ASD.

5   Conclusion and Future Challenges

In this paper we discussed possible guidelines for developing accessible websites or mobile applications for users with ASD. We have also analysed and compared many of the existing websites and applications in order to check which comply with all or parts of these guidelines.

As future challenges, we have noticed that all the sites and applications that we have tested lack of a feature that represents an innovative challenge: Adaptivity towards users. Automatically, the systems should be able to adapt their behaviour, considering the history of the users' interaction, their requests, needs and preferences. Another issue is related to the present synthesizers available in different applications. We have noticed that many of them produce sounds which are not easily recognisable by users with limited comprehension. The adaptation of the language and also of the voices would highly improve the quality of these applications. Finally, our future work will be dedicated to refine our proposal of guidelines for ASD accessibility, explicitly considering the usability: accessibility does not imply usability, i.e., a website or an application might be accessible, but not usable. Combining usability and accessibility for new *usable accessibility* guidelines are our next aim.

References

1. Ambitions about autism. https://www.ambitiousaboutautism.org.uk/
2. Apps for autism. http://edninja.com/
3. Asd in new zealand schools. http://asdinnzschools.org.nz/
4. Asd info wales. http://www.asdinfowales.co.uk/
5. Autism education trust. http://www.autismeducationtrust.org.uk/
6. Autism ihelp. https://www.facebook.com/AutismiHelp/
7. Autism nz. http://www.autismnz.org.nz/home
8. Autism somerset. http://www.autismsomerset.org.uk/
9. Autism spectrum australia. https://www.autismspectrum.org.au/
10. Autism wessex. http://autismwessex.org.uk
11. Cell symposia. http://www.cell-symposia-autism.com/
12. Findme. http://www.interface3.com/findme/
13. The founders centre. http://thefounderscenter.org/
14. The global health network. https://grand.tghn.org/
15. Hacs. http://www.hacs.org.uk/
16. Leisure for autism. http://www.leisureforautism.org/
17. The national autistic society. http://www.autism.org.uk/
18. New struan school. http://www.newstruanschool.org/
19. Niki talk. http://www.nikitalk.com/
20. Proloquo apps. http://www.assistiveware.com/
21. Scottish autism. http://www.scottishautism.org/
22. Specialist autism services. http://www.specialistautismservices.org/
23. St giles school. http://www.st-giles.notts.sch.uk/
24. Sunderland city council. http://www.sunderland.gov.uk/
25. Supporting students with asd. http://www.autismsupportpackage.education.nsw.gov.au/home
26. Titanic belfast. http://titanicbelfast.com/
27. Touch autism. http://touchautism.com/
28. Convention on the rights of persons with disabilities (2006). http://www.un.org/disabilities/convention/conventionfull.shtml
29. Web content accessibility guidelines 2.0 (2008). https://www.w3.org/TR/WCAG20
30. Department of Health (UK). Basic Guidelines for People Who Commission Easy Read Information (2009). http://www.easy-read-online.co.uk/media/10612/comm%20basic%20guidelines%20for%20people%20who%20commission%20easy%20read%20info.pdf
31. Proloquo2go (2014). https://itunes.apple.com/it/app/proloquo2go-symbol-based-aac/id308368164?mt=8
32. Pyramid educational consultants, inc. (2014). http://www.pecs-canada.com/
33. Cognitive accessibility user research, w3C (2015). http://www.w3.org/TR/coga-user-research/
34. An interview with Jamie Knight: autism and accessible web design (2015). http://www.iheni.com/an-interview-with-jamie-knight-autism-and-accessible-web-design/
35. W3 consortium (2016). http://www.w3.org
36. Abou-Zahra, S.: How people with disabilities use the web: overview (2012). https://www.w3.org/WAI/intro/people-use-web/
37. American Psychiatric Association (ed.): The Diagnostic and Statistical Manual of Mental Disorders: DSM 5. BookpointUS (2013)

38. Baxter, A.J., Brugha, T., Erskine, H., Sheurer, R., Vos, T., Scott, J.: The epidemiology and global burden of autism spectrum disorders. Psychol. Med. **45**(3), 1601–1613 (2014)
39. Britto, T., Pizzolato, E.: Towards web accessibility guidelines of interaction and interface design for people with autism spectrum disorder. In: The Ninth International Conference on Advances in Computer-Human Interactions, ACHI 2016, Venice, Italy, 24–28 April 2016
40. Darejeh, A., Singh, D.: A review on user interface design principles to increase software usability for users with less computer literacy. J. Comput. Sci. **9**(11), 1443–1450 (2013)
41. Dattolo, A., Luccio, F.: Modelling volo, an augmentative and alternative communication application. In: The 8th International Conference on Advances in Computer-Human Interactions, ACHI 2015, Lisbon, Portugal, 22–27 February 2015
42. Dattolo, A., Luccio, F., Pirone, E.: Webpage accessibility and usability for autistic users: a case study on a tourism website. In: The 9th International Conference on Advances in Computer-Human Interactions, ACHI 2016, Venice, Italy, 24–28 April 2016
43. Fletcher-Watson, S.: Evidence-based technology design and commercialisation: recommendations derived from research in education and autism. TechTrends **59**(1), 84–88 (2015)
44. Frauenberger, C., Makhaeva, J., Spiel, K.: Designing smart objects with autistic children: Four design exposes. In: Proceedings of the Conference on Human Factors in Computing Systems, CHI 2016, pp. 130–139. ACM, New York (2016)
45. Friedman, M.G., Bryen, D.N.: Web accessibility design recommendations for people with cognitive disabilities. Technol. Disabil. **19**(9), 205–212 (2007)
46. Grandin, T.: How does visual thinking work in the mind of a person with autism? A personal account. Philos. Trans. R. Soc. **364**(1522), 1437–1442 (2009)
47. Kamaruzaman, M.F., Rani, N.M., Nor, H., Azaharia, M.: Developing user interface design application for children with autism. Procedia - Soc. Behav. Sci. **217**, 887–894 (2016)
48. Lisa Seeman, M.C.: Techniques for the the cognitive and learning disabilities accessibility task force (COGA). W3C (2016). https://w3c.github.io/coga/techniques/
49. McQuiggan, S., McQuiggan, J., Sabourin, J., Kosturko, L.: Mobile Learning: A Handbook for Developers, Educators, and Learners, 1st edn. Wiley, Hoboken (2015)
50. Pavlov, N.: User interface for people with autism spectrum disorders. J. Softw. Eng. Appl. **7**(2), 128–134 (2014)
51. Putman, C., Chong, L.: Software and technologies for people with autism: what the users want? In: 10th International ACM SIGACCESS Conference on Computers and Accessibility, ASSETS 2008, Halifax, Canada, pp. 3–10, 13–15 October 2008
52. Sicile Kira, C.: What is sensory processing disorder and how is it related to autism? (2010). http://goo.gl/1naVTp
53. Still, K., Rehfeldt, R., Whelan, R., May, R., Dymond, S.: Facilitating requesting skills using high-tech augmentative and alternative communication devices with individuals with autism spectrum disorders: a systematic review. Res. Autism Spectr. Disord. **8**, 1184–1199 (2014)
54. Yaneva, V., Temnikova, I., Mitkov, R.: Accessible texts for autism: an eye-tracking study. In: Proceedings of the 17th International ACM SIGACCESS Conference on Computers Accessibility, ASSETS 2015, pp. 49–57. ACM, New York (2015)

Analysis of Stereoscopic Visualization in a Consumer-Oriented Head Mounted Display

Cinzia Vismara, Marco Granato, Laura Anna Ripamonti, Dario Maggiorini, and Davide Gadia(✉)

Department of Computer Science, University of Milan, Milan, Italy
cinzia.vismara@studenti.unimi.it, marco.granato@unimi.it,
{ripamonti,dario,gadia}@di.unimi.it

Abstract. The upcoming availability of advanced Head Mounted Displays (HMDs) dedicated to the consumer market has lead to a great interest in the design and development of dedicated media, like e.g. immersive video games and movies. As a consequence, Virtual Reality is becoming more accessible to a wider audience, with a large number of potential applications and integrations with already existing smart technologies and devices. HMDs use stereoscopic visualization to enhance the sense of realism and immersivity in a virtual scene. However, a correct stereoscopic visualization requires an accurate consideration of different parameters related to the production and display stage. In this paper, we analyze the stereoscopic setup of a HMD, in order to highlight its main visualization characteristics in relation with the known issues and requirements of a correct stereoscopic visualization, and to establish some preliminary guidelines for an optimal creation of stereoscopic contents.

Keywords: Head Mounted display · Oculus Rift · Stereoscopy · Stereoscopic media production · Stereo Window Violation

1 Introduction

Virtual Reality (VR) has been one of the most investigated research topics of the last years. Several applications of VR have been proposed in particular in industrial research (e.g., for the training of personnel involved in critical situations in dangerous environments [1]), or in medicine, due to the advanced visualization and simulation capabilities [2]. VR is largely used also in perceptual psychology, in order to replicate realistic situations in a controlled virtual setup [3]. Different approaches and technologies for VR visualization and interaction [4–6] have been proposed: the final choice of the most appropriate tools and solutions requires an accurate analysis of the goal of the simulation, of the number of users involved in the virtual environment, of the provided level of interaction, etc. [7,8].

Several works in the VR field are focused on the use of HMDs, because of their advanced immersivity and relatively affordable cost (if compared to large

© ICST Institute for Computer Sciences, Social Informatics and Telecommunications Engineering 2017
O. Gaggi et al. (Eds.): GOODTECHS 2016, LNICST 195, pp. 274–283, 2017.
DOI: 10.1007/978-3-319-61949-1_29

projection-based VR systems). However, due to the technological limits of the HMD models available until some years ago, one of the most discussed research topics has been the evaluation of the appropriateness of HMDs in presenting stereoscopic information [9]. In fact, the limited Field of View (FOV) of the previous generation of HMDs has often been considered one possible reason of the relevated underestimation of depth and distances in VR environments [10,11], even if other works [12,13] have suggested that this effect can be mitigated if the user can look around the environment without constraints.

However, a new generation of HMDs is becoming increasingly more available. These new devices are assembled using high quality electronic components already available for the construction of mobile or portable devices, and they are characterized by low latency, high resolution displays, and large FOV, with a price range relevantly lower than the previous HMD models. Moreover, some portable HMDs are even using smartphones as the main processing and visualization units. The target of these devices is mainly the consumer market for entertainment, which is currently focused on the definition of an integrated "ecosystem" of portable devices and smart objects.

As a consequence, there is a growing interest in the production of dedicated media specifically designed to enhance the peculiar characteristics of HMDs, like e.g., immersive video games, and 360° stereoscopic movies. However, the production of stereoscopic media requires an accurate knowledge of all the aspects related to the acquisition/generation setup, and of the visualization parameters of the 3D display, in order to obtain an optimal representation of depth, and to avoid annoying perceptual issues like e.g., excessive parallax on screen, or window violations [14,15].

In this paper, we will present an analysis of the stereoscopic setup of the Oculus Rift DK2 (Development Kit 2), in order to understand its visualization characteristics and stereoscopic performances, and to determine some preliminary guidelines for an optimal creation of stereoscopic contents. Moreover, to better evaluate the technical peculiarities of these devices, we will present a comparison of the stereo parameters of the Oculus Rift DK2 with the visualization setup typical of a 3D monitor.

2 Stereoscopic Parameters

Stereoscopic visualization is used to create an illusion of depth in the observer, by means of two images corresponding to two different perspective views of a scene, each sent only to the left or right eye of the viewer using specific hardware solutions. If the observer has an adequate stereoscopic ability [16], her visual system will process the binocular disparity between the two views (i.e., the horizontal different positions of an object in the two images), elaborating the perception of depth.

In the last few years, several solutions for the acquisition, elaboration and visualization of stereoscopic movies [14,15,17] and video games [18–20] have been proposed. In the presented analysis of the stereoscopic characteristics of a HMD, we will consider three crucial parameters: the *native parallax* of the display, the *maximum positive parallax* on screen, and the presence of *window violations* in the stereoscopic setup.

Native Screen Parallax. The native screen parallax (NP) is a parameter describing the stereoscopic characteristics of a 3D display, independently from the settings regarding the acquisition and visualization of the stereo content [14]. It is calculated as:

$$NP = \frac{iod}{sw} \tag{1}$$

where *iod* is the human interocular distance (approximately 2.56 in/65 mm), and *sw* is the screen width. NP can be interpreted as the percentage of screen width which will equal the human interocular distance, i.e. the maximum amount of pixel disparity on screen before having a painful *divergent parallax* situation [21].

Maximum Parallax on Screen. The production of a stereoscopic content requires an accurate comprehension of all the parameters and settings of both the acquisition/generation and visualization setups. The main goal is to avoid perceptual discomfort in the observer. One of the main source of discomfort is an excessive positive parallax on screen, which makes the process of fusion of the two views difficult, if not impossible, to the viewer. The native parallax NP gives the threshold, for a given 3D display, before having a problematic situation, while the maximum parallax on screen (MPP) provides the measure of the actual maximum horizontal positive disparity on screen given a specific acquisition and visualization setup. As described in [21]:

$$MPP \propto \frac{M \cdot f \cdot iax}{d_0} \tag{2}$$

where f is the focal length of the stereoscopic cameras, *iax* is the interaxial distance between left and right camera, d_0 is the distance between the stereoscopic camera and the convergence plane, and M is the screen magnification factor, i.e. the ratio of the display width to the width of the camera sensor.

If the MPP value of a given stereoscopic setup is lower than the native parallax NP of the display, then it is not possible to have an excessive positive parallax presented to the observer. If MPP is greater than NP, then it is possible that the positive parallax on screen of some objects will exceed the average human interocular distance, leading to a stereoscopic image painful to view. Particular care must be given to avoid these situations by changing the parameters of the stereoscopic acquisition or generation setup, or changing the content of the scene, by moving the objects at a less critical depth.

Window Violation. Window violation is a problem related to the visualization of objects with negative parallax on screen (i.e., perceived in front of the screen).

When these objects are "cut off" by the stereoscopic window, then there is a mismatch between the perception of depth elaborated using the parallax information (which tells that the object is in front of the screen) and the perception of depth given by the occlusion by the image frame (which tells that the object is behind the window border) [14,17].

In stereoscopic movie production, the Dynamic Floating Window (DFW) technique [17] is usually used to remove window violations. The technique is based on the application of black masks at the borders of the frame to cover the visual information leading to the perceptual mismatch. In most of the cases, the black masks are applied in post-processing to the stereoscopic frame, even if recent works [22,23] have investigated the automatic detection of window violations, and the procedural application of the DFW technique. Moreover, some works have been presented on the application of this technique in real-time applications [24].

3   Stereoscopic Visualization in the Oculus Rift DK2

The Oculus Rift DK2 is the second pre-production version (Development Kit) provided by Oculus VR to the developers community, in order to allow them to design, test and develop immersive VR contents prior to the availability of the final consumer version.

The DK2 model is equipped with a 1920 × 1080 OLED display with a width of 125.77 mm and a height of 70.74 mm [25]. Pixel density is 15.26 pixel/mm. Stereoscopic visualization is achieved by presenting left and right view in a side-by-side format on the screen, and allowing each eye to see only the corresponding half of the screen. The declared distance between the eyes and the screen is 49.8 mm. To bring the image into focus and to achieve a wide FOV (106.19 vertically and 94.16 horizontally, as stated in Oculus SDK documentation [26]), two wide-angle lenses are placed in front of the observer's eyes (Fig. 1). The lenses apply a pincushion effect on the images, that is compensated by applying a pre-warping (barrel distortion) of the image through a pixel shader [27].

The distance between the lenses can be adjusted between 55 and 75 mm, with 65 mm as default value [26].

To analyze the stereoscopic characteristics of the Oculus Rift DK2, we have modeled a simple test scene in Blender [28], composed by a cube (with size 1.5 m) and a room (with a length from the camera of 30 m). A checker texture (composed by 25 × 25 cm squares) has been assigned to the floor material. A preview of the scene can be seen in Fig. 2. We have chosen Blender as the production tool for our analysis because, despite the fact its internal Game Engine mode is not officially supported by Oculus VR as are other game engines, it is the only tool allowing to modify the parameters regarding the interocular distance and the camera FOV.

We have started our analysis by determining the native parallax of the Oculus Rift DK2 screen, and the maximum positive parallax on screen considering the overall production pipeline. Considering that each eye sees only one half of the screen, we determine the native parallax of the DK2 display applying Eq. 1 as:

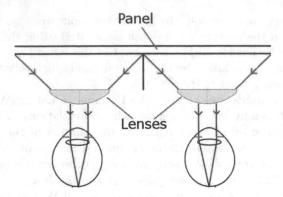

Fig. 1. Screen separation for left and right image visualization, and lenses placement inside the Oculus Rift DK2.

$$\mathrm{NP}_{DK2} = \frac{65}{125.77 \cdot 0.5} = \frac{65}{62.885} \sim 1.0336$$

As a consequence, the screen of the Oculus Rift DK2 can not display parallax values equal or greater than the average human interocular distance, and thus it is free from perceptual issues related to divergence situations on the background. To have a more precise measure of the actual maximum parallax achievable on the DK2 screen, we have applied Eq. 2, considering the default dimension (32 mm) of the virtual sensor of the Blender camera to determine $M = 62.885/32 = 1.96$ and using $f = 14.88$, which is the focal length value corresponding to the 94.16 horizontal FOV of the Oculus Rift DK2:

$$\mathrm{MPP}_{DK2} = \frac{1.96 \cdot 14.88 \cdot 65}{49.8} \sim 38.066\,\mathrm{mm}$$

Therefore, the maximum parallax achievable on the Oculus Rift DK2 is only the 58% of the human interocular distance. As a consequence, the placement of objects in the virtual environment in the far background will never lead to perceptual issues or eye strain. In our preliminary tests, all the users have been able to correctly perceive objects placed at the bottom of our test scene. By considering the minimum (55 mm) and maximum (75 mm) values for the interaxial distance of the DK2 lenses, we obtain $MPP_{DK2} = 32.2102$ mm and $MPP_{DK2} = 43.9228$ mm, respectively.

A peculiar characteristic of HMDs is that the placement of the "convergence plane" (i.e., where the parallax value is zero, and the objects are perceived on the screen) is not equal to the physical distance between the observer's eyes and the screen, as it occurs in projection-based or monitor-based stereoscopic setups. To determine the virtual distance from the camera to the convergence plane in the Oculus Rift DK2, we have applied an empyrical approach: we have gradually moved away from the camera the cube in our test scene, and we have analyzed the final disparity value given its position in the left and right views. When the

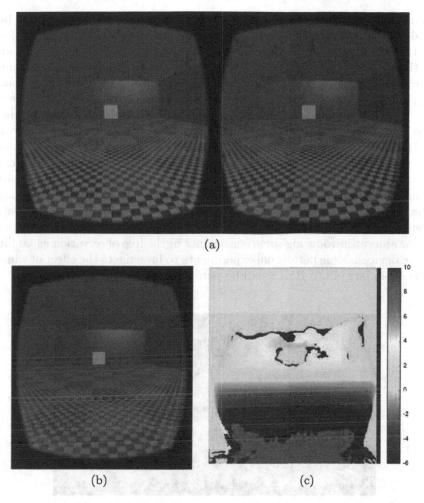

(a)

(b)   (c)

Fig. 2. The test cube placed at the depth of the convergence plane (with interaxial distance 65 mm). Figure 2(a) shows the rendered test scene with barrel distortion applied before the visualization in the Oculus Rift. Figure 2(b) shows an anaglyph of the image: the parallax of the cube is zero, thus its depth is the depth of the convergence plane. Figure 2(c) shows a disparity map of the scene to confirm the placement of the cube (see the cyan area in the center of the map, please notice that the presence of the black area at the borders due to the application of the pre-warping distortion has introduced some artifacts in the bottom of the map.)

disparity value of the cube becomes zero, then the depth position of the cube gives the distance of the convergence plane. By using this approach, we have determined that, for the default interaxial distance of 65 mm, the convergence plane is at 2 m from the virtual camera. For the interaxial distances of 55 mm and 75 mm, the convergence plane distance becomes 1.60 m and 2.20 m, respectively. In Fig. 2 we show the cube in the test scene, placed at the convergence distance, and we show the map of the disparities in the scene.

Finally, a preliminary analysis of the presence of window violations has been considered. Having determined the distance of the convergence plane, we know that there is a negative parallax range of about 2 virtual meters. In this area, it is theoretically possible to have window violations: Fig. 3 shows an example where our cube has been placed between the camera and the convergence plane, only partially inside the view frustum of the camera. It is evident that the two views have different visual information, because part of the cube is not visible in the right image. However, these kind of window violations are less perceivable in a HMD than in other stereoscopic devices, because of the larger horizontal FOV, which moves the window violations at the periphery of sight, and because of the head tracking capabilities, which allows a continuous change of the visual information observed. However, for some immersive but not-interactive media, as the new kind of immersive movies currently produced for the new generation of consumer-oriented HMDs, this is an aspect to consider, if for some reasons the director aims at introducing some constraints in the free observation capabilities of these devices. Some perceptual experiments to investigate the effect of window violations in large FOV HMDs will be performed in the next months.

Fig. 3. An example of window violation in the Oculus Rift DK2.

4   Stereoscopic Setup of a Standard 3D Display

We have decided to compare the stereoscopic characteristics of the Oculus Rift DK2 with a standard setup used for stereoscopic visualization with a 3D monitor. We have considered a 27" LCD monitor (Asus VG278H 3D), with resolution 1920 × 1080 and physical dimensions of 600 mm × 340 mm, equipped with an active stereoscopy system. We have set the observation distance at 1.02 m, following the convention to calculate the optimal viewing distance for a Full HD panel as 3 times the panel height. Following this setup, we have adapted our virtual test scene in Blender by setting the distance of the convergence plane at 1.02 m from the camera (i.e., setting a correspondence between the physical distance between the eyes and the screen and the virtual distance between the camera and the convergence plane), and the FOV value at 32.78 (the view angle subtended by this visualization setup).

Applying Eq. 1, the native parallax of the LCD display is:

$$NP_{LCD} = \frac{65}{600} \sim 0.1083$$

As for the Oculus Rift DK2, we have calculated the maximum parallax achievable on the LCD monitor. We have applied Eq. 2 with $M = 600/32 = 18.75$ and $f = 54.4$:

$$MPP_{LCD} = \frac{18.75 \cdot 54.4 \cdot 65}{1020} \sim 65 \text{ mm}$$

Thus, with a parallax on screen of approximately 208 pixels (only 10.83% of the screen width), the disparity is already equal to the average human interaxial distance. As a consequence, a higher level of attention must be given during the production of stereoscopic contents, to avoid perceptual issues in the final results. In fact, from the preliminary visualization tests, observers have reported relevant difficulties to correctly perceive stereoscopic images with screen parallaxes greater than 3 cm. These issues are due to the combination of the narrow FOV, display size and coarser pixel density of the LCD panel. Regarding window violations, even if the negative parallax range is almost half of the range of the Oculus Rift DK2, the presence of this perceptual issue is more relevant, due to the absence of head tracking, and to the narrower FOV (the objects placed at the border of the screen are more evident because they fall in a more central retinal area). In Fig. 4 we show a graphical comparison between the two different stereoscopic visualization setups.

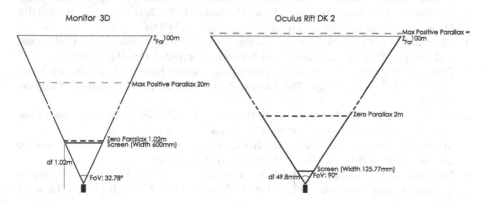

Fig. 4. Schemes of the different stereoscopic setups of the Oculus Rift DK2 and a standard 3D monitor.

5   Conclusion

In the next future, the consumer market for entertainment will see an increasing diffusion of Virtual Reality-based devices and stereoscopic content, due to the introduction of a new generation of advanced and affordable HMDs. With the probable establishment of a complex and articulated interaction between different smart technologies and devices, the production and development of dedicated content designed to exploit the peculiarities of these new visualization devices is mandatory. In this paper, we have presented an analysis of the stereoscopic characteristics of the Oculus Rift DK2, as a representative of this new generation of HMDs. We have determined that this kind of devices does not present issues related to possible excessive parallax values on screen, giving a relevant freedom to the developers to create immersive content without worrying about the final stereoscopic perception of objects placed in the background. Some additional accurate investigations are needed in order to evaluate if stereoscopic window violations are actually perceived in a relevant way, or if they are limited to some very specific configurations. Moreover, with the upcoming interest for online 3D interactive environments, it is also mandatory to extend our analysis to online collaborative applications, as already hinted in [29].

References

1. Ayala García, A., Galván Bobadilla, I., Arroyo Figueroa, G., Pérez Ramírez, M., Muñoz Román, J.: Virtual reality training system for maintenance and operation of high-voltage overhead power lines. Virtual Reality **20**(1), 27–40 (2016). Springer
2. Ruthenbeck, S.G., Reynolds, J.K.: Virtual reality for medical training: the state of the art. J. Simul. **9**(1), 16–26 (2015)
3. Wilson, C.J., Soranzo, A.: The use of virtual reality in psychology: a case study in visual perception. Comput. Math. Methods Med. (2015). Article ID 151702. https://www.hindawi.com/journals/cmmm/2015/151702/
4. Sherman, W., Craig, A.: Understanding Virtual Reality: Interface, Application, and Design. The Morgan Kaufmann Series in Computer Graphics (2002)
5. Craig, A., Sherman, W., Will, J.: Developing Virtual Reality Applications: Foundations of Effective Design. The Morgan Kaufmann Series in Computer Graphics (2009)
6. Bowman, D., Kruijff, E., LaViola, J., Poupyrev, I.: 3D User Interfaces: Theory and Practice. Addison-Wesley/Pearson Education, Boston (2004)
7. Marini, D., Folgieri, R., Gadia, D., Rizzi, A.: Virtual reality as a communication process. Virtual Reality **16**(3), 233–241 (2012). Springer
8. Barricelli, B.R., Gadia, D., Rizzi, A., Marini, D.: Semiotics of virtual reality as a communication process. Behav. Inf. Technol. **35**(11), 879–896 (2016). Taylor & Francis
9. Wann, J.P., Rushton, S., Mon-Williams, M.: Natural problems for stereoscopic depth perception in virtual environments. Vis. Res. **35**(19), 2731–2736 (1995)
10. Loomis, J.M., Knapp, J.M.: Visual perception of egocentric distance in real and virtual environments. In: Virtual and Adaptive Environments, pp. 21–46. CRC Prees (2003)

11. Kline, P.B., Witmer, B.G.: Distance perception in virtual environments: effects of field of view and surface texture at near distances. Hum. Factors Ergon. Soc. Annu. Meet. Proc. **40**, 1112–1116 (1996)
12. Knapp, J.M., Loomis, J.M.: Limited field of view of head-mounted displays is not the cause of distance underestimation in virtual environments. Presence: Teleoper. Virtual Environ. **13**(5), 572–577 (2004)
13. Willemsen, P., Gooch, A.A., Thompson, W.B., Creem-Regehr, S.H.: Effects of stereo viewing conditions on distance perception in virtual environments. Presence: Teleoper. Virtual Environ. **17**(1), 91–101 (2008)
14. Mendiburu, B.: 3D Movie Making: Stereoscopic Digital Cinema from Script to Screen. Focal Press, Waltham (2009)
15. Mendiburu, B., Pupulin, Y., Schklair, S.: 3D TV and 3D Cinema: Tools and Processes for Creative Stereoscopy. Taylor and Francis, Park Drive (2012)
16. Gadia, D., Garipoli, G., Bonanomi, C., Albani, L., Rizzi, A.: Assessing stereo blindness and stereo acuity on digital displays. Displays **35**(4), 206–212 (2014). Elsevier
17. Gardner, B.R.: Dynamic floating window: new creative tool for three-dimensional movies. J. Electron. Imaging **21**(1), 011009 (2012)
18. Schild, J.: Deep Gaming - The Creative and Technological Potential of Stereoscopic 3D Vision for Interactive Entertainment. CreateSpace Independent Publishing Platform (2014)
19. Bickerstaff, I.: Case study: the introduction of stereoscopic games on the Sony PlayStation 3. In: Stereoscopic Displays and Applications XXIII, Proceedings of SPIE, vol. 8288, p. 828815 (2012)
20. Weaver, J., Holliman, N.S.: Interlopers 3D: experiences designing a stereoscopic game. In: Stereoscopic Displays and Applications XXV, Proceedings of SPIE, vol. 9011, p. 90110F (2014)
21. Lipton, L.: Foundations of the Stereoscopic Cinema. Van Nostrand Reinhold, New York (1982)
22. Poulakos, S., Monroy, R., Aydin, T., Wang, O., Smolic, A., Gross, M.: A computational model for perception of stereoscopic window violations. In: Seventh International Workshop on Quality of Multimedia Experience (QoMEX), pp. 1–6 (2015)
23. Scalabrin, M., Ripamonti, L.A., Maggiorini, D., Gadia, D.: Stereoscopy-based procedural generation of virtual environments. In: Stereoscopic Displays and Applications XXVII, Proceedings of IS&T's 28th Symposium on Electronic Imaging: Science and Technology (2016)
24. Stanfield, B., Zerebecki, C., Hogue, A., Kapralos, B., Collins, K.: Impact of floating windows on the accuracy of depth perception in games. In: Stereoscopic Displays and Applications XXIV, Proceedings of SPIE, vol. 8648, p. 864814 (2013)
25. Oculus Rift DK2 Screen. http://www.theverge.com/2014/7/31/5956589/new-oculus-dev-kit-uses-front-of-galaxy-note-3-for-display. Accessed Mar 2016
26. Oculus Rift Developer Documentation. https://developer.oculus.com/documentation/intro-vr/latest/concepts/book-bp/. Accessed Mar 2016
27. Pohl, D., Johnson, G.S., Bolkart, T.: Improved pre-warping for wide angle, head mounted displays. In: Proceedings of the 19th ACM Symposium on Virtual Reality Software and Technology, pp. 259–262 (2013)
28. Blender homepage: http://blender.org. Accessed Mar 2016
29. Gerla, M., Maggiorini, D., Palazzi, C.E., Bujari, A.: A survey on interactive games over mobile networks. Wireless Commun. Mob. Comput. **13**(3), 212–229 (2013)

The Use of Wearable Devices
in the Workplace - A Systematic Literature
Review

Jayden Khakurel[✉], Simo Pöysä, and Jari Porras

Lappeenranta University of Technology, Lappeenranta, Finland
{jayden.khakurel,jari.porras}@lut.fi

Abstract. The aim of this Systematic Literature Review is to provide a heuristic overview on the recent trends of wearable technology and to assess their potential in workplaces. The search procedure resulted a total of 34 studies. In more details, 29 different types of wearable devices were obtained from the studies. Categorization revealed that obtained wearable devices were used for monitoring: 18 types (e.g. for mental stress, progress, etc.), augmenting: 3 types (e.g. for data, images), assisting: 3 types (e.g. to uplift their work), delivering: 2 types (e.g. for vital information contents) and tracking: 8 types (e.g. sedentary behaviour). To sum up, though wearable technology has already gained momentum for personal use to monitor daily activities, our studies shows that it also has potential to increase work efficiency among employees, improve worker's physical well-being and reduce work related injuries. Further work in terms of privacy, usability, security, policies, cost of devices and its integration to the existing system is required in order to increase the adoption rate of wearable devices in workplaces.

Keywords: Wearable technologies · Wearable devices · Workplace · Benefits · Occupational health · Wearable robotics · Systematic literature review

1 Introduction

Evolution of technologies such as computers, smart phones, has dramatically reshaped the workplace over the past couple of decades. This evolution has also occurred at the workplace as most job descriptions have changed from manual labor to predominantly physically inactive duties (e.g., desk jobs, automated assembly lines, etc.) [18]. At the same time, employees are working longer hours *to meet the requirements of the job, anticipation/expectation of higher earnings in the future, increasing volumes of work, job insecurity, employee's preference, occupational commitment and career enhancement* [12, 16]. This can potentially have enormous effect on physical well-being of employee, likelihood of occupational injuries and illness [6]. According to Baka, "Occupational accidents still occur, despite technical developments in the occupational safety field at large" [1]. A potential injury occurs at the industrial environment due to complex, hazardous conditions [1, 8, 13] and fatigue. Studies conducted by various researchers and managers have generally recognized that health and well-being can

© ICST Institute for Computer Sciences, Social Informatics and Telecommunications Engineering 2017
O. Gaggi et al. (Eds.): GOODTECHS 2016, LNICST 195, pp. 284–294, 2017.
DOI: 10.1007/978-3-319-61949-1_30

potentially affect both workers and organizations in negative ways [5]. Kritzler states that, "companies suffer significant financial losses every day due to illness and poor health of their employees [1, 13]. Therefore, there is need for improvement in health and safety, which can bring benefits to both company as well as employees.

Companies have started incorporating ICT based approaches in to their health and safety promotion programme designed to improve worker's health and safety, and reduce health care costs [4, 14, 20]. Currently there is a great inclination to modify well-being concept and health care by changing the technology in "wearable" [7]. These technologies have gained increasing traction in recent years for personal use to track data about everyday lives and physical well-being. Following the same tendency, we assume that this technology could be immediately useful in workplace.

Wearable technology also called wearable devices or gadgets, as an autonomous, powerful system that are worn in human body or attached to clothing worn by human to perform the specific task or function [9]. Wearable Technology offers new opportunities to monitor human activity continuously with the miniature wearable sensors embedded [3] in garments. A key benefit of wearable technology is to improve in productivity, efficiency, connectivity, health and wellness [19].

The question then becomes how wearables could strike out potential benefits in the work place. In order to unfold potential benefits, firstly, it is necessary to discover what types of wearable devices can be used in workplaces, how these wearables devices can be integrated in to day business activities *(i.e. to increase safety, level of physical activity, reduce their stress and increase productivity and efficiency)* based on previous researches, we performed the systematic literature review guided by Kitchenham and Charters [10].

This study provides an overview on the research trends and patterns and the usage pattern of wearable technologies for workplaces from 2000 to 2016. The paper is organized as follows: Sect. 2: *how research process been conducted*; Sect. 3: *findings of this study and presents an interpretation of our results*; Sect. 4: *discussions*; and Sect. 5: *concludes the paper.*

2 Research Methods and Questions

– **Research Process:** A systematic literature review has been adopted and applied, in line with Kitchenham and Charters [10] guidelines, terminology and Petersen et al. [17]. According to Kitchenham and Charters a systematic literature review can be defined *"as means of identifying, analyzing and interpreting all available data relevant to the particular research question or topic area in an unbiased way"* [10]. The overview of the adopted process consists of following phases:

  • *Definition of the research question, based on the objective of the research.*
  • *Conduct a search of articles for primary studies by using search strings on scientific libraries, databases. Tools like NAILS bibliometric software [11] can also be utilized for this purpose.*
  • *Screening the initial set of articles, by applying inclusion and exclusion criteria to determine whether each potential study should be included.*

- *Classification of articles based on the keywords from the abstracts of selected articles.*
- *Classification and categorization of articles based on the final set of keywords.*

Petersen et al. [17] recommends researchers doing systematic reviews to investigate and make use of alternative ways of presenting and visualizing their results. Finally, the results were consolidated from the relevant articles and presented in the form of graphs, tables, or other form of graphical representations.

- **Research Questions:** The overall objective of the systematic literature review is to identify the types of wearable technologies that can be utilized in workplaces and whether these technologies can be beneficial for different business stakeholders (corporate, internal and external). Hence, given that we specified three research questions (RQs) together with a rationale for each one to obtain more inclusive overview on the topic:

  - **RQ1:** *What types of wearable technology are mentioned in literature in between 2000–2016 that can be used in the workplace? To what extent wearable technology can be utilized in workplaces?*
    Rationale: *identifies the range of wearable technologies under study in recent time and possible areas of future development.*
  - **RQ2:** *What benefit does wearable technology give for the company and employees?*
    Rationale: *indicates the extent to which whether wearable technology can be beneficial for companies and employees, which provides information about the likelihood of development in wearable technology.*
  - **RQ3:** *What challenges still remain and need further investigation by research communities?*
    Rationale: *provides information that can be serve as a basis for ascertaining future research direction.*

- **Search Design Process:** We started the primary studies search by using the search strings on online search databases. The following electronic databases were searched: ACM digital library, IEEE Xplore, Science direct[1] and web of knowledge. We have chosen the stated databases because they are identified as relevant to information technology field. From the identified papers, we also manually browsed the citations [21]. The search strategy used to formulate the search terms (ST) was composed of following 4 phases as described in (Fig. 1):

  In **phase 1**, we formulated the search terms based on research question using PICO criteria[2]. In our studies, we have discarded comparison and outcome as we not comparing any devices or measuring anything in our study. In **phase 2**, we identified possible synonyms and acronyms or alternative words for search terms (i.e. ("wearable"; "wearable device"; "wearable computing"; "wearable

---

[1] www.sciencedirect.com.

[2] PICO Criteria: http://learntech.physiol.ox.ac.uk/cochrane_tutorial/cochlibd0e84.php.

Fig. 1. Search string formulation process

technology"), ("workplace"; "work"), ("benefit"; "advantage"). In **phase 3**, we merged all the identified synonyms and acronyms or alternative words of search terms by using the Boolean "OR". Finally, in **Phase 4**, we connected all the major terms to form the final search string using the Boolean operators AND, the relevant articles whose publication date was since 2000 onwards, as *(""wearable*" or "wearable device*" or "wearable computing" or "wearable technology*") **AND** (""workplace*" or "work") **AND** ("benefit*" or "advantage*") **AND** ("publication year > 2000").*

By utilizing the above predefined digital databases sources with their search utility, and formulated final search string, we conducted the initial search process in March 2016 and the final set of search in 30/06/2016. Additionally, search was also conducted using the Google scholar in order to find any relevant articles as well as to cross check the final sets of retrieved papers to determine the relevance of each paper.

- **Article Selection Process:** The aim of the article selection process was to find those articles that are relevant to the objective of this systematic literature review based on inclusion and exclusion criteria. Thus we applied the following set of inclusion and exclusion criteria to select the relevant publications to answer our research questions. The inclusion criteria (IC) formulated and applied are: **IC1:** *Publication date between 1/1/2000–30/06/2016;* **IC2:** *Includes answers for at least one of the research questions;* **IC3:** *Includes if study conducted related about workplace, using wearable technology;* **IC4:** *If several papers reported by same author, only the most recent one is included;* **IC5:** *Only papers written in English.* The exclusion criteria (EC) formulated and applied are: **EC1:** *Paper that limited discussion about wearables;* **EC2:** *If it doesn't cover the enhancement of workplace productivity;* **EC3:** *Technical documentation or reports that are available in the form of abstracts and secondary literature reviews.*

In the beginning, automated search led to 359 articles from *IEEE Xplore (166), ACM digital Library (7), Science direct (181)* and *web of knowledge (5).* After refining the results based on the above predefined exclusion and inclusion criteria, such as keywords, abstract, full text, titles were in English and duplicate articles, final 34 studies were selected for data extraction and analysis.

- **Data Extraction:** Template was used to register the relevant information from the final set of reviewed articles. The data extraction (DE) process included following input from each selected primary resources: Metadata: *Study ID (S1, S2...,), Author* (s), Year of Publication, Paper title, Name of the Conference or Journal in which study has been presented, Keywords, Topic, Database in which study was found. Because we are interested to find and analyze the data with respect the RQ, we extracted the data as: *Types of wearables (if Applicable); RQ2, Utilizations (if Applicable): RQ2; Wearing position (if Applicable): RQ2; Benefits: RQ3.*

Overall, 12 data fields were created to extract data from selected articles. (See APPENDIX: A).[3]

3 Results

We gathered and analyzed the data from 34 articles (see APPENDIX: B)[4] from 2000 to 2016. Based upon the analyzed data, results related to the systematic literature review are presented in this section. Even though, search was limited, between 2000 to 2016, relevant articles only started to appear around 2009. This seems to indicate that recently there has been growing interest among researchers in this topic. The following section highlights the important results:

RQ 1: What types of wearable technology are mentioned in literature in between 2000–2016 that can be used in the workplace? To what extent wearable technology can be utilized in workplaces?

The main objective of this research question is to identify the range of wearable technologies that has been extensively mentioned in recent years. The first part of research question concerned what types of wearables has been addressed in workplaces. The search led to the identification of 29 types of wearables from relevant papers. These identified devices are listed in APPENDIX: C[5]. Literature review revealed that there are five ways how wearable technologies has been utilized in workplaces which are explained below:

1. **Monitoring** *[Study ID S3, S5, S6, S7, S8, S10, S11, S12, S15, S19, S20, S27, S28, S29, S33, S34]:* It allows employees to collect ongoing health information via series of activities using the devices. We have found out most of the selected studies used wearable devices in their workplace to monitor work related stress [S12], [S15], [S19], [S27], [S28], individual and social behaviour [S10] [S12], progress [S3].
2. **Assisting** *[Study ID S4, S14]:* It allows employers to provide external tools which are worn in body to control their posture, or lift heavy items. We also discovered that some of the studies used hydraulic and electric powered exo-skeletons to assist the workers in order to uplift the heavy load [S4] as well as to control posture of the workers [S14]. Exo-Skeleton is defined by Looze et al. [15] as *a wearable, external mechanical structure that enhances the power of a person.*

---

[3] APPENDIX A: http://step.lut.fi/data/uwd/Appendix_A.pdf.
[4] APPENDIX B: http://step.lut.fi/data/uwd/Appendix_B.pdf.
[5] APPENDIX C: http://step.lut.fi/data/uwd/Appendix_C.pdf.

3. **Augmenting** *[Study ID S1, S9, S12, S13, S21]:* It allows employers to deliver digital information, such as: images, text, videos on devices such as HMD's, glasses while wearer views the real world. According to Gartner Research[6], wearable augmented device is going to be an important tool for companies to enhance key business activities such as business process, training, etc. Experiments conducted by [S12] [S13] found out that by augmenting, employers can improve employee performance by initiating training tools. We have discovered that employers can use the AR devices for employer's productivities [S12], [S13], remote guidance [S26], health and safety improvement [S1], industrial design [S13], [S21], and maintenancework [S1].

4. **Tracking** *[Study ID S6, S7, S10, S16, S17, S18, S24, S25, S30, S31, S32, S34]:* Through this usage, employers will be able to track worker's position, movement through the use of devices deployed on the body (e.g. arm movement, distance travelled). For example: Study conducted by [S24] [S25] used devices [T15] to track employee's sedentary behavior.

5. **Delivering** *[Study ID S3, S9, S21]:* It allows employers to deliver the content and to the users via device allowing them to read, listen or watch context provided by third parties. Based on Chen et al. [S3], wearable can provide just-in-time information which are currently not possible with paper on-site construction processes.

By implying the utilization of wearables in workplaces, we clustered the obtained wearables type under categories *(C1): Monitoring; (C2): Assisting (C3): Augmenting; (C4): Tracking; and (C5): Delivering.* From the categorization, we found that various types of wearables devices were used for monitoring: 18 types, augmenting: 3 types, assisting: 3 types, delivering: 2 types and tracking: 8 types. Based on the findings, we have created the usage of wearable framework in workplaces (See APPENDIX. D)[7]. We have also discovered that, three devices were utilized for multiple purpose.

Studies shows that simpler devices such as digital pedometer [T15], smartwatch [T1] can help employer to get minimal data from tracking the worker's activities whereas advanced technologies such as EEG devices [T8], EMG sensor nodes [T9] can help employer to gather complex data in order to create and deploy effective physical well-being strategy. We have also found out that same wearable devices such as HMD's [T21], EEG devices [T8], Digital pedometer [T15] can be utilized for multiple purposes while other can fit for only specific purpose.

RQ2: What benefit does wearable technology give for the company and employees?

As described in previous section, wearable technologies can be utilized for multiple purpose. In this section, we analysis how wearable technologies can be beneficial and provide long lasting effects in work place. From the primary studies we found out that, the benefits of wearable technologies in the workplace is highest when they are introduced to:

---

[6] http://www.gartner.com/newsroom/id/2649315.

[7] Appendix D: http://step.lut.fi/data/uwd/Appendix_D.pdf.

– **Monitoring physcological and physiological factors of the employees:** Many employers are unaware of their employee's physio-social and physical-stress levels and the effects it at the workplace. One of the quotes by Dr. Deming [2] *"if you can't measure it, you can't manage it"* fully implies in workplace. Unless employer monitors working environment it is difficult for them to know if their employees are getting worse or better with regards to performance level.

Wearable technology can be valuable tool in workplace to monitor and refine the wellness initiatives of the employees. From the study, we found out that many devices have been used for tracking physio-social stress (stress about the job) and physical stress (working hard with the equipment's) or tracking the physical activities of the worker. One of the benefit of wearable technology is active monitoring by taking the advantage of the data delivered by wearable devices. With those data, employers could take active steps towards assisting their employees either via discussion about the issues or creating physical activities. This will help employees to relieve stress, tension and live physically and mentally fit.

– **Enhance operational efficiency:** Wearable devices such as HMD's (such as smart glass, Microsoft HoloLens) can be utilized for remote guidance. By using HMD user's hands are totally free and the user's vision is unobstructed. The person who is giving the guidance can see exactly the same things as the one who is being guided, through the camera in the mounted device. This means that one giving guidance can see the real world and the created 3D images from the camera. 3D images can be created into real world surfaces for the guided person to see and they can be interacted with different types of touch gestures [S26]. With the help of AR, communication becomes more accurate and easier to understand which also effects on work performance.

– **Workplace safety and security:** Employee's safety is always important in any workplace, especially in hazardous jobs where employee is for example working in a mine, operating heavy machinery, construction site or in a job where employee is dealing with high voltages. From the literature review, we found out that safety and security can be improved with the help of accurate monitoring using wearables.

Yang et al. [S33] found in their study that, it is possible to detect the dangerous working spots (places where happens the most near-miss falls) with the collected data from wearable devices. Another study conducted by Sole et al. [S30] found out that RFID tags can be used to improve workplace safety and to limit false alarms. Baka et al. [S2] explained in their paper that, wearable could be used to detect and warn the user when step voltage hazard exists. According to them, two sensors (transducers) can be attached to user's feet so that they are in contact with skin. These sensors can detect the user's body current and work as monitoring system, when the dangerous potential differences are starting to occur. When the user is approaching dangerous zone, the device warns the user. This clearly shows that wearable use in workplace has clear benefits to improve workplace safety for employees.

– **Industrial designing:** Wearables integrated AR technology can be used for example designing construction plans [S13], blueprints [S13], building information modeling [S13] and aircraft cabins [S21]. As a result, task can be done virtually without any extra cost such as over-head, travelling, onsite meeting. Study conducted by [S21] discovered that AR can be used in manufacturing purposes for maintenance and measuring the wires for vehicles before installations which will lead to save time and cost.

- **Improve worker's health:** Working posture are always problematic for all kind of jobs. However, computer related jobs, construction works, mining can be taken as the examples due to lots of physical strain it can cause to the backside of body. When the working posture is bad for years, it is highly likely to cause low back disorders, more so in more physically demanding workplaces as mentioned. Eurofound also observed that level to exposure to some risks such as (particularly 'tiring and painful positions' and 'repetitive hand or arm movements') has shown an upward trend [16]. Luo et al. [S14] conducted study on this issue where he designed WSAD (Wearable Stooping-Assist Device) for stooped work. As the name imply, this device reduces the strain from a stooping posture and so it prevents the risks having a low back disorder. Chu et al. [S4] also experimented wearable robots (exo-skeleton) to improve worker's health in shipbuilding work. [S4] used exoskeletons to decrease the muscle strain on lower limb muscles of workers and to support vertical load. This type of support helps preventing possible musculoskeletal disorders. In this study [S4] used two different prototype exoskeletons, i.e., standard type and gooseneck type. Exoskeleton's mobility and usability was tested for several hours. Though exoskeletons had certain limitations, such as lifting capacity and maximum walking speed, the workers did confirm that the exoskeletons improved work efficiency and seemed to help preventing muscular diseases.

RQ3: What challenges still remain and need further investigation by research communities?

Data analyzed from the studies have shown that, wearable devices can have benefits to the workplace. However, there are still some remaining challenges which needs to be investigated and resolved. During our primary studies, we have identified following open challenges that still needs to be further investigated by research communities:

- **Usability:** It has been established from the research work of Khakurel et al. [9], device characteristics (size, battery life, modalities, etc.) were the most discussed usability issues that have limited the ways in which users can interact with the wearable devices. Hence, in this study, we have also found out that size and battery life [S3], [S20], [S31] are the most important parameters. In order to increase adoption of wearable devices at workplaces and improve the usability of the users, re-searcher should further investigate on how size and energy consumption of the system can be minimized by increasing the memory size [9].

- **Privacy:** One major issue identified in the studies [S11], [S12], [S16], [S34] is the violation of privacy because data generated from wearable devices contains, vital information of employees, such as heart rate, number of steps taken, etc. Researcher's needs to investigate what kind of data employees would like to handover and create further guidelines related to which type of wearables can be applied in workplace and what kind of data can be extracted and analyzed.

- **Adoption:** One of the challenges, we found from the studies is the adoption of wearables [S12], [S20], [S22] by both employees and employers. The adoption of wearables and also the willingness to share the data with employees would require vast amount of awareness. Further research should investigate new incentives, motivation and workplace performance model with the integration of wearables.
- **Cost factors**: Other key challenges for employers is the complexity and cost of integration with existing system. Chen et al. [S3], found out for companies it is necessary that Return of Investments (ROI) exceeds the cost of obtaining information wirelessly. Research communities should investigate the ways to developing and integrating low cost wearable devices to the existing system.
- **Accuracy:** From the studies [S19], [S21], [S28], we have found out that data delivered by wearable devices are not 100% accurate. Also from the studies made by Khakurel et al. [9], one of the usability issues for wearable devices is accuracy. Therefore, there is need for further studies to develop the higher accuracy sensors and algorithms to ensure that quality and accuracy of data remains creditable.
- **Security:** Like all other technologies, wearables are vulnerable to hackers. From the studies, we have found that employers are concern from possible cyberattacks which can lead to breach of security data. Further research on how this possible attacks can be eradicated after implementing devices in workplaces.

4 Discussion

The focus of this section is to discuss the results obtained during the systematic literature review and are based on interpretation and exploration of the retrieved data.

Based on this literature review, we can clearly see that wearable technology is not only popular for entertainment purposes but it is also starting to be a valid solution for workplace needs. Our findings show that the majority of the reviewed papers reported several devices (e.g., smart watch [S11] [S33], digital pedometers [S7] [S22] [S29], electronic shirts [S33] and HMD'S [S3] [S21] that are being used for entertainment or lifestyle purposes, can also be applied for workplace usage.

Carrying and detaching multiple technologies on the body could lead more stress for workers. It is necessary for workplace to investigate and combine multiple technologies to create single service to monitor the employees. For example, use of wristbands which can monitor the activities, to get through doors in work-place or as a timestamp device. This way the wearable device would not feel like a thing that an employee has to wear every day just to be monitored.

In some cases, it was also noted that using wearable devices also increased work performance. This was the case for using exoskeletons and HMD's. Exoskeletons also help preventing muscular diseases by lowering the physical strain on the body. So this type of device has actually two great benefits. The problem with wearable exoskeletons is however the fact that the safety standards for them in workplace usage are still in progress and they are still more in experimentation stage. In the near future however, wearable exoskeletons would be a great asset especially in industrial and construction type of work where there are a lot of heavy lifting.

Having healthy employees are important for the company and being healthy is obviously a desirable thing. As this work indicated, this type of monitoring can be used for finding out the cause for stress and then possibly limiting it by taking necessary actions. Also by monitoring physical changes in body, it may be possible to detect possible illnesses and get proper treatment for them, before they get more serious. By using wearable devices, the safety of workplaces can also be improved as it turned out in the text.

5 Conclusion

The aim of this study was to provide systematic literature review of the current trends of research and future perspectives of wearable technology in workplaces. Following predefined criteria, we identified and analyzed around 34 relevant articles.

Results revealed that there has been many experimentations and implementations for several types of wearable devices in different kind of workplace environments. To achieve research goal, we identified the types of wearables and categorized in terms their mode of use. We also observed that some wearables can be used for multiple purposes while some can be used for specific purpose. Findings revealed that, most of the identified devices are still in prototype stages but have the potential and will be definitely a useful tool in workplaces in the near future.

Most of the benefits of wearable devices in workplace addressed focus on employee's health, workplace safety and improved work performance. However, wearable technology has limitations which need to overcome, with regards to technology, privacy, cost, accuracy, adoption and design.

In conclusion there are a various types of wearables that can be utilized in workplaces for different purposes. Wearable technology in the workplace are relatively new concept to improve health and safety of the workers and have gained significant momentum over the last few years. Although, wearable technologies have been great assets for personnel use, it is still a relatively new area of research for use in the workplace where issues such as usability, privacy, cost factors, data accuracy issues are yet to be resolved.

References

1. Baka, A.D., Uzunoglu, N.K.: Protecting workers from step voltage hazards. IEEE Technol. Soc. Mag. **35**(1), 69–74 (2016)
2. Best, M.: W Edwards Deming: father of quality management, patient and composer. Qual. Saf. Health Care **14**(4), 310–312 (2005)
3. Ching, K.W., Singh, M.M.: Wearable technology devices security and privacy vulnerability analysis. Int. J. Netw. Secur. Appl. **8**(3), 19–30 (2016)
4. Cook, R.F., et al.: A field test of a web-based workplace health promotion program to improve dietary practices, reduce stress, and increase physical activity: randomized controlled trial. J. Med. Internet Res. **9**, 2 (2007)

5. Danna, K., Griffin, R.W.: Health and well-being in the workplace: a review and synthesis of the literature. J. Manag. **25**(3), 357–384 (1999)
6. Dembe, A.E., et al.: The impact of overtime and long work hours on occupational injuries and illnesses: new evidence from the United States. Occup. Environ. Med. **62**(9), 588–597 (2005)
7. Ferraro, V., Ugur, S.: Designing wearable technologies through a user centered approach. In: Proceedings of 2011 Conference on Designing Pleasurable Products and Interfaces, pp. 5:1–5:8 (2011)
8. Kenn, H., Bürgy, C.: "Are we crossing the chasm in wearable AR?" - 3rd workshop on wearable systems for industrial augmented reality applications. In: Proceedings of International Symposium on Wearable Computers: Adjunct Program, ISWC, pp. 213–216 (2014)
9. Khakurel, J., et al.: Usability issues related to wearable devices: a systematic literature review (Submitted)
10. Kitchenham, B., Charters, S.: Guidelines for performing systematic literature reviews in software engineering. Engineering **2**, 1051 (2007)
11. Knutas, A., et al.: Cloud-based bibliometric analysis service for systematic mapping studies. In: Proceedings of 16th International Conference on Computer Systems and Technologies, pp. 184–191 (2015)
12. Kodz, J., et al.: Working long hours: a review of the evidence. vol. 1—Main report, DTI Employ. Relations Res. Ser. ERRS16. 1, 16, (2003)
13. Kritzler, M., et al.: Wearable technology as a solution for workplace safety. In: Proceeding of 14th International Conference on Mobile and Ubiquitous Multimedia (MUM 2015). Mum, pp. 213–217 (2015)
14. Loeppke, R.R., et al.: Integrating health and safety in the workplace: how closely aligning health and safety strategies can yield measurable benefits. J. Occup. Environ. Med. **57**(5), 585–597 (2015)
15. de Looze, M.P., et al.: Exoskeletons for industrial application and their potential effects on physical work load. Ergonomics **139**(December), 1–11 (2015)
16. Parent-Thirion, A., et al.: Eurofound. In: Fifth European Working Conditions Survey (2012)
17. Petersen, K., et al.: Systematic mapping studies in software engineering. In: EASE 2008, Proceedings of 12th International Conference on Evaluation and Assessment in Software Engineering, pp. 68–77 (2008)
18. Monitoring and Evaluation of Worksite Health Promotion Programs - Current State of Knowledge and Implications for Practice. Background paper prepared for the WHO/WEF Joint Event on Preventing Noncommunicable Diseases in World Health Organisation, pp. 1–42 (2007)
19. PricewaterhouseCoopers BV: Consumer Intelligence Series The Wearable Future (2014)
20. Sole, M., et al.: Control system for workplace safety in a cargo terminal. In: 2013 9th International Wireless Communications and Mobile Computing Conference, IWCMC 2013, pp. 1035–1039 (2013)
21. Webster, J., Watson, R.T.: Analyzing the past to prepare for the future: writing a literature review. MIS Q. **26**(2), xiii–xxiii (2002)

Radio Link Planning Made Easy with a Telegram Bot

Marco Zennaro[1]([✉]), Marco Rainone[2], and Ermanno Pietrosemoli[1]

[1] ICTP Telecommunication/ICT4D Lab, Strada Costiera 11, Trieste, Italy
mzennaro@ictp.it
[2] SolviTech, Udine, Italy

Abstract. Traditional radio planning tools present a steep learning curve. We present BotRf, a Telegram Bot that facilitates the process by guiding non-experts in assessing the feasibility of radio links. Built on open source tools, BotRf can run on any smartphone or PC using Telegram. Running it on a smartphone has the added value that the Bot can leverage the internal GPS to capture the current coordinates. BotRf can be used in low bandwidth environments as the generated data traffic is very limited. We present an example of its use in Venezuela.

Keywords: Telegram · Bots · Radio frequency planning · Simulator · Terrain profiles · Propagation models

1 Introduction

One aspect that is paramount in the planning of wireless links is the determination of the attenuation introduced by the terrain between the transmitter and the receiver, which ultimately determines the feasibility of a given link. There are many commercial programs meant to solve this problem, most of them making use of digital elevation maps. Some of them are quite costly and others restrict their usage to the radios and antennas of a particular manufacturer.

We still miss an easy to use, open source tool that can be used to assess the feasibility of wireless links. Taking advantage of the capabilities of the Bot technology and given the broad use of mobile devices, we developed a tool that minimizes the amount of data that the user needs to input and that does all the processing in the remote server, making it particularly suitable for low bandwidth environments. BotRf is platform independent as Telegram runs on smartphones (Android, iOS or Windows phones) and laptops/desktops (Windows, OSX and Linux). It provides a simulation of the terrain profile for different atmospheric refraction index values, calculating the path loss in a wireless point to point link. It shows the results in an easy to grasp interface and gives a numerical value of the link margin in dB when the radio and antenna parameters are also inserted.

We believe this tool could be particularly useful to setup Community Wireless Networks [1]. Community wireless network have sprouted in many countries,

© ICST Institute for Computer Sciences, Social Informatics and Telecommunications Engineering 2017
O. Gaggi et al. (Eds.): GOODTECHS 2016, LNICST 195, pp. 295–304, 2017.
DOI: 10.1007/978-3-319-61949-1_31

addressing needs that are not satisfied by commercial operators, either due to the lack of a high enough return on investment or because commercial operators were not well suited to address social aspects unrelated to profits.

2   RF Propagation Models

In [2], a thorough analysis of 30 propagation models used for the estimation of path loss is performed, reaching the conclusion that there is not a single one that can offer the best results in every case. Some models make use of digital elevation maps and ray tracing techniques to estimate the path loss, while other use a completely empirical approach, based on many measurements performed in a variety of environments at different frequencies. Then there is the hybrid approach, that combines terrain information with statistical inference from field measurements. They end up stating that *"..the landscape of path loss models is precarious: typical best-case performance accuracy of these models is on the order of 12–15 dB root mean square error (RMSE) and in practice it can be much worse"*. Therefore, in our work we stick with the well known Longley-Rice Irregular Terrain Model (L-R ITM) [3], which has been widely used since its original publication in 1968. The advantage of the L-R ITM is that by making use of the terrain profile between transmitter and receiver (derived from digital elevation maps), it will readily detect any obstruction that might preclude the link. So if the model suggests that a links is unfeasible, we accept this result and search for an alternative such as raising the antenna height or looking for an alternate location. On the other hand, when the model finds a path unobstructed, we declare it a "maybe" until further information is available. In particular, the uncertainty is more significant when using SRTM3 DEM data that have a high chance of ignoring obstacles that are less than 90 m in size. This strategy has been quite successful over a number of links that we have simulated and later deployed. The path attenuation result of the L-R ITM is calculated by modifying the free space loss by incorporating the effects of diffraction and dispersion, as well as statistic losses that have been estimated based on many empirical measurements at different frequencies and over different types of terrain.

A very important factor that must be borne in mind when dealing with RF propagation is that the refraction index of the atmosphere causes a bending of the radio beam. This bending normally causes the radio horizon to extend 4/3 beyond the optical horizon, and this is accounted for by multiplying the real radius of curvature of the earth by a $K = 4/3$ factor and then draw the radio beam as a straight line. The atmospheric refraction index can change unexpectedly as it is affected by factors like temperature, humidity, water vapor content and so on, so the K factor might adopt temporarily other values. The International Telecommunications Union (ITU) [4] recommends that for critical links in which a very high reliability is required, the obstacles of the terrain must be cleared even for K less than 1 for distances below 100 km. For K less than 1, the effective radius of the earth is smaller than the real radius, so the radio horizon is closer that the optical horizon. BotRf allows for easy modification of the K factor.

Lastly, and more importantly, we must also note that electromagnetic waves occupy a volume in space called the Fresnel ellipsoid, extending from the transmitter to the receiver, with maximum girth at midpoint between the two. The radius of this ellipsoid is called the Fresnel zone radius and is proportional to the wavelength. In order to capture most of the power contained in radio waves, at least 60% of the Fresnel zone must be cleared. In a wireless link, we try to avoid that any obstacle protrudes more than 40% in the Fresnel zone, this means that the antennas must be raised above the minimum required to draw an unobstructed line from the transmitter to the receiver (the optical LOS).

3 RF Planning Tools

There are many RF planning tools available on the market, and they can be categorized as Commercial, Vendor Specific, Free and Open.

- Commercial tools use proprietary models and digital elevation maps of varying degrees of resolution. They run on PCs, are usually quite expensive and require heavy downloads. They are therefore not well suited to the needs of developing countries.
- Vendors like Motorola, Ubiquiti Networks, Cambium and Mimosa (among many others), offer radio propagation planning tools free of charge. They are usually associated to the specific of their radios and antennas offering, often require registration in their site and in general are quite cumbersome to use. They are usually based on web interfaces and are not designed to be used on mobile devices.
- Several free radio frequency planning tools are available. In our trainings and deployments we have used extensively the Radio Mobile program developed by Roger Coude [5]. It provides very valuable information, but it is built for the Windows operating system only, and requires considerable effort to install and to use. There is also an easier to use on-line version, but it works only for the frequencies allotted to the radio amateur service and does not specify the amount of first Fresnel zone clearance [6]. As the tool is free but not open, there is no guarantee that it will be maintained in the future.
  "Hey whats that path" profiler [7] is another free on line tool that can quickly draw terrain profiles between two or more points. It does not calculate the attenuation, but allows to change the frequency and the atmospheric refraction index and show how this affects the radio beam.
  The Communications Research Centre Canada offers the Radio Coverage Prediction [8] using the Longley-Rice model, but it is only for point to area, and will not work for point to point links. Its coverage is limited regions up to 5° in latitude and 10° in longitude.
  The Polish National Institute of Telecommunications developed PIAST (Platform IT for an Analysis of Systems in Telecommunications) [9], a web based tool for point to point RF links planning that will provide a path profile and estimates of the attenuation, using the ASTER GDEM v2 maps.

4   Splat! An Open Source RF Planning Tool

John Magliacane wrote Splat! [10] (Signal Propagation, Loss, And Terrain Analysis), an open source Linux based tool offered under the GNU license. It uses both the Longley-Rice Irregular Terrain Model and the Irregular Terrain with Obstructions Model to simulate the attenuation between the transmitter and the receiver as well as to estimate the point to area coverage of a transmitter for the frequencies between 20 MHz and 20 GHz. Splat! has been ported to Windows and is also the basis of QRadioPredict, an experimental software for VHF-UHF propagation prediction and radio coverage analysis.

Splat! uses the SRTM3 [11] digital elevation maps (DEM) which have a resolution of 90 m. As the maps are very heavy to download and we want to serve users in low-bandwidth environments, we downloaded the maps of the entire world in our server so that users don't have to do it. This account for more than 65 GB of data. We optimized the Splat! code to work directly with the native file format of the digital elevation maps to make the calculations quicker.

5   Telegram and Telegram Bots

Telegram [12] is a cloud-based instant messaging service, similar to Whatsapp. Telegram clients exist for smartphones (Android, iOS, Windows Phone, Ubuntu Touch) and desktop systems (Windows, OSX, Linux). It differs from Whatsapp in that it does not support voice calls, but unlike Whatsapp it can be used without a phone. The client is free and has no limits on the size of media that can be exchanged. Servers are distributed in many locations around the world.

In June 2015, Telegram launched a platform for third-party developers to create Bots [13]. Bots are Telegram accounts operated by programs that respond to messages or mentions and can be integrated in other programs. They mimic the behavior of a human being in specific applications, like a help desk. Telegram acts as a "middle man" between users with a Telegram client and a server where the Bot is running. As all the processing is done in the Bot server, no powerful computer is required, only a smartphone or a tablet.

6   BotRf Usage

Once Telegram is installed on a smartphone or PC, the preliminary step is to add BotRf as a contact (as would be done with a friend or colleague), as shown in Fig. 1.

The first step to check the feasibility of a wireless link is to set the working frequency. This is done by using the `freq` command and entering the frequency in MHz. So if you are going to use the 5.8 GHz frequency for you link, you have to write (the system is case insensitive) `freq 5800`, as shown in Fig. 2.

The second step is to insert the information about the two sites you want to link. If you are using Telegram on a PC, you have to enter the information about the sites manually. For example: `site mountain_1 -4.3409 55.7450 5,`

Fig. 1. Preliminary step: add BotRf as a contact.

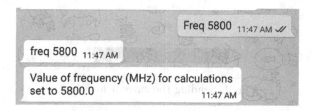

Fig. 2. Entering the frequency in MHz.

where mountain_1 is the name of the site, −4.3409 is the latitude in decimal degrees, 55.7450 is the longitude in decimal degrees, and 5 is the height of the antenna above the ground in meters. The same has to be done for the second site. If the second site is called mountain_2, then enter `site mountain_2 -4.6205 55.4413 16`.

If you are using Telegram on a smartphone, you can enter your current location with the click of a button, by selecting the paperclip icon (beware that different smartphones have slightly different setups), clicking Location and then Send your current location, as shown in Fig. 3. You will then be asked to enter the site name and the antenna height in meters.

Now you have all the information required to check if the path is clear or obstructed from the radio signal viewpoint, by using the `calc` command. Enter `calc mountain_1 mountain_2` to check the link between mountain_1 and mountain_2, at the frequency you previously selected. You will obtain the result shown in Fig. 4, which tells you that the link is feasible since there is no obstruction due to terrain.

You can select the graph and analyze it carefully elsewhere. The graph is shown in detail in Fig. 5.

The blue line represents the curvature of the earth, modified by the refraction index. The red line is the terrain profile as seen by the radio wave. In cyan we have the first Fresnel zone contour. The magenta line is the 60% of the first Fresnel zone.

If there is an obstruction that can be cleared by raising the antenna, you can use the command `alt` to choose a new value for the antenna height.

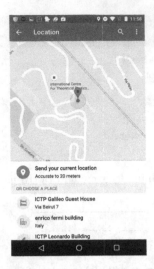

Fig. 3. Sending the current location

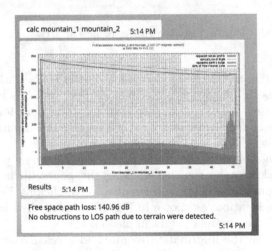

Fig. 4. Result of the link simulation: there is no obstruction

For instance enter `alt mountain_1 30` to change the antenna height of the site called mountain_1 to 30 m.

At any point, you can ask for help to the Bot using the `/hlp` command.

7   BotRf Usage in Venezuela

BotRf was used to plan the wireless links needed to extend the university network from the administrative building to the printshop at Universidad de los Andes in Merida, Venezuela. There are many buildings that block the line of sight

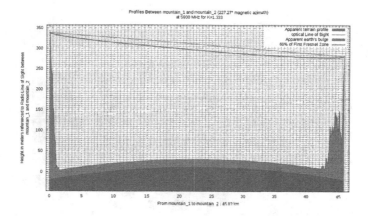

Fig. 5. Graph showing the earth curvature, terrain profile and Fresnel zone (Color figure online)

between the end points so a two legs solution had to be devised. Plan del Morro was chosen as repeater site since due to its altitude it offers an unencumbered view of both ends. Figure 6 shows the layout of the two ends points and the proposed repeater site.

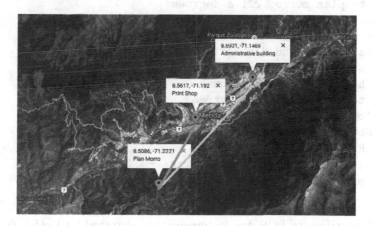

Fig. 6. Layout of the two legs link from administrative building to the printshop, Merida Venezuela.

Entering the coordinates and antennas heights of the administrative building and of Plan del Morro in BotRf and using the `calc` command, Fig. 7 was produced in few seconds showing an unobstructed line of sight.

Entering `rep` in BotRF produces an extensive text report:

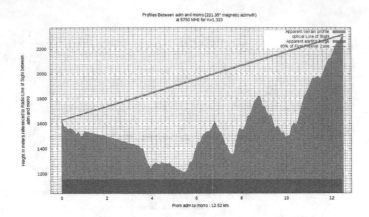

Fig. 7. Terrain profile between administrative building and Plan del Morro, Merida Venezuela.

```
Transmitter site: edif_adm
Site location: 8.5931 North/71.1469 West
Elevation: 1582 m above sea level,
Antenna height: 50 m above ground
Distance to plan morro: 12.52 km
Azimuth to plan morro: 221.3 degrees
Elevation: +3.1 degrees
Receiver site: plan_morro
Site location: 8.5086 North/71.2221 West
Elevation: 2311 m above sea level,
antenna height: 6 m above ground
Azimuth to edif_adm: 41.3 degrees,
depression angle: -3.2 degrees
Free space path loss: 129.69 dB
Longley-Rice path loss: 129.55 dB
Attenuation due to terrain shielding: -0.13 dB
Mode of propagation: Line-Of-Sight
The first Fresnel zone is clear.
```

No obstructions to LOS due to terrain were detected by BotRf, as per the last line of the report.

Similarly, the link between Plan del Morro and the printshop was simulated with BotRf and proved to be feasible. As both links are feasible from the LOS point of view, the link will work provided that the system gain of the radios and antennas is greater than 130 dB plus the required link margin.

The pow command in BotRf is used to obtain the power levels in the link. The user needs to input the name of the transmitter site, the name of the receiver site, the transmitter power output in dBm, the cable loss between the transmitter and the antenna in dB, the gain of the transmitter antenna in dBi (dB with respect to an isotropic antenna), the gain of the receiver antenna in dBi, the cable loss in dB between the antenna and the receiver and the receiver sensitivity in dBm. Using the data from our equipment, we have:

```
pow edif_adm plan_morro 20  0  24 24 0 -87
```

which will automatically generate the graph in Fig. 8.

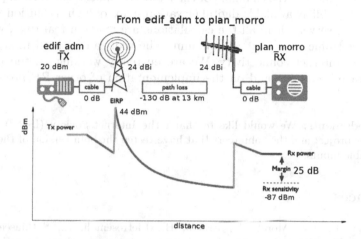

Fig. 8. Power versus distance of the link between administrative building and Plan del Morro

We can see the values of the EIRP (Equivalent Isotropic Radiated Power), as well as the link margin, 25 dB, providing a quite reliable signal that will support the highest modulation schemes. The path loss used is derived directly from the free space loss previously calculated by BotRf. The additional attenuation that might be present must be considered in each case and added to the free space loss to obtain the new margin.

It is worth noting that all the input data, as well as the results, are stored in the server under each user's account, so they can be retrieved for future use. BotRf `list` command provides a list of all the sites ever entered by the user with their respective coordinates.

8   Bandwidth Usage

We measured the bandwidth usage of BotRf by installing a network monitoring application [14] on a smartphone. Entering information for two sites using the "Send your current location" and running one simulation requires 750 kB to be transferred over the network. This is a very limited amount of data, making BotRf usable in low-bandwidth environments.

9   Conclusions and Future Works

We have presented a user friendly and platform independent tool that can be used for the planning of RF links even by people with limited telecommunications background. BotRf can also be used as a learning tool to asses the impact of the different elements of the communication channel in the final performance. In particular, the apparent radius of curvature of the earth can be modified to determine the effect of the changing of the refractive index. The terrain profile is derived from publicly available digital elevation maps of high resolution that are housed on the server where all the calculations are made in real time, whereby the Internet traffic used is at a minimum. The tool can be used in sites with very limited Internet connectivity. We are currently working on the point to area coverage prediction and on the implementation of other RF propagation models.

Acknowledgments. We would like to thank the Internet Society (ISOC) for supporting this project and the volunteers that have tested the beta version of the Bot for their valuable inputs.

References

1. Saldana, J., Arcia-Moret, A., Braem, B., Pietrosemoli, E., Sathiaseelan, A., Zennaro, M.: Alternative network deployments: taxonomy, characterization, technologies, and architectures. RFC 7962, August 2016. doi:10.17487/RFC7962. http://www.rfc-editor.org/info/rfc7962
2. Phillips, C., Sicker, D., Grunwald, D.: Bounding the practical error of path loss models. Int. J. Antennas Propag. **2012**, 21 p. (2012). Article ID 754158, Hindawi Publishing Corporation
3. Longley, A.G., Rice, P.L.: Prediction of tropospheric radio transmission loss over irregular terrain. ESSA Technical report ERL 79-ITS 67 (1968)
4. Propagation data and prediction methods required for the design of terrestrial line-of-sight systems. ITU-R P.530 (2015)
5. Radio Mobile. http://www.cplus.org/rmw/english1.html
6. Radio Mobile On-Line. http://www.cplus.org/rmw/rmonline.html
7. HeyWhatsThat Path Profiler. http://www.heywhatsthat.com/profiler.html
8. CRC Radio Coverage Prediction. http://lrcov.crc.ca/main/
9. PIAST. http://piast.edu.pl/
10. SPLAT! http://www.qsl.net/kd2bd/splat.html
11. SRTM3 - Shuttle Radar Topography Mission Global Coverage. http://www.webgis.com/srtm3.html
12. Telegram. https://telegram.org
13. Wikipedia entry for Internet Bot. https://en.wikipedia.org/wiki/Internet_bot
14. Databit. https://itunes.apple.com/al/app/databit/id1052616692?mt=8

Enabling Social- and Location-Aware IoT Applications in Smart Cities

Marco Govoni[1(✉)], James Michaelis[2], Alessandro Morelli[1],
Niranjan Suri[2,3], and Mauro Tortonesi[1]

[1] Department of Engineering, University of Ferrara, Ferrara, Italy
{marco.govoni,alessandro.morelli,
mauro.tortonesi}@unife.it
[2] United States Army Research Lab (ARL), Adelphi, MD, USA
{james.r.michaelis2.civ,niranjan.suri.civ}@mail.mil
[3] Florida Institute for Human and Machine Cognition, Pensacola, FL, USA
nsuri@ihmc.us

Abstract. In the last decade, governments, municipalities, and industries have invested large amounts of funds on research on smart cities with the main goal of developing services to improve people's quality of life. Many proposals focus on a Cloud-centric network architecture in which all the data collected from a myriad of sensors devices is transferred to the Cloud for processing. However, this approach presents significant limitations when faced with the formidable traffic generated by the Internet of Things and with the need for low-latency services. The deployment of IoT devices in compact groups, connected to the smart city network infrastructure by relatively powerful "gateways", opens the possibility to depart from the centralized architectures and move the computation closer to the data sources. To this end, this paper proposes SPF, a new middleware solution that supports IoT application and service development, deployment, and management. SPF runs IoT services on capable devices located at the edge of the network and proposes a programming model that enables to take advantage of decentralized computation resources in a seamless fashion. SPF also leverages an information dissemination solution designed for constrained network environments and adopts Value-of-Information based methods to prioritize transmission of essential information.

Keywords: Internet-of-Things (IoT) · Smart cities · Social- and location-aware IT services

1 Introduction

Governments, municipalities, and industries around the world are investing large amounts of money to improve the quality of life in modern cities, as numerous research projects in the field of smart cities demonstrate [1]. The Yokohama Smart City Project (http://www.city.yokohama.lg.jp/ondan/english/yscp/) and the LIVE Singapore project (http://senseable.mit.edu/livesingapore/) in Asia, the SmartSantander (http://www.smartsantander.eu/), CITYKEYS (http://citykeys-project.eu), and Open Cities (http://www.opencitiesproject.org) projects in the European Union, and the City Science

© ICST Institute for Computer Sciences, Social Informatics and Telecommunications Engineering 2017
O. Gaggi et al. (Eds.): GOODTECHS 2016, LNICST 195, pp. 305–314, 2017.
DOI: 10.1007/978-3-319-61949-1_32

Initiative in the USA (https://sap.mit.edu/article/standard/city-science-initiative-media-lab) are just a few examples of the many ambitious research projects that focus on one or more of the six aspects that, in accordance with the official European Union website on smart cities (http://www.smart-cities.eu), characterize modern urban realities: environment, living, mobility, governance, economy, and people [1].

Many research efforts and commercial solutions for smart cities propose complex network architectures with a Cloud-centric infrastructure [2–4]. At the edge, a multitude of sensors acquire raw data, which is continuously transferred over the Internet to the Cloud, where enough resources are available for storage and processing. From there, consumers (including citizens and policy makers) can access derived information by connecting to IT services hosted in Cloud data centers.

Despite showing early promise, Cloud-based architectures present significant limitations for use in emerging smart city infrastructures. Usage of heterogeneous and pervasive sensing and computing resources in IoT infrastructures deployments of IoT devices in smart cities produce a huge amount of information, with forecast studies predicting that, by 2019, IoT devices will generate 507.5 ZB of data per year [5]. It is very costly and inefficient to transfer, process, and store this formidable amount of raw data in Cloud-based data center.

At the same time, it is possible to envision a new generation of social- and location-aware IT services that leverage fully decentralized communication and information processing infrastructures to deliver functions that improve the citizens' quality of life significantly. Through better efficiency in existing health care environments, for instance, next-generation wellbeing oriented services can leverage remote health provision, enabling people to monitor their own health during the day, and better management of conditions such as stress [6].

In terms of preventive care, new services could take advantage of wearable activity trackers like FitBit (www.fitbit.com), which monitor heartbeat, levels of aerobic activity, and hydration status, and cross-correlate that information with the data provided by large, free Cloud datasets like OpenData (www.opendatafoundation.org), to look for and analyze specific trends and unpredictable anomalies. The study of activity tracker data across a city could give valuable insights on the "walkability" and the public safety of particular areas, favoring the detection of areas that have poor quality sidewalks, where residents suffer from a higher risk of robbery/assault, or have a lower quality of health.

In smart cities, IoT devices are often deployed in groups such as sensing systems and connected using short-range and low-power wireless communications, e.g., IEEE 802.15.4 or Bluetooth LE. These IoT networks are connected to the smart city networking infrastructure through one or more "gateway" devices that build on top of capable microprocessors, e.g., ARM Cortex A, and enable the execution of sophisticated and computationally hungry services, while still remaining fairly energy efficient.

In IoT infrastructures, gateway devices represent a promising location to deploy information processing tasks, with continuous reconfiguration of the task allocation according to real-time environmental conditions and service characteristics. In order to fully unleash the potential to develop disruptive innovations in IT services, there is the need for new models for information processing, information dissemination, and application programming.

This paper presents an analysis of opportunities and challenges involved in the development of social- and location-aware IoT services in smart city environments. The manuscript then introduces SPF, a new middleware solution to support IoT application and service development, deployment, and management. SPF enables application developers to take advantage of decentralized computation resources in a seamless fashion. To this end, SPF runs IoT services on devices at the edge of the network, proposes a programming model, leverages information dissemination solution designed for constrained network environments, and adopts Value-of-Information based concepts to prioritize information transmission.

2 Next-Generation IoT Services in Smart Cities

In a smart city, as depicted in Fig. 1, applications, storage, and processing capabilities are typically concentrated in Cloud data centers at the core of the network. Connected through heterogeneous communication means to the smart city infrastructure, edge networks include Wireless Sensor and Actuators Networks (WSANs), WiFi and other public networks that provide free Internet access to the mobile citizens, smart grids for smart energy management that connect factories, buildings, and houses, smart roads with sensors and actuators to monitor and manage traffic, and so forth. The fast-paced deployment of a myriad of heterogeneous IoT devices (e.g., traffic cameras, actuators, and sensors for measuring CO_2, temperature, and acoustics) and the increasing presence of personal wireless devices such as wearables and smartphones in smart city

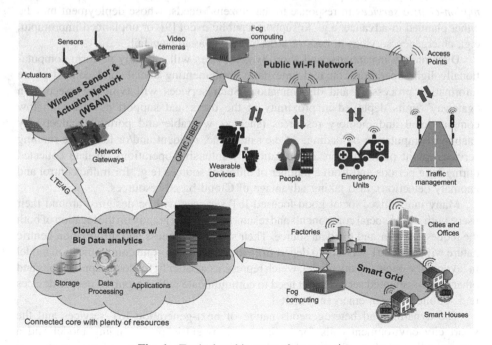

Fig. 1. Typical architecture of a smart city.

environments both represent an increasing burden for communications infrastructures [7]. The functionality of smart city systems is directly impacted by communication infrastructure capability, in-turn affected by growing data transmission to and from Cloud services. Users might experience slower service response times, real-time data processing and information transmission to client systems might become unfeasible, and user-submitted requests may be dropped. Such conditions are particularly unacceptable for time-sensitive applications like emergency-response.

One of the most interesting approaches to reduce network bandwidth consumption and thus increase the quality of services offered to the citizens is to move data processing and computation towards the edge of the network. This idea is at the basis of the *fog computing* concept [8], which aims at integrating computational and storage resources on the Cloud with those available at the network edge. However, fog computing proposes the same application programming and management model of Cloud computing, which was designed for reliable and high-bandwidth networking and does not interact well with the heterogeneous wireless communications at the edge of the smart city network infrastructure. Instead, it is critical that any proposed solution that supports social good-oriented IoT services takes into consideration existing design features and infrastructure of smart cities, selectively adapting and extending these resources as needed.

The pervasive computing scenario enabled by IoT technology goes beyond the "decentralized data centers" vision proposed by fog computing and stands to enable the development of a new generation of IT services that significantly improves quality of life within smart cities. In fact, large and high-density IoT installations create a distributed sensing and computation infrastructure for deploying *a wide range of information-centric services* in response to the citizens' needs, whose deployment may be either planned in-advance, e.g., to support a public event [9], or unplanned/impromptu, e.g., emergency services in case of a flash mob or a subway fail.

Dynamically instantiated and short-lived services will typically perform computationally light operations on real-time data, implementing social- and context-aware information processing and dissemination. Such services will typically execute on "gateway" units deployed in proximity of the users and support devices with low computational and memory resources (such as wearable and portable gadgets) by enabling computation offloading. At the same time, resident and/or long-time running services might perform more computationally intensive operations on data collected during long periods and from a number of different sources (e.g., for traffic control and anomaly detection), also taking advantage of Cloud-based resources.

Many innovative, social good-focused IoT services will be designed around their users, with strong social components and results that depend greatly on the location of both the requesting user and the data source. Their social-awareness and information-centric nature will cause IoT services to depart from the usual one-to-one communication model in favor of the one-to-many model, which represents a better fit for social applications and other citizen-oriented services that need to communicate with a group of people/devices (e.g., public safety or emergency alerts).

The dynamic and heterogeneous nature of next-generation IoT services and the smart city environment calls for an information-centric programming model and a corresponding platform that enable and simplify the deployment and management of applications and information processing tasks across the smart city. This would considerably reduce the times and costs for the allocation/deallocation of resources to/from specific services, for instance to respond to peaks in the demand or idle times, and for the on-demand deployment and instantiation of new services, to address needs that arise only in specific situations, e.g., during a concert, a sport match, or any other social event. In addition, information-centric platforms for IoT services could provide developers with the possibility to register and deploy their own applications. In this case, those solutions need to offer a set of basic features on which applications can be built and expose a well-defined API to allow applications running on users' devices to issue requests. Besides that, the API will also have the essential task of hiding any complexities that might derive from the system architecture, the location of remote applications with respect to the data sources, the allocation/deallocation of resources, etc.

Therefore, there is the need for solutions to manage network resource consumption and reduce traffic between the nodes at the edge and the Cloud. The final target is to maximize the usefulness of the offered services as perceived by the citizens of the smart city by having a scalable system that is capable to adapt to changes in the demand and make a smart usage of all the available resources.

3 SPF

SPF (as in "Sieve, Process, and Forward") is a middleware solution for the development, deployment, and management of dynamic IoT applications in urban computing environments [9]. SPF adopts a distributed computation approach that aims at addressing the continued growth of IoT data collection by applying needed processing at the edge of the network, in close proximity to the data source.

The two main components of SPF are the SPF Controller, deployed in the core part of the smart city infrastructure, and the Programmable IoT Gateway (PIG), which is deployed in several "gateway" devices at the edge/core border of the smart city networking infrastructure, as depicted in Fig. 2. The SPF Controller provides an information-centric programming model and an accompanying development toolchain that allow to define IoT applications and to deploy them on the PIGs, where they are actually executed. At the same time, the SPF Controller is responsible for receiving service requests from application users, identifying the most appropriate course of action in terms of IoT services to activate or reconfigure, and dispatching corresponding instructions to relevant PIGs. This allows for dynamic behavior that triggers the execution of information processing and dissemination only when they are actually needed.

PIGs provide both information processing and dissemination functions, which leverage the set of filtering and communication functions implemented by the software platform according to the instructions received by the SPF Controller. PIGs could be deployed directly on the gateway nodes that connect 6LoWPAN networks to the Internet or on dedicated hardware placed in the gateway nodes proximity.

In order to save processing resources on the PIGs and further reduce network usage, SPF employs a content-based filtering on the input data. More specifically, when new data arrives at the PIG from the WSAN, it goes through a filter component that compares the new piece of information with a reference, i.e., the last piece of

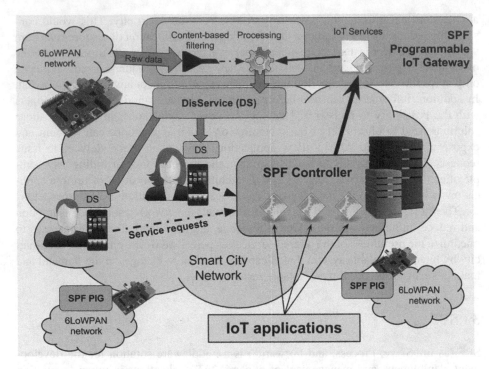

Fig. 2. Adoption of SPF in smart city scenario.

information processed by the PIG. A difference threshold τ determines if the difference between the new data and the reference is significant. In a positive case, the PIG processes the new data, which then becomes the new reference. Note that SPF allows each application to define the value for τ that best suits determined targets.

Following data processing, the PIG can deliver the extracted information to the requesting users. SPF relies on the DisService component of the Agile Computing Middleware (ACM) for the dissemination of responses [10]. DisService is a P2P communication middleware that handles the dissemination of the information using ad hoc communication links to set up a P2P network and deliver messages to nodes. DisService leverages network interfaces such as Bluetooth, WiFi, and other device-to-device (D2D) techniques that have already proven effective in pursuing mobile offloading [11, 12]. This way, DisService enables the offloading of the network infrastructure and ensures delivery even when the mobile network is congested or the signal is absent or bad, e.g., when one cell provides connectivity for too many devices. In addition, DisService enables the fine-tuning of delivery policies, thus allowing applications to reply with responses that are user-specific, or with responses that target larger sets of people.

The SPF platform identifies three main figures (or stakeholders): SPF administrators, application developers, and users. SPF administrators have the important task of managing deployed SPF platforms, and other tasks that include: deployment of gateways, allocation of resources for the applications, and configuration of the SPF controller. Application developers are responsible for defining and configuring IoT applications. Finally, the users need to install client versions of the IoT applications on their devices to have access to the SPF platform. Applications send requests to SPF Controllers and receive responses from the PIGs. The typical SPF user will be on a mobile device, so application requests will normally arrive at the SPF Controller via 4G/WiFi networks, while responses can reach their destinations using the peer-to-peer (P2P) ad hoc networks composed of nodes running SPF. Additionally, SPF allows for the definition of multiple user types, each one with different priorities and permissions, such as emergency units, police, and citizens. This enables the definition of applications that only a specific set of users can run and eases the allocation of bandwidth for dissemination based on the type of user that made a request. In the context of smart city infrastructures, declaration of user types can aid in prioritizing bandwidth usage for particular purposes, such as emergency response or law enforcement.

4 Application Development Lifecycle in SPF

SPF defines an IoT Application as a collection of related IoT services with the same priority and the same target users. SPF allows application developers to define IoT applications and takes care of their installation and dynamic activation (and deactivation) on the PIG components. This enables the definition of several concurrent applications, each with different services and priority levels.

SPF provides developers with a dedicated Domain Specific Language (DSL) that allows the rapid definition of IoT applications and services. Each application has several aspects that can be configured, such as name, priority level, a set of allowed service types provided to users, and a set of service configurations and dissemination policies. In this way, application developers can differentiate between critical and best-effort applications, define how the application deals with user service requests, and define which dissemination policies are needed.

In SPF, IoT services are developed according to a strictly information-centric perspective: each service is implemented by 2 components that run in a sequential fashion and respectively define the processing of raw data (typically collected from IoT sensors) and the dissemination of the resulting Information Objects (IOs) behaviors for the service. Low-level raw data manipulation functions are provided by specialized components of SPF, namely the information processors, or *pipelines*. The lifetime of services mainly depends on users' requests: applications receive user service requests forwarded by an SPF Controller and activate services on PIGs accordingly, in an on-demand fashion. In addition, if users do not request a specific service for a certain amount of time, the PIG deactivates that service, which will be reactivated only upon reception of new user service request, thus allowing resource saving.

Whenever a PIG first activates a service, that service registers itself with all required pipelines. From that point on, and until the service is deactivated, running pipelines continuously analyze raw input data to obtain higher-level IOs to feed the registered services. This phase could also involve data reduction, compression, and discretization, resulting in IOs smaller than their corresponding raw data and containing only relevant information.

Once a service is deactivated, it unregisters itself from all pipelines. This also determines the pipelines' lifecycle: the PIG keeps pipelines active as long as they still have services registered with them; when all services have unregistered from some processing pipeline, the PIG deactivates it. Examples of information processors are the Optical Character Recognition (OCR), face recognition, car recognition, object tracking, and audio identification pipelines.

Another fundamental aspect in SPF is the reuse and sharing of pipeline and services. In SPF, applications can define services that take as input the output of another service and, similarly, it is possible to design processing pipelines that work in series with other pipelines. Ultimately, this enables the creation of cascades of reusable components and the sharing of processing resources in SPF. These characteristics contribute to give a very dynamic behavior to SPF, with services and pipelines as true autonomous entities that cooperate among them and that consume resources only when needed.

The dissemination of IOs follows a prioritization rule that takes into account the Value of Information (VoI) of IOs. VoI is a measure of the estimated utility of information to consumers based on their situational context, which represents one of the most promising evolutions for information filtering and prioritization in IoT applications. Services calculate VoI according to various factors: some of them are common between all services, but there is also the possibility to define service-specific factors. There are four common parameters: *Application Priority (Pa)*, *Normalized Number of Requests (RN)*, *Timeliness Relevance (of Request) Decay (TRD)* and *Proximity Relevance (of Request) Decay (PRD)*. If available, SPF also takes into consideration the geographic distance between a consumer and the location corresponding to an IO to compute its VoI. Besides common factors, developers can also define service-specific (SS) factors for VoI calculation. For example, the calculation of the VoI of an Audio Identification service could also involve an accuracy parameter that represents the quality of the audio match. The value of such a parameter could be provided, for instance, directly by the Audio Identification pipeline.

Based on the factors discussed above, SPF defines the following formula for VoI calculation:

$$VOI(o, r, t, a) = SS(o) * PA(a) * RN(r) * \\ TRD(t, OT(o)) * PRD(OL(r), OL(o))$$

where o is an Information Object, r the requestor recipient, t the current time, a the application, and OT and OL are operators that return the time and location of origin of objects and requestors, respectively. The result is the tuple <*IO, VoI*>, which is dispatched to the Dissemination Component for forwarding.

5   Conclusions and Future Works

The decentralized computing and information-centric approaches adopted by SPF seem to be effective in enabling the development of social good-oriented and citizen-focused IoT applications and services. Comforted by the first positive results, we are planning to extend our work in several directions.

One direction to be further investigated in SPF is on the usage of semantics based methods for defining and supporting IoT applications. Semantic Web technologies [13] focus on enabling both integration of data and corresponding machine interpretation, through use of Ontologies (structured representations of domain knowledge) and reasoning engines. In prior IoT research efforts, usage of semantics in data representation has been applied in a variety of settings that include: dynamic service discovery [14], pervasive computing infrastructures [15], and context-aware asset search [16].

We are also planning to evaluate the adoption of the ICeDiM middleware (http://endif.unife.it/dsg/research-projects/icedim) as an alternative to DisService for information dissemination. ICeDiM is an innovative solution that leverages the concept of virtual dissemination channels with tunable permeability to facilitate the delivery of public and/or unclassified information and, at the same time, enable the constraining of sensitive information to a subset of authorized devices.

Another interesting future objective is to define an extended, acceleration-aware programming model for IoT applications and services that allows their efficient execution on high performance gateways with accelerator-based heterogeneous hardware. More specifically, the acceleration-aware programing model should provide developers with abstractions and functions to write code that can be easily and efficiently run in a parallel fashion on a wide range of parallel hardware platforms and whose parallelism can be safely changed at run time (acceleration-friendly code). This programming model will also provide functions that enable the code to inquire at run time the current computational resources available on the hardware platform and request the PIGs to increase or decrease the execution parallelism dynamically, e.g., for performance, cost, and/or energy saving purposes (acceleration-aware code). This would enable to take advantage of highly innovative, computationally capable, and relatively low-energy consuming hardware solutions based on neuro-morphic processors (such as IBM's True North Chip), hybrid CPU/manycore (such as Adapteva's Parallela board) or CPU/FPGA architectures (such as Xilinx's Zynq-7000 SoC), thus significantly improving the performance of IoT applications.

References

1. Khatoun, R., Zeadally, S.: Smart cities: concepts, architectures, research opportunities. Commun. ACM **59**(8), 46–57 (2016)
2. Fu, Y., Jia, S., Hao, J.: A scalable cloud for Internet of Things in smart cities. J. Future Trends Comput. **26**(3), 63–75 (2015)
3. Alamri, A., Ansari, W.S., Hassan, M.M., Hossain, M.S., Alelaiwi, A., Hossain, M.A.: A survey on sensor-cloud: architecture, applications, and approaches. Int. J. Distrib. Sens. Netw. **9**(2), 917–923 (2013)
4. Huawei Technologies Co., Ltd.: Huawei Smart City Solution. White paper. http://enterprise. huawei.com/ilink/cnenterprise/download/HW_315743
5. CISCO: Cisco Global Cloud Index: Forecast and Methodology, 2014–2019 White Paper, April 2016. http://www.cisco.com/c/en/us/solutions/collateral/service-provider/global-cloud-index-gci/Cloud_Index_White_Paper.pdf

6. Biggs, P., Garrity, J., LaSalle, C., Polomska, A., Pepper, R.: Harnessing the Internet of Things for global development. In: 8th Annual Conference on Information and Communication Technologies for Development (ICT4D) (2016). http://www.itu.int/en/action/broadband/Documents/Harnessing-IoT-Global-Development.pdf

7. Zaslavsky, A.B., Perera, C., Georgakopoulos, D.: Sensing as a service and big data. In: Proceedings of the International Conference on Advances in Cloud Computing (ACC), July 2012

8. Dastjerdi, A.V., Buyya, R.: Fog computing: helping the Internet of Things realize its potential. Computer 49(8), 112–116 (2016)

9. Tortonesi, M., Michaelis, J., Morelli, A., Suri, N., Baker, M.A.: SPF: an SDN-based middleware solution to mitigate the IoT information explosion. In: IEEE Symposium on Computers and Communication (ISCC 2016), pp. 435–442 (2016)

10. Benincasa, G., Morelli, A., Stefanelli, C., Suri, N., Tortonesi, M.: Agile communication middleware for next-generation mobile heterogeneous networks. IEEE Softw. 31(2), 54–61 (2014). ISSN 0740-7459

11. Orsino, A., Araniti, G., Militano, L., Alonso-Zarate, J., Molinaro, A., Iera, A.: Energy efficient IoT data collection in smart cities exploiting D2D communications. Sensors 16(6), 836 (2016)

12. Morelli, A., Stefanelli, C., Suri, N., Tortonesi, M.: Mobility pattern prediction to support opportunistic networking in smart cities. In: 6th International ICST Conference on MOBILe Wireless MiddleWARE (MOBILWARE 2013), November 2013

13. Barnaghi, P., Wang, W., Henson, C., Taylor, K.: Semantics for the Internet of Things: early progress and back to the future. Int. J. Semant. Web Inf. Syst. (IJSWIS) 8(1), 1–21 (2012)

14. Chun, S., Seo, S., Oh, B., Lee, K.: Semantic description, discovery and integration for the Internet of Things. In: 2015 IEEE International Conference on Semantic Computing (ICSC), pp. 272–275 (2015)

15. Kiljander, J., D'elia, A., Morandi, F., Hyttinen, P., Takalo-Mattila, J., Ylisaukko-Oja, A., Soininen, J., Cinotti, T.S.: Semantic interoperability architecture for pervasive computing and Internet of Things. IEEE Access 2, 856–873 (2014)

16. Perera, C., Zaslavsky, A., Christen, P., Compton, M., Georgakopoulos, D.: Context-aware sensor search, selection and ranking model for Internet of Things middleware. In: IEEE 14th International Conference on Mobile Data Management, vol. 1, pp. 314–322 (2013)

Connected Vehicles for Safety Enhancement: Reliability of Beaconing in Urban Areas

Alessandro Bazzi, Barbara M. Masini, and Alberto Zanella$^{(\boxtimes)}$

CNR - IEIIT, v.le Risorgimento, 2, Bologna, Italy
{alessandro.bazzi,barbara.masini,alberto.zanella}@cnr.it

Abstract. Safety enhancement is the main objective to pursue through the exploitation of connected vehicles. To this aim, the exchange of periodic beacon messages through vehicle-to-vehicle (V2V) communications is essential to guarantee a timely and reliable alert, whatever is the targeted safety application. In this paper, we focus on beaconing in vehicular networks and we evaluate the reliability of beacons exchange between vehicles in realistic urban scenarios. Specifically, IEEE 802.11p, which is the actual standard *de facto* for vehicular communications, is considered as radio access technology and the impact of distance and obstacles on beacons reliability is evaluated. Results obtained through detailed simulations highlight the high impact of distance and obstacles, to be carefully taken into account in the application design.

Keywords: Connected vehicles · Vehicular networks · Safety · Vehicle-to-vehicle (V2V) · Beaconing · IEEE 802.11p

1 Introduction

The internet of everything is changing the world in terms of both new enabled applications (from e-health, to home automation, smart grid/traffic/lighting, etc.) and new volume of data traffic on wireless networks channels. Globally, mobile data traffic will grow 8-fold from 2015 to 2020, with a compound annual growth rate of 53% [1]. It is expected that a big part of mobile data traffic will be produced by vehicles equipped with OBUs, able to transmit and receive information through a wireless interface, thus enabling a variety of new services addressing safety, traffic management, environment monitoring, urban surveillance, Internet access, etc.

Among all these services, those related to safety gather most of the attention of both standardization bodies and governative administrations with the ambitious objective to reduce the number of road accidents. Over 1.2 million people are, in fact, killed annually because of road accidents. Studies predicted that road accidents would become the sixth largest cause of death in the world in 2020 even with the use of many safety devices, whereas it was the ninth largest cause of death in 1990 [2].

© ICST Institute for Computer Sciences, Social Informatics and Telecommunications Engineering 2017
O. Gaggi et al. (Eds.): GOODTECHS 2016, LNICST 195, pp. 315–324, 2017.
DOI: 10.1007/978-3-319-61949-1_33

Safety, so as most of the services enabled by transport-related information, can be obtained through cooperative vehicle-to-vehicle (V2V) wireless communications which allow vehicles to directly communicate with each other and to largely extend their awareness range beyond autonomous on-board capabilities. To this aim, a crucial role is played by the periodic transmission of packets, normally called beacons, carrying information about the vehicle type, state, position and speed.

The importance of beaconing has been recently investigated, especially focusing on its impact on channel congestion and vehicles density, possibly proposing to adapt the beacon periodicity (BP). In [3,4], for example, BP is investigated for channel congestion reduction with different radio access technologies. In [5] the impact of some parameters (such as vehicle dynamics and channel load) on safety when performing adaptive beaconing is proposed. In [6] the impact of the application requirements on the communication settings of each vehicle, and on the overall channel load generated is investigated. In [7] the effect of multi hop propagation on the reliability of a forward collision warning application is studied with the objective to show that network-coding-based propagation yields an improvement of reliability with respect to a randomized forwarding strategy. In [8], the performance of beaconing in safety applications under MAC challenging conditions is deepen in highway scenarios. Beacons reliability has been investigated in [9] as a function of different radio propagation models and different vehicular density for the cooperative collision warning application. In [10] a transmission power control scheme is proposed to let each vehicle obtaining the position information of its neighboring vehicles at a sufficient frequency for avoiding collision, showing that the beacon reliability is improved with respect to constant transmission power and that the length of consecutive failures of beacon reception from distant vehicles is reduced.

Differently from the recent literature, in this paper we focus on a scarcely investigated aspect of beaconing, which is its dependance on the inter-vehicular distance and on what happens in the presence of obstacles, such as near intersections. At the best of the author knowledge, the impact of inter-vehicular distance has been recently investigated in [10], where the focus however is on a beacon transmission power control scheme in highway scenarios without realistic mobility models. In this work, we investigate, by simulation in realistic urban scenarios, the dependance of beacons reliability on the inter-vehicular distance and obstacles taking into account real road maps and vehicular traffic.

2   Wireless Access for Connected Vehicles

The importance and the increasing interest in V2V communications, has triggered standardization efforts in both US and in Europe. As a result two families of standards have been completed, wireless access in vehicular environment (WAVE) with the IEEE 802.11p as the physical and MAC layer standard in 2010 in the US, and the first release of the ETSI cooperative-intelligent transport systems (C-ITS) called ETSI-ITS G5 in 2013 in Europe. In early 2014, different working groups within 3GPP have also started studying V2X as an additional feature for LTE-Advanced [11–13]. All these standards specify a V2V feature to address road safety, so that cars can benefit from low latency by sending each other awareness beacons. Values of BP and tolerable latency for these messages are usually fixed for a given use case to guarantee the right level of safety for a specific scenario.

3GPP started considering to enable vehicular communications through the cellular networks as one key feature of 5G. This is made possible by the low end-to-end latency guaranteed by LTE and by the supported speed are around 350 km/h [14]. One of its main advantages is the fact that the network has already been deployed (whereas, in case of large deployment of IEEE 802.11p roadside units the investment could be not negligible). However, the current implemented release of LTE lacks of a native V2V communication. A direct mode with emphasis on public safety (LTE-D2D, or Proximity Services - ProSe) has been specified within Rel. 12 and from Rel. 13 onward. Vehicular communications are explicitly introduced only from LTE Rel.14, whose standardization process is still ongoing, with the name of LTE-Vehicular (LTE-V2V) [11,12].

Thus, although LTE-V2V may represent an interesting solution for connected vehicles in the long term, thinking to short term safety applications IEEE 802.11p has an a higher degree of maturation and remains the only consolidated solution to enable V2V communications. WAVE/IEEE 802.11p (or its European version, C-ITS) represents the actual standard *de facto* for V2V communications: it was born to enable ad hoc short range communications also in high speed vehicular scenarios, with simplified signaling and low latency. This is made available by the *WAVE mode* that allows the transmission and reception of data frames with the wildcard basic service set (BSS) identity (ID) value and without the need of belonging to a particular BSS. This feature enables a fast exchange of contextual data, including position and speed. The access technology layer is based on CSMA/CA and operates in the 5.9 GHz frequency band. At the physical layer, IEEE 802.11p is based on orthogonal frequency division multiplexing (OFDM) modulation, with channels of 10 MHz and data rates between 3 and 27 Mb/s.

3   Safety Requirements

Several applications have been imagined for an improved safety, better traffic management, and entertainment to passengers. Focusing on safety applications, all of them are based on two types of messages, in spite of the names given by the various standards: single-hop periodic messages that cars broadcast containing information about the speed, position, etc., and event-driven messages whose purpose is to disseminate safety information in a specific geographical region. In this work we focus on periodic messages, called for example cooperative awareness messages in ETSI [15] and basic safety messages in IEEE [16], that are hereafter denoted beacons.

With reference to the safety applications enabled by the transmission of beacons, in Table 1, we summarize the applications foreseen by three of the main

Table 1. Safety applications and requirements for NHTSA, ETSI, and 3GPP.

Safety application	Beacon periodicity [Hz]	Communication range [m]	End-to-end latency [ms]
NHTSA			
Wrong way driver warning	10	500	100
Cooperative forward collision warning	10	150	100
Lane change warning	10	150	100
Blind spot warning	10	150	100
Highway merge assistant	10	250	100
Cooperative collision warning	10	150	100
Highway/rail collision warning	1	300	1000
Cooperative glare reduction	1	400	1000
ETSI			
Emergency electronic brake lights	10	N/A	100
Safety function out of normal condition warning	1	N/A	100
Emergency vehicle warning	10	N/A	100
Slow vehicle warning	2	N/A	100
Motorcycle warning	2	N/A	100
Vulnerable road user warning	1	N/A	100
Overtaking vehicle warning	10	N/A	100
Lane change assistance	10	N/A	100
Co-operative glare reduction	2	N/A	100
Across traffic turn collision risk warning	10	N/A	100
Merging traffic turn collision risk warning	10	N/A	100
Intersection collision warning	10	N/A	100
Co-operative forward collision warning	10	N/A	100
Collision risk warning from roadside units	10	N/A	100
3GPP			
Forward collision warning	10	N/A	100
Control loss warning	10	N/A	100
V2V use case for emergency vehicle warning	10	N/A	100
V2V emergency stop use case	10	N/A	100
V2I emergency stop use case	10	N/A	100
Queue warning	N/A	N/A	100
Warning to pedestrian against pedestrian collision	N/A	N/A	N/A
Vulnerable road user safety	1	N/A	100

international institutions and their requirements in terms of BP, communication range, and end-to-end latency. Table 1 only refers to V2V communications with periodic transmission of beacons, whereas applications based on event-driven messages and vehicle-to-infrastructure (V2I) communications are not shown.

In particular, Table 1 reports the studies of NHTSA, ETSI, and 3GPP. The numbers from NHTSA report the results of studies done during a project, in which 34 safety and 11 non-safety scenarios have been described, providing the definition and the description of each application and indicating the communication modalities and requirements in terms of end-to-end latency, BP and transmission range [17]. Requirements from ETSI can be found in [18], whereas the 3GPP working group SA1 published in [11] its first study.

As it can be observed, most safety applications are guaranteed by a BP of 10 Hz. Regarding the required communication range, requirements are only provided by NHTSA, with values from 150 to 500 m; however, such numbers appear focused on an highway scenario, and may not apply to urban scenarios. Looking at the last column of Table 1, all institutions agree that an end-to-end latency of 100 ms is required by most applications.

At the end, once the BP is fixed, the only requirement is in the latency. However, it should be remarked that such latency is easily achievable by single hop communications, even in highly congested conditions, unless the message is lost. Indeed, even if no specific requirement has been provided by the listed institutions on the reliability of beacon reception, such metric is what most studies focus on.

4 Beaconing Performance in Realistic Urban Scenarios

With the aim to investigate the performance of beaconing and the feasibility of safety services in large scale deployments, we performed simulations in the realistic scenarios hereafter detailed. The main settings are summarized in Table 2.

Table 2. Main simulation settings.

Parameter	Value
Equivalent radiated power	23 dBm
Receiver sensitivity	−85 dBm
Receiver antenna gain	3 dB
Minimum SINR	10 dB
Transmission range (LOS)	∼740 m
Packet length	160 byte
Beacon periodicity	0.1 packet/s

4.1   Settings

Simulations refer as a case study to the center part of the Italian city of Bologna (sketched in Fig. 1(a)), with the position of vehicles provided by realistic vehicular traffic traces obtained using the road traffic simulator VISSIM (more details can be found in [19–22]). Both fluent traffic and congested traffic conditions are considered, as summarized in Table 3.

Table 3. Scenarios.

Scenario	Area	Average number of vehicles
Bologna, fluent traffic	$2.88\,\text{km}^2$	455
Bologna, congested traffic		670

Simulations are application independent, since they focus on the beacon transmission reliability. In particular, each OBU periodically transmits a beacon in broadcast to all the vehicles under its radio coverage. The beacon period is set to 10 Hz, which is the value considered for most applications (as discussed in Sect. 3). Beacons of 160 byte are assumed. As an output, the beacon delivery rate (BDR) is calculated, which is the rate of packets that are correctly received. In all the performed scenarios, correctly received beacons observed an end-to-end latency well below the requirement of 100 ms, and it is thus not shown here for brevity.

The IEEE 802.11p technology is simulated taking into account the sensing and random access procedures, with collisions and retransmissions, also including hidden terminals, exposed terminals, and capture effects. The most reliable mode is used, thus the nominal bit rate is 3 Mb/s. As detailed in [23], we assume a path loss proportional to the distance raised to the power of 2.2 in line of sight (LOS) conditions [24] and we add an attenuation when buildings impair the LOS [25]; specifically, 9 dB loss per each external wall and 0.4 dB/m loss inside the buildings are assumed [25]. A packet is correctly received if both the received power is higher then the receiver sensitivity of −85 dBm and the signal to noise and interference ratio (SINR) is higher than a threshold of 10 dB. With an assumed equivalent radiated power of 23 dBm and antenna gain at the receivers of 3 dB, it follows an average radio range of nearly 740 m. As a consequence, the number of vehicles in the radio range of an OBU can exceed 200 in congested traffic conditions, as observable in Fig. 1(b), where the statistic of number of vehicles within coverage of each OBU is shown.

4.2   Results

Impact of Distance and Obstacles. In Fig. 2, the BDR is shown varying the transmitter-receiver distance[1] for the two considered scenarios. To better

---

[1] Per each transmission and per each receiver, the success or loss of the packet is stored with the related transmitter-receiver distance. At the end of the simulation, the BDR is then averaged as a function of such distance.

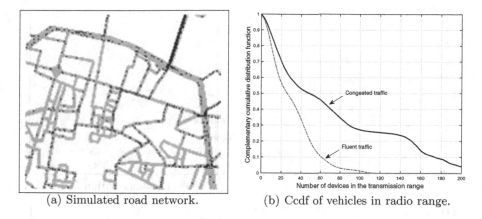

(a) Simulated road network.   (b) Ccdf of vehicles in radio range.

Fig. 1. Simulated road network with the position of vehicles in a random instant (congested traffic) and complementary cumulative distribution function (ccdf) of the number of vehicles in the radio range of the OBUs.

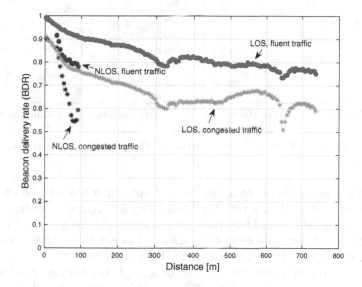

Fig. 2. Beacon delivery rate vs. transmitter-receiver distance.

highlight the impact of obstacles on the communication reliability, results under LOS and non line of sight (NLOS) conditions are shown separately.

As expected, the BDR worsens with an increasing distance (due to heavier impact of interferers) as well as an increasing vehicular density, and is significantly impacted by the presence of buildings impairing the LOS. The high attenuation caused by buildings at 5.9 GHz is shown to reduce the range from nearly 740 m in LOS conditions to a maximum of nearly 100 m in NLOS conditions.

(a) Performance within 20 m.   (b) Performance within 50 m.

(c) Performance within 100 m.   (d) Performance within 200 m.

Fig. 3. Beacon delivery rate as a function of the position of receiving OBUs.

The shown results imply that beaconing from connected vehicles can hardly be implemented at 10 Hz if a very high reliability is targeted. Looking at Fig. 2, in fact, a 95% reliability in LOS conditions is achievable only up to 35 m in the fluent traffic conditions and cannot be achieved in congested traffic conditions. Moreover, the BDR is further reduced in NLOS conditions.

However, it can be noted that the loss of a single beacon may not be so critical. Please note, for example, that a 75% reliability implies that the probability to loose all of 10 consecutive beacons (covering 1 s) is below 10^{-6}. Targeting 75% reliability, almost 120 m in LOS conditions and 50 m in NLOS conditions are obtained in the congested traffic case. In the same case, distances increase to more than 600 m and 90 m in the fluent traffic case, respectively.

Impact of Receiver Position. To observe the effect of the position of vehicles in the scenario, in Fig. 3 the BDR is related to the location of the receivers for the case of Bologna congested. Colors express the BDR in each position, considering the receivers that are within a parametric distance d^* from the transmitter.

If we focus for example on $d^* = 50\,\text{m}$, it can be observed that the BDR remains above 98% in most roads and junctions of the scenario, and is approximately 95% in the main junction, where a congestion involving multiple lanes is occurring. Worse conditions, with average BDR below 80% can be only observed with $d^* = 200\,\text{m}$ in the main junction.

5 Conclusion

In this paper, we investigated the performance of V2V beaconing using IEEE 802.11p for safety purposes. Through detailed simulations in realistic scenarios, it is shown that the achievable range is limited if a 95% or more reliability is targeted in areas where obstacles may impair the LOS (like buildings aside of junctions). It is however observed that single losses may not cause safety risks, thus a reduction of the reliability requirement could be accepted, with significant increase of the achievable distance. In the case a higher reliability is mandatory at large distances, the outcomes reveal that additional solutions might be needed, such as multi-hop communications or the use of infrastructure (either cellular base stations or roadside units).

Acknowledgments. This work was partly funded by the project "Development of European ETSI message set compliant V2X system and applications based on ITS-G5", N046100011, funded by KIAT (South Korea).

References

1. Cisco: Cisco visual networking index: global mobile data traffic forecast update, 2015-2020 white paper. Cisco, Technical report, February 2015. http://www.cisco.com/c/en/us/solutions/collateral/service-provider/visual-networking-index-vni/mobile-white-paper-c11-520862.html
2. World Health Organization: The top 10 causes of death. WHO (2014). http://www.who.int/mediacentre/factsheets/fs310/en/
3. Sommer, C., Tonguz, O., Dressler, F.: Traffic information systems: efficient message dissemination via adaptive beaconing. IEEE Commun. Mag. **49**(5), 173–179 (2011)
4. Bansal, G., Kenney, J., Rohrs, C.: Limeric: a linear adaptive message rate algorithm for DSRC congestion control. IEEE Trans. Veh. Technol. **62**(9), 4182–4197 (2013)
5. Schmidt, R., Leinmuller, T., Schoch, E., Kargl, F., Schafer, G.: Exploration of adaptive beaconing for efficient intervehicle safety communication. IEEE Netw. **24**(1), 14–19 (2010)
6. Sepulcre, M., Gozalvez, J.: On the importance of application requirements in cooperative vehicular communications. In: 2011 Eighth International Conference on Wireless On-demand Network Systems and Services (WONS), pp. 124–131. IEEE (2011)
7. Librino, F., Renda, M.E., Santi, P.: Multihop beaconing forwarding strategies in congested ieee 802.11p vehicular networks. IEEE Trans. Veh. Technol. **65**(9), 7515–7528 (2016)
8. Kloiber, B., Strang, T., Röckl, M., de Ponte-Müller, F.: Performance of CAM based safety applications using ITS-G5A MAC in high dense scenarios. In: 2011 IEEE Intelligent Vehicles Symposium (IV), pp. 654–660, June 2011

9. Tian, D., Wang, Y., Ma, K.: Performance evaluation of beaconing in dense VANETs. In: 2010 IEEE Youth Conference on Information Computing and Telecommunications (YC-ICT), pp. 114–117, November 2010

10. Okamoto, K., Ishihara, S.: Highly reliable data distribution scheme for location information in vehicular networks using cyclic beacon transmission power patterns. In: 2013 IEEE Vehicular Networking Conference, pp. 55–62, December 2013

11. 3GPP: Study on LTE support for V2X services. TR 22.885 V14.0.0, December 2015

12. 3GPP: Study on LTE-based V2X services. TR 36.885 V0.4.0, November 2015

13. Bazzi, A., Masini, B.M., Zanella, A.: Performance analysis of V2V beaconing using LTE in direct mode with full duplex radios. IEEE Wirel. Commun. Lett. 4(6), 685–688 (2015)

14. METIS: Scenarios, requirements and KPIs for 5G mobile and wireless system. D1.1, May 2013

15. Intelligent Transport Systems (ITS); Vehicular Communications; Basic Set of Applications; Part 2: Specification of Cooperative Awareness Basic Service. ETSI TS 102 6372 V1.1.1 (2010)

16. DSRC message communication minimum performance requirements: basic safety message for vehicle safety applications. Draft Std. J2945.1 Revision 2.2, SAE. SAE International DSRC Committee (2011)

17. National Highway Traffic Safety Administration (NHTSA): Vehicle safety communications project task 3 final report - identify intelligent vehicle safety applications enabled by DSRC, March 2005

18. Intelligent Transport Systems (ITS); Vehicular Communications; Basic Set of Applications; Definitions. TR 102 638 V1.1.1, June 2009

19. SHINE: http://www.wcsg.ieiit.cnr.it/people/bazzi/SHINE.html. Accessed November 2016

20. Bazzi, A., Pasolini, G., Gambetti, C.: SHINE: simulation platform for heterogeneous interworking networks. In: IEEE International Conference on Communications, ICC 2006, vol. 12, pp. 5534–5539 (2006)

21. Bazzi, A., Masini, B., Zanella, A., Pasolini, G.: Vehicle-to-vehicle and vehicle-to-roadside multi-hop communications for vehicular sensor networks: simulations and field trial. In: 2013 IEEE International Conference on Communications Workshops (ICC), pp. 515–520, June 2013

22. Bazzi, A., Masini, B.M., Zanella, A., Pasolini, G.: IEEE 802.11p for cellular offloading in vehicular sensor networks. Comput. Commun. 60, 97–108 (2015)

23. Bazzi, A., Masini, B.M., Zanella, A., Calisti, A.: Visible light communications as a complementary technology for the internet of vehicles. Comput. Commun. 93, 39–51 (2016). (Multi-radio, Multi-technology, Multi-system Vehicular Communications). http://www.sciencedirect.com/science/article/pii/S0140366416302626

24. Karedal, J., Czink, N., Paier, A., Tufvesson, F., Molisch, A.F.: Path loss modeling for vehicle-to-vehicle communications. IEEE Trans. Veh. Technol. 60(1), 323–328 (2011)

25. Sommer, C., Eckhoff, D., German, R., Dressler, F.: A computationally inexpensive empirical model of IEEE 802.11p radio shadowing in urban environments. In: 2011 Eighth International Conference on Wireless On-demand Network Systems and Services (WONS), pp. 84–90, January 2011

Early Training in Programming: From High School to College

Ugo Solitro[1](✉), Margherita Zorzi[1], Margherita Pasini[2],
and Margherita Brondino[2]

[1] Department of Computer Science, University of Verona, Verona, Italy
{ugo.solitro,margherita.zorzi}@univr.it
[2] Department of Philosophy, Education and Psychology, University of Verona,
Verona, Italy
{margherita.pasini,margherita.brondino}@univr.it

Abstract. Informatics is recognized as a fundamental discipline in education at all levels. It is also an indispensable subject for scientific and technical studies. Some abilities connected to informatics learning *(computational thinking)* has being considered to provide "fundamental skills for everyone". Programming or, more generally, the ability of solving problems by algorithmic methods is one of these skills. In Italy, many scientific degree courses offer, at the first year, at least an introductory course in programming. Digital expertize and a basic attitude to computational thinking are in general expected. The present study, has been conducted at the University of Verona, in the context of the course *Programming with laboratory* of Applied Mathematics curriculum. We focus on first period of lessons, when the fundamentals of programming are introduced. Most of the students come from secondary schools, in particular *Liceo*, a secondary school with emphasis science or humanities, and where the role of informatics is in general not central. So, an academic course in programming can be a difficult task for students. In this paper, we analyze how the *"cultural"* background influences the learning of programming and the performance of students.

Keywords: Computational thinking · Programming · Coding · Extreme apprenticeship · Motivation

1 Introduction

The relevance of informatics as an autonomous discipline and the computational thinking as a general methodology has been pointed out in several papers and reports [6,9,16].

In the last twenty years, the importance of information technology in school courses has been emphasized also in the Italian educational landscape: this attention involves school courses at all levels, from primary school to University. The introduction of informatics in Italian school has a long history. In the Nineties,

© ICST Institute for Computer Sciences, Social Informatics and Telecommunications Engineering 2017
O. Gaggi et al. (Eds.): GOODTECHS 2016, LNICST 195, pp. 325–332, 2017.
DOI: 10.1007/978-3-319-61949-1_34

an experimental project called **PNI** - *Piano Nazionale dell'Informatica* (in English, Computer Science National Project) has been proposed and implemented as a pedagogical avant-garde: the main objective was to align Italian curricula to European and American educational trends, in which "technological skills" have a central role.

However, the effective presence of informatics in different courses and levels is heterogeneous, with an emphasis on digital literacy and the use of digital tools. Even if the role of computer science education has been largely recognized (recent Italian ministerial recommendations are clearly ITC-oriented), the acceptance of the "digital culture" as a central subject of didactical curricula still encounters some obstacles. Many difficulties are related to the lack of resources and teachers' specific educational training. Also, computer science curricula for high school are diversified; and, with only a few exceptions, informatics is still treated as a "subordinate science". Consequently, the majority of students face academic courses without a solid preparation in principles of informatics. Regarding that issue, a crucial and interesting case study is represented by first-level courses of programming [9,11].

Programming abilities and computational thinking involve many skills, such as, for instance: reading comprehension, critical and systemic thinking, cognitive meta-components identification, planning and problem solving, creativity and intellectual curiosity, mathematical skills and conditional reasoning, procedural thinking and temporal reasoning, analytical and quantitative reasoning, as well as analogical, syllogistic and combinatorial reasoning. Teaching programming at university, particularly in introductory courses, seems to be a challenge. A promising perspective in promoting computational thinking is the *Cognitive Apprenticeship* (**CA**) learning model, a method inspired by the apprentice-expert model in which skills are learned within a community, through direct experience and practice guided by an expert of the subject [7]. An extension of the Cognitive Apprenticeship model, *eXtreme Apprenticeship* (**XA**), was proposed in introductory programming courses by a team of University of Helsinki [14,15]; **XA** emphasizes communication between teacher and learners during the problem-solving process. This methodology has been successfully applied also in different contexts: operating systems [2,3], databases [4], mathematics [8] and, more recently, in secondary schools. A "light" version of XA technique has been introduced for students in *Applied Mathematics* and *Computer Science* at the University of Verona [13].

Students' cultural background could impact the effectiveness of teaching programming. This cultural background, mainly connected with the educational experience during the secondary school, could also define in some way the possibility to achieve good results. Some authors classify students as *science-oriented* and *humanities-oriented* according to their approach to problem solving [1]. Students can also be classified on the bases of the teaching method adopted (traditional teaching method, cognitive apprenticeship, extreme apprenticeship and so on). In this paper we analyze early performances in learning programming of students enrolled at the first year of the course in *Applied Mathematics*. The aim of this pilot study is to verify the impact of different educational experiences on students' achievement measured by a partial test covering the first part of the course Programming with Laboratory. A subset of students was trained with a traditional teaching methods, whereas a second subset was trained using **XA**.

2   Method

The sample consisted of 140 students (51.4% males, mean age 20.3) enrolled at the first year of the bachelor degree in Applied Mathematics in Verona throughout the last three academic years. The traditional teaching methodology of the past years has been updated in the current course introducing the eXtreme Apprenticeship (XA), so that some students of the current year in the sample (68,6%) was trained with a traditional teaching method and the others with XA teaching method. Concerning students' cultural background, participants came from different kind of schools. Most of them (59,3%) are from a secondary school which emphasizes mathematics and sciences. Another group of students (27,1%) come from technical and professional schools, with different curricula emphasizing technical and professional skills. The third group, the smallest one (13,6%), comes from humanistic studies (humanities, language and social sciences high schools). In order to preliminarily evaluate students' previous skills, we asked them to fill out a questionnaire to collect informations about their school experience in informatics. We can qualitatively describe the result in the following way: in most cases (about 75%) informatics was not a subject of the last year and in general was not treated autonomously; about 50% of them (think to) know the notion of algorithm and programming language, but the great majority have no relevant experience in programming in a specific language.

2.1   Research Design and Data Analysis

At the end of the initial period of the course Programming with Laboratory, students took a partial exam (in the following, *test*) considered as part of the final examination. The following parameters are considered for the evaluation: correctness of the solution, logical structure and good programming practices. The test consists of two parts: a general theoretical section (TH), in which the knowledge of fundamental notions (e.g. the definitions of compiler, interpreter, specification...) are verified; a practical, programming section (PR), where students must solve a few exercises of increasing difficulty about programming competences and problem solving skills. The evaluation of the test produced a quantitative score, which was normalized in the range 0–1 to allow the comparison among the three different groups of cultural background and the comparison between the theoretical and the programming outcomes. At the end, two different-even if related-quantitative dependent variables were considered: theoretical score (TH), and programming score (PR). A quasi-experimental design was used, with two between-subject factors: 1. educational background (with three conditions: science, humanities, and technical/professional); 2. the teaching method (with two conditions: XA and TT), and the two learning outcomes as the dependent variables (TH and PR). A mixed 3X2X2-ANOVA (Fisher's ANalysis Of VAriances, see e.g. [5]) were run, with the school group as a three-level between-subject factor, the teaching method as a two-level between-subject factor, and the two different scores as the within-subjects factor (hence the classification 3X2X2).

In the following, we will adopt the standard general form to write ANOVA results, i.e. $F(a, b) = c; p \bullet d$, where: $\bullet \in \{<, >, =\}$; the ratio c of the F-statistic depends on a, b, that represent the degrees of freedom of the between-subject variables and of the within-subject variables respectively; p is the *p-value* and d is a threshold (traditionally set to .05). When $p < d$, observed data can be considered statistically meningful. Another statistical measure we use is the *effect size*, a standard measure that can be calculated from any number of statistical outputs. Informally, effect size expresses the mean difference between two groups in standard deviation units, and will be denoted as η^2. For further details, see [5].

2.2   Results

A mixed 3X2X2-ANOVA was run to check for statistical differences among groups' means. The main effect of the secondary school was significant ($F(1,134) = 3.424$; $p < .05$) even if with a small effect size ($\eta^2 = .05$), with students from scientific high school performing better than technical/professional students, and than humanities students, which showed the worst overall

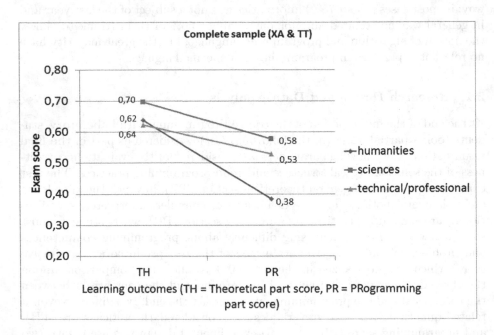

Fig. 1. Average test scores considering the two learning outcomes (TH and PR) for the three school groups (sciences, technical/professional, humanities) in the whole sample.

performance. The main effect of the teaching method was also significant $(F(1,134) = 20.979;\ p < .001)$ with a medium effect size $(\eta^2 = .14)$: students trained with XA performed better than students trained with the traditional teaching method. The main effect of test $(F(1,134) = 60.003;\ p < .001)$ with a medium effect size $(\eta^2 = .31)$ showed students performed better on the theoretical part than in the programming part. An interesting result concerns the interaction between the kind of learning outcomes and the secondary school $(F(1,134) = 3.68;\ p < .05)$ even if with a small effect size $(\eta^2 = .05)$. This effect is showed by Fig. 1, which represents the average test score considering the two learning outcomes (TH and PR) for the three groups (sciences, technical/professional, humanities). For all the three groups the programming part is more difficult than the theoretical one, but for students from humanities schools this gap was higher. No other results were statistically significant, but an interesting trend is shown by Figs. 2 and 3, showing learning outcomes in TH and PR in the three different school groups distinguished by teaching method. XA seems more effective for students coming from humanities high school, mainly for the theoretical test. Students coming from technical/professional schools showed the lowest level of benefit from the XA teaching methodology.

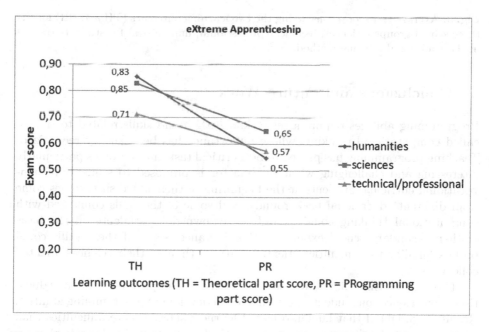

Fig. 2. Average test scores considering the two learning outcomes (TH and PR) for the three school groups (sciences, technical/professional, humanities) for students with XA.

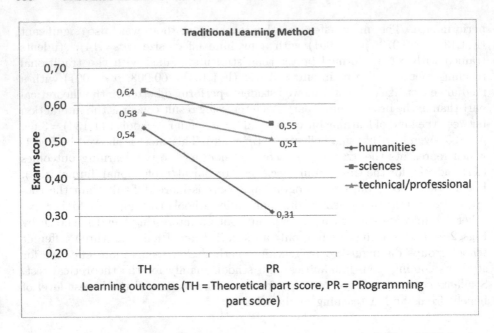

Fig. 3. Average test scores considering the two learning outcomes (TH and PR) for the three school groups (sciences, technical/professional, humanities) for students trained in the traditional learning method.

3   Conclusions and Future Work

Programming abilities require a set of knowledges and skills related to the so-called computational thinking, whose importance has been largely recognized. Teaching programming has proved to be a critical task, and becomes particularly interesting and challenging when this matter is proposed to students of non-vocational curricula. Students at the beginning of their university studies come from different educational backgrounds, and some of the skills connected with computational thinking could be differently owned by students on the basis of their secondary school experience. For instance, some of these skills could be less familiar to humanities-oriented learners than to their sciences-oriented colleagues.

The aim of this pilot study was to verify the impact of different educational experiences on students' performance in developing programming abilities. Results highlighted that human-oriented learners showed more difficulties than sciences-oriented colleagues, more in practical tasks than in theoretical ones. Is this gap insurmountable? A promising perspective to face this issue seems to be the use of appropriate teaching methodology, as for example the Cognitive Apprenticeship learning model, and particularly eXtreme Apprenticeship, a learning model which emphasizes communication between teacher and learners during the problem-solving process. In the present pilot research, the gap between humanities-oriented and sciences-oriented students has been reduced in the group who attended programming courses with XA.

An improved of teacher and peer-wise support combined with automated scaffolding [10] and an enhancement on the motivation side [12] could produce better results.

Further studies are needed. First we aim to verify whether this result in this small sample can be replicated and generalized. Second, it will be interesting to enrich the ANOVA with further subjects such as genres and high-school final evaluation. Finally, we plan to better understand the underlying mechanism which allows this improvement in computational thinking.

References

1. Billington, J., Baron-Cohen, S., Wheelwright, S.: Cognitive style predicts entry into physical sciences and humanities: questionnaire and performance tests of empathy and systemizing. Learn. Individ. Differ. **17**(3), 260–268 (2007)
2. Del Fatto, V., Dodero, G., Gennari, R.: Assessing student perception of extreme apprenticeship for operating systems. In 2014 IEEE 14th International Conference on Advanced Learning Technologies (ICALT), pp. 459–460. IEEE (2014)
3. Del Fatto, V., Dodero, G., Gennari, R.: Operating systems with blended extreme apprenticeship: what are students' perceptions? Interact. Des. Archit. J. (IxD&A), special issue (2015)
4. Del Fatto, V., Dodero, G., Lena, R.: Experiencing a new method in teaching databases using blended extreme apprenticeship. Technical report (2015)
5. Freedman, D.A.: Statistical Models. Theory and Practice, 2nd edn. Cambridge University Press, Cambridge (2009)
6. Gander, W., Petit, A., Berry, G., Demo, B., Vahrenhold, J., McGettrick, A., Boyle, R., Mendelson, A., Stephenson, C., Ghezzi, C., et al.: Informatics education: Europe cannot afford to miss the boat. ACM (2013)
7. Ghefaili, A.: Cognitive apprenticeship, technology, and the contextualization of learning environments. J. Educ. Comput. Des. Online Learn. 1–27 (2003)
8. Hautala, T., Romu, T., Rämö, J., Vikberg, T.: Extreme apprenticeship method in teaching university-level mathematics. In: Proceedings of the 12th International Congress on Mathematical Education, ICME (2012)
9. Katai, Z.: The challenge of promoting algorithmic thinking of both sciences-and humanities-oriented learners. J. Comput. Assist. Learn. **31**(4), 287–299 (2015)
10. Pärtel, M., Luukkainen, M., Vihavainen, A., Vikberg, T.: Test my code. Int. J. Technol. Enhanc. Learn. 2 **5**(3–4), 271–283 (2013)
11. Pears, A., Seidman, S., Malmi, L., Mannila, L., Adams, E., Bennedsen, J., Devlin, M., Paterson, J.: A survey of literature on the teaching of introductory programming. In: Working Group Reports on ITiCSE on Innovation and Technology in Computer Science Education, ITiCSE-WGR 2007, pp. 204–223. ACM, New York (2007)
12. Solitro, U., Pasini, M., Brondino, M., Raccanello, D.: The challenge of learning to program. In: PPIG 2016, September 2016

13. Solitro, U., Zorzi, M., Pasini, M., Brondino, M.: A "light" application of blended extreme apprenticeship in teaching programming to students of mathematics. In: Caporuscio, M., De la Prieta, F., Di Mascio, T., Gennari, R., Rodríguez, J.G., Vittorini, P. (eds.) Methodologies and Intelligent Systems for Technology Enhanced Learning. AISC, vol. 478, pp. 73–80. Springer, Cham (2016). doi:10. 1007/978-3-319-40165-2_8
14. Vihavainen, A., Luukkainen, M.: Results from a three-year transition to the extreme apprenticeship method. In: 2013 IEEE 13th International Conference on Advanced Learning Technologies (ICALT), pp. 336–340. IEEE (2013)
15. Vihavainen, A., Paksula, M., Luukkainen, M.: Extreme apprenticeship method in teaching programming for beginners. In: Proceedings of the 42nd ACM Technical Symposium on Computer Science Education, pp. 93–98. ACM (2011)
16. Wing, J.M.: Computational thinking. Commun. ACM **49**(3), 33–35 (2006)

A Smart Wearable Navigation System for Visually Impaired

Michael Trent, Ahmed Abdelgawad, and Kumar Yelamarthi[✉]

School of Engineering and Technology, Central Michigan University,
Mt. Pleasant, MI 48859, USA
{trentlma, abdella, yelamlk}@cmich.edu

Abstract. Smart devices are becoming more common in our daily lives; they are being incorporated in buildings, houses, cars, and public places. Moreover, this technological revolution, known as the Internet of Things (IoT), brings us new opportunities. A variety of navigation systems has been developed to assist blind people. Yet, none of these systems are connected to the IoT. The objective of this paper is to implement a low cost and low power IoT navigation system for blind people. The system consists of an array of ultrasonic sensors that are mounted on a waist belt to survey the scene, iBeacons to identify the location, and a Raspberry Pi to do the data processing. The Raspberry Pi uses the ultrasonic sensors to detect the obstacles, and provide audio cues via a Bluetooth headset to the user. iBeacons will be deployed at different locations with each having a unique ID. In the cloud, there is a database for all the iBeacons attached with the corresponding information e.g. address and information about the place. The Raspberry Pi detects the iBeacon's ID and sends it to the cloud, accordingly the cloud sends back the information attached to this ID to the Raspberry Pi that converts the text to audio and plays it via a Bluetooth headset to the user. Tests demonstrate that the system is accurate within the threshold radius and functions as a navigational assistant.

Keywords: Ultrasonic sensor · Audio feedback · Visual impairment · Navigation assistance

1 Introduction

A variety of portable/wearable navigation systems has been developed to assist blind people during navigation indoor/outdoor environments. These systems can be categorized into three main types: Electronic Travel Aid (ETA), Electronic Orientation Aid (EOA), and Position Locator Device (PLD) [1]. There are many systems that deal with the autonomous navigation for blind people. These systems are using GPS [2], RFID [3], Ultrasonic sensor [4], camera [5], and Kinect sensor [6]. However, some of these systems present some drawbacks e.g., accuracy of GPS is not reliable for indoor use, the camera needs a high bandwidth, Kinect is not working for outdoor use. In addition to the system drawbacks, blind and visually impaired people are handicapped in achieving the desired level of mobility and context-awareness, especially in unknown environments. They rely on their previous knowledge of an environment to navigate and usually get help from guide dogs or white canes [7].

© ICST Institute for Computer Sciences, Social Informatics and Telecommunications Engineering 2017
O. Gaggi et al. (Eds.): GOODTECHS 2016, LNICST 195, pp. 333–341, 2017.
DOI: 10.1007/978-3-319-61949-1_35

In the future, everything is expected to be integrated into the IoT, where sensor node dynamically joins the Internet and uses it to collaborate and accomplish its task. The IoT is an expansion of the Internet and incorporates with network connections to allow data transmission between objects and the Internet. The IoT enables researchers to efficiently process and store data to ensure accurate situation analysis. These results can lead to recognizing extremes, anomalies, and trends over periods of time. Overall, the IoT stimulates an increased level of awareness about the surrounding environment and serves as a mean to monitor and respond to the changing environmental phenomenon [8]. Accordingly, the IoT is estimated to become the largest device market in the world in the next few years.

Applications that support navigation in unfamiliar places are very helpful for the blind and visually impaired. Therefore, the development of the IoT navigation system for the visually impaired can not only enrich mobility of them but can also bring an additional sense of security and safety. This paper presents the design and implementation of an IoT-enabled wearable navigation system for the visually impaired to operate in both familiar and unfamiliar environments. This navigation system helps the blind person solve many problems such as, leaving home by themselves in a safe and convenient way and participating in more social and civic activities to improve the quality of life. At the same time, the reliable portable navigation system represents a civilized, harmonious, progressive society, and a service oriented project for the engineers.

2 Proposed System

The proposed system is focused on low-power and low-cost design principles. A reasonable expectation is that the power would last throughout the day and could be recharged at night. The system cannot rely on a large battery because it must remain portable enough for the user to carry comfortably and without significant burden. There is also a high incentive to use low-cost components in the design of the device. As the price of the device falls, it becomes more accessible to people of low economic standing.

The architecture of the proposed system consists of five modules as shown in Fig. 1. The first module is a Bluetooth Low Energy (BLE) iBeacon transmitter [9]. As the user might navigate both indoors and outdoors, the environment is tagged with these iBeacons, and each is loaded with location information. While operating in the BLE mode, each iBeacon can function on a single coin cell battery for extended periods of time without any problems. When a user comes in proximity to any of these iBeacons, the navigation system reads the ID of each iBeacon and sends this information to the cloud server. This information is processed in the cloud to identify the location and responds to the navigation system with the location information.

The second module in the system is an array of three HC-SR04 ultrasonic sensors mounted on the waist belt of the user, and can detect obstacles at a range of 20–4000 mm, with an accuracy of 3 mm [10]. As there is a mismatch in operating voltage between these ultrasonic sensors and Raspberry Pi, an interface circuit as presented in Fig. 2 is designed for reliable communication between the ultrasonic sensors and Raspberry Pi.

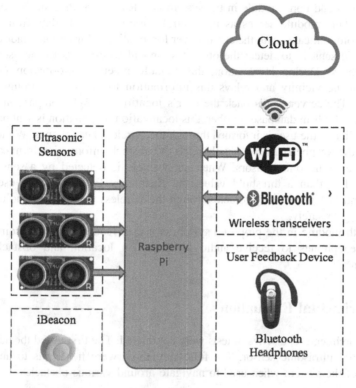

Fig. 1. System architecture of the proposed navigation system

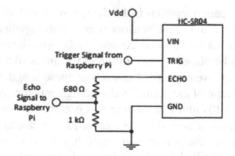

Fig. 2. Interface circuit between ultrasonic sensor and Raspberry Pi

The third module in the system is a set of wireless transceivers, BLE, and Wi-Fi. The BLE transceiver is used to localize the system through iBeacons, and provide feedback to the user through Bluetooth headphones. The Wi-Fi transceiver is used to communicate with the server on localization information, and any other information as requested by the server.

The fourth and core module in the system is a Raspberry Pi 2 single board computer [11]. This module serves as the central command, reads data from the BLE iBeacons, communicates with the cloud server for location information, reads data from the ultrasonic sensors to detect the obstacles, and also responds to the user through audio feedback. During localization, this module receives information from BLE iBeacons in the vicinity and relays this information to the server through a Wi-Fi transceiver. The server sends back the user's location through comparison of information with a built-in database. Further, this localization information is sent back to the Raspberry Pi, and the user is informed through the wireless headphones. While the user is moving, the Raspberry Pi continually reads the obstacle information from each of the three onboard ultrasonic sensors. When an obstacle is detected by a sensor whose distance is less than a threshold value, the Raspberry Pi informs the user on the direction and distance of the obstacle through the wireless headphones and allows the user to navigate safely.

The fifth module in the proposed system is a user feedback device, comprised of wireless headphones to receive audio feedback on location and obstacle profile information.

3   Experimental Evaluation

Using this architecture, a series of tests were conducted. The first tested the accuracy of the HC-SR04 ultrasonic sensor. The following three were field tests to analyze the efficiency of the system when used to navigate around various obstacles.

3.1   Detection Accuracy

As one of the system's main operations is the detection of obstacles, a test was used to verify the accuracy of the ultrasonic sensors used in this application. As stated, the HC-SR04 can detect obstacles between 20 and 4000 mm. Because of this range, an obstacle was chosen to be placed at three different distances (0.5 m, 1 m, and 3.8 m). After setup, 500 readings were recorded at each of these lengths. Following the collection, a distribution graph of the normalized readings was formed and can be seen in Fig. 3. Further, an HC-SR04 ultrasonic sensor was used to measure the distance to four different types of materials at three distances each. Each test was setup by placing the object directly in front of the sensor and capturing 1000 readings. The results in Table 1 show that the HC-SR04 is able to detect objects within 1 m and 2 m with a probability of 1. On the other hand, the probability of detection starts to drop at 3 m, as presented. This outcome was used in the decision making of the safety distance to be used in field tests.

3.2   Navigation and Obstacle Avoidance Field Tests

This was the first of three navigation tests. In this scenario, the threshold value for sensor readings was selected to be 0.8 m and all sensors readings were capped at 3 m.

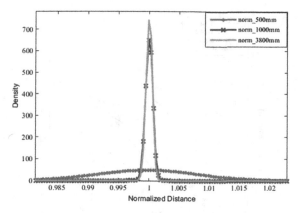

Fig. 3. Data distribution of ultrasonic sensor with obstacles at different

Table 1. Obstacle detection sensor accuracy.

Material	Actual distance (cm)	Measured distance (cm)	Error (%)	Probability of detection
Aluminum	100	99.2	0.79	1.00
	200	198.6	0.70	1.00
	300	294.9	1.70	0.99
Plastic	100	100.3	0.29	1.00
	200	197.1	1.45	1.00
	300	296.5	1.16	1.00
Styrofoam	100	96.9	3.09	1.00
	200	197.6	1.20	1.00
	300	296.3	1.23	0.83
Paper	100	98.1	1.90	1.00
	200	201.3	0.65	1.00
	300	294.9	1.70	0.58

Two users were asked to navigate to a particular location with the system. To give a sense of their initial spacing, they were told which direction the ending location was in. Figure 4 shows the path taken by each user along with an optimal path that would potentially be taken by someone with clear vision.

Figure 5 displays the paths that were taken by each user in the second test and an optimal path was chosen, similar to test 1. The last field test also used the same parameters as test 1 and 2 but had a different route for the users to take. As in the previous tests, the users' paths and an optimal path are pictured in Fig. 6. After the conduction of the third test, the distance for each path in every test was compared to its optimal route to determine how much additional distance was traveled, and results are presented in Table 2.

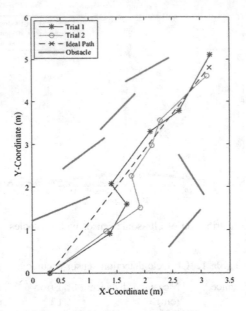

Fig. 4. Navigation Field Test-1 Path

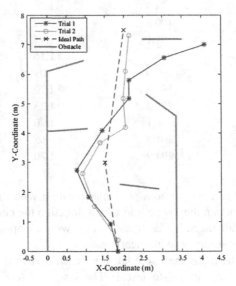

Fig. 5. Navigation Field Test-2 Path

3.3   Localization Using BLE Beacons

One of the primary purposes of the navigation system is to localize the user and inform him/her on the location with respect to a known landmark. Accordingly, the proposed system was programmed to read the ID of BLE beacons in the vicinity, and relay this

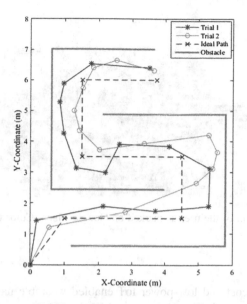

Fig. 6. Navigation Field Test-3 Path

Table 2. Comparison of distance & time traveled.

Test #	Additional distance traveled compared to ideal path (%)		Time to reach destination (minutes)	
	Trial 1	Trial 2	Trial 1	Trial 2
1	12.09	2.33	0.58	0.63
2	15.47	5.18	1:11	1:13
3	21.28	6.85	3:33	2:19

information to the cloud server. The server localizes the user, compares his/her location with landmarks as presented on Google Maps, and sends this information back to the Raspberry Pi device. The Raspberry Pi device relays this information to the user through the BLE headphones and allows him/her to navigate to the next location accordingly. Figure 7 shows a snapshot of the server web page with the location of the user marked by the blue dot and the red circle. This information is stored in the cloud, so any other family member can track the user.

Fig. 7. Location of the user as marked on Google Maps (Color figure online)

4 Conclusion

In this paper, a low-cost and low-power IoT enabled wearable navigation system for blind people was proposed. The system consists of an array of ultrasonic sensors to survey the scene, iBeacon to identify the location, and a Raspberry Pi. The Raspberry Pi uses the ultrasonic sensors to detect the obstacles, and provides audio cues via a Bluetooth headset to the user. Each deployed iBeacon has a unique ID that is related to the location. On the cloud, there is a database for all the iBeacons attached with the corresponding information e.g. address and information about the location. The Raspberry Pi detects the iBeacon ID and sends it to the cloud, accordingly the cloud sends back the information attached to this ID to the Raspberry Pi that converts the text to audio, and plays it via a Bluetooth headset to the user. Experimental tests validate the proposed system and proof that it functions as a navigational assistant for the blind and the visually impaired.

Acknowledgment. Authors would like to thank the Faculty Research and Creative Endeavors Committee (FRCE) and the Office of Research and Graduate Studies (ORGS) at Central Michigan University (CMU) for their support.

References

1. Dakopoulos, D., Bourbakis, N.G.: Wearable obstacle avoidance electronic travel aids for blind: a survey. IEEE Trans. Syst. Man Cybern. Part C (Appl. Rev.) **40**(1), 25–35 (2010)
2. Baranski, P., Strumillo, P.: Field trials of a teleassistance system for the visually impaired. In: 8th International Conference on Human System Interaction (HSI), Warsaw, pp. 173–179 (2015)
3. Kassim, A.M., Jaafar, H.I., Azam, M.A., Abas, N., Yasuno, T.: Design and development of navigation system by using RFID technology. In: IEEE 3rd International Conference on System Engineering and Technology (ICSET), Shah Alam, pp. 258–262 (2013)

4. De silva, S.A., Dias, D.: A sensor platform for the visually impaired to walk straight avoiding obstacles. In: 9th International Conference on Sensing Technology (ICST), Auckland, pp. 838–843 (2015)
5. Tian, Y., Liu, Y., Tan, J.: Wearable navigation system for the blind people in dynamic environments. In: IEEE 3rd Annual International Conference on Cyber Technology in Automation, Control and Intelligent Systems (CYBER), Nanjing, pp. 153–158 (2013)
6. Yelamarthi, K., Laubhan, K.: Navigation assistive system for the blind using a portable depth sensor. In: IEEE International Conference on Electro/Information Technology (EIT), Dekalb, IL, pp. 112–116 (2015)
7. Lapyko, A.N., Tung, L.P., Lin, B.S.P.: A cloud-based outdoor assistive navigation system for the blind and visually impaired. In: Wireless and Mobile Networking Conference (WMNC), Vilamoura, pp. 1–8 (2014)
8. Ul Huque, M.T.I., Munasinghe, K.S., Jamalipour, A.: Body node coordinator placement algorithms for wireless body area networks. IEEE Internet Things J. 2(1), 94–102 (2015)
9. What is iBeacon. https://support.apple.com/en-gb/HT202880. Accessed 5 May 2016
10. Ultrasonic Ranging Module HC-SR04. http://www.micropik.com/PDF/HCSR04.pdf. Accessed 5 May 2016
11. Raspberry Pi 2 Model B. https://www.raspberrypi.org/products/raspberry-pi-2-model-b/. Accessed 5 May 2016

Enabling Smart Objects in Cities Towards Urban Sustainable Mobility-as-a-Service: A Capability – Driven Modeling Approach

George Bravos[✉], Pericles Loucopoulos, George Dimitrakopoulos, Dimosthenis Anagnostopoulos, and Akrivi Kiousi

Department of Informatics and Telematics, Harokopio University of Athens, 9, Omirou street, 17778 Athens, Greece
{gebravos,ploucopoulos,gdimitra,dimosthe}@hua.gr, Akrivi.Kiousi@intrasoft-intl.com

Abstract. Economic growth in Europe has been, strongly associated with urbanization, overwhelming cities with vehicles. This renders mobility inside cities problematic, since it is often associated with large waste of time in traffic congestions, environmental pollution and accidents. Cities struggle to invent and deploy "smart" solutions in the domain of urban mobility, so as to offer innovative services to citizens and visitors and improve the overall quality of life. In this context, the paper discusses on the basic challenges that cities face when trying to enable smart objects, focusing on the particular area of mobility and presenting a capability – driven enterprise modeling approach towards enabling Smart Objects for Smart City Operations (SCO). Moreover, a process towards linking capability models to simulation ones is presented, trying to set the basis for effective SCO based on Smart Objects deployment.

Keywords: Smart cities · Smart City Operations · Mobility · Enterprise modeling

1 Introduction

It is widely accepted that citizens inside large cities at a worldwide level are "bombed" by large amounts of uncorrelated and non-synchronized data, from innumerable sources and through various devices in a complex manner. Citizens are thus not in position to efficiently handle them, this resulting in severe inefficiencies associated with their mobility, such as (i) fragmented travel solutions/lack of door-to-door solutions, especially when dealing with multimodal transportation, as well as (ii) inadequateness in providing real-time, whilst individualized services. Those drawbacks often result in losses of time, decrease in the level of safety in mobility, pollution, degradation of life quality, and huge waste of nonrenewable fossil energy. Moreover, they affect not only citizens, but all relevant stakeholders, such as also public authorities and businesses.

At the same time, cities keep on becoming smarter and smarter, trying to offer traditional services with unconventional methods (e.g. via Information and

© ICST Institute for Computer Sciences, Social Informatics and Telecommunications Engineering 2017
O. Gaggi et al. (Eds.): GOODTECHS 2016, LNICST 195, pp. 342–352, 2017.
DOI: 10.1007/978-3-319-61949-1_36

Communication Technologies – ICT), as well as completely novel services, often enabled again by ICT. This trend is reflected on a concept coined by IBM, namely the "smart cities" concept [1, 2].

Considering that transportation inside large cities is rapidly increasing, alongside with the addition of new transport media (carpooling, car sharing, etc.), it is among a city's priorities to improve the quality of living inside them, providing smart services to their citizens and visitors. As such, it would be of great interest to place a special focus on a "smart" city and try to revolutionarize mobility in the aforementioned context. Further, the above necessitate research towards improving novel mobility practices for citizens/policymakers/businesses. This can be done only by engineering innovative strategies for aggregating large amounts of data from versatile sources (conventional and new ones), intelligently processing it and providing accurate directives associated with actual mobility status and potentials, in a multimodal and concurrently individualized fashion [3].

This data aggregation can only be carried out effectively through Smart Objects and IoT (Internet of Things). The application of the IoT paradigm to an urban context is of particular interest, as it responds to the strong push of many national governments to adopt ICT solutions in the management of public affairs, thus realizing the so-called Smart City concept [13]. Although there is not yet a formal and widely accepted definition of "Smart City," the final aim is to make a better use of the public resources, increasing the quality of the services offered to the citizens, while reducing the operational costs of the public administrations. This objective can be pursued by the deployment of an urban IoT, i.e., a communication infrastructure that provides unified, simple, and economical access to a plethora of public services, thus unleashing potential synergies and increasing transparency to the citizens. An urban IoT, indeed, may bring a number of benefits in the management and optimization of traditional public services, such as transport and parking, lighting, surveillance and maintenance of public areas, preservation of cultural heritage, garbage collection, salubrity of hospitals, and school. Furthermore, the availability of different types of data, collected by a pervasive urban IoT, may also be exploited to increase the transparency and promote the actions of the local government toward the citizens, enhance the awareness of people about the status of their city, stimulate the active participation of the citizens in the management of public administration, and also stimulate the creation of new services upon those provided by the IoT [14]. Therefore, the application of IoT technologies and Smart Objects to a Smart City is particularly attractive to local and regional administrations that may become the early adopters of such technologies, thus acting as catalyzers for the adoption of the IoT paradigm on a wider scale.

Based on all the above, the contribution of this paper is manifold, as it (a) gathers and summarizes all fundamental challenges that arise towards enabling Smart Objects for the implementation of Smart City Operations (SCOs); (b) describes a capability – driven enterprise modeling approach to deal with the aforementioned challenges and (c) creates the basis for the simulation, design and implementation of such models.

The rest of this paper is organized as follows. Section 2 provides an overview on the relevant research challenges that arise in SCOs. Section 3 briefly discusses the role of Smart Objects for the implementation of such operations, and Sect. 4 presents a detailed analysis of the capability – driven enterprise modeling approach, followed by a method to link capability models to simulation models in Sect. 5. Concluding remarks are drawn in Sect. 6, along with an outlook on future research activities.

2 Smart Cities and Smart City Operations Challenges

Cities tend to become increasingly smarter through leveraging on (often ICT-enabled) insights to transform their systems and operations delivery to citizen-centered service delivery [1]. To be able to continue advancing in this area and consolidate a solid "smart" background", several fundamental requirements need to be addressed from an operational point of view [4]. A set of requirements/challenges that affect the design of Smart City Operations, is described below.

(1) Social Considerations

Intelligence ("smartness") might be a difficult concept to sketch from various viewpoints. As such, a city should appropriately consider a priori the desired levels of smartness to be achieved at short, medium and long time scale. This depends of course to a number of services that a city wants to provide to its citizens and visitors, especially during large scale events. In such cases, a city should consider the needs, plans and opinions of all stakeholders involved in its operations, such as (i) citizens, (ii) service providers, (iii) businesses, (iv) municipal authorities and (v) national standards. At the same time, all economic, environmental and people oriented viewpoints should be considered. This means achieving a balance not just between the interests of the particular city's stakeholders, but also taking into account relationships with neighboring cities affected by the events. The above seem as a complex algorithmic process with multiple variables ([7]).

(2) Technological Considerations

As technology constitutes the primary driver towards the provision of Smart City Operations during large scale events, technological requirements should be treated as having high significance. This implies the deployment of solutions of a new generation of integrated hardware, software, and network technologies that provide IT systems with real-time awareness of the real world and advanced analytics to help visitors and citizens (during the events) make more intelligent decisions about alternatives and actions that will optimize business processes and business balance sheet results [8].

In more detail, certain factors when implementing ICT with regard to resource availability, capacity, and institutional willingness should be considered [9]. Ebrahim and Irani [10] have outlined some of the challenges of using technologies in smart cities, including lack of employees with integration skills and culture, lack of cross-sectoral cooperation and inter-departmental coordination, politics and others.

More detailed technical challenges are related to specific technologies required for smart city operations. For instance, UAVs are key technology aspects for smart transportation systems. Technical considerations in that field include (i) adaptable middleware to ensure smooth operation, (ii) development of fail-safe systems, to guarantee high safety confidence levels in the event of aircraft failure, (iii) development of very efficient, low vibration, engines and a gyro-stabilized platform technology, for high resolution imaging and accurate measurements of gravitational field strength, (iv) development of automated image data compression algorithms, stitching of aerial imagery and others [11]. Similarly, a number of technology considerations is related with privacy and data protections issues. Data collection, information sharing, security risk management, malicious attacks and human errors are only some of the security aspects to be considered within the framework of a Smart City [12].

(3) Economic Considerations

The contribution of large scale events to the economic growth of a city seem as a fundamental prerequisite for any kind of smart city operation to be provided. From a high level, economics viewpoint, a city can be thought of as an entity that enables internally operating business groups to obtain income from outside its geographical region, and then enables the obtained revenues to circulate within its region. This of course can function the other way round (extroversion).

Accordingly, the economic performance of a city during and after the events can be viewed from two viewpoints: its industrial competitiveness relative to other regions, and the soundness of the finances within its region.

In this respect, it is essential that when planning and designing the provision of smart city operations, one must take a holistic, long term approach (i.e. way after the events). In particular, the assessment of strengths, weaknesses, opportunities and threats needs to look 10 or even 20 years ahead. Such a process will allow a city to continue attracting immense attention for businesses, whilst being comfortable and secure for its citizens [7].

3   Smart Objects in Smart City Operations

A key role in IoT, as well as in smart city scenarios and services, is played by the concept of smart object, first introduced in [15], which is a physical/digital object having a unique identifier that is used to digitally manage physical things (e.g., sensors), to track them throughout their lifespan and to annotate them (e.g., with descriptions, opinions, instructions, warranties, tutorials, photographs, connections to other objects, and any other kind of contextual information imaginable), and to consciously handle its relationships with other smart objects and with remote systems. In sum, a smart object is a physical/digital object augmented with sensing/actuating, processing, and networking capabilities that may embed human behavioral logic [16].

Smart objects are typically part of a Smart Environment, which is "a physical world that is richly and invisibly interwoven with sensors, actuators, displays, and computational elements, embedded seamlessly in the everyday objects of our lives, and connected through a continuous network" [18]. Smart Environments are often based on a suitable middleware that enables communication and management of smart objects in distributed applications ([17, 19, 20]). Enabling Smart Objects and realizing Smart Environments is critical in order to provide efficient SCO. It is important to define accurate and effective modeling approaches towards enabling Smart Objects – in the following section, we describe in detail such a capability – driven approach.

4 A Capability Driven Approach

The notion of 'capability' can be found in *strategic management* where one can distinguish between two prevailing views namely those of the Resource Based View (RBV) [21, 22] and the Dynamic Capability View (DCV) [21]. In the field of *Information Systems* modeling enterprise capabilities has been proposed by both academia [23, 24] and practice [25] as the lynchpin to connecting strategic objectives and high level organizational requirements to technological artifacts. From a service orientation perspective a business capability is defined in [26] as: "A particular ability or capacity that a business may possess or exchange to achieve a specific purpose or outcome. A capability describes what the business does (outcomes and service levels) that creates value for customers; for example, pay employee or ship product. A business capability abstracts and encapsulates the people, process/procedures, technology, and information into the essential building blocks needed to facilitate performance improvement and redesign analysis".

The Framework
We propose the adoption of an Enterprise Modeling approach in order to enable smart objects in SCO, based on the notion of 'capability' within a framework that considers 5 interrelated viewpoints as shown in Fig. 1. This is based on a paradigm [27], which is partly influenced by previously developed schemes in Enterprise Modeling e.g. [28], and extended with new features that offers opportunities for a greater level of analysis [27]. Within this modeling framework, developers can follow a process that is depicted graphically in Fig. 2.

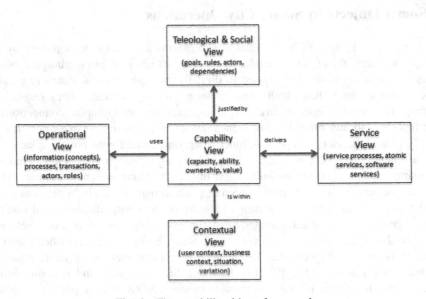

Fig. 1. The capability-driven framework

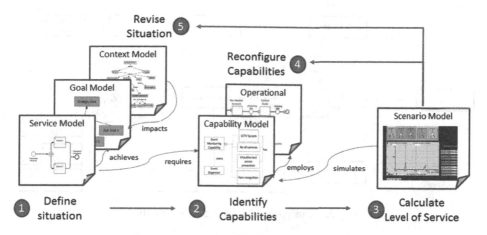

Fig. 2. The process of enterprise modeling

(Step 1) define the enterprise situation in terms of the enterprise goals and the services that achieve these goals in a specific context; (step 2) identify required capabilities as a configuration of resources; (step 3) calculate the level of service based on capabilities; (step 4) reconfigure capabilities and (step 5) revise situation, if necessary.

For example, a strategic goal is to 'Smooth traffic in rush hours', which is achieved by the 'Traffic control service' provided by the 'Traffic control Smart objects Division'. The contextual parameters affecting the delivery of this service include the particular traffic/geographical characteristics, the type and number of expected cars in specific locations and the expected routes, etc. (Step 1). Provision of the 'Traffic control service' requires 'Route screening capability' which is based in smart objects around the city and in turn employs a number of screening stations, having certain throughput, i.e., number of cars crossing a specific point per time unit (Step 2). Analyzing the 'Route screening capability' in the current context (referred to as scenario modeling) signifies the level of service that is achieved in terms of delay time per car (Step 3). Depending on the estimated level of service it might become necessary to reconfigure the 'Route screening capability' (e.g., increase number of screening stations and/or add 'route management capability') (Step 4) or even revise the situation (e.g., allocate/propose additional routes) (Step 5).

The Ontology

The key concepts that need to be considered in a capability-oriented approach have been defined in [29] and are summarized in the meta-model of Fig. 3.

A capability enables an enterprise to provide a *service* in order to achieve a *goal* in a specific *context*. We refer to this triplet (goal, context, service) as *situation*. In the traffic management example mentioned above, the 'Route screening capability' enables the provision of the 'Traffic control service' in order achieve the goal 'Smooth traffic in rush hours in the context of specific traffic/geographical characteristics with 5 screening points per Km, with specific expected car entrance rate in the monitored area.

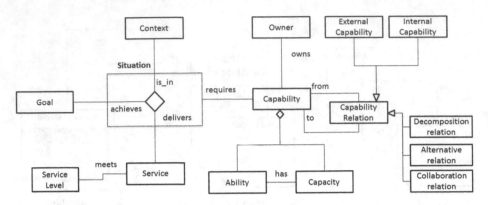

Fig. 3. A meta-model focusing on capability

A capability is associated to a certain *owner* (an entity such as a department, an organisation division, a person, a system). In the traffic control example, the 'Traffic control Smart objects Division' owns the 'Route screening' capability.

A capability denotes the *capacity* and *ability* of its owner for realising certain *level of service* targeted in a given situation. The level of service targeted in our example might refer to the average delay time per car with respect to no-traffic route time.

Capacity encapsulates the resources (processes, people, technology, information) employed by the capability owner for the purpose of possessing this capability, while ability is a measure of this capacity in terms of quantity or level of quality. For example, the 'Route screening capability' encapsulates the capacity of a number of screening stations, whose ability can be measured in terms of the number of cars screened per unit of time (throughput).

Capabilities may be *owned* by different actors (e.g. the Traffic control Smart objects Division and the Route Management Division, respectively). A capability owner may be external to the enterprise (e.g., the Traffic control authority might decide to use the Route Management Capability of an external company). Thus, there is a need to distinguish between capabilities owned by the enterprise (*internal capability*) and capabilities where the owner is external to the enterprise (*external capability*).

Capabilities may be related, making a distinction between *collaboration, decomposition* and *alternative* capability relations. The collaboration relation denotes inter or intra organization integration of capabilities towards the realization of a common end result. Decomposition expresses the fact that in order to own a composite capability one needs to acquire all its component capabilities. Finally, the alternative relation is used to represent the diverse capabilities that can be used to bring about the same end result.

5 Linking Capability Models to Simulation Models

The simulation results comprise quantitative, time-based and cost-related information about process execution and resource usage, e.g. waiting times, throughput times, resource utilization. In output analysis, it can be interesting to evaluate the data at a certain point in time, e.g. the number of completed process instances at the end of the simulation time, or over time, e.g. the development of waiting times after a peak in demand. The specific type of data to be generated by simulation and how it is analyzed depends on the analysis goal.

In the capability-driven approach, capabilities need to be expressed in terms of output analysis goals. As a capability enables an enterprise to provide a service in order to achieve a goal in a specific context, we need to investigate whether the triplet (goal, context, service) may be fulfilled. This means that all three attributes need to be expressed in simulation terms. To ensure validity, the description of both the level or service and the context needs to be very specific.

For this purpose, the following steps are proposed to ensure mapping of the (goal, context, service) triplet to the simulation environment.

1. Express context in terms of simulation parameters, decisions variables or other model aspects, e.g. in a specific Avenue there are 5 smart objects for car screening, mean car velocity is 15 km/h, distribution is exponential
2. Express level of service requirements in terms of specific simulation output parameters, e.g. level of service is the percentage of cars finding a route faster than the average
3. Express goals in terms of output analysis goals, e.g. percentage of cars finding a route faster than the average = 100%
4. Perform experimentation to determine if output analysis goals may be satisfied at the required level of service

To provide extensive design support through simulation, we also consider employing goal driven simulation. In goal driven simulation (GDS), we may automate many of the output analysis and experimental design tasks of a simulation study. This may include determining parameters to change, suggesting a rate of change, and testing these changes against a pre-established set of goals. To accomplish goal driven simulation, we need to integrate techniques such as object-oriented design, knowledge based systems and neural nets. In this case, there are still several issues to resolve including the type of interaction between these techniques and output analysis.

Goal driven simulation may be employed when goals are not met at the required level of service for a specific context, to indicate alternative contexts where goals may be met. In this case, we may then examine whether this context may be realistic in terms of design, cost etc. constraints.

To provide this capability, we add an extra step:

5. Experiment with different model parameters (decision variables) or the model itself to test various process and environment scenarios, to determine alternative contexts where goals may be met.

Our overall proposed approach for linking capability models with simulation modeling and experimentation is presented in Fig. 4.

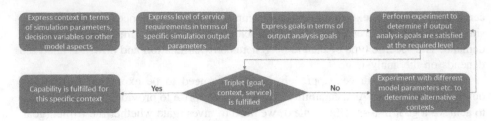

Fig. 4. Steps towards capability fulfillment

6 Conclusions and Future Directions

This paper discussed on a capability – driven modeling approach, towards enabling Smart Objects and providing SCO, focusing on smart mobility services. As such, it first provided some basic challenges that cities face when designing SCOs. Then it focused on the role of Smart Objects for the implementation of such operations, and presented a detailed analysis of the capability – driven enterprise modeling approach, followed by a method to link capability models to simulation models.

Overall, smart cities are continuously getting smarter. This naturally requires capital expenditure and calls for novel solutions in various areas, especially regarding Smart Objects and similar infrastructure. Transportation is an area where SCO find prosperous ground since it can increase the quality of living in large cities.

Several exciting areas are yet to be explored in the area of mobility offered in the context of SCOs. In particular, the further exploitation of intelligent transport systems principles in SCOs can lead to a 100% real-time assessment of traffic congestions, a priori identification of forthcoming dangers, as well as to the provision of open APIs and interfaces for intermodal MaaS inside cities/regions. Moreover, city-wide services can inform drivers on city-specific events (cultural, etc.), as well as on city-specific incidents (e.g. protests, works, etc.) and offer also targeted/focused ads and infotainment. Last, the exploitation of modern mobile communication infrastructures (e.g. 5G D2D) with which cities are more or less equipped, can naturally reduce deployment costs and provide low-latency emergency management services.

Acknowledgment. The authors wish to acknowledge the Qatar National Research Fund project i-Doha (Proj. No. NPRP 7-662-2-247) project, under the auspices of which the work presented in this paper has been carried out.

References

1. Dimitrakopoulos, G., Demestichas, P.: Intelligent transportation systems based on cognitive networking principles. In: IEEE Vehicular Technology Magazine (VTM), March 2010
2. Toppeta, D.: The Smart City Vision: How Innovation and ICT Can Build Smart,"Livable", Sustainable Cities, The Innovation Knowledge Foundation (2010). http://www. thinkinnovation.org/file/research/23/en/Toppeta_Report_005_2010.Pdf

3. http://www.ibm.com/smarterplanet/us/en/smarter_cities/overview/. Accessed 13 June 2016
4. http://www.hitachi.com/products/smartcity/download/pdf/whitepaper.pdf. Accessed 13 June 2016
5. BIS: The smart city market: opportunities for the UK. In: Department of Business, Innovation and Skills (2013)
6. Naphade, M., Banavar, G., Harrison, C., Paraszczak, J., Morris, R.: Smarter cities and their innovation challenges. IEEE Comput. **44**(6), 32–39 (2011)
7. Hogan, J., Meegan, J., Parmar, R., Narayan, V., Schloss, R.J.: Using standards to enable the transformation to smarter cities. IBM J. Res. Dev. **55**(1.2), 4:1–4:10 (2011)
8. Walravens, N., Ballon, P.: Platform business models for smart cities: from control and value to governance and public value. IEEE Commun. Mag. **51**(6), 72–79 (2013)
9. Odendaal, N.: Information and communication technology and local governance: understanding the difference between cities in developed and emerging economies. Comput. Environ. Urban Syst. **27**(6), 585–607 (2003)
10. Ebrahim, Z., Irani, Z.: E-government adoption: architecture and barriers. Bus. Process Manag. J. **11**(5), 589–611 (2005)
11. Mohammed, F., Idries, A., Mohamed, N., Al-Jaroodi, J., Jawhar, I.: UAVs for smart cities: opportunities and challenges. In: 2014 International Conference on Unmanned Aircraft Systems (ICUAS), Orlando, FL, pp. 267–273 (2014)
12. Commisioner for Privacy and Data Protection: Smart Cities: Privacy and Security (2015). https://www.cpdp.vic.gov.au/images/content/pdf/privacy_week/Smart_Cities_Background_Paper.pdf
13. Schaffers, H., Komninos, N., Pallot, M., Trousse, B., Nilsson, M., Oliveira, A.: Smart cities and the future internet: towards cooperation frameworks for open innovation. In: Domingue, J., et al. (eds.) FIA 2011. LNCS, vol. 6656, pp. 431–446. Springer, Heidelberg (2011). doi:10.1007/978-3-642-20898-0_31
14. Cuff, D., Hansen, M., Kang, J.: Urban sensing: out of the woods. Commun. ACM **51**(3), 24–33 (2008)
15. Kallman, M., Thalmann, D.: Modeling objects for interaction tasks. In: Arnaldi, B., Hégron, G. (eds.) Eurographics, pp. 73–86. Springer, Heidelberg (1998). doi:10.1007/978-3-7091-6375-7_6
16. Kortuem, G., Kawsar, F., Sundramoorthy, V., Fitton, D.: Smart objects as building blocks for the Internet of Things. IEEE Internet Comput. **14**(1), 44–51 (2010)
17. Fortino, G., Guerrieri, A., Russo, W., Savaglio, C.: Middlewares for smart objects and smart environments: overview and comparison. In: Fortino, G., Trunfio, P. (eds.) Internet of Things Based on Smart Objects. IT, pp. 1–27. Springer, Cham (2014). doi:10.1007/978-3-319-00491-4_1
18. Poslad, S.: Ubiquitous Computing Smart Devices, Smart Environments and Smart Interaction. Wiley, Hoboken (2009)
19. Fortino, G., Guerrieri, A., Russo, W.: Agent-oriented smart objects development. In: Proceedings of 2012 16th IEEE International Conference on Computer Supported Cooperative Work in Design (CSCWD 2012), Wuhan, China, 22–25 May (2012)
20. Fortino, G., Guerrieri, A., Lacopo, M., Lucia, M., Russo, W.: An agent-based middleware for cooperating smart objects. In: Corchado, J.M., et al. (eds.) PAAMS 2013. CCIS, vol. 365, pp. 387–398. Springer, Heidelberg (2013). doi:10.1007/978-3-642-38061-7_36
21. Barney, J.: Firm resources and sustained competitive advantage. J. Manag. **17**, 99–120 (1991)
22. Teece, D.J., Pisano, G., Shuen, A.: Dynamic capability and strategic management. Strateg. Manag. J. **18**, 509–533 (1997)

23. Stirna, J., Grabis, J., Henkel, M., Zdravkovic, J.: Capability driven development – an approach to support evolving organizations. In: Sandkuhl, K., Seigerroth, U., Stirna, J. (eds.) PoEM 2012. LNBIP, vol. 134, pp. 117–131. Springer, Heidelberg (2012). doi:10.1007/978-3-642-34549-4_9

24. Iacob, M.-E., Quartel, D., Jonkers, H.: Capturing business strategy and value in enterprise architecture to support portfolio valuation. In: 16th International Enterprise Distributed Object Computing Conference (EDOC 2012), pp. 11–20 (2012)

25 Ulrich, W., Rosen, M.: The business capability map: the "Rosetta Stone" of business/IT alignment. Enterp. Archit. **14**(2) (2014)

26. Homann, U.: A Business-Oriented Foundation for Service Orientation. Microsoft Developer Network (2006)

27. Bērziša, S., Bravos, G., Gonzalez, T., Czubayko, U., España, S., Grabis, J., Henkel, M., Jokste, L., Kampars, J., Koc, H., Kuhr, J.-C., Llorca, C., Loucopoulos, P., Juanes, R., Pastor, O., Sandkuhl, K., Simic, H., Stirna, J., Zdravkovic, J.: Capability driven development: an approach to designing digital enterprises. Bus. Inf. Syst. Eng. **57**(1), 15–25 (2015)

28. Loucopoulos, P.: Experiences with modelling early requirements. In: Soderstrom, P.J.E. (ed.) Information Systems Engineering. IGI Publishing, Hershey (2008)

29. Loucopoulos, P., Kavakli, E.: Capability oriented enterprise knowledge modeling: the CODEK approach. In: Karagiannis, D., Mayr, H.C., Mylopoulos, J. (eds.) Domain-Specific Conceptual Modeling, pp. 197–215. Springer, Cham (2016). doi:10.1007/978-3-319-39417-6_9

Crowd Sensing of Weather Conditions and Traffic Congestion Based on Data Mining in Social Networks

Rita Tse[1], Lu Fan Zhang[1], Philip Lei[1,2,3], and Giovanni Pau[2,3(✉)]

[1] Computing Program, Macao Polytechnic Institute,
Rua de L. Gonzaga Gomes, Macao, China
{ritatse,philiplei}@ipm.edu.mo,
vivianppmonkey@gmail.com
[2] Computer Science Department, University of California, Los Angeles, USA
gpau@cs.ucla.edu
[3] Lip6 – University Pierre et Marie Curie, Paris, France

Abstract. In recent years, the growing prevalence of social networks makes it possible to utilize human users as sensors to inspect city environment and human activities. Consequently, valuable insights can be gained by applying data mining techniques to the data generated through social networks. In this work, a practical approach to combine data mining techniques with statistical analysis is proposed to implement crowd sensing in a smart city. A case study to analyze the relationship between weather conditions and traffic congestion in Beijing based on tweets posted on Sina Weibo platform is presented to demonstrate the proposed approach. Following the steps of raw dataset pre-processing, target dataset processing and statistical data analysis, analytic corpus containing tweets related to different weather conditions, traffic congestion and human outdoor activity is selected to test causal relationships by Granger Causality Test. The mediation analysis is also implemented to verify human outdoor activity as a mediator variable significantly carrying the influence of good weather to traffic congestion. The result demonstrates that outdoor activity serves as a mediator transmitting the effect of good weather on traffic congestion.

Keywords: Smart city · Social networks · Data mining · Weather condition · Traffic congestion · Mediation analysis

1 Introduction

Social networks are becoming increasingly popular in the information era, with the ability to allow people sharing their perspectives upon different areas of urban life. People can communicate with each other and express their own voice through those platforms. Most importantly, the emergence of social networks makes it possible to study human life in a new way due to the fact that the tweets posted on the social networks can reflect people's opinions and emotions [1]. Recently, it has become a new and effective way to research in data mining field by leveraging social media data

© ICST Institute for Computer Sciences, Social Informatics and Telecommunications Engineering 2017
O. Gaggi et al. (Eds.): GOODTECHS 2016, LNICST 195, pp. 353–361, 2017.
DOI: 10.1007/978-3-319-61949-1_37

sources in smart cities. These researches involve tackling the challenge of social science, public health, and also weather and traffic conditions at urban management scale in a view of smart city [2–5]. Wang et al. [6] investigated the value of Chinese social media for monitoring air quality trends and the related public perceptions and response. The study verified quantitatively that message volume in Sina Weibo is indicative of true particle pollution levels. Pan et al. [7] described the detected traffic anomaly by mining representative terms from the social media that people posted when the traffic anomaly happened. Also, they demonstrated the effectiveness and efficiency of the method using a dataset of tweets collected from Sina Weibo, a Twitter-like social site. Cool et al. [8] established an approach to use the traffic intensity data originated from minute-by-minute data coming from single inductive loop detectors to analyze the relationship between weather, road safety, traffic speed, and traffic intensity and then investigated the impact of various weather conditions on traffic intensity. Zeng et al. [9] constructed a dynamic evolution network of traffic congestion by the tweets of the online users of social media. The present work aims to propose a simple solution which incorporates statistical analysis into data mining processes to crowd sense traffic conditions in a smart city [10]. The analysis is based on the tweets about weather conditions, traffic congestion and human outdoor activity posted on Sina Weibo platform. The work proceeds to reveal the relationship between weather conditions and traffic congestion in Beijing city of China.

2 Methodology

There are three primary stages in this work: data pre-process stage, data process stage and data analysis stage. Initially, the raw dataset needs to be preliminarily refined in the data pre-process stage to remove noise and to be reformatted prior to further processes. Then the refined dataset can carry on some fundamental mining procedures like word segmentation and frequency analysis to help construct lexicon used in selecting target dataset (analytic corpus). Next, the target dataset is filtered out based on the lexicon and a daily based tweets count file associated with weather conditions, outdoor activity and traffic congestion is generated during the data process stage, which is then served as source file for data analysis. In the last stage, Granger Causality Tests are performed to make sure there are causal relationships between weather and traffic variables. To figure out the indirect relationship between weather conditions and traffic congestion, outdoor activity is introduced as a mediator, and also mediation analysis is conducted to model the relationships among weather conditions, outdoor activity and traffic congestion.

As demonstrated in Fig. 1, data pre-process stage contains two main tasks: data cleansing and lexicon generation. Next, target dataset (analytic corpus) is selected as well as daily based tweets count CSV file is generated in the data process stage. Lastly, Granger Causality Test and mediation analysis are conducted in the data analysis stage.

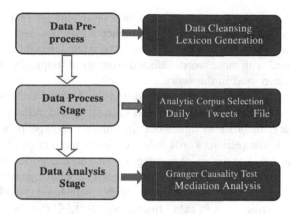

Fig. 1. Data mining major steps.

2.1 Data Pre-processing

To begin with, the data integrity of the raw dataset needs to be checked before any further operations. Since the raw dataset was crawled from the Internet through Sina Weibo API, some redundant tweets may occur during the crawling process. After removing redundant tweets, we used various regular expressions to detect and remove different types of noise data that were not useful in current study. These included picture and video sharing, check-in and empty tweets.

2.1.1 Lexicon Generation

The basis of this work is to develop appropriate lexicon used for filtering out analytic corpus. Unlike sentimental lexicon, it is difficult to find comprehensive and authoritative domain lexicon for weather conditions/outdoor activity/traffic congestion on the Internet. Consequently, the lexicon used in this work is a joint effort of both the initial lexicon of weather conditions, outdoor activity and traffic congestion collected from the Internet and keywords (related to weather conditions, outdoor activity and traffic congestion) with relatively high occurrences selected from the result of word frequency analysis.

Initially, lexicons related to weather conditions, outdoor activity and traffic congestion are collected from Internet which serves as the first part of the lexicon used in this work. Prior to word frequency analysis, content of tweets in the refined dataset are segmented using Rmmseg-cpp, a powerful Chinese word segmentation tool fully implemented by C++. Although there are many word segmentation tools based on different segmentation algorithms available on the Internet, they are mainly designed for English contents. However, most users of Sina Weibo are Chinese which means most tweets in Sina Weibo are written in the Chinese language. Therefore, the Rmmseg-cpp is selected to perform this Chinese word segmentation task in this work due to less memory consumption and fast segmentation speed. Additionally, Rmmseg-cpp is a Ruby gem which can be easily incorporated with Ruby environment and this work is mainly implemented by Ruby. The output of word segments are stored in one TXT file and then a word frequency analysis program is implemented to count each distinct word occurrence in the file, in which the words are rearranged based on their frequencies to select words related to weather conditions, outdoor activity and traffic congestion with high frequency. In the end, the initial lexicons collected from the Internet are combined with those words selected from word frequency analysis to serve as the ultimate lexicon used in this work.

In the relationship between weather conditions and traffic congestion, there are three main categories: weather conditions, outdoor activity and traffic congestion in the combined dictionary. In order to figure out the direct relationship between weather conditions and traffic congestion, words reflect different weather conditions and traffic congestion are selected. For the weather category, two subcategories are preliminarily divided: good weather and bad weather. Good weather contains words or expressions with respect to normally good weather, like '阳光' (sunshine), '明媚' (radiant and enchanting), '晴朗' (serene), '天气真好' (nice day), '好天气' (lovely weather). On the contrary, bad weather contains words or expressions related to severe weather which may have influences on human outdoor activities, such like '下大雨' (pour), '下大雪' (snow heavily), '寒风' (cold wind). As to the traffic congestion category, words like '堵车' 堵车(traffic jam), '堵塞' (choked), '堵死' (block off) are selected.

On the other hand, the indirect relationship between weather conditions and traffic congestion via outdoor activity is studied. As mentioned before, the outdoor activity serves as the mediated bridge between the weather conditions and traffic congestion where weather conditions have influence on human outdoor activities, and also human outdoor activities affect the traffic congestion. Therefore, for the outdoor activity words which may have impact on the traffic congestion are selected, like '逛街' (hang out), '出去吃饭' (eat out), '出发' (leave for) or words may indicate outdoor activities like '购物中心' (shopping center), '饭店'(restaurant) and '公园' (park).

2.2 Data Processing

The first task in this stage is to select the target dataset (analytic corpus). Tweets whose contents contain the words in the lexicon built in the previous stage are selected separately into four intermediate tables. Each of them contains tweets related to one subcategory: good weather, bad weather, outdoor activity, and traffic congestion. Next, a Ruby program computed the daily tweet counts for the four tables and saved them in CSV format.

2.3 Data Analysis

The core part of the whole work is data analysis stage. Since the mediation model is a causal model in nature, the causal relationships between weather conditions and traffic congestion, weather conditions and outdoor activity and outdoor activity and traffic congestion are determined first using Granger Causality Test. Afterwards, mediation analysis is conducted to model the relationships among weather conditions, outdoor activity and traffic congestion.

2.3.1   Granger Causality Test

The Granger Causality Test is a statistical hypothesis test for determining whether one time series is useful in forecasting another [11]. Basically, Granger Causality Test is used to determine if one time series variable X has causal relationships with another time series variable Y. In other words, it can be used to test the possibility to make prediction on one time series Y based on another time series X. Additionally, there is one basic assumption that must be fulfilled in order to use Granger Causality Test: time series X and time series Y should be stationary. Stationary time series keeps statistical properties such as mean, variance, autocorrelation, etc. constant over time. Therefore, meaningful sample statistics such as means, variances, and correlations with other variables can be obtained if the time series is stationary.

In this work, all four variables are time series variables since the values of each variable are collected at constant interval. Each data record is unique from other records and dependent only on time fields. Therefore, three groups of causal relationships are checked through this test: different weather conditions and traffic congestion, different weather conditions and outdoor activities as well as outdoor activities and traffic congestion.

As Fig. 2 shows, stationarity of the four time series variables are tested prior to the Granger Causality Test performed and only if the result shows independent variable and dependent variable are stationary, then the Granger Causality Test can be applied. Otherwise, the non-stationary variables must be transformed to stationary variables if either variable of the pair is non-stationary.

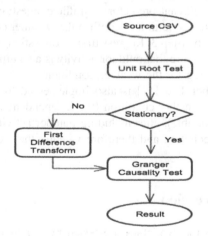

Fig. 2. Granger Causality Test mechanisms.

2.3.2   Mediation Analysis

As stated before, the mediation model is a causal model in nature. Therefore, the mediation analysis can be conducted once the causal relationships among weather conditions, outdoor activity and traffic congestion are determined. From the perspective of statistics, a mediation model is to identify an observed relationship between an independent variable and a dependent variable via the inclusion of a third variable, known as mediator. Besides the direct relationship between the dependent variable and the independent variable, mediation model hypothesizes that the independent variable influences the mediator which in turn influences the dependent variable [15]. In other words, the mediator transmits the effect of an independent variable on a dependent variable. As demonstrated in Fig. 3, the effect of the independent variable on the dependent variable may be mediated by a mediator while the direct effect still remains.

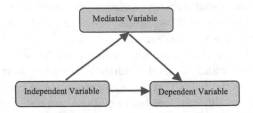

Fig. 3. A sample of mediation model

As against Fig. 3, the corresponding relationship in this work is: weather condition refers to the independent variable, traffic congestion refers to dependent variable and outdoor activity refers to the mediator.

To determine if outdoor activity is the mediator in this model, there are three major steps [16]: Step 1, Regress traffic congestion on the weather condition to ensure that weather condition is a significant predictor of traffic congestion. Step 2, Regress outdoor activity on the weather condition to confirm that weather condition is a significant predictor of outdoor activity. Step 3, Regress traffic congestion on both outdoor activity and weather condition to ensure that outdoor activity is a significant predictor of traffic congestion while controlling for the weather condition.

Additionally, the Sobel Test [17] is also implemented to determine whether the reduction in the effect of weather condition (the independent variable) on traffic congestion (the dependent variable), after including outdoor activity (the mediator) in the model, is a significant reduction and therefore whether the mediation effect is statistically significant.

3   Results and Discussion

The stationarity of these four variables are tested by Augmented Dickey–Fuller test (ADF) [12] and the results indicate that good weather and bad weather are stationary time series while outdoor activity as well as traffic congestion are non-stationary time series where the first difference of them are stationary. Consequently, the modified first differences of these non-stationary variables are used in the further analysis.

The Pairwise Granger Causality Tests are conducted using EViews, having the stationarity of both dependent and independent variables fulfilled. The test results demonstrate that prediction can be made on traffic congestion based on the good weather time series with the P value (probability) of the null hypothesis at 3.E−06.

Likewise, there are causal relationships between good weather and outdoor activity with P value of the null hypothesis at 8.E−09 as well as outdoor activity and traffic congestion with P value at 4.E−05. On the contrary, bad weather time series can be used to predict the traffic congestion (P value 0.0028) while it shows no obvious causal relationships with outdoor activity according to the test result (P value 0.0659).

Figure 4 illustrates the positive correlation between occurrence of daily tweets mentioning good weather and traffic congestion and outdoor activities. Each data point represents a day. On having social media can reflect people's opinions or thoughts to some extent, it can be inferred that there are more chances for people talking about traffic congestion when the weather is good and that people are more likely to do outdoor activities when the weather is good.

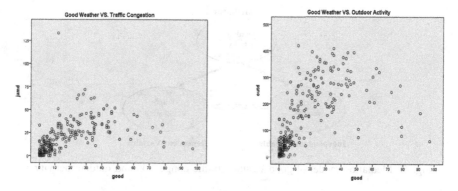

Fig. 4. Scatter chart of good weather vs. traffic congestion and outdoor activity

Similarly, the scatter chart in Fig. 5 demonstrates the positive trend between outdoor activity and traffic congestion. In accordance with the common sense, it can be seen clearly that more outdoor activities will cause more traffic congestions.

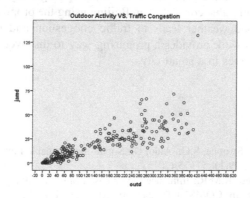

Fig. 5. Scatter chart of outdoor activity vs. traffic congestion

On having mediation model is a causal model in nature, the mediation model of good weather, outdoor activity and traffic congestion is then constructed after determining the causal relationships among these three time series variables. Based on the method to test whether outdoor activity can act as a mediator between good weather and traffic congestion, the regression results suggest that the significance of good weather on predicting traffic congestion decreases greatly when the outdoor activity intervenes. In addition, the Sobel Test result also indicates the mediation effect of outdoor activity is statistically significant with respect to the relationship between good weather and traffic congestion. Therefore, outdoor activity carries the effect of good weather on traffic congestion, which means it is a mediator in the mediation model shown in Fig. 6.

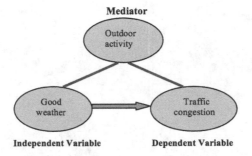

Fig. 6. Mediation model of good weather, traffic congestion and outdoor activity

4 Final Remarks

A practical approach that combines data mining techniques with statistical analysis is proposed to study the relationship between weather conditions and traffic congestion based on social networks. Following the general data mining procedures, statistical analysis can be incorporated with the final analysis stage. By crowd sensing the weather conditions and traffic congestion in Beijing using the proposed approach, it has been proved that good weather leads to traffic congestion and the direct cause is outdoor activity. This work provides a promising way to discover latent relationships between various activities in a smart city.

References

1. Derek, D., Karl, S., Swapna, S.G., Aldo, D.: Social media enabled human sensing for smart cities. AI Commun. **29**(1), 57–75 (2015)
2. Anjaria, M., Guddeti, R.M.R.: Influence factor based opinion mining of Twitter data using supervised learning. In: COMSNETS, January 2014, pp. 1–8 (2014)
3. Wu, X., Xie, F., Wu, G., Ding, W.: Personalized news filtering and summarization on the web. In: Proceedings of the 2011 IEEE 23rd International Conference on Tools with Artificial Intelligence, Washington, DC, USA, pp. 414–421 (2011)

4. Nathan, K.C., Amanda, L.G.: Health behavior interventions in the age of Facebook. Am. J. Prev. Med. **43**(5), 571–572 (2012)

5. Fisher, J., Clayton, M.: Who gives a Tweet: assessing patients' interest in the use of social media for health care. Worldviews Evid Based Nurs. **9**(2), 100–108 (2012)

6. Wang, S.L., Paul, M.J., Dredze, M.: Social media as a sensor of air quality and public response in China. J. Med. Internet Res. **17**(3) (2015)

7. Pan, B., Zheng, Y., Wilkie, D., Shahabi, C.: Crowd sensing of traffic anomalies based on human mobility and social media. In: ACM SIGSPATIAL GIS pp. 344–353 (2013)

8. Cools, M., Moons, E., Wets, G.: Assessing the impact of weather on traffic intensity. Weather Clim. Soc. **2**, 60–68 (2010)

9. Zeng, K., Liu, W.L., Wang, X., Chen, S.H.: Traffic congestion and social media in China. Intell. Syst. **28**(1), 72–77 (2013)

10. Chifor, B.C., Bica, I., Patriciu, V.V.: Sensing service architecture for smart cities using social network platforms. Soft Comput. **21**, 1–10 (2016)

11. Granger, C.W.J.: Investigating causal relations by econometric models and cross-spectral methods. Econometrica **37**(3), 424–438 (1969)

12. Dickey, D.A., Fuller, W.A.: Distribution of the estimators for autoregressive time series with a unit root. J. Am. Stat. Assoc. **14**(366), 427–431 (1979)

13. Box, G.E.P., Jenkins, G.M., Reinsel, G.C.: Time Series Analysis: Forecasting and Control, 3rd edn. Prentice Hall, Englewood Cliffs (1994)

14. Anderson, O.: Time Series Analysis and Forecasting: The Box-Jenkins Approach. Butterworths, London (1976)

15. MacKinnon, D.P.: Introduction to Statistical Mediation Analysis. Erlbaum, New York (2008)

16. MacKinnon, D.P., Fairchild, A.J., Fritz, M.S.: Mediation analysis. Annu. Rev. Psychol. **58**, 593–614 (2007)

17. Sobel, M.E.: Asymptotic confidence intervals for indirect effects in structural equation models. Sociol. Methodol. **13**, 290–312 (1982)

Physical and Cognitive Training of Children with Down Syndrome Using Video Games

Elif Surer[✉]

Graduate School of Informatics, Middle East Technical University,
06800 Ankara, Turkey
elifs@metu.edu.tr

Abstract. In this study, a video-games based training platform that aims to provide user-specific physical and cognitive tasks is developed so that children with Down Syndrome can continue their training autonomously at home. For this purpose, a set of video games which addresses physical activities (balance and feet coordination) and cognitive tasks (abstraction, memory and word-forming) are being designed and implemented. During the gameplays, center of pressure, brain activity and electrodermal activity measurements are done to identify the specific needs of the child and to tailor a training programme that addresses these difficulties.

Keywords: Down Syndrome · Serious games · Video games

1 Introduction

Down Syndrome (DS) is a genetic disorder usually stemming from an extra chromosome 21 [1]. Children with DS in general has physical (posture, balance, motor skills) and cognitive (language, arithmetic, short term memory) impairments and to overcome these impairments and to make them become autonomous adults, special education and exercise programmes exist [2–5]. However, these programmes are being held with therapists during the day and there lacks a training program that is tailored for the necessities of the kid which he/she can continue to perform at home, autonomously. The purpose of this study is to provide kids with DS a specialized physical and cognitive training platform which is composed of video games. This platform is customized with sensors and measures the requirements of the child and creates a training program to handle those requirements. Besides, given that video games create a sensation of flow [6], the training programs aim to motivate the child to follow the training program for a longer period of time and with enthusiasm. In this ongoing study, physical and cognitive video games are being developed. The following sections describe the methodology (game descriptions and instrumentation), data acquisition, evaluation and future work of the study.

© ICST Institute for Computer Sciences, Social Informatics and Telecommunications Engineering 2017
O. Gaggi et al. (Eds.): GOODTECHS 2016, LNICST 195, pp. 362–365, 2017.
DOI: 10.1007/978-3-319-61949-1_38

2 Methodology

In this section, proposed video games for physical training, for cognitive training and the instrumentation used, are presented in detail. The games are developed with Unity3D game engine given that it provides multi-platform support and a powerful layer to handle multiple devices.

2.1 Video Games for Physical Training

Hopscotch Game (Feet Coordination): Hopscotch is a game which is played with Wii Fit. The user is guided with the numbers in order to understand on which square to put the foot on. While one foot is put on the correct square, the other foot has to be removed from the platform, which requires the user to be in balance with only one foot. The purpose of the game is to enable feet coordination, to pay attention to the correct foot and to be fast while doing the exercise. As the difficulty of the game increases, the directions of the movements are not only limited to the right or left side, but to forward and backward as well. Besides, the frequency of the numbers, the duration of staying on one foot increases as the difficulty of the game progresses (Fig. 1).

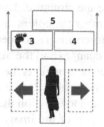

Fig. 1. Gameplay representation of the Hopscotch game.

Kite Game (Balance): In this game, the user sees her silhouette as a kite. The purpose of the game is to stabilize the kite in a given area and stay still during the task. The game is played with Wii Fit and the direction of the kite changes due to the center of pressure. When the user is in balance, the kite remains still, but when the center of pressure is moved to right or left, wind appears on the direction of the center of pressure and the kite moves to that direction as well. As long as the kite is not met to the center, the user loses points. To ensure safety, the screen is divided into three different areas and when the user starts to enter the risky areas, the game stops. When the difficulty of the game increases, the width of the areas diminishes and extra factors such as birds and clouds enter the screen and try to distract the user.

2.2 Video Games for Cognitive Training

Word Tetris (Attention): As in the traditional game of Tetris, there are different types of blocks that move on the screen. The main difference is that, each block has letters on them and the main purpose is to form a meaningful word fitting the blocks to the correct place. Depending on the level difficulty, the complexity of the words increases and the blocks move faster. On the right side of the screen, there is a hint of the word to be formed. The main purpose of this game is to make the child perform attention tasks and to increase the word memory [7] (Fig. 2).

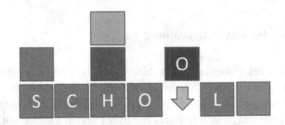

Fig. 2. Gameplay representation of the Word Tetris game.

Lego Game (Attention, Memory and Abstraction): At the beginning of the game, the user chooses a picture of which a lego-like structure is to be built. The chosen image is mapped to a 3D empty lego-like structure and the user is expected to put the correct colored pieces in order to complete the structure. During the game, the picture disappears to challenge the user to remember the colors and the picture reappears randomly again to remind the user of the chosen image. Depending on the difficulty level, the complexity of the proposed images changes and the 3D structure is seen from a different depth. While in the first levels, the camera angle is the same as the picture's angle, when the difficulty increases, the camera viewpoint also changes. This challenges the user to map the 2D image to a 3D structure and to envision the image in 3D. When the colors of lego blocks do not match the given part of the image, the user loses points [6].

2.3   Instrumentation

- **Microsoft Kinect:** In the games targeting physical training, Microsoft Kinect is used. Users interact with the game via their avatar and their movements are reflected on the game in real-time. The ideal range of motion data is set due to the therapists' suggestions and when the children are about to overdo that range, the game is stopped in order to prevent injuries. Feedback regarding the risky movements is displayed on the screen.
- **Wii Fit:** For the balance-oriented games, users use Wii Fit and right and left foot movements are recorded accordingly. The gameplay depends on the correct selection of the foot for a given amount of time.
- **BioSignalsPlux EDA Sensors:** During the gameplay of cognitive games, electrodermal skin activity (EDA) of the user is recorded so that the tasks which overwhelm the user most are recognized. These data are used to create a tailored training program for the specific necessities of the user.

- **BioSignalsPlux EEG Sensors:** During the gameplay of cognitive games, neuroactivities of the user are also recorded to understand which brain waves are activated and which cognitive tasks require more time to be completed. Combined with the data of EDA sensors, these data provide a clearer picture to design a specific training program for the user.

3   Data Acquisitions, Evaluation and Future Work

The proposed work is still in progress and the video game set will be enlarged so that the physical training set will include three games and the cognitive part will include four games in total. So far, usability tests with healthy users have been started for the games presented in this work and the same procedure will be applied to the new games as well. Then, the games will be tested with children with DS and the outcomes of the training will be monitored using biofeedback sensors and questionnaires. At least 10 autonomous DS children (7–17 ages) will be recruited and the ethical permission procedure has already been completed.

Acknowledgements. This work is fully supported by The Scientific and Technological Research Council of Turkey (TÜBİTAK) under TÜBİTAK 2232 – Reintegration Research Fellowship Program and the Project ID is: 115C088.

References

1. Korenberg, J.R., et al.: Down syndrome phenotypes: the consequences of chromosomal imbalance. Proc. Nat. Acad. Sci. **91**(11), 4997–5001 (1994)
2. Weijerman, M.E., De Winter, J.P.: Clinical practice. Eur. J. Pediatr. **169**(12), 1445–1452 (2010)
3. Chapman, R.S.: Language development in children and adolescents with Down syndrome. Ment. Retard. Dev. Disabil. Res. Rev. **3**(4), 307–312 (1997)
4. Cronk, C., et al.: Growth charts for children with Down syndrome: 1 month to 18 years of age. Pediatrics **81**(1), 102–110 (1988)
5. Chapman, R.S., Hesketh, L.J.: Behavioral phenotype of individuals with Down syndrome. Ment. Retard. Dev. Disabil. Res. Rev. **6**(2), 84–95 (2000)
6. Csikszentmihalyi, M.: Flow and the Psychology of Discovery and Invention. Harper Collins, New York (1996)
7. Sürer, E.: Video-games based framework designed for the cognitive rehabilitation of children with Down syndrome. In: 2016 24th Signal Processing and Communication Application Conference (SIU). IEEE (2016)

Author Index

Printed in the United States
By Bookmasters